P9-EMB-783

DISCARDED

LINDLEY J. STILES
Dean of the School of Education, University of Wisconsin
ADVISORY EDITOR TO DODD, MEAD & COMPANY

Secondary School Administration:
Theoretical Bases of Professional Practice

Secondary School Administration

New York

Toronto

1965

Theoretical Bases of Professional Practice

Lloyd E. McCleary

Stephen P. Hencley

University of Illinois

DODD, MEAD & COMPANY

Copyright © 1965 by Dodd, Mead & Company, Inc.

All rights reserved

No part of this book may be reproduced in any form
without permission in writing from the publisher

Library of Congress catalog card number: 65-11948

Printed in the United States of America

Editor's Introduction

POLICIES and practices for administering secondary schools have grown largely in Topsy-like fashion. Typically, a strong principal evolves procedures that are emulated by others. Too frequently, personal charm and individual aggressiveness are the foundations of leadership, and pragmatic efficiency is the goal of school organization. Under such conditions, the man with the personal power to keep a school on schedule and pupils under control is considered the good administrator. Educational qualifications and leadership skills, if they are considered at all, are secondary.

The need for a theoretical base for secondary school administration is apparent. Until such direction is provided, quality in educational leadership—and hence in learning—is left to chance. Without a theory of the role and function of administration, accountability is a matter of speculation. Without theoretical orientation, research to establish superior practices is without bench marks. Without a theory of its mission, secondary school administration remains a trade rather than a profession.

This volume brings to the student of secondary administration an introduction to the theory of his art. In writing this book, the authors have assumed that given a sound theoretical grounding the administrator can move toward judgments of policies and practices suitable for quality secondary schools. Hence, the book is not simply a catalogue of administrative practices and patterns; it rather is a treatment in depth of the forces, functions, and responsibilities that shape the character of leadership for secondary schools. The result of this approach is an entirely new type of book in secondary school administration, one that promises to point the way toward the quality in administration needed for high schools in the years ahead.

Professors Lloyd E. McCleary and Stephen P. Hencley are no ivory tower theoretical scholars. Both have prepared for this writing through experience in secondary school administration. Both are familiar with the work of secondary school principals throughout the United States—in small as well as large schools. Both have been active in testing ad-

v

ministrative theory in real situations. Such experiences combined with sound acquaintance with recent research on administrative theory and awareness of the changes in educational dogma taking place have made possible the formulation of a theory of administration that focuses on qualitative ideals for secondary schools. Yet the authors are highly sensitive to the practical problems that administrators face in their day-to-day assignments. For both the prospective and the experienced administrator this book will provide refreshing insights and useful guidelines for the improvement of administration of secondary schools.

LINDLEY J. STILES

Preface

THE substance of junior and senior high school administration derives from many sources. Objectives, content, and processes of education; forms and procedures that make up the institutional structure of the school; concepts and mechanisms of general administration and their specific applications to administrative practice in the secondary schools; and selected knowledge of the behavioral sciences—all contribute to an understanding of secondary school administration and to its practice. None of the elements that form the substance of the field are static, however. By 1960, fundamental influences within each area were sufficiently well advanced to permit the assertion that secondary schools were about to enter a phase of radical transformation. The belief that secondary school administration should become a significant force in that change, and thus should itself be transformed, became the motivation for this work.

Having served earlier as administrators in secondary schools, both authors in 1961 were completing periods of intensive study directly relating to secondary school administration. Stephen P. Hencley until 1962 was Associate Director of the University Council for Educational Administration; and Lloyd E. McCleary as Professor of Educational Administration at the University of Illinois was completing a three-year study of secondary education with Lindley J. Stiles and Roy Turnbaugh in the production of the book *Secondary Education in the United States*. The two authors began a period of discussion of the problems of secondary school administration, and an exchange of papers relating to influences and directions of development led to the production of this book.

In its preparation, the authors consciously attempted to spare the book from becoming a compendium of current information or a treatment of descriptions and principles cast in the mold of existing works. The purpose was clear from the beginning—that the compelling interest of secondary school administration lay in the directions of its future development and in the constructs that illuminate its problems. Dean

Stiles gave his full support to this emphasis by providing helpful criticism and advice.

The authors wish to acknowledge the interest of Alonzo Grace, Dean of the College of Education, University of Illinois, who helped with several specific problems and gave reactions to Chapter 1; Professor Van Miller, University of Illinois, and his seminar on educational leadership in providing the opportunity to try out certain ideas and materials; and members of the faculty of the University of Illinois who contributed at numerous points. Of this latter group, the work of Professor Harry Broudy in the area of curriculum theory was invaluable in the preparation of Chapter 8. The authors are also indebted to Mrs. Karen Skilbred, Secretary to the University's Department of Educational Administration, for her aid in the preparation of the manuscript, and to Mr. Rafael Lewy, administrator in the public schools of Israel and doctoral student in educational administration, for his work as research assistant.

L. E. McC.
S. P. H.

Contents

Part I
Secondary Education and Administration

Chapter 1
Administration in
Secondary Schools

T HE administrative function as a distinct feature of education arose
out of the need to give direction to development and operation
of schools. Increasing complexity, both in size and diversity of program,
ultimately stimulated attempts to specify and put into practice systematic
administrative procedures. From these efforts, descriptions of successful
practice and sets of principles were derived. Building on this base, educators have begun a serious effort to evolve a theory and science of educational administration. This development includes the formulation and testing of theoretical propositions, systematic investigation of practice, and
the application of theories from other social and political fields to the
problems of educational administration. Promising new concepts of the
nature and function of administration required for secondary schools
are resulting from these approaches.

Today, forces acting upon secondary schools are accelerating the rate
of expansion of their responsibilities and making their operation more
complex. Larger operating units, closer and more direct relationships
with other social agencies and with the school's patrons, as well as with
other units of the school system, make administrative knowledge and
skills imperative. At the same time, new knowledge and widespread
appeals for excellence highlight the importance of secondary education.
These factors serve to expand administrative services and to make them
more complex and sophisticated. As a consequence, past conceptions of
administrative practice are no longer adequate. New conditions and new
insights into the administrative function require a reformulation of the

meaning and purpose of administration required for secondary schools. To provide such a statement is the purpose of this book.

CONTEXT OF SECONDARY SCHOOL ADMINISTRATION

At present there are more than 26,000 secondary schools in the United States and its territories. These include four-year high schools, two- and three-year junior high schools, two- and three-year senior high schools, and combined junior-senior high schools. The search for an understanding of the kind of administration needed by each type of school has become an urgent task.

Search for the Meaning of Administration

Authorities generally agree that the quality of administrative service within a school is the most significant determinant of the level of effectiveness of the total educational program. This is so because administration penetrates every phase of school life. Administrative actions have the potential to support, enhance, and develop or to discourage, disrupt, and confuse any or all parts of a school organization.

The importance of secondary school administration requires that care be exercised in the selection and training of administrators for secondary schools. The effectiveness of the administrator is determined largely by the extent to which he and those associated with him understand the purposes, processes, techniques, and skills of administration as they are applied to secondary schools. The essential nature of secondary school administration, properly identified and described, should, then, become a major area of study of the potential administrator and those who would understand his work.

Variation in Administrative Services Due to Local Characteristics

Certain factors influence significantly the nature and extent of provisions for administrative service to secondary schools. Size of school enrollment, legally prescribed organizational patterns, fiscal arrangements, program features resulting from local community conditions, ability and willingness of the community to support the educational effort, and quality of educational leadership—all are factors that account for gross differences in administrative provisions among schools. To illustrate how these factors produce variation, two of them—size of enrollment and organizational patterns—are described.

SIZE OF SCHOOL ENROLLMENT. Secondary school sizes range from about 10 students (for example, Lake Alice High School, Scottsbluff, Nebraska, or Errol Consolidated High School, Errol, New Hampshire) to over 6,000 students (Erasmus Hall High School, Brooklyn). In smaller schools, the chief administrator is a teacher who also handles administrative duties. In the larger schools, a full-time principal is assisted by a relatively large staff of specialized administrators.

PATTERNS OF ORGANIZATION. More than 1,200 high schools of the four-year type are organized as separate high school districts with their own boards of education. In these districts the high school principal is responsible directly to the board of education for all administrative matters, including those usually borne by a superintendent of schools. The remaining secondary schools, approximately 24,000, are organized into a variety of unit systems.[1] In these schools the duties of the secondary school administrators are determined within an administrative structure that includes a superintendent and a central-office staff as well as administrative officers of other schools in the system.

Numerous other variations in the nature of secondary administration derive from the factor of legally prescribed organizational patterns. For example, Chicago has a subdistrict pattern, all schools are organized within twenty-one subdistricts, each of which is administered by a district superintendent who in turn is directly responsible to the central office. Many large cities use specialized high schools for vocational programs, for the gifted, or for those talented in the arts. Certain New England states have the supervisory district system; in the county system typical of the South and West certain services and supervisory functions are performed by what might be termed intermediate districts. All of these arrangements have produced variation in the nature and extent of administrative services within the local administrative unit.

GENERAL FORMULATION NEEDED TO GUIDE STUDY AND PRACTICE

The close relationship between the practice of educational administration and its study is easily understood. In fact, educational administration

1. More than 24,000 secondary schools are organized within approximately 12,000 school districts which also include, as part of their organization, elementary schools, junior colleges, and the like. Each of these districts has a superintendent as chief administrative officer.

as a social science derives its character from the context in which it is practiced. It is performed within a matrix of ideals, values, and purposes of a given group of people. It functions through a system of laws and customs. Furthermore, it is conditioned by the practices of teaching, organization, and management of education itself. Is secondary school administration, then, particularistic in character and, hence, impossible to describe in terms of general concepts and principles? Can the general dimensions of the kind of administration needed by the secondary schools be defined? Can a theoretical formulation of secondary adminis-tration be constructed and employed to identify the essential meaning and purpose of administration, regardless of the idiosyncrasies of local practice? The authors believe that an affirmative answer can be given to all these questions.

Administration in the Local Secondary School

To move closer toward definitive answers to the questions posed above requires an analysis of the work of the local school principal. It should be clear that the local situation for each of some 26,000 schools, earlier termed the context of secondary school administration, does have import for administration. School administration is a part of a social setting, particularly that provided by the local community and the school itself. It is most important, however, that school administration is af-fected by the setting and, at the same time, is intended to *change* that setting.

The work of the principal takes place "under orders"—not in a direct and detailed manner from a "boss" but from a complex assortment of policies, requests, expectations, and requirements of those who are joined in the network of associations of the school and the school system. In most cases a superintendent and a central-office staff have immediate authority over the principal. Experience dictates, however, that wide dis-cretion must be left to the principal and his staff. The competent princi-pal, to a large extent, writes his own "orders"; thus, he both directs and is directed by the context within which he works.

To say that a principal writes his own orders does not imply that he should do so arbitrarily. First of all, he exercises judgment within a framework of principles and rules. This framework, the authors contend, should be developed by the administrator as a result of serious profes-sional study and guided experience. Second, the principal by himself can anticipate only a few of the possible consequences of his decisions and actions. He must rely upon the reports and judgments of others, and he must communicate back to them in order that all those who are involved in a particular decision or course of action will understand how they are affected by it.

The principal and other administrative officers in the secondary school can no longer claim expert knowledge of all the special, technical activities of the modern comprehensive school. Rather, theirs is a complex task of defining goals and purposes, allocating staff and material resources, planning and managing the achievement of the purposes of the school, and evaluating its accomplishments.

The secondary school administrator is not only a planner, a decision maker, and a key participant in complex group processes, he is above all a "doer." He is the person directly responsible for the operation of a school. Grand educational slogans, pious statements of policy, even state laws and school board resolutions do not in themselves create and execute detailed plans for the kind of education such statements embody. Administration of a school requires not only knowledge of a variety of processes, operations, and skills but the judgment to use them— the test of the administrator is in accomplishment.

Evidence of Administrative Failure

A large and ever increasing number of secondary school administrators exhibit the kind of leadership which characterizes the highest form of professional service. Nevertheless, secondary school administration reveals areas of weakness and failure as well as areas of steady and substantial progress. Since knowledge of shortcomings often provides the best means of improvement, it is in this light that they are noted here.

By and large, administrative failures in the secondary schools result from inadequate understanding of the nature of administration as well as from ignorance of specific technical knowledge and lack of essential skill. The fault is not completely the practicing administrator's, but resides as well with scholars in the field of educational administration. In addition to the human frailties of the practitioner, certain serious gaps in theory and research have hampered better understanding of the substance of administration as a field of study.

Critical examination of the factors producing diversity, as they relate to the total context of school administration, reveals a system enormous in size and extent, operated within unrelated and inconsistent organizational patterns, directed through fragmentary and poorly coordinated systems of controls, inadequately and unequally financed, and tampered with in various ways by numerous agencies of at least three levels of government. More damning still are the critics of American secondary education who charge that the school administrator has exhibited a singular lack of understanding of the essential nature of the educational programs demanded by the conditions of contemporary life. As the reader is likely to be painfully aware, ideas and principles have, in practice, often become widely accepted without sufficient examination. Frequently, sheer innovation rather than thoughtful study has been the source of change. Conditions produced by change which is mere innovation represent administrative failure that cannot be attributed to a perverse public, unfavorable social conditions, or cruel acts of fate. They stem directly from shortcomings in administrative knowledge and skills.

Both types of criticism—that bearing upon chaotic organizational and fiscal arrangements and that charging a lack of program leadership—strike at the heart of the administrative function. There is just enough truth in these criticisms to suggest that the successful school administrator cannot merely accept the context of the particular situation within which he finds himself and proceed to administer the existing educational program as efficiently as possible. Rather, the administrator must supply the vision and leadership to modify and redirect the forces, both internal and external to the local school, that impede the effectiveness of the educational program. He must be able to *change* as well as *control.* Out of a view of the total context of secondary school administration, the dimensions of administration needed for the modern secondary school emerge.

DIMENSIONS OF SECONDARY SCHOOL ADMINISTRATION

The immediate working environment of the administrator is the school organization. The administrator occupies a defined position within the organization—the principalship is the chief administrative position in each school. A position—whether that of principal, assistant principal, dean, director, department chairman, teacher, or counselor—becomes defined first in terms of generally accepted practice. Positions become defined in detail according to the specific needs of a particular school and, within limits, by the personal qualities of the individual occupying the position.

General conceptions relating to the kind of administration required by secondary schools provide important guides to its study as a specialized field of professional service. They seem to reveal four general dimensions. Two dimensions the authors choose to call "executive dimensions"; two, "leadership dimensions."

Executive Dimensions

Two dimensions of educational administration, into the present decade, serve as central focuses for the orientation of the field. One dimension comprises the technical-managerial skills of "running a school." It includes the tasks involved in the administrator's roles as supervisor of teachers, schedule maker, disciplinarian, and business manager. The second dimension encompasses curriculum and guidance skills. It entails knowledge of discrete fields of study, translation of that knowledge into sequential programs of instruction, and the relating of students to the resulting plan.

In the past these dimensions provided pivotal points of orientation to the principal as he attempted to give meaning to the many, apparently unrelated and disparate tasks which made up his job. These executive dimensions also became the basis for college programs constructed for the training of school administrators, and they corresponded quite nicely to citizens' expectations of the school administrator in many local communities.

Broadly conceived, they have served the administrator well. When coupled with an agreeable personality, a dedication to the job, and an intuitive grasp of the sociology of the local community, they have won him praise as an effective executive. They have not, however, served as a sufficient base to give professional stature to his position.

Leadership Dimensions

Two additional dimensions of professional competence are required. First is the necessity to relate educational administration to the wider field of public administration. Second is the need for administrators to arm themselves with the knowledge and leadership skills to design, advocate, and bring about imaginative educational programs rooted in a realistic appraisal of current practice and based upon a sound conception of administrative processes.

The four dimensions of educational administration emerge from an appraisal of the current educational scene. The school administrator faces the choice of becoming (1) an able and dedicated servant, one who can do well what he is "expected" to do; or (2) a student of the crucial problems and issues of his field, one who places himself in a position of leadership through his knowledge and ability. In the former case, the administrator often becomes a victim of his job, overwhelmed by details and problems referred to him by others. In the latter instance, he affords himself the opportunity to participate in the definition of his own professional role; he exercises choice in the problems to be attacked and finds satisfaction in putting into effect programs in whose formulation he has shared major responsibility.

GENERAL FORMULATIONS OF SCHOOL ADMINISTRATION

Research and study, intensively conducted during the past decade, tend to validate the usefulness of describing educational administration within the categories of (1) administrative tasks, (2) administrative processes, (3) situational factors, and (4) administrator behavior. The reader will find these categories in general use in the professional literature. Research in administration has been conducted largely within the framework of each category, and the results of this research form the basis of the presentation in this section.

Administrative Tasks

One fruitful means of describing educational administration is to gather data about what administrators actually do on the job and the aspects of their work which they feel to be most important in providing good schools. Numerous studies of this kind have been conducted, using interview, observation, questionnaire, and other techniques.

One study, fairly representative in its final listing of tasks, resulted from an attempt to define areas of competency. The study was conducted by the Southern States Cooperative Program (SSCP) in Educational Administration.[2] The task areas identified are:

1. Instruction and curriculum development
2. Pupil personnel
3. Community-school leadership
4. Staff personnel

2. Southern States Cooperative Program in Educational Administration, *Better Teaching in School Administration* (Nashville, Tenn.: George Peabody College for Teachers, 1955).

5. School plant
6. Organization and structure
7. School finance and business management [3]

Studies of the kind just mentioned do reveal broad categories for giving structure to the content of school administration. It must be noted, however, that such studies reveal what administrators tend to be doing without providing a basis for judging what they *should* be doing or in what manner they are performing their tasks.

Administrative Process

A second descriptive formulation of administration is in terms of the administrative process.[4] This approach emphasizes administrative behavior, the activities of administration rather than the tasks. Aside from its value in describing administration, it is a useful illustration of the relationship of educational administration to the total field of administration, particularly public administration.[5]

The administrative process is defined by the Commission on Staff Relations in School Administration as follows: "Administration, then, may be defined as the total of the processes through which appropriate human and material resources are made available and made effective for accomplishing the purposes of an enterprise. It functions through the behavior of persons." [6]

The Commission then lists what it terms the crucial constituent functions of the process:

1. *Planning,* or the attempt to control the future in the direction of the desired goals through decisions made on the basis of careful estimates of the probable consequences of possible courses of action.

3. One area omitted here relates to school transportation and seems too specific to be listed as a discrete task. The authors would incorporate this item as an element of business management wherever it becomes a task for a school principal.
4. Excellent and exhaustive treatment of this topic as it relates to educational administration may be found in Russell Gregg, "The Administrative Process," in Roald Campbell and Russell Gregg (eds.), *Administrative Behavior in Education* (New York: Harper & Bros., 1957), Chapter VIII, pp. 269-317.
5. Fayol, a Frenchman, first used this formulation of administration in 1916 to describe general industrial management. His formulation was later adapted and widely applied to public administration. Although the formulation has not been useful as a basis for scientific studies of administration, it has uses not only in description but in the analysis of administrative problems either in actual field situations or in case studies.
6. American Association of School Administrators, *Staff Relations in School Administration, Thirty-third Yearbook* (Washington, D.C.: the Association, 1955), p. 17.

2. *Allocation,* or the procurement and allotment of human and material resources in accordance with the operating plan.
3. *Stimulation,* or motivation of behavior in terms of the desired outcome.
4. *Coordination,* or the process of fitting together the various groups and operations into an integrated pattern of purpose-achieving work.
5. *Evaluation,* or the continuous examination of the effects produced by the ways in which the other functions listed are performed.[7]

Gregg's formulation [8] of the administrative process and an alternative formulation suggested by Campbell, Corbally, and Ramseyer [9] are given in skeletal form in Table 1-1. Note that "decision making" has been made the first item on each list. In the second list, Gregg's "planning" and "organizing" items are labeled "programming," and his terms "communicating" and "influencing" are subsumed in the term "stimulating."

Table 1-1.   Comparison of Formulations of the Administrative Process as Applied to Educational Administration

I	II
Gregg	Campbell, Corbally, and Ramseyer
1. Decision making	1. Decision making
2. Planning	2. Programming
3. Organizing	3. Stimulating
4. Communicating	4. Coordinating
5. Influencing	5. Appraising
6. Coordinating	
7. Evaluating	

All of the formulations, despite the differences in number of elements and exact terminology, are surprisingly similar and apparently reflect a high degree of unanimity relative to the kinds of organizational behaviors expected of administrators.

Unlike the descriptions of tasks, which were derived from actual accounts of what administrators were doing or said they were doing, the process formulations result from a conceptualization of the administrative act. Although descriptive terms are used, the terms imply a theoreti-

7. *Ibid.*
8. Gregg, *op. cit.,* p. 274.
9. Roald Campbell, John Corbally, and John Ramseyer, *Introduction to Educational Administration* (Boston: Allyn and Bacon, 1958), p. 179.

cal definition of what administration is. Logically, then, to the extent that the administrators do not do these things, or, put another way, to the extent that they are doing things they cannot label with these terms, *they are not administering.* As with the task descriptions, there is no attempt to place qualitative meanings upon these descriptive terms. How each element is performed in the secondary school setting, what emphasis it is to have, how it relates to other elements, and many other questions remain to be answered.

Situational Factors and Administrator Behavior

Formulations of tasks and processes provide approaches to an understanding of the common elements of secondary school administration at a general, descriptive level. They indicate categories rather than dynamic relationships. When applied to the study of actual situations, they yield only static listings. Until recently, the study of educational administration was hampered by a lack of formulations appropriate to systematic analysis and understanding of the dynamic elements known to exist. Many students of the field despaired of ever developing the means of understanding administration at a level of sophistication appropriate to the analysis of dynamic situations. Fortunately, developments in the social sciences have contributed knowledge that begins to fill this gap. These formulations permit greater understanding of administration through analysis of situational factors and administrator behavior.

In such analysis, both elements—situational factors and administrator behavior—must be considered together. Hollis Moore indicates their close interrelationship: ". . . investigators became convinced that the only way to arrive at a definition of educational administration, or, for that matter, to analyze clearly the functions performed by school administrators, was to do so by observing them in actual situations, and to describe them in the situational terms, not according to traits or personal qualities." [10] Selected studies can be cited to illustrate this approach and reveal factors of the situation and of administrator behavior that are likely to be significant.

The Ohio State University School-Community Development staff conducted an investigation of administrator behavior and situational factors significant to the solution of certain educational problems. Factors

10. Hollis A. Moore, *Studies in School Administration* (Washington, D.C.: American Association of School Administrators, 1957), p. 28.

which seemed to affect problem solutions were: (1) the administrator himself, (2) the persons with whom the administrator works, (3) the relationship between the administrator and the individuals and groups with which he works, (4) the instructional organization or pattern in which administrator behavior takes place, (5) the mores already established in the school community, and (6) the physical characteristics and legal provisions of the community itself. It is interesting to note, in light of the lists of administrative processes presented in the preceding section, that problems arose in the following areas: (1) making policy, (2) setting goals, (3) determining roles, (4) coordinating administrative functions and structure, (5) working with community leadership to promote improvements in education, (6) using educational resources of the community, (7) involving people, (8) communicating, and (9) appraising effectiveness.[11] These problem areas correspond quite closely to the list of processes presented in Table 1-1.

SCHEMATIC MODEL OF ADMINISTRATION. A group from Teachers College, Columbia University, developed a model to provide a unifying concept of administration. The model, called "The Tri-Dimensional Concept of Educational Administration," is composed of three interrelated elements: the administrator's job, the man he is, and the social setting in which he operates. Although developed for use in studies of the superintendency, it is of value as a tool for research on the principalship as well. According to the model, the *job* of school administration requires knowledge of specific content, which, in turn, requires skills and abilities for successful performance. The *man* brings to the job his total capacities, plus his total behavior patterns. The *social setting* provides stimulations and limitations to the *job* and affects the *man* in various ways. The *man* modifies the job; the *job* influences the man; both are encompassed in the *society*. This model implies intricate but largely unidentified sets of relationships, and, to this extent, it fails to provide a scheme for direct analysis. As a model within which specific problems can be structured for study, it does have use.

THEORETICAL MODEL OF ADMINISTRATION. From the schematic formulations of situational factors and administrator behavior, efforts have grown to construct rigorous, hypothetical-deductive formulations by

11. John Ramseyer, Lewis Harris, Millard Pond, and Howard Wakefield, *Factors Affecting Educational Administration,* School-Community Development Monograph, No. 2 (Columbus, Ohio: The Ohio State University Press, 1955).

which more meticulous study of administrator behavior may be undertaken. To the extent that such theoretical models can be constructed and tested, they can reveal the essential nature of administration and provide a scientific base for the guidance of practice in the field. Representative of this movement is the work of Daniel Griffiths. He has exerted the most persistent, and perhaps produced the most useful, effort in this direction.

Griffiths posits decision making as the heart of organization and the process of administration. According to Griffiths, decision making is central in that *all* administrative functions can be interpreted in terms of the decision-making process. He maintains that all organizational activity, even the form of the organization, depends upon dimensions of the decision-making process. Because the decision-making process controls the allocation of resources, communications, informal and formal groupings in the organization, achievement of goals, and power and authority are all ordered in relation to that process. Therefore, an understanding of the decision-making process is the key to understanding the essential nature, personnel relationships, and modes of operation of any organization.

Griffiths defines the steps in decision making as similar to the following:

1. Recognize, define, and limit the problem.
2. Analyze and evaluate the problem.
3. Establish criteria or standards by which solutions will be evaluated or judged as acceptable and adequate to the need.
4. Collect data.
5. Formulate and select the preferred solution or solutions.
6. Put into effect the preferred solution.
   a. Program the solution.
   b. Control the activities in the program.
   c. Evaluate the results and the process.[12]

Griffiths conceives of administration as a thoroughgoing problem-solving activity. He reduces leadership functions, executive managerial functions, and human relations or group maintenance functions of administrator behavior to problem-solving acts. His steps in decision

12. The reader is encouraged to study the complete presentation of the theory in Daniel E. Griffiths, *Administrative Theory* (New York: Appleton-Century-Crofts, 1959).

making, when viewed in this light, become closely analogous to the formulations of administrative process by Gregg and others. Griffiths' contribution is much greater, however, than a mere reformulation of a conception of administrative process. He has attempted to construct a unitary, logical system which can be used in generating hypothetical statements amenable to empirical testing. This is an important point of departure for the scientific study of educational administration.

FORMULATION OF ADMINISTRATION FOR SECONDARY SCHOOLS

As a means of placing in perspective the formulations of administration given in the previous section, and in an effort to present a comprehensive formulation of administration appropriate to the secondary school, the authors offer their own formulation in this section.

Secondary school administration, as a field of specialized professional service, exists within three interrelated areas of human concern. In the context of administration and of secondary school administration in the local setting, the three areas might be identified and characterized by the following statements:

One area is the setting for secondary education—social, educational, political, economic—changing at an ever accelerating pace due to powerful and pervading forces. The immediate environment of the school is the community, and it is through the community that the impact of the total environmental setting is interpreted and brought to bear upon the school.

The second area is secondary education itself—its purposes, organization, methodologies, and content—now being transformed in startling fashion by innovations, discoveries, and the growth of knowledge. The major effect upon the school from this area is likely to be from professional sources through the knowledge and competencies of the total school staff, including the administrator. It is in this area that administration and staff can give expression to their understanding of the best education possible with the resources available.

The third area is composed of the fundamental processes, techniques, operating principles, and ethical values of educational administration—now undergoing thorough reexamination and reformulation. Each area possesses a unique identity; yet, to the knowledgeable administrator, all three are intertwined in significant ways.

Any formulation of secondary school administration must not only define the substance of administration but indicate its relevance to the other two areas. The reader is encouraged to analyze critically the following and other formulations, not as an intellectual exercise but as a means of constructing a frame of reference for his own use. The formulation presented below may be considered a means of orientation for the study of the remainder of this volume.

Phases of Administrative Activity

The authors believe that the secondary school administrator is involved in three fundamentally different, though related, phases of activity: (1) participation in broad policy making, (2) organizational leadership, and (3) technical management.

MODEL OF SECONDARY SCHOOL ADMINISTRATION. Figure 1-1 represents the authors' version of a formulation of administration appropriate to the secondary schools. The reader will note three levels of administrative activity encompassing the program of the school. These three levels indicate the substantive activities of the three phases listed above.

The first level of administrative activity—participation in broad policy making—is represented by the tasks grouped on the outer circle. This activity is largely political in nature. It represents the administrator's professional responsibility to influence the forces which shape the direction and emphasis of public education in the community.

The second level of activity—organizational leadership—involves translating broad policies into organizational action within the school. These tasks, between the outer and inner circles of the model, represent major leadership tasks of the principal as he works with his professional staff. This phase of activity, the authors will contend, represents the central focus of secondary school administration.

The third phase—technical management—is indicated by the tasks grouped on the inner circle. They are slightly altered in terminology from the list provided by the Southern States Cooperative Program study. Here, "supervision" is preferred to the term "staff personnel," while the combined term "facilities and management" carries a more general meaning than that of the SSCP's "school plant" and "school finance and business management" terms.

Finally, all of these tasks are affected by the situational factors derived from the profession, the school, and the community. These situ-

Figure 1-1. Model of Administration for Secondary Schools

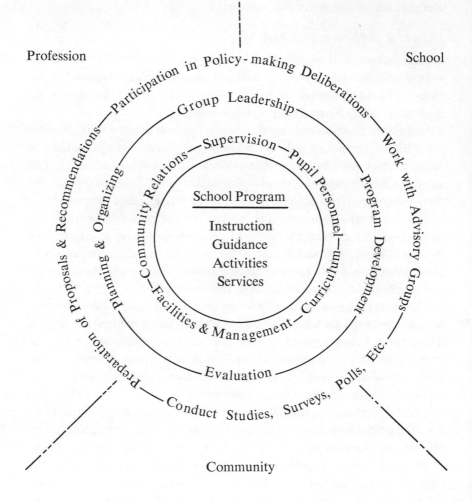

ational factors were described in the introduction to this section. Each task is shaped by the values, knowledge, and expectations brought to the task from each area.

All three levels of tasks are performed in terms of the administrative processes examined earlier. In this model, secondary administration is conceptualized as tasks. In Chapter 4, these same phases of administration are treated as functions in an analysis of a total administrative performance system. When this is done, the administrative processes are treated as a fourth dimension.

PARTICIPATION IN BROAD POLICY MAKING: FIRST PHASE OF ADMINISTRATIVE ACTIVITY. Education is often discussed as being outside the realm of politics. Nothing could be further from the truth. Education is kept as far from bureaucratic political control as possible, even to the provision of a completely separate system of government for its legal operation. At its base, however, education is a public concern, and all policy matters relating to it come within the purview of political bodies representative of the citizens who support the schools.

In theory, a school administrator does not make policy; he executes it. According to the principle of the separation of policy making and administration, all the ethical premises upon which schools operate are formulated by public bodies—some by the people themselves, some by legislatures, others by boards of education. Some of the basic policy questions include: Who has a right to attend school? What is to be taught? What educational services are to be provided? In theory, professional discretion is left only to decide how the public mandates are to be carried out, and here discretion is limited to questions of fact. For example, choice of a particular method of teaching biology is left to professional discretion because this should be a matter that can be decided by expert opinion based upon factual data. As the reader well knows, the principle is frequently violated in practice. Legislatures and school boards often go well beyond the bounds of policy making, and school administrators often enforce policies untested by public judgment.

The violation of the principle of the separation of policy making and administration does not mean, however, that the principle is valueless. Democratic institutions are the only just and final means of creating policy; there is no "expert" or "scientific" way for doing so. Rather, the problem is to find procedures which, on the one hand, enable administrators to contribute to sound policy development for education and, on the other hand, make it possible for the public to review administrative decisions.[13]

The model (Figure 1-1) reveals representative kinds of administrative activity that pertain to participation in policy decisions. The administrator should continuously seek the results of research as the basis of proposals to the appropriate policy-making agencies. Whenever possible, he should give service by participating in the deliberations of lay councils and formally constituted bodies. At this level, the administrator is not in control of decision-making processes; his role is to understand what processes are to be used in a given situation and how he can ethically contribute to policy development.

ORGANIZATIONAL LEADERSHIP: SECOND PHASE OF ADMINISTRATIVE ACTIVITY. Administration is often thought of as "the art of getting things done." Too often ignored is the choice of *what* is to be done, a step that must precede action. The problems of choice in complex human enterprises such as a school have become the overriding concern of administration. Solutions to problems and issues which lead to lines of action are no longer simple or easily agreed upon. The total formulation being presented here perhaps can best be interpreted as focusing upon the administrator as a decision maker or, at least, as one whose chief concern is with the decision-making process of an organization. Even at the technical management level, it is proposed that the school administrator *decide* upon appropriate procedures; administration largely ceases when procedures become routine.

Planning and organizing, growing out of program evaluation and development, form the major tasks of the organizational leader. This phase of administrative activity may best be understood with reference to the concept "organization." The organization takes form from the interrelationships of the individuals—teachers, students, administrators, and nonprofessional staff—and from the allocation of things—equipment, supplies, and facilities—to accomplish the purposes of the school. One major area of decisions relates to the specification of purposes and the design of the educational program to accomplish them. Whenever certain outcomes are sought, planning takes place; decisions are "planned" when

13. The reader may find a more detailed treatment of this problem in Van Miller, *The Public Administration of American School Systems* (New York: The Macmillan Co., 1965), pp. 61-143.

they are based upon an assessment of consequences—in this case, the achievement of educational purposes.

Educational planning leads to organizational decisions. The administrator exercises organizational power and influence to rearrange the relationships of people and the distribution of resources. In fact, the administration *decides* the distribution of power and influence, insofar as it is possible to do so, within the school organization and in its external relationships. Whenever an administrator makes a decision, he organizes and accepts rcsponsibility for school leadership.

Care must be taken to maintain the view that the administrator is part of a group and that decisions emerge from a group process. The administrator is caught up in a host of relationships that bear upon his role as a leader. He receives communications of the judgments and decisions of others, and he uses them as a basis for his own actions. It is in this sense that decision making at any level of the administrative hierarchy is only a part of an extended process.

One facet of decision making, accounted for in the model but often overlooked, is the role of evaluation. Decisions are generally expected to bring a matter to a final conclusion. Actually, most decisions should become part of a process of assessment and review. Most decisions— whether part of planning, organizing, leading, or program formulating —should be employed to test current practices and new ideas. These decisions, rather than settling an issue once and for all, may later become proposals as their consequences become known. In this sense, decisions can be viewed as part of an evaluation process.

TECHNICAL MANAGEMENT: THIRD PHASE OF ADMINISTRATIVE ACTIVITY. The phase of administrative activity immediately bearing upon the operation of a school may best be characterized as managerial. It entails the administrative decisions and activities which ensure the successful conduct of instruction, guidance, student activities, and services. The administrative work in this phase involves scheduling, assigning, directing, supervising, expediting, inspecting, and correcting. Administrative action is primarily that of creating or approving procedures, communicating and clearing instructions, resolving unforeseen conflicts, and assessing results.

At the technical management level, many of the procedural matters become routine, and rightly so. Established, efficient routines, well understood by the staff, are essential to effective operation. It is in this phase of activity, however, that the administrator often permits himself to become involved in clerical tasks, with a resultant loss of effectiveness. As procedural matters become routine, the administrator must withdraw or become a clerk. He should make periodic checks and provide the means for review of procedures, but he must not assume the detailed execution of procedural matters.

REFERENCES

Albright, A. D., *et al., School Administration and the Human Sciences* (Lexington, Ky.: University of Kentucky, 1961).

Bennis, Warren G., "Leadership Theory and Administration Behavior," *Administrative Science Quarterly,* Vol. 4, No. 3, December, 1959, pp. 259-301.

Culbertson, Jack, Jacobson, Paul, and Reller, Theodore, *Administrative Relations* (Englewood Cliffs, N.J.: Prentice-Hall, 1960).

Griffiths, Daniel, *Administrative Theory* (New York: Appleton-Century-Crofts, 1959).

McLure, William P., and Miller, Van (eds.), *Government of Public Education for Adequate Policy Making* (Urbana, Ill.: Bureau of Educational Research, University of Illinois, 1960).

Miller, Van, *The Public Administration of American School Systems* (New York: The Macmillan Co., 1965).

Simon, Herbert A., *Administrative Behavior* (New York: The Macmillan Co., 1959).

Wengert, E. S., *et al., The Study of Administration* (Eugene, Ore.: School of Business Administration, University of Oregon, 1961).

Chapter 2
Secondary Schools
as Social Institutions

S ECONDARY schools—both junior and senior high schools—represent the most advanced educational institutions attended by the majority of youth. If society is to equip the immature to participate fully, responsibly, and happily in adult life, it must accomplish that task during the period devoted to secondary education. The characteristics of the educated person are rarely acquired by random experience; rather, they are acquired through planned, carefully directed programs of instruction. This implies educational planning geared to cultural values and beliefs and to social needs and trends in terms of a coherent philosophy of education and a theory of learning.

In periods of cultural stability and social tranquility, it is easy to identify society's demands for its schools. Strong institutionalized practices can be developed to insure that these expectations are met. But during the past two decades the rapidity of cultural change has produced varied and continually revised expectations for the secondary schools. Heightened by external threat to the social order, the need to reformulate the functions of secondary education has taken on a note of urgency.

A second and more subtle element has further confused the picture. During the same period, a scientific and technological revolution has drastically altered the *content* and the *uses* of knowledge in the secondary school curriculum. Until after World War II the content of instruction in the secondary schools was largely of a traditional nature, and it was intended for associative and replicative use—that is, the minimum essentials of the subject fields were taught to be stored and applied later in situations closely resembling the conditions under which they were learned in school. Today, however, with the rapid shift to technical and specialized uses of knowledge, the learner must select and apply what he knows in situations quite different from those in which he learns.

Although this is an oversimplification of the problem, the content and uses of knowledge have drastically changed at the same time that the socially determined functions of the secondary schools have come to require reexamination. Thus it has become imperative that the administrators of secondary schools understand the problems they face in guiding secondary education into a new and challenging phase of development.

A compatible relationship between the secondary schools and the broader society is essential. Secondary education receives its *raison d'être* from American society and is a primary instrument of cultural advance. The society–school relationship is a focal point of administrative attention. The administrator seeks to mediate between the goals set by the school and the expectations held for it. He wishes to improve its impact upon the community and the broader society; he seeks to create a better understanding of the educational function and why it should be more fully used.

If the secondary school administrator is to be an educational leader, he needs to understand the perspectives within which the school formulates its program. He needs to understand cultural patterns and values of society in order to relate educational goals to societal needs. He needs to know the means by which controls over schools are established and how they function. He needs to gain a perspective of the status of secondary education—its function in American society and the direction of its development.

SECONDARY EDUCATION: CURRENT GUIDELINES

Leaders of secondary schools attempt to fashion programs of instruction and provide the institutional arrangement to make them effective educational instruments. To do this, they require a clear idea of what secondary schools are to accomplish—a conception of the purposes and functions of the schools and of the machinery, forms, and processes for achieving the desired goals. There are currently—and likely to be for some time to come—major disagreements within the profession and among the public at large about both functions and purposes of secondary education and the nature of the institution required to achieve them.

A brief examination of each of the two elements may serve to clarify current issues and conflicts.

Statements of Educational Purposes: Social Policy for Secondary Education

Statements of purpose for secondary education throughout the nation's history provide an interesting documentation of the beliefs and aspirations of individuals and groups. Many of these statements have attained the status of educational classics. Their importance derives from their ability to consolidate opinion, both lay and professional, upon the direction to be given to the development of educational programs. When they express values around which support can be mustered sufficient to obtain necessary resources, they become influential in policy development. From them specific operational goals can be formulated at the local level to guide the planning of instruction.

The reader is probably familiar with the content of many of the more important statements of purposes. Among them are several from the period since World War II:

General Education in a Free Society (The Harvard Report), 1946.
Report of the White House Conferences on Education, 1956, 1960.
The Pursuit of Excellence (The Rockefeller Report), 1958.
The Contemporary Challenge to American Education (Educational Policies Commission), 1958.
The American High School Today (The Conant Report), 1959.

Taken together, these statements yield a list of purposes for the secondary schools which include the following:

1. Develop intelligence, character, and personality.
2. Provide a fund of important knowledge and ideas of this and other cultures.
3. Foster social and political cohesion and loyalty to democratic ideals.
4. Provide vocational preparation.
5. Promote mental and physical health.
6. Improve the individual's powers of self-improvement, particularly in the use of leisure time.

Formulations of purposes are intended to provide criteria for assessing the effectiveness of schools and to give direction by providing a framework within which specific instructional goals can be established and priorities assigned. Purposes are viewed as the expectations of society at large for the education of its youth. Latitude is left to local determination in matters of curriculum, and the wide diversity of abilities and interests of youth mitigate against highly detailed or specific statements. Nevertheless, such statements have powerful impact in establishing both scope and direction for planning and development.

Conflicts over Purposes

Many issues relating to secondary education center upon conflicting views of the functions of secondary education and, hence, the purposes to be served. Differences relating to purposes have always existed, and certain of them have now become intensified. In addition, new and sharp differences in points of view about purposes have been introduced by fundamental changes in the social order.

EDUCATION AND MATERIAL WELFARE. Formulations of purposes are framed as idealized goals. As such, they are difficult to use in assessing the effectiveness of public education. Any set of purposes, when expressed as ideal goals and used to evaluate schools, tends to make schools appear relatively ineffective. Public spokesmen and many individuals in the profession have come to see the direct relationship of education to the material welfare of society. They seriously question idealized statements of purposes as suitable to educational planning. Social ills, national manpower shortages in technical fields, and concern for national survival are only a few conditions whose solutions seem to depend directly upon secondary education. Strong pressures have developed to require secondary schools to devote more attention to societal demands and to reshape purposes in accordance with them.

INCREASING COMPLEXITY OF KNOWLEDGE. Present formulations of goals offer little help in establishing priorities. All areas of knowledge appear to be given equal status. In these circumstances, considerable pressure is brought to bear by various groups to increase emphasis upon their particular preference—among others, the sciences, humanities, health and physical education, and foreign languages all vie for favored status. General statements of purposes provide no standards or criteria to resolve such conflicts, and each school is left to shift for itself. In effect, traditional formulations of purposes are not serving as effective statements of social policy.

NEW INFLUENCES ON SECONDARY PROGRAMS. New influences, particularly at the national level, have entered the scene. National examinations, Federal programs, and the work of private foundations, to name only a few, are effecting fundamental changes without regard to the total development of secondary education. Massive movements are under way to reduce secondary education to a crass instrument of the momentary economic, social, and political ends of special-interest groups. In this regard, formulations of purposes have failed to provide a basis for the intelligent design of sound educational programs. At present there seems to be no rationale to harmonize these forces and control them in terms of a sound theory of secondary education. Statements of purposes rely upon consensus for their implementation. Special-interest groups have found more direct means of influencing program development than through integrated social policy.

DIVERSITY AND UTILITY AS SOURCES OF CONFLICT. Purpose formulations, since the famed Seven Cardinal Principles of 1918, have tended to emphasize diversity and utility as concepts in the development of educational programs. Both of these concepts are now being seriously questioned by some groups, defended by others. Those opposed to diversity believe that the secondary schools are attempting to encompass all youth functions within a program of formal education. They point to student activities that have been incorporated into the instructional program and to the lack of a well-defined core of common studies as evidence that the desire for diversity has watered down and eroded educational programs.

A charge equally serious is leveled against the concept of utility in programs of secondary education. A consistent effort stemming from correctionist and behavioral psychology has caused educators to stress the direct application of knowledge. Psychological studies into transfer of training established that skills and knowledge are transferred most readily when the largest number of identical elements are present in both the learning situation and the testing situation. A pragmatic philosophy incorporated the findings of these studies into its position that the student should learn in real life situations. The concept of utility became accepted as a major criterion for determining content in secondary education—that which had the most immediate use and could be taught in real life situations became most important to learn.

Objection to the concept of utility is based upon the argument that technic has been given preference over basic knowledge. What is needed according to this view is a concept of utility that stresses principles and concepts appropriate to an explanation of the widest range of facts and conditions. Real life situations stress specific skills and factual materials of a low order of generality, whereas broad and general laws, principles, and concepts provide fundamental knowledge of most lasting value.

Comprehensive School: Model of Secondary Education

The term "comprehensive school" refers to particular forms, arrangements, and an organizational structure for the conduct of secondary education in the United States. As an idealized concept, it is the model upon which local secondary schools are patterned.

Features of the comprehensive school are so well known that certain of them do not need detailed examination here. Those which are reasonably standard throughout the country include the pattern of required and elected subjects, the pattern of the school day and year, organization of pupils into grade levels, standard grouping arrangements, teacher course loads, marking system, credits for graduation, and examination system. Although these features have typically been the focus of attention of the administrators—lengthening the school day and year, altering the Carnegie unit, creating high- and low-ability sections of standard courses, instituting the organizational trappings of team teaching, and the like—they are not the significant components of what is meant by the comprehensive school.

The concept of the comprehensive school includes certain troublesome features. Competent students of secondary education have attempted to clarify some of the difficulties and suggest improvements.[1] Since World War II, and particularly during the post-Sputnik period of 1957-1962, considerable public concern has been expressed about the effectiveness of the secondary schools. Within the ranks of laymen and educators alike, there are those who seek a penetrating examination of certain aspects of the comprehensive school and a clarification of its meaning in current terms.

NEED FOR A DEFINITION OF SECONDARY EDUCATION. When one wishes to examine and improve secondary education, certain questions are ap-

---

1. The most recent effort to examine seriously the current conception of secondary education was made by James B. Conant in his studies *The American High School Today* (New York: McGraw-Hill Book Co., 1959) and *Education in the Junior High School Years* (New York: McGraw-Hill Book Co., 1960).

propriate: What is meant by a secondary education? What sorts of learnings are essential to a secondary education? What prerequisite knowledge, skills, and behavior patterns are necessary to begin secondary education, and which are symptoms of its completion? Such questions imply that some agreement exists concerning starting and ending points for a given student, content and learnings to be dealt with during the process of secondary education, and expectations established for levels of competence in learning. In short, secondary education as a concept should be amenable to definition in educational terms.

There is no question that each junior and senior high school by its practices has defined secondary education in operational terms. Some have done so explicitly and in a highly sophisticated manner. Throughout the profession generally, however, the concept of the comprehensive school has had built into it certain corollaries which have precluded persistent, scholarly examination of a definition (or definitions) of secondary education. This shortcoming has left the profession in a weak position for examining critically the adequacy of secondary education either to current educational demands or to alter the definition in light of new conditions.

Corollaries that have come to be built into the concept of the comprehensive school and that seem to impede work toward a satisfactory definition of secondary education include the following:

1. Secondary education is specified in terms of six years of study— each year organized as a grade level. Typically, the junior high school is composed of grades 7 through 9; high school is composed of grades 10 through 12. All students must complete all grades in order and in time sequence.

2. The educational program is defined in terms of subjects organized into courses. Subjects are studied daily for a school year.

3. Common (or required) studies are defined as courses (see Item 2 above), not as learner competencies or knowledge and skills to be acquired by all students. Passing a certain minimum of required courses is evidence that the student has acquired an acceptable education in the common studies.

4. Elective subjects are provided to permit exploration, specialization, and tailoring of programs to individual interests and needs.

5. Common studies define minimal requirements; the remainder of each student's program of study is to comprise elective courses. Approxi-

mately half of a sixteen-Carnegie-unit high school program is required; the remaining half is elective.

6. The program of secondary education should include studies to meet the interests and ability levels of all youth. Courses of a given subject, whether required or elective, are to be so constructed in content and level of difficulty that the poorest student may meet the minimum requirements. Courses are ordinarily structured more in terms of content than in terms of learner competencies; hence a low-ability course in a given subject may not resemble in any fundamental way the regular or honors course of the same subject and grade level.

Secondary school administrators, the authors contend, do in fact define secondary education in terms of the above list and in terms of idealized purposes as examined in an earlier section of this chapter.[2]

NEED FOR AN ADEQUATE CURRICULUM THEORY. The curriculum is one of the means by which schools educate youth. Schools, as institutions, also educate through organized activities, school services, climates created by various formal and informal relationships, and many other means. But the curriculum is, or ought to be, the primary means by which schools influence the development of youth. The curriculum consists of content—concepts, ideas, facts, values, norms, rules, principles, and the like—organized into units of instruction, usually by subject. Through instruction, the curriculum brings about changes in the mental makeup of students. The authors attempt to spell out an adequate theoretical model of curriculum in Chapter 8. Into the present period, however, no systematic and consistent theory has guided the development of the curriculum.

There are at least three approaches to curriculum development in the secondary schools. These may be identified briefly as follows:

First, the curriculum is determined by the continuous study of the development of the culture, the aims of society, and the needs of developing youth. Curriculum is specific in objectives, and outcomes are expressed in behavioral terms. Learning is conceived basically as problem-solving activity and is centered in contemporary situations and circumstances. Subject matter of a given course is drawn from several domains to be applied to an understanding of the situations posed.

2. For example, see American Association of School Administrators, *The High School in a Changing World, Thirty-sixth Yearbook* (Washington, D.C.: the Association, 1958).

Second, curriculum construction is largely an effort to identify the best fruits of the disciplines, collect and organize them, and formulate patterns by which they can be most effectively transmitted to youth. Concomitant with the transmission of knowledge is the obligation to impart a spirit of inquiry, the structure of logical reasoning associated with the subject, and insight into the methods of investigation indigenous to that field. Where pressing social needs require direct attention by the school, the disciplines serve as resources. Curriculum content becomes flaccid under the constant shifts and changes of the disciplines caused by rapid advances of knowledge, and it is believed that this problem is minimized by focus upon conceptual structure and the rigor, precision, and thoroughness characteristic of the disciplines.

Third, the curriculum is determined by the teacher. No matter how well conceived the program or how detailed the course of study, the teacher decides what the materials will be like as they reach the student, how they will be interpreted, and to what depth they will be studied. Three problems are central to this point of view: what is to be taught, what materials are to be provided for instruction, and what teachers need to know if they are to handle the instructional materials available to them. Those who hold this view believe that teaching is composed of two elements: (1) knowledge, and (2) knowledge about knowledge. The more the teacher knows *about* knowledge, the more competent he is to teach. Under this view, the curriculum is usually defined by the interests and competencies of the staff rather than by a curriculum plan for the school being staffed. Traditional subjects form the central or stable portion of the school offering, with numerous subjects—for example, horticulture, photography, earth science, crafts, and the like—being added or subtracted according to the staff available.

At the operational level—the point at which pupils and teachers must be brought together for instructional purposes—the three approaches to curriculum development have not been synthesized. Rather, each has been accommodated by various, often ingenious, piecing together of courses. The result, however, has been a patchwork arrangement unsatisfactory at major points from any single point of view. Under these circumstances only two alternatives are possible: (1) continuing conflict, or (2) a reconstruction of the curriculum based upon a rationale which resolves the central issues encompassed by the three points of view.

PRESSURES FOR A RATIONAL DESIGN OF THE TOTAL INSTITUTION. In addition to pointing out the need for a workable curriculum theory, some educators have expressed concern about the dimensions of the institution itself. Here, the problems relate to the extent of pupil and staff services, student activities, community functions, and a host of institutional facilities and arrangements that extend far beyond those necessary to support curriculum needs. Into the present period, the concept of the comprehensive school has meant a community-oriented school. Institutional arrangements and the addenda of community services continue to be determined almost completely by local needs and demands and by the willingness of local citizens to provide resources.

The role of professional leadership, under these conditions, is to encourage local effort to study needs, formulate programs to meet the needs identified, and generate political support for them. This pattern of community-based activity has much to commend it. Citizen interest and involvement, local initiative and responsibility, and provision of local political machinery backed by a competent professional staff are only a few of the elements of strength in this process. No one can depreciate its effectiveness in creating a remarkable system of universal, free, public education—one that is a unique American contribution. One must ask the question, however, whether or not this is an adequate pattern for current and future conditions.

What are the effects of attempting to meet regional, national, and international problems on a local level with a locally oriented educational institution under conditions in which local and even state resources have become grossly inadequate to the task? What shall be the guidelines for deciding the development of the secondary school as an institution?

SECONDARY EDUCATION: CURRENT STATUS

The constant rise in level of education of the general population is a source of pride to the nation and an inspiration to other countries. The high standard of living in all spheres of activity is viewed as a direct function of education rather than of natural wealth. All nations with literate populations have high per capita incomes and high levels of living standards; whereas no nation with an illiterate population—despite great natural resources—has achieved high productivity. According to a survey of Alva Myrdal of the relation of education to economic growth in

Western nations, "education has, in the nations that have advanced rapidly and firmly, been rather a predecessor than a follower in the table of progress." [3]

The direct relationship of secondary education to individual development and the group welfare is obvious, though difficult to measure. The role of education, particularly in economic growth, is becoming an area of serious study. Important facts are coming to light to contribute to an assessment of secondary education in the United States. Some of these facts reveal great successes, while others indicate sources of weakness. Certain areas of strength and weakness have been selected for review in this section as a means of examining the current status of secondary education.

Enrollment and Retention

The high value placed upon obtaining a secondary education for all youth stems from many sources. Emphasis upon individual perfectibility is deeply rooted in the American tradition. Perhaps more important is the realization that a sound, general education is vital to a free society. Whatever the societal pressures and incentives to provide secondary education and the individual motivations to attain it, secondary schools have multiplied their enrollments ten times during the past fifty years while the secondary school age population has doubled. Table 2-1 contains the data on enrollments with estimates to 1970. In 1962, almost 90 percent of the fourteen- to seventeen-year age group was in attendance.

Approximately sixty-five of each one hundred youth seventeen years of age graduated from high school in 1962. Actually, the graduating age is not uniformly at age seventeen, and this figure is therefore slightly higher. Estimates place the total number of high school graduates in a given year at slightly over 70 percent.

Table 2-1 also reveals the extent of the problem of youth who do not complete high school and graduate—the dropouts. Approximately one-third of the youth of the nation do not complete a secondary school education. Some implications of this problem are illustrated in a later section of this chapter.

3. As reported in John K. Norton, "Education and Economic Development," *Indiana Journal of Educational Administration and Research,* No. 1, Spring, 1961, p. 13.

Table 2-1. Secondary School Enrollment Data, 1890 to 1970

Year	Population 14-17 years of Age	Public School Enrollment Grades 9-12*	Nonpublic School Enrollment Grades 9-12*	Percent of Enrollment in Nonpublic Schools	Total Number Enrolled per 100 14-17 Years of Age	Number Graduated per 100, 17 Yrs. of Age
1890	5,355,000	203,000	95,000	32	6.7	3.5
1900	6,152,000	519,000	111,000	18	11.4	6.4
1910	7,220,000	916,000	117,000	11	15.4	8.8
1920	7,736,000	2,200,000	214,000	9	32.3	16.8
1930	9,341,000	4,399,000	341,000	8	51.4	29.0
1940	9,720,000	6,635,000	488,000	6	73.3	50.8
1950	8,405,000	5,758,000	695,000	10	76.8	59.0
1960	11,155,000	8,600,000	1,100,000	11	87.0	64.2
1962†	12,027,000	9,600,000	1,200,000	12	89.8	64.8
1970‡	14,500,000	11,745,000	1,450,000	14	91.0	67.0

*Number rounded to nearest 1,000.

†Preliminary data for 50 states and the District of Columbia.

‡Estimated.

SOURCE: U.S. Office of Education, Biennial Survey of Education in the United States (Washington, D.C.: U.S. Department of Health, Education, and Welfare, 1960).

Adequacy of Secondary School Programs

Secondary schools now enroll youth comprising the full range of motivation, educability, occupational goals, racial and ethnic groups, and socioeconomic status. A brief examination of Table 2-1 reveals the change from small, selected enrollments to the large, diverse ones of today. Retention of youth under these conditions is not enough. Secondary school programs must provide an education adequate to the needs of all youth—adequate in terms of both the immediate learning environment and the long-range uses of schooling.

SCHOOL DROPOUT AS A MEASURE OF ADEQUACY. The dropout provides an interesting means of appraisal of some of the shortcomings of the secondary school and, equally important, of the community in which large numbers of dropouts occur. Some of the findings of the National Education Association Project on School Dropouts are revealing of conditions conducive to low retention:

1. The average dropout is not uneducable. He does tend to score lower on IQ tests than his in-school counterpart, but a nationwide study conducted by the U.S. Department of Labor showed that 70 percent of the dropouts surveyed had registered IQ scores above 90, clearly in the educable group. An intensive six-year study in the State of New York revealed that 13 percent of the dropouts had IQ scores above 110. This rating should permit high school graduation and some post-high school training.

2. The average dropout is at least two years retarded in reading ability by the time he quits school. Reading remains the fundamental educational skill; without it no student can perform adequately in school. The consequences of retardation in reading are obvious: dropouts fail three times as many courses as "stay-ins," and 9 of every 10 dropouts have been retained in some grade at least one extra year.

3. The majority of dropouts are from lower socioeconomic families. They often come from families where the father is missing, where cultural background and horizons are limited, where education is viewed with indifference, distrust, or open resentment. Any redemptive or preventive effort of the school will have to take account of the student's total environment and will depend heavily on the school's staff of guidance counselors and school-community coordinators.

4. There is a high percentage of dropouts among minority groups. This fact was detailed as follows at the 1961 Conference on Unemployed, Out-of-School Youth in Urban Areas:

Estimates of the number of Mexican-American youth who leave school before getting to high school range as high as 50 percent in the major cities.

Today, two-thirds of all Negroes live in urban areas, one-third in urban areas outside the South.

In a slum section composed almost entirely of Negroes in one of our largest cities the following situation was found. A total of 59 percent of the male youth between the ages of 16 and 21 were out of school and unemployed. They were roaming the streets. Of the boys who graduated from high school, 48 percent were unemployed in contrast to 63 percent of the boys who had dropped out of school.

An even worse state of affairs was found in another special study in a different city. In a slum area of 125,000 people, mostly Negro, a sampling of the youth population shows that roughly 70 percent of the boys and girls ages 16-21 are out-of-school and unemployed.

The problem of unemployed youth in the large cities is in no small part a Negro problem. We do not facilitate its solution by trying to find phrases to hide this fact.

5. Dropouts are not entirely from minority groups. Of the four special surveys made for the Conference on Unemployed, Out-of-School Youth in Urban Areas, two dealt with racially mixed urban school districts where the majority of the dropouts interviewed were white. Like the minority group dropouts, however, most of these white boys and girls belonged to lower income families who had recently arrived in the city. Theirs were families who had left subsistence farms, families said to be among the nation's least educated, with a lack of motivation no less deadening than that of darker-skinned families from depressed areas. But the problem of school dropouts is not confined to the big cities. It exists in small towns. It is particularly acute in rural areas, and the problems of the rural areas and the big cities are closely related.[4]

SCHOOL OFFERINGS AS AN INDEX OF ADEQUACY. Numerous studies have been made employing an inventory of courses actually completed by high school youth of recent graduation. In particular, two studies conducted by James Conant employing this approach have received nationwide attention.[5] The studies, taken together, indicate that wide variations exist in educational opportunity among schools as measured by offering. Marked differences are found between (1) small, rural schools which tend to have very limited offerings; (2) large city schools which tend to have undifferentiated programs; and (3) large, suburban schools which

4. National Committee for Support of the Public Schools, *Changing Demands on Education and Their Fiscal Implications* (Washington, D.C.: the Committee, 1963), pp. 57, 58.

5. Conant, *The American High School Today, op. cit.,* and *Slums and Suburbs* (New York: McGraw-Hill Book Co., 1961).

tend to have extensive offerings and differentiated programs in terms of individual student abilities and goals. Table 2-2 summarizes a sample of student inventories taken from six selected schools—five suburban, one special city high school—showing academic offering.

There seems to be general agreement that the following program features are highly desirable:

Junior High School—Grades 7–9

1. Required programs to include: three years of English and social studies, three years of mathematics, at least two years of science with a minimum of one laboratory science, health and physical education.
2. Required study in art and music with specialized study for the talented.
3. Elective study in foreign languages, art, music, crafts, typing, home economics, and shop.

Senior High School—Grades 10–12

1. Required programs to include: three years of English, one year of social studies—two if none is taken in grade 9, one year of science, one year of mathematics as minimums, health and physical education.
2. Elective subjects: two years' minimum study of a foreign language for all students who show facility in foreign language in the junior high school, art and/or music, home economics, business and secretarial,, and shop in ordered sequences.
3. Programs arranged so that students may study five subjects each year rather than the traditional four subjects, plus physical education.

Elements for Both Junior and Senior High School

1. Planning of student programs on an individual basis.
2. Ability grouping, subject by subject.
3. Developmental reading program with systematic appraisal of students' reading abilities and performance.
4. Provisions for diagnostic and remedial work by specialists.
5. Guidance, counseling, and testing services for all students, with planned parent conferences.
6. Special facilities and staff for slow learners and the handicapped.
7. Provision of summer school for all levels of student interests and needs.
8. Vocational training extending into community occupations.

OCCUPATIONAL SUCCESS: MEASURE OF ADEQUACY. Since occupational success is a measure of the potential of the individual to attain the material aspects of the good life, individual income has long been used as a measure of the adequacy of education. The latest of a long series of stud-

Table 2-2. The High School Program and Post-High School Occupation
of the Typical (Median)* Student in Each IQ Group in Six Selected Schools

IQ Group	75-89			90-104			105-114			115-129			130+			All IQ's		
B-Boys, G-Girls, T-Total	B	G	T	B	G	T	B	G	T	B	G	T	B	G	T	B	G	T
No. in Category	26	23	49	102	123	225	213	209	422	488	255	743	549	192	741	1378	802	2180
Post-High School Occupation: C-College, E-Employment	E	E	E	C	C-E	C	C	C	C	C	C	C	C	C	C	C	C	C
(Figures are numbers of courses, grades 9-12.)																		
Total Courses	22	22	22	22	24	22	23	23	23	24	24	24	26	26	26	24	24	24
Total Academic Courses†	12	12	12	14	14	14	16	16	16	16	18	16	19	19	19	17	17	17
1. English	4	4	4	4	4	4	4	4	4	4	4	4	4	4	4	4	4	4
2. Total Foreign Lang.	0	0	0	2	2	2	2	3	3	2	4	3	3	3	3	3	3	3
3. Social Studies	4	4	4	4	4	4	4	4	4	3	4	3	4	4	4	4	4	4
4. Mathematics	2	2	2	3	2	3	4	3	3	4	3	4	4	4	4	4	3	4
5. Science	2	2	2	2	2	2	3	2	3	3	2	3	4	4	4	3	2	3
Total Nonacademic Courses†	10	10	10	8	10	8	7	7	7	8	6	8	7	7	7	7	7	7
1. Physical Education	4	4	4	4	4	4	4	4	4	4	4	4	4	4	4	4	4	4
2. Art, Music, Home Economics, Business and Secretarial, Shop	6	6	6	4	6	4	3	3	3	4	2	4	3	3	3	3	3	3

*A median represents a midpoint. For example, the typical student takes 24 total courses, but as many students take more than 24 courses as take fewer than 24 total courses. This is another way of looking at the figures presented in the previous table for all six schools combined.

†The totals do not necessarily equal the sum of the individual parts. This happens in a composite picture drawn from different students with different programs. For example, the total of academic subjects for all students is 17, but the components add up to 18. With nonacademic subjects, except for physical education, the students distribute themselves so that in few cases do as many as 50 percent of the students take a particular course.

SOURCE: James B. Conant, Slums and Suburbs (New York: McGraw-Hill Book Co., 1961), p. 130.

ies comparing individual income with level of education is summarized
in Table 2-3. Herman Miller conducted the study based upon "derived"
figures representing conditions in 1958. Under 1958 conditions, the average graduate of elementary school could expect a lifetime income of
about $182,000 or $3769 per year, whereas an average secondary school
graduate could expect about $258,000 or $5567 per year. The difference
associated with a high school education amounts to 42 percent.

Table 2-3. Estimated Earnings from Age Eighteen to Death,
and Level of Education Completed

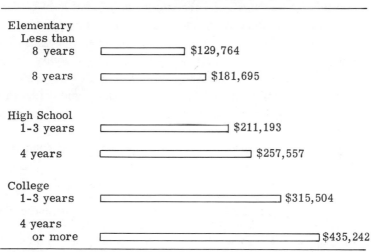

Elementary
Less than
8 years $129,764

8 years $181,695

High School
1-3 years $211,193

4 years $257,557

College
1-3 years $315,504

4 years
or more $435,242

SOURCE: Herman P. Miller, "Annual and Lifetime Income in Relation
to Education," American Economic Review, Vol. 50, No. 5,
December 1960.

Miller reports, "Although the income levels have changed considerably during the past twenty years, the basic relationship between the
extent of schooling and income appears to have remained relatively the
same." [6] It is particularly significant to note this finding with reference
to Table 2-1. Even though large masses of the population have been
brought into the secondary schools and colleges, the relative effectiveness
of individuals to attain levels of income commensurate with levels of education is unchanged. The effect of mass education appears to be to ele-
vate the total economic potential of the nation.

6. Herman P. Miller, "Annual and Lifetime Income in Relation to Education,"
American Economic Review, Vol. 50, No. 5, December 1960, p. 4.

Unmeasurable Contributions of Secondary Education

The apparently insurmountable task of specifying and measuring the total effects of education seems to leave definitive answers concerning adequacy dangling in the air. Changing conditions defy the establishment of criteria by which one can judge whether educational institutions are more effective now than they were in the past. Both the content and the uses of schooling have changed dramatically in the past and are undergoing a pervasive change now. Such influences as the mass media, new opportunities for travel, and the rise in the general level of the culture have an impact which is an added inducement to education and is facilitative of it. On the negative side, educational effectiveness is reduced by conditions stemming from population growth and mobility, inequalities in financial support of education, shortages of well-trained teachers and of classrooms, unsolved social problems of slums and of discrimination against minority groups, and unresolved debates over the purposes of education.

Nevertheless, most would agree that there have been solid, though statistically unmeasurable, gains for education in general and secondary education in particular. Some of these contributions might be listed as:

1. Dramatic lifting of the general educational level of the entire population—an essential ingredient of a modern, civilized society.
2. Development of a route for each individual to improve himself and gain access to the good life.
3. Achievement of democratic aims through the preparation of the individual for intelligent participation in public affairs.
4. The acceptance of change—to value new knowledge and resist superstition and ignorance—and the creation of a climate of acceptance of the scientific solution of problems.
5. Direct improvement of public health, agriculture, and family life.
6. Contribution to the preparation of the pool of trained manpower to operate the scientific and technological systems that support the nation.
7. Development within the individual of the attitudes and skills necessary for continued learning.

These are but a sampling of items that critics of secondary education have attributed to it in their writings. Whatever measures are made of achievements or shortcomings, significant elements remain that can only be enumerated.

PROBLEMS AND CLIMATES OF DECISION

Throughout this chapter the authors have pointed to specific inadequacies of secondary education as well as to its strengths and accomplishments. Assessments of adequacy are of little use, except to historians, unless they provide insight into potentials for solving problems. Certain persistent, unresolved problems, as well as those that are currently developing, will be resolved or not within a complex pattern of decision making. Action within the local secondary school is determined by decisions—individual, political, and professional—that create climates within which the local school functions.

Figure 2-1. Framework of Decisions Affecting Local Schools

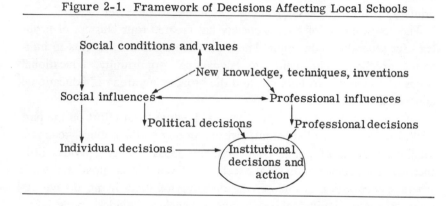

The three types of decisions are shown in Figure 2-1. Political decisions at local, state, and national levels shape the programs and institutional arrangements in each school district. Compulsory attendance laws, fixing of tax rates, assignment of responsibility for certain specific courses, and a host of other legal requirements create climates of operation for the secondary schools. Professional decisions to prepare teachers in certain ways, develop instructional materials, and conduct studies reflect the kinds of decisions made within professional circles. Similarly, a cumulative effect is produced by the enormous number of individual decisions made relative to schools. These range from individual adult voting decisions to course selections by students representing choices of occupational preparation. Each is independent; yet each affects the others, and together they produce climates of operation for the schools.

The impact of social conditions and values is particularly significant for understanding of persistent problems and issues to be dealt with in this section. The impact of new knowledge, techniques, and inventions (see Figure 2-1) is treated in Chapter 3.

Educational Problems Due to Mass Society

Long-term social changes toward centralization of government and industry, breakup of traditional community patterns, increased population, population mobility, urbanization, basic shifts from middle-class to so-called "affluent" values—all are deep-rooted symptoms of the development of what sociologists call "mass society." Intense specialization due to the demands of a technological age, mass media of communications, and rapid, large-scale transportation are usually singled out as the primary causes of these radical changes in the social order.

The development of a mass society has created four clusters of problems for secondary education. These problem areas are: threats to individual excellence, inequality in educational opportunity, educational needs of a scientific technology, and the broadening arena of educational concern.

THREATS TO INDIVIDUAL EXCELLENCE. Despite great effort on the part of the profession—and apparent, insistent urging by the public—to create quality programs of public education, our mass society provides little incentive for general, individual excellence. Except in occupational fields where specialization is intense, the demands of daily living do not require or reward individual excellence. Television provides ample information and entertainment without the effort of reading. Home appliances, autos, and mechanical conveniences are so finely adjusted and so complex that the owner dares not attempt to service them even if he understands the nature of their construction. Automation supplants the need for most skills and precludes the necessity of understanding—even computing one's change at the check-out counters of stores can now be handled automatically.

Youth readily perceive the lack of necessity to acquire basic skills and broad, general knowledge beyond a rudimentary level. Where motivation depends upon obvious application and immediate utility, schools are hard pressed to justify sophisticated, abstract learning for the purposes of a sound general education.

BURDEN OF INEQUALITY IN EDUCATIONAL OPPORTUNITY. Perhaps the most serious persistent problem cluster, and the one that has the most pervasive effect, is the matter of unequal educational opportunities. The matter becomes particularly serious at the secondary school level where programs become differentiated and higher degrees of specialized learnings are involved. Inequalities arise from several principal sources:

1. Limited programs of the small rural secondary schools and those of numerous communities geared to local industry and to basic college-oriented subjects.

2. Community conditions in depressed areas, in communities where various forms of discrimination are practiced, and in places where family aspirations or social values sharply restrict the range of educational offering and curtail the ability of the school to adjust instruction to the learning needs of students.

3. Sharp area differences in levels of support, both within and between states; there is ample evidence of a direct relationship between level of support and quality of educational program—support of education in wealthy districts is well over one hundred times that in poorer districts of the nation, based upon equated dollars.

GEARING SECONDARY EDUCATION TO A SCIENTIFIC TECHNOLOGY. The fabric of modern mass society is sustained by a technology powered by science. The interdependence of large numbers of specialists creates at certain points critical balances of trained manpower. The educational system of the country is now directly involved in sustaining and improving the standard of living, for education is the essential ingredient in technological advance. The rapid shift expected in occupational manpower needs during the 1960's is shown by Table 2-4.

Professional and technical occupation needs will increase more than 40 percent during the 1960's. The need for unskilled workers will show no change, and the need for farm workers will decrease almost 20 percent. The relationship of education to these needs is shown in the right side of Table 2-4. Note that average years of schooling for occupational groups are tabulated for the year 1959. There is strong reason to expect that these educational levels proved inadequate, even for 1959, and that demands for improvement of the whole occupational force call for increased years of schooling all down the line.

SECONDARY EDUCATION IN AN EVER BROADENING ARENA. A cluster of problems centers around the fact that secondary education can no longer be oriented, organized, and supported primarily in terms of the local community. Until World War II, public education might have been char-

Table 2-4. Percent Change in Employment, 1960-1970, and
Average Level of Schooling by Occupational Group, 1959

Occupation Group	Percent Change in Employment 1960-1970	Average Years of School Completed, 1959
	−20 −10 0 10 20 30 40 50	
Professional & technical		16.2
Proprietors & managers		12.4
Clerical & sales		12.5
Skilled		11.0
Semiskilled		9.9
Service		9.7
Unskilled		8.6
Farmers & farm workers		8.6

SOURCE: U.S. Department of Labor, Manpower: Challenge of the 1960's
(Washington, D.C.: U.S. Government Printing Office, 1961), p. 11.

acterized as provincial education, but the immediacy of national and
international communities now requires a reexamination of program,
organization, control, and support to insure a broad orientation. In the
area of program alone, a simple illustration may suffice to show this
need. Many secondary schools today offer little or no study in geography
and often little more than an acquaintance with history and the cultural
background of the United States. What seems to be needed is deeper
knowledge of the development of Western civilization—including languages, political theories, and economics, a study of the cultures of emer-
gent nations, of at least physical and economic geography, and of communist ideology.

There is little doubt that controls and support are now shifting dramatically toward state and national governments and away from the local
community. The amount of state support has now reached 40 percent
of the total expenditures for education, and state departments as well as
universities are organizing to take a more direct interest in the affairs of

public education. National interests are continuously being pressed through foundations, national testing programs, and government-supported programs. These efforts are as yet operated on a piecemeal basis, with danger of overemphasis in specialized areas such as science, mathematics, and vocational training. The trends away from purely local controls are clear.

Direction, Support, and Control: Need for Social Commitment

From the previous section it should be clear that rapid social changes have radically altered the role of secondary education. The needed reorientation of secondary education and redefinition of its meaning in a new age are basically professional decisions. But before the work of the profession can move ahead, a number of fundamental decisions of public policy must first be made. These broad policy decisions are of three kinds: (1) directions for the development of secondary education, (2) levels of support, and (3) structures of organization and control.

The question of direction and priorities is still a matter of intense public debate. Conflict over purposes has been examined in an opening section of this chapter. Most authorities agree that this struggle is symptomatic of deep social unrest, and early solutions are not anticipated. Unclear purposes represent a source of both weakness and danger to public education. Without clear public mandates, program planning becomes undirected and disorganized, and no basis is provided for assessment. In such a climate the public schools are vulnerable to attack by irresponsible groups, and they easily become embroiled in fruitless conflict.

Structures of organization and control are examined in some detail in Chapters 6 and 7. There is ample evidence that present provisions for the organization of public education and its control are inadequate to the task ahead. The profession—as represented both in professional organizations and among leading administrators—has not provided continuous aggressive leadership to seek adequate organizational structures, and special interest groups and advocates of local autonomy have retarded progress in this field. Gross inequalities exist between school districts, and inadequate and costly organizational arrangements are maintained. Reorganization—from the local district level to the U.S. Office of Education—can be effected only through public expression and formal decisions.

Perhaps in no other area—including debate over purposes—is there as much misinformation and general lack of public understanding as in the matter of support for education. Attacks upon Federal expenditures for education, opposition to general support of education by the Federal Government, disagreement over proper ratios of state and local support, publicity about dramatically rising educational costs, and widespread voter revolts against increases in educational support at the local level are common knowledge. Although many side issues enter the picture, two general notions are given widespread attention. One is that modern education costs much more than it did in the past. Another holds that public education is analogous to a sponge and that further expenditures would not bring commensurate returns.

Table 2-5. Daily Per Pupil Current Expenditure for Public
Primary and Secondary Education

Year	Daily Per Pupil Cost in 1954 Dollars
1900	$1.48
1910	1.48
1920	1.50
1930	1.43
1940	1.49
1950	1.40
1958	1.45

SOURCE: Werner Z. Hirsch, <u>Analysis of Rising Costs of Public Education</u>, U.S. Congress Joint Economic Committee, Study Papers 4 and 5 (Washington D.C.: U.S. Government Printing Office, 1959), p. 34.

The belief that modern education costs more than it did in the past appears to be myth. Recent studies have developed measures by which costs of education may be equated and compared. One measure, that of *income elasticity of education,* reflects the cost of education per pupil in average daily attendance in school. Thus the numbers of students, days in the school year, and other factors are held constant. Table 2-5 provides data of educational costs based upon this measure by ten-year periods since 1900. The year of highest cost was 1942 (not given in the table), when the cost was $1.49 per pupil, per day. The year of lowest cost was 1922 (also not given in the table), when the cost was $1.37 per pupil, per day.

The amazingly stable level of expenditures is obvious. One can only conclude that the public is unwilling to buy education at a higher rate than it did in 1900, despite large increases in real income per citizen during the past sixty years.

The second belief commonly expressed, that increased expenditures are not likely to yield increased quality, appears to be as much a myth as was the first. The Institute of Administrative Research of Teachers College, Columbia University, has conducted an extensive review of studies attempting to relate educational costs to quality of school programs. John Norton summarizes this research as follows:

A number of lines of research indicate that higher per pupil expenditure is a major and essential factor in achieving quality education, regardless of one's definition of quality. This appears to be true among favored school districts, all of which are well above average in financial support. Apparently adequacy of support as a factor in increasing educational quality has not reached a point of diminishing returns among schools with the highest levels of cost.[7]

In the important areas of direction, control, and support—areas that depend upon public policy decisions—secondary education appears to be seriously hampered. Professional leadership is necessary to study educational needs in these areas and to challenge the public to commit itself seriously to the task of public education.

REFERENCES

Association for Supervision and Curriculum Development, *New Dimensions in Learning* (Washington, D.C.: the Association, 1962).

Campbell, Roald, and Bunnell, Robert A., *Nationalizing Influences on Secondary Education* (Chicago: Midwest Administration Center, University of Chicago, 1963).

Chandler, B. J., Stiles, Lindley J., and Kitsuse, John I. (eds.), *Education in Urban Society* (New York: Dodd, Mead & Co., 1962).

Conant, James B., *Slums and Suburbs* (New York: McGraw-Hill Book Co., 1961).

National Committee for Support of the Public Schools, *Changing Demands on Education and Their Fiscal Implications* (Washington, D.C.: the Committee, 1963).

President's Committee on Youth Employment, *The Challenge of Jobless Youth* (Washington, D.C.: U.S. Government Printing Office, 1963).

Stiles, Lindley J., McCleary, Lloyd E., and Turnbaugh, Roy, *Secondary Education in the United States* (New York: Harcourt, Brace & World, 1962).

7. National Committee for Support of the Public Schools, *op. cit.,* p. 80.

Suffirn, Sidney C., *Issues in Federal Aid to Education* (Syracuse, N.Y.: Syracuse University Press, 1962).

U.S. Department of Labor, *Manpower Challenge of the 1960's* (Washington, D.C.: U.S. Government Printing Office, 1961).

U.S. Office of Education, *Progress of Public Education in the United States of America, 1961-1962* (Washington, D.C.: U.S. Department of Health, Education, and Welfare, 1962).

Vaizey, John, *The Economics of Education* (New York: Free Press of Glencoe, 1962).

Chapter 3
Emergent Forces and
New Directions

AMONG the many forces presently shaping the character of American education, three appear to possess sufficient impact to create new educational institutions, new devices and processes of instruction, new curricula, and entirely new patterns of instruction. The three forces presently restructuring American education are (1) the rapid growth and mobility of population, (2) the stress of international tensions, and (3) the accelerated development of automation, technology, and new knowledge.

IMPACT OF POPULATION GROWTH AND MOBILITY

Population figures in the United States are showing unparalleled increases. Rising birth rates added 28 million new persons to the population of this country in the decade between 1950 and 1960—an increase comparable to the nation's total population at the outbreak of the Civil War.[1] Moreover, predictions concerning the current "population explosion" indicate that 26 million new young people will surge into the job market during the next decade. By 1970, one out of three persons in the United States will have been born after World War II.

The rapidly increasing population of the United States is being paralleled by unusual population mobility and a sustained rush to great centers of population. Already one fourth of all Americans live in states other than those in which they were born, and the proportion of the

1. Conrad Taeuber, "Some Current Population Trends in the United States," in *Financing Education for Our Changing Population* (Washington, D.C.: Committee on Educational Finance, National Education Association, 1961), p. 11.

nation's population living on farms has fallen from 37 percent to just over 10 percent. The "gray areas" of metropolitan centers are presenting problems of ever increasing complexity; urbanization in America has become a phenomenon of dramatic proportions. Predictions indicate that millions will live in vast regional cities similar to the Atlantic Coast strip-city from Boston to Washington, which presently houses nearly 30 million individuals.

The Challenge of Numbers

American education has already felt the impact of these powerful forces. The educational enterprise now involves one fourth of the nation's population and requires an annual operating budget of billions of dollars. In the decade ending in 1960, public school enrollments increased from 24 to 36 million; teacher requirements rose from 913,000 to 1,-300,000; and yearly costs of maintaining the educational enterprise increased from $5.8 billion to $15.6 billion.[2]

There is every indication that the phenomenal growth of public education will continue through the 1960's. Estimates indicate that elementary and secondary public school enrollments will reach 44 million by 1969-1970. College and university enrollments will rise a spectacular 70 percent.[3] Indeed, the enrollment rise of 2.7 million at the level of higher education during the 1960's will encompass 44 percent of all the nation's eighteen- to twenty-one-year age group.

Such figures indicate that the provision of adequate school facilities in the 1960's will be fully as critical as it was in the preceding decade. The problem of staffing the schools with competent and qualified teachers will continue unabated, and program development to meet the needs of great numbers of pupils will pose demanding problems. Moreover, the cost of financing the expanding educational enterprise will tend to keep alive the debate over sources of financial support and will bring increasing demands for Federal participation in meeting school costs.

2. The staff of the School Administration Branch, United States Office of Education, "Educational Administration in the Decade Ahead," *School Life,* January 1961, pp. 2-6.
3. Committee on Mission and Organization of the U.S. Office of Education, *A Federal Education Agency for the Future* (Washington: U.S. Government Printing Office, 1961), p. 39.

Effect on Administrative Units

Population mobility and the growth of great centers of population indicate that education in metropolitan areas will become increasingly important in coming years. Of the increases in school enrollment, 75 percent will be localized in some 200 metropolitan centers and population complexes. Such centers will face unusual demands in terms of school plant facilities, district and staff organization, finance, and program development to meet altered circumstances.

It appears likely that many metropolitan centers will follow the lead of cities like Chicago where twenty-one subdistricts were created in an effort to decentralize a tremendously complex school operation. District superintendents were appointed to assist in the management of the subdistricts encompassing attendance areas of approximately 25,000 elementary and secondary pupils. Benjamin Willis, the General Superintendent of Schools, noted that "increasingly serious problems of growing enrollments, staffing the schools, and housing of pupils necessitate the most effective plan of administration and supervision which can be developed in order that appropriate emphasis may be given to our primary concern, viz., that of instruction." [4] Moreover, the new departmental and subdistrict plan of organization was implemented to "improve coordination and communication, and further the effectiveness of the instructional program within the Chicago Public Schools. It will develop more effective working relationships between administrative and supervisory personnel, and the schools and communities whose pupils they serve." [5]

The philosophy of strong central control, however, is likely to remain in force in large cities even where subdistricts have been created.

In other words the whole system must be orderly, patterned, and integrated. There can be only one school system in any one city. The district budget makes this fact obvious, for regardless of the autonomy of the local unit, there is but one budget. Since any school budget is merely an instrument of policy, the relationship of local units to the larger unit in terms of policy control and unity of program is clear.[6]

4. Excerpt from the *Proceedings of the Board of Education of the City of Chicago,* April 13, 1955.
   5. *Ibid.*
   6. American Association of School Administrators, "Decentralization of Administrative Processes in Large School Districts," *School District Organization,* a report of the AASA Commission on School District Reorganization (Washington, D.C.: the Association, 1958), p. 304.

Despite the lead of cities such as Chicago, patterns of decentralization in big-city districts are still largely unexplored. Such new patterns are likely to receive increased attention and impetus as metropolitan areas cope with the problem of meeting local educational and instructional needs in large urban complexes.

The trend toward decentralization in large cities is likely to be paralleled by different organizational trends in nonurban areas. With the continuing centralization of population, rural areas will necessarily face problems associated with rapidly declining enrollments. The 42,000 school districts existing in the United States in the 1960's may well be reduced to half that number in future years. Continuing interest in district reorganization in rural and suburban areas may result in greater consolidation and centralization and the creation of school districts encompassing both elementary and secondary education. County units are also likely to increase in number in areas of population scarcity. Such reorganization trends may radically affect the size of many present-day secondary schools; the coming trend will apparently be toward large centralized high schools with enrollments of 1500 to 4000 pupils and greatly augmented programs. It seems clear that the role of intermediate units may be extensively redefined: in many states such units are likely to be restructured to provide extended special services and consultant help to supplement and assist the efforts of local districts. Moreover, state departments of education should assume new positions of prominence as state educational activities are expanded, as more and more chief state school officers become board-appointed, and as state department powers and functions are broadened.

The adequacy, effectiveness, and efficiency of administrative organizations will undergo severe tests as increased population mobility reduces rural enrollments and bursts the seams of available school facilities in urban and suburban areas. The task of maintaining quality in the face of rising costs and rising enrollments will create new administrative problems to affect and test all administrative levels—local, intermediate, and state.

IMPACT OF INTERNATIONAL TENSION

Satellite competitions, cold wars, and worldwide ideological conflicts in recent years have repeatedly emphasized the important role of education and scholarship in the affairs of men. In many countries, education and scholarship have come to be viewed as critical national resources essential to successful competition in the world struggle for power and supremacy.

In the United States, growing realization of education's important mission has precipitated a decade of controversy concerning the adequacy of the American educational enterprise. Increased attention has been directed not only to the existing alignment of educational priorities, purposes, and goals but to educational patterns, functions, and needs. Important challenges have been posed concerning the substance, process, spirit, and aims of education. In the past few years new educational goals have emerged: society has increasingly insisted that quantity in education be matched with quality, that universality be paralleled by excellence,[7] and that schools become the vehicles of national survival. The emergence of new societal goals has prompted critical appraisal of means for identifying and releasing student potential; for improving and upgrading curricula and teaching personnel; for providing more effective tools and techniques in the teaching process; for implementing more flexible and efficient ways to deploy pupils and teachers; for improving the organization and quality of the teaching-learning process; for upgrading the quality of educational organization and leadership; and for creating educational institutions capable of producing "masses of intellectuals." [8]

The Changing Curriculum

The new criterion of excellence, the growth of public concern over the quality and breadth of educational programs, and the demand for education of masses of intellectuals will tend to direct increasing attention toward the intellectual aims of secondary education during the coming decade. The rapid obsolescence of knowledge is already discrediting the notion that the curriculum can consist of a static body of knowledge and ideas which, when mastered, will prepare the individual for effective living. The changing nature of knowledge is bringing realization that today's facts and ideas may be totally inadequate for meeting the challenges of the future.

Important new directions in curriculum reconstruction will emerge during the coming decade to meet the criteria of quality and excellence.

7. See Francis S. Chase, "Universality Versus Excellence in Education," in *Education Looks Ahead* (Chicago: Scott, Foresman & Co., 1960).

8. Charles E. Silberman, "The Remaking of American Education," *Fortune*, Vol. LXIII, No. 4, April 1961, p. 127.

Acquisition of facts will become secondary to the development of abilities for using knowledge, analyzing evidence, exercising critical judgment, and reaching sound conclusions. There will be increasing emphasis upon the pursuit of new knowledge and upon the ability to fit ideas to changing situations and circumstances.[9] Students will learn to apply the important concepts in mathematics and science and the basic themes in the humanities and the social sciences in progressively complex problem situations. Creativity in the use of knowledge will become paramount as emphasis is placed upon developing critical judgment, fertile hypotheses, and reasoned conclusions. Thus, quality and excellence will demand not only new criteria for selecting basic ideas and concepts in each subject area but new patterns for the scope and sequence of learning experiences. Content in various subject matter fields will require careful assessment to determine what should be taught and the best way to teach it.

Considerable progress has already been made in the development of new instructional and curricular materials to improve the teaching-learning process. New courses and instructional materials for school use are being made available by Yale University's School Mathematics Study Group, the National Science Foundation, the Wayne State University Foreign Language Project, the Biological Sciences Curriculum Study at the University of Colorado, and the Physical Science Study Committee at the Massachusetts Institute of Technology.

Complete "packaged courses[10] have been developed in a number of subject areas. Jerrold Zacharias, for example, spearheaded a project aimed at a complete revision of content and methods in the area of high school physics. With support from the National Science Foundation, Zacharias and the Physical Science Study Committee (PSSC, since renamed Educational Services, Inc.) developed a revolutionary new course which is presently being used in many high schools. As a result of its work the PSSC made available complete new textbooks, comprehensive teacher's guides, and a set of sixty films explaining and demonstrating scientific concepts and phenomena.

An entirely new mathematics curriculum for each of the grades 4 through 12 is being prepared by Yale University's School Mathematics Study Group. The program seeks to develop the computation skills of stu-

9. Chase, *op. cit.*, p. 31.
10. See Henry C. Ruark, Jr., "Technology and Education," *Phi Delta Kappan,* Vol. XLII, No. 9, June 1961.

dents and to increase their understanding of the logic of the number system. The high school English curriculum is receiving attention from the Commission on English headed by Harold C. Martin of Harvard University. The Commission, set up by the College Entrance Examination Board, is directing major attention to developing writing abilities among high school students. Progress is also under way in curriculum revision in chemistry and biology. Filmed courses in such subjects as physics, mathematics, biology, and chemistry are already available for use in high schools.

School Staffs

Efforts to raise the quality of education in tomorrow's schools will result in new standards for the selection, preparation, deployment, and performance of professional workers in education. Large numbers of well-qualified young people will be attracted to the field by raised professional standards, better pay, and opportunities to achieve high personal and professional goals. More and more teachers will be trained in liberal arts colleges and universities rather than in teachers colleges. Programs for preparing teachers will stress the acquisition of substantial bodies of organized knowledge, and there will be increased emphasis on processes of intellectual inquiry as bases from which knowledge may be extended and generated.

In like manner, professional training programs for administrators will stress not only technical competencies but social, process, and conceptual competencies. The basic disciplines will receive more and more emphasis, and there will be provision for intensive study of human relations, leadership, and administrative theory. Internships, community study, and simulation [11] will become increasingly important, as will the study of motivation, communication, power structures, perception, decision making, and leader behavior.

THE TEACHER'S ROLE. As the professional and nonprofessional functions of teachers are defined, instructional staffs will undoubtedly be liberated from present burdens of custodial, clerical, and police duties. Much greater emphasis will be placed upon the teacher's professional competence for motivating and guiding learning. Teaching functions will

11. See Jack A. Culbertson, "Simulated Situations and Instruction: A Critique," in *Simulation in Administrative Training* (Columbus, Ohio: University Council for Educational Administration, 1960).

be clearly differentiated and opportunities to bypass many routine and drill tasks will be increased with new programmed materials, teaching machines, films, and television. Moreover, special proficiencies of teachers will be more broadly utilized through the introduction of teaching teams.

Emerging patterns of staff deployment and utilization are already having major impact in selected schools across the nation. Experimental approaches to team teaching, for example, are introducing new roles such as "master" teacher, "team" leader, and "senior" teacher. These newly defined roles are creating opportunities for teachers to advance along an instructional rather than an administrative route. One writer defines a team-teaching relationship as follows:

A team relationship occurs when a group of teachers and students, as an organized unit, accept and carry out decision-making responsibility for a set of instructional variables such as time, space, group size, group composition, teacher assignment, and resource allocation. In addition to the variables normally under control of the teacher, the team unit permits delegation to the instructional team of decisions usually made by the principal and the use of variables not present in the smaller single teacher-class unit of organization.[12]

No one pattern of team teaching is dominant at the present time; patterns range from two-teacher teams in one subject area to larger interdisciplinary teams in which teachers from several subject areas are represented. A complex team operation may include many features: a team leader or coordinator, teachers from different subject fields, teacher aides or assistants, a large group of pupils, extensive technological media, block scheduling, varied instructional materials, flexible physical surroundings, flexible patterns of pupil grouping, and new administrative and guidance arrangements. Team operations encompass face-to-face instruction in large group settings, in divided group settings, and in small discussion seminars. As new patterns of instruction are incorporated, teachers are finding more opportunities to influence pupil actions, motivations, decisions, and perceptions through direct interaction with individual students.

The liberation of teachers for professional tasks is proceeding along still another route—through the use of teaching aides and assistants.

12. Robert E. Ohm, "Toward a Rationale for Team Teaching," *Administrator's Notebook,* Vol. IX, No. 7, March 1961, p. 1.

For example, arrangements such as the following are being used in a number of school districts: "contract" correcting of test papers and student compositions by specially hired readers; use of undergraduate and graduate students for supervision of classes, study halls, laboratory sessions, and playgrounds; employment of clerks to relieve teachers of nonprofessional tasks such as record keeping and duplication of materials; and assignment of teaching assistants to handle routine tasks associated with team teaching.

New patterns of staff utilization [13] are creating changes whose effects will require careful assessment. New roles are being created for teachers, principals, and students. Authority and status relationships are undergoing changes. Teaching patterns, motivations, and reward systems are being affected. Change has become an important dimension in the teaching-learning process, and the study and evaluation of such change will be an important task for the future.

THE PRINCIPAL'S ROLE. There are indications that changes in instructional patterns and emphases will create major shifts in program and personnel policies in school districts. Personnel administration will become much better organized and there will be clearer delineation of the responsibilities of principals, central-office personnel, and superintendents. Systemwide written policies and regulations will become more common, and increased time and effort will go into the development of policies designed to strengthen educational programs. Principals will assume major responsibilities for improvement of school instructional programs. Decentralization in school districts will lead increasingly to the addition to secondary school staffs of competent professionals who will assist principals with instructional leadership.

As instructional leaders of their schools, principals will spend a great deal of time supervising personnel, coordinating total learning resources, developing curriculum, improving settings for teaching and learning, and conducting research and evaluation.[14] In addition, principals will carry major responsibilities for the in-service education of teachers in new teaching methods, for new patterns of staff deployment, and for the use of new media in classroom instruction. Systematic in-service education

13. J. Lloyd Trump, *Guide to Better Schools* (Chicago: Rand McNally & Co., 1961), pp. 83-87, 131-135.

14. J. Lloyd Trump, "Image of the Future Secondary School Principal," *California Journal of Secondary Education,* Vol. 35, No. 8, December 1960, p. 518.

of teachers under the direction of competent professionals will take on new meaning and significance in the school of the future.

IMPACT OF TECHNOLOGY AND AUTOMATION

New developments in technology, automation, and communication are presently paving the way for startling changes and innovations in all areas of the teaching-learning process. Whereas yesterday's school transmitted knowledge through books, oral presentations, radios, filmstrips, slides, and disc recordings, the schoool of tomorrow will augment these with airborne television, closed-circuit television, video and audio tapes, language laboratories, teaching machines, programmed materials, and computer-based autoinstructional devices. Many of the new media are already part of the instructional process in many schools across the country.

Three directions are clearly evident in the development of technology and new media, and each will have major impact on the school of tomorrow. One area of development is probing the nature and use of new instructional media for mass instruction. A second is exploring possibilities for individual self-instruction through the use of automated teaching devices. The third is emphasizing the development of programmed materials in various subject areas. Finn has predicted that such developments will "hit education with a million-pound thrust." [15]

These developments have been motivated in part by the search of professional groups and foundations for improved methods of utilizing the time and energies of both pupils and teachers. The search for excellence has brought under critical review matters such as the quality of instruction; the efficient deployment of staff, pupils, and instructional materials; and the use of new media in instruction.[16]

Technology and Mass Instruction

The impact of new media on education can be gauged in part by the tremendous expansion presently taking place in the audiovisual (AV)

15. James D. Finn, "Automation and Education: III, Technology and the Instructional Process," *Audiovisual Communication Review,* Vol. 8, No. 1, Winter 1960, pp. 5-26.
16. See the Fund for the Advancement of Education, *Teachers for Tomorrow,* Bulletin No. 2, 1955; Trump, *Guide to Better Schools, op. cit.;* and Francis S. Chase and Harold A. Anderson (eds.), *The High School in a New Era* (Chicago: University of Chicago Press, 1958).

field: in accelerated technological and media developments; in the growth of local, state, and national AV associations; and in the progress of research in this area. The 1960 edition of the *Encyclopedia of Educational Research,* for instance, lists nearly three times the number of AV research references listed by the 1950 edition.

Even though schools have been characteristically slow to accept audiovisual materials,[17] there are indications that the current 20 million dollar annual expenditure for new media equipment and services will rise precipitously in the next decades. In 1954 there were fewer than 10 schools using television instruction. By 1960 there were over 600, and the number has been rising sharply each year. The number of schools using language laboratories [18] jumped from 64 to 458 in the two-year period between 1958 and 1960; such installations will be commonplace by 1970. Nearly 100 different teaching machines are now on the market, and it is estimated that autoinstructional devices will be a billion-dollar business by 1970.[19] Moreover, grants from the Ford Foundation, the Carnegie Foundation, and the U.S. Office of Education are presently supporting the development of over 100 programmed courses in psychology, mathematics, genetics, languages, philosophy, music theory, physics, chemistry, engineering, and other areas. Textbook publishers are bringing out "programmed books" in increasing numbers; and many companies, including Bell Telephone, Hughes Aircraft, American Telephone and Telegraph, Eastman Kodak, Polaroid, International Business Machines, and the Logistics Management Center in Fort Lee, Virginia, are using programmed teaching methods to educate personnel.

The growing impact of technology on mass education is indicated by other unique developments. Several hundred thousand persons continue to view college courses in subjects such as statistics, chemistry, and physics on NBC telecasts of Continental Classroom; great numbers of these viewers are enrolled for college credit. The "stratovision technique" used by the Midwest Council on Airborne Television, in which a DC-7 aircraft broadcasts instructional television programs to classrooms, indicated that regional and even national educational television (ETV)

17. Educational Policies Commission, National Education Association, *Mass Communication and Education* (Washington, D.C.: the Association, 1958), p. 87.
18. Gene C. Fusco, "Technology in the Classroom, Challenges to the School Administrator," *School Life,* March and May 1960, p. 4.
19. Launor F. Carter, "The Impact of Automation and Technology on Education," System Development Corporation, SP-282, March 1961, p. 1.

networks can be created.[20] The "stratovision technique" has already made it possible for one aircraft to telecast programs on video tape to several million potentiaľ students in 13,000 schools and colleges located in six different states. Courses on video tape originating from Purdue University are transmitted to the DC-7 for rebroadcasting to schools in Wisconsin, Illinois, Ohio, Kentucky, Indiana, and Michigan.

Pros and Cons of Mass Instruction

The increasing use of ETV, closed-circuit television, and other mass instructional media has led to controversy concerning the advantages and disadvantages accruing from their use. Proponents maintain that ETV makes possible "exposure to greatness" and brings the expert, the master teacher, into every classroom. Moreover, the medium is highly adaptable for the presentation of intimate details of laboratory work in the physical sciences to large numbers of students at the same time. In the social sciences the medium permits students to become acquainted with a wide range of phenomena which are difficult to present through the printed word. ETV is an economical method for presenting education material, and it also makes possible a great deal of flexibility in the teaching-learning process.

Limitations in ETV have also been noted. Education should have much wider scope than mere exposure to factual information: evaluation, interpretation, and application of information are fully as important. Moreover, ETV and other mass instructional media have not met the need for interaction that is necessary to social adjustment and the acquisition of values, ethics, and moral codes. Mass instructional situations make little provision for active participation by students and the give-and-take necessary in spirited inquiry. Finally, mass education media have difficulty meeting the need for progressively graded presentations to take care of individual differences among pupils.

ETV appears to be well suited for certain types of teaching: for demonstrations and presentation of factual material in a wide variety of subject areas. It may hold less promise, however, where interpretations

20. A regional ETV network is operating in the New England States. State networks are operating in Oklahoma, Alabama, and North Carolina. Other states such as New York, Oregon, Georgia, Minnesota, and Louisiana are developing ETV networks. Still other states are presently studying the feasibility of such networks.

of material are necessary; where fine shades of meaning must be drawn; where analysis, clarification, and judgment are necessary; or where interaction with others is necessary.

Technology and Individualized Instruction

Like television, autoinstructional devices are creating unlimited possibilities for new educational patterns in tomorrow's schools. These devices have the capacity to individualize instruction.

TEACHING MACHINES. The idea of teaching machines is not new: S. L. Pressey's writings on self-instructional devices began in 1926. More recently, B. F. Skinner at Harvard University has stimulated development in this area.[21] Although the teaching machine is relatively in its infancy, there are already dozens of different kinds in existence utilizing mechanical, electrochemical, or paper devices in their operation. Most self-instructional machines have three features in common. (1) They display learning items to pupils. (2) They have some method for the student to indicate responses to questions. (3) They either check the correctness or incorrectness of responses or show pupils a model response for comparison.

Early teaching machines utilized programmed materials consisting of sequences of questions revealed one at a time through a window. Pupils wrote the answer to each question, pulled levers to move the written answer into a position where it could be viewed but not altered, and compared their written answer with the correct response provided by the machine. After pressing a lever which totaled incorrect answers, the pupils could move to the next question in the series.

In the development of more satisfactory teaching devices, attention will be directed not only to the form and content of the material to be taught but also to the design of the machine. The development of content alone is a major undertaking which opens great numbers of alternatives. The material to be taught must be broken down into its concept elements, and each concept may require up to 40 items for instructional purposes. Thus a single course may require as many as 20,000 items if instruction is to be orderly and effective. Moreover, linear programs must make provision for individual differences and learning rates of students. Hence

21. See B. F. Skinner, "The Science of Learning and the Art of Teaching," *Harvard Educational Review,* Vol. 24, No. 2, Spring 1954, pp. 99-113.

"branching" or "contingent" items must be made available in programs so that students who experience difficulty may go over items through a succession of smaller or simpler steps until mastery is demonstrated.

LANGUAGE LABORATORIES. The increased use of self-instructional devices in the teaching-learning process is exemplified in the rapid growth of language laboratories. Electronic devices and audiolingual methods are now making it possible for high school students in many parts of the country to develop conversational skills in a number of different foreign languages. The electronic components permit instantaneous correction of pronunciation errors, provide drill as required, and allow each student to progress at his own speed.

The essential components of such learning laboratories are (1) the monitor center which permits contact between the teacher and each of the pupil stations,[22] and (2) the program center which makes it possible for instructors to direct programs with complete control. Different programs—tape, radio, phonograph, or audio portions of telecasts—can be circuited directly or selectively to each pupil station. Each student is provided with a booth, headset, microphone, and recording facilities. These facilities are often augmented by visual aids such as motion picture projectors, overhead projectors, and slide and filmstrip projectors.

SYSTEMS APPROACHES. New developments at the Learning Resources Institute [23] (Princeton, New Jersey), and at the System Development Corporation (Santa Monica, California), indicate that "systems approaches" will be developed to relate the science of learning to modern communications media. A systems approach has been described as follows:

> Any arrangement of men and machines bound together to produce a specifiable output can be referred to as a "system." The output of an educational system is, of course, educated people. Thus Pythagoras and his stick with which he taught theorems to students by drawing in the sand is an early man-made system; just as a university with its physical plant, its teachers, blackboards, books, card-punch machines, etc., is also a man-machine system.

22. The instructor can "listen in" without disturbing the student, or he can carry on a two-way conversation. Annunciators permit students to contact the instructor.
23. LRI is supported by foundations and private corporations and devotes its efforts to finding improved instructional uses for films, radio, TV, autoinstructional devices, and programmed materials.

Generally speaking, the output of a modern educational system is a result of a complex of interrelated factors. The systems approach to this complexity is to functionally describe the men and equipment in the system; analyze both the informal and formal communication channels and the informational needs of those involved in the system (in this case educators, students, and parents); determine costs of the present system requirements; and relate costs to the output of the system.

Two methods of systems analysis have been in general use. Neither of them is entirely new to education. One involves mathematical modeling and the other simulation techniques.[24]

The shape of things to come in systems approaches to teaching and learning may be foreshadowed by the Computerized Laboratory for Automated School Systems (CLASS) facility at System Development Corporation. CLASS, which at present is devoted to educational research and development in systems technology, integrates (1) individual automated instruction; (2) automated and conventional group instruction; and (3) centralized data processing for administration, guidance, and planning functions.

The primary aim in designing CLASS has been flexibility, and thus the central control of the system is a large Philco 2000 digital computer. Associated with the computer is a switching mechanism called a real-time input-output transducer. This transducer acts as an intermediary between (1) the Philco 2000 and the instructional materials being presented to students, and (2) the recording of student responses by the computer. Other components of the system at the present time include an alphanumeric printer, output units, and pupil desks equipped with film viewers and response devices. It is anticipated that a card punch, a flexowriter, and electrical typewriters connected to the computer will be installed at a later date to improve information processing. At present, the CLASS facility includes an administrative area, a counseling-observation area, and a large automated classroom. Each area has facilities for communicating with the computer.

CLASS's output unit can be an individualized filmed-item display unit, a random-access slide projector and viewing device, closed-circuit television, or the teacher. The closed-circuit television and the random-access slide projector can display any type of audiovisual material to

24. Don D. Bushnell and John F. Cogswell, "A Computer-Based Laboratory for Automation in School Systems," System Development Corporation, SP-256, March 1961, p. 1.

the whole class. A control tape containing all the instructions can be loaded on the computer to instruct it as to the way in which student responses should be handled. The tape also tells the computer the order of item presentation, when items may be skipped, and when remedial material is necessary. Moreover, the tape contains instructions about feedback messages for the student. Both the random-access slide projector and the closed-circuit television can be operated by either the computer or the teacher.

The input unit in this system is a five-key box which students use to select responses to the programmed material presented in instructional sessions. Changing of responses is possible with the use of an "enter" bar; no response is recorded by the computer until this bar is pressed.

Since both the administrative area and the guidance area have access to the computer, the principal and counselor may also use the Philco 2000 in a number of ways. The principal can call upon the computer for information about attendance, registration, classroom scheduling, bus scheduling, teachers' records, financial accounting figures, individual student progress, or any other data amenable to punch-card processing. The information stored on magnetic tape in the computer can also be used by the counselor to give immediate access to grade records, student performance, test scores, biographical data, and student progress at different periods.

The whole system is planned to provide flexibility in the instruction of a classroom of pupils. Since the system provides means for individual presentations to students, it will be possible to teach students either individually or in a group. Moreover, simultaneous, controlled individual instruction will be possible in several subject areas. It will be possible for some students, for example, to study physics while others are studying geometry or a foreign language. The computer can be programmed in each subject to present each student with material appropriate to his level of proficiency. Thus a system using a moderately large computer could easily tutor 1000 or more students simultaneously. If students are receiving the same instructional material concurrently, the number who can be taught depends only on the nature of the student performance analysis required or requested by teachers and administrators.

The goal behind the development of systems such as CLASS is not to replace classroom teachers but to increase teaching effectiveness with the assistance of advanced technology. Since immediate information about student performance is available in such a system, teachers can diagnose pupils' difficulties immediately and direct attention and instruction to areas of weakness. Since most clerical tasks, grading, and drill can be handled by the system, teachers are liberated to perform tasks of a professional nature: to motivate learning, to foster analysis of evidence, to develop use of critical judgment, to extend understanding, and to challenge imagination and creativity.

Technology and School Facilities

Projections of enrollment for the next decade indicate the need for over 600,000 new classrooms and auxiliary facilities if expanding school populations are to be properly housed. The need for additional school facilities is further complicated in that conventional school spaces do not easily lend themselves to effective utilization of new increased-enrollment patterns, team teaching, new instructional media, and the individualization of instruction.

Both the National Association of Secondary-School Principals Commission on the Experimental Study of the Utilization of the Staff in the Secondary School [25] and the School Building Commission of the American Association of School Administrators state that present "classroom cubicles" in school buildings will give way to various types and sizes of instructional spaces designed to accommodate pupil groups ranging in size from 15 to 150. New schools will stress such features as teaching-material centers, which will include teachers' offices, meeting rooms, workrooms, rooms for assistants and clerks, and supply rooms. There will be provision for large-group instruction in auditorium-sized rooms containing an audiovisual core, a stage, and possibilities for easy subdivision into four or more rooms capable of accommodating 150 pupils each. The new schools will also contain spaces designed for independent pupil study [26] and smaller rooms that may be used for seminar groups and small discussion groups. Moreover, provision will be made for learning resource centers for students in subject areas; foreign language, English, and special studies laboratories; banks of automated instructional devices; rooms for reading, listening, and viewing; and excellent library resources.

25. See J. Lloyd Trump, *New Directions to Quality Education* (Washington, D.C.: National Association of Secondary-School Principals, 1961).

26. Edward Anderson and John C. Harkness, "Planned Variability," *The Nation's Schools,* April 1960, pp. 83-91.

School architecture will stress flexibility and adaptability to accommodate changing teaching methods and pupil scheduling patterns: walls will be movable, and large spaces will be divisible to accommodate groups of many sizes. Emerging school designs will explore the use of large spaces for instruction with new media; [27] "Q" spaces for individual students, enclosed on three sides and capable of accommodating a television screen and self-instructional devices; [28] windowless schools with unique ventilating and lighting arrangements; space-saving "schools in the round"; and movable rooms constructed of modular sections. New school designs will be more economical, more adaptable to quick construction, and more attractive. They will also be relatively more expensive to operate. Maintenance of expensive equipment, increased electrical consumption to operate many electrical devices and air-conditioning systems, and the initial cost of new media installations will all tend to increase operating costs.

EMERGING HIGH SCHOOL IMAGE

The forces shaping tomorrow's school are creating new educational designs and patterns that may shatter many traditional and popular conceptions of secondary education. Little in the emerging image suggests a continuance of uniform, lockstep, mass education procedures rooted in traditions of past centuries. Rigid group-instructional practices and outmoded concepts of "class" and "grade" may find little place in tomorrow's secondary schools.

Whereas schools of the past emphasized teaching, the schools of the future will emphasize learning. Whereas yesterday's schools emphasized the imparting of knowledge, tomorrow's schools will emphasize new learning resources and comprehensive means to motivate, facilitate, systematize, and evaluate learning. Whereas traditional schools stressed lockstep, mass education practices, the new schools will stress individualized instruction to accommodate pupil differences. Whereas yesterday's teaching techniques stressed "chalk and talk," tomorrow's learning techniques will stress independent study, motivated self-learning, and wide use of new instructional media and self-teaching devices. Whereas the schools of the past emphasized basic building blocks of teacher-class

27. John R. Boice *et al.* (eds.), *Coordinated Schools and Community Planning* (Stanford, Calif.: School Planning Laboratory, December 1959), pp. 43-58.

28. See Charles W. Brubaker and Lawrence B. Perkins, "Sketch Book—Space for Individual Learning," *School Executive*, February 1959.

units, the schools of tomorrow will emphasize the flexibility of teaching teams and instructional groups of many sizes.

1. *The high school of the future will reaffirm the intellectual aims of education.* Increased needs both for literacy and for the exercise of critical judgment in most occupations in industry, government, the military, the professions, and elsewhere will require a quality and excellence of education equal to the task of educating masses of intellectuals. The increasing growth of technology and automation will seriously limit future occupational opportunities for the uneducated and the unskilled. Secondary education is rapidly approaching the era when it will "need to provide for many a quality of education at least as good as that offered to a small elite in the most advanced nations of the world." [29]

2. *The high school of the future will make increasing provision for individual differences among learners.* Rigid mass instructional practices will give way to increased use of a variety of pupil-grouping patterns and de-emphasis of present "class" and "grade" structures. Ability grouping of students according to achievement and intellectual ability will be combined with organizational patterns that will enable pupils to progress at varying rates. Greater attention will be given to vertical and horizontal enrichment to accommodate differences in pupil maturity and learning capacity. Not only will special programs be established for gifted, average, and slow learners, but there will also be increased opportunity for pupils to engage in independent study, individual library research, and self-instruction with autoinstructional devices. Increased recognition of pupil differences will result in augmented guidance services aimed at reducing pupil dropouts and tailoring of programs to suit the capabilities of individual learners. Self-realization for each pupil will be a major goal in tomorrow's secondary schools.

3. *The high school of the future will incorporate new instructional and learning patterns.* Large-group teaching under the guidance of teaching teams utilizing mass media to augment instruction will be commonplace. Small classes and seminar groups with fifteen or fewer pupils will be used extensively. Individualization of instruction will be accommodated through self-teaching devices and programmed materials. Computer-based learning and instructional patterns utilizing a systems

29. Chase, "Making the School a Place for Learning," in Francis S. Chase and Harold A. Anderson (eds.), *The High School in a New Era* (Chicago: The University of Chicago Press, 1958).

approach will provide new avenues to teaching-learning effectiveness.

4. *The high school of the future will use new instructional materials and media extensively.* ETV, closed-circuit television, films, audio and video tapes, teaching machines, programmed materials, and computer-based teaching-learning systems will augment audiovisual aids already familiar to the schools. Learning laboratories in many subject areas will be commonplace. Filmed courses in most subjects will be widely available.

5. *The high school of the future will utilize new advances in curriculum construction.* The rapid obsolescence of knowledge will direct increasing attention to the teaching of basic concepts and to the building of pupil competence in the use of these concepts in progressively complex problem situations. The acquisition of facts will become secondary to the development of abilities to use knowledge creatively, to analyze evidence, to use critical judgment, to advance fertile hypotheses, and to reach reasoned conclusions.

6. *The high school of the future will emphasize the professional role of the educator.* New standards of competence, knowledge and specialization will emerge as the professional and nonprofessional functions of educators become clearly defined. Custodial, clerical, and police functions will become the province of assistants, clerks, and machines. Teachers will use their professional knowledge and skill to direct intellectual inquiry and to motivate and guide learning. Ability to marshal total learning resources will receive increased emphasis. New roles, such as "team" leader and "master" teacher, will recognize individual differences among teachers and will provide new avenues for advancement along an instructional route.

7. *The high school of the future will house many new types of facilities.* New buildings will incorporate multisized instructional spaces capable of accommodating individual, small-group, and large-group instructional patterns. Instructional materials centers will be common. There will be provision for student learning resource centers; learning laboratories in various subject matter areas; banks of automated instructional devices; rooms for viewing, listening, and reading; and easily accessible libraries and learning materials. Movable walls will increase opportunities to adapt spaces to various instructional uses.

8. *The high school of the future will emphasize flexibility in scheduling and in the availability of teaching-learning resources.* Typical groups

of students will engage in a variety of activities during the day. Following registration, some may move directly from home rooms to independent cubicles equipped with books, tapes, records, and teaching machines. Others may move to small-group instructional settings or seminars where groupings are based upon achievement and intellectual ability. From seminars and independent study, pupils may move in several directions: to small-group discussions led by teachers or other students; to automated laboratories in various subject areas; to libraries containing books, listening rooms, viewing rooms, reading rooms, and a variety of new media for individual and small-group use; to physical education, health, and recreation centers; and to practical and fine arts centers. Students will reassemble for large-group instruction in instructional spaces capable of accommodating large numbers of pupils. Such spaces will be divisible and will contain facilities for team teaching and media for large-group instruction such as overhead and film projectors, ETV, and closed-circuit television.

REFERENCES

American Educational Research Association, "Instructional Materials: Educational Media and Technology," *Review of Educational Research,* Vol 32, No. 2, April 1962.

Beggs, David, III (ed.), *Team Teaching—Bold New Venture* (Indianapolis, Ind.: Unified College Press, 1964).

Boice, John R., *et al.* (eds.), *Coordinated School and Community Planning* (Stanford, Calif.: School of Education, Stanford University, 1959).

Brown, Frank B., *The Nongraded High School* (Englewood Cliffs, N.J.: Prentice-Hall, Inc., 1963).

Educational Facilities Laboratory, *Design for ETV, Planning for Schools with Television* (New York: Dave Chapman, Inc., Industrial Design, 1960).

Finn, James D., "Automation and Education: III, Technology and the Instructional Process," *Audiovisual Communication Review,* Vol. 8, No. 1, Winter, 1960.

Finn, James D., and Perrin, Donald G., *Teaching Machines and Programmed Learning, 1962: A Survey of the Industry,* Occasional Paper No. 3, Technological Development Project (Washington, D.C.: National Education Association, 1962).

Fry, Edward B., *et al.,* "Teaching Machines: An Annotated Bibliography," *Audiovisual Communication Review,* Supplement I, Vol. 8, No. 2, 1960.

Holz, Robert E., *School Scheduling Using Computers* (Cambridge: Massachusetts Institute of Technology, 1964).

Lumsdaine, A. A., and Glaser, Robert (eds.), *Teaching Machines and Programmed Learning: A Source Book* (Washington, D.C.: Department of Audiovisual Instruction, National Education Association, 1960).

National Association of Secondary-School Principals, National Education Association, "New Horizons in Staff Utilization," "Exploring Improved Teaching Patterns," and "Progressing Toward Better Schools," *The Bulletin of the National Association of Secondary-School Principals,* January issues, 1958, 1959, and 1960.

Schramm, Wilbur, *Programed Instruction: Today and Tomorrow* (New York: Fund for the Advancement of Education, 1962).

Silberman, Charles E., "The Remaking of American Education," *Fortune,* Vol. LXIII, No. 4, April 1961.

Trump, J. Lloyd, and Baynham, Dorsey, *Guide to Better Schools* (Chicago: Rand McNally & Co., 1961).

Part II
Leadership, Structures, and Controls

Chapter 4
Functional View
of Administration

THE secondary school principalship is obviously a well-established position in educational administration. And yet views concerning the appropriate and important functional responsibilities of this post are by no means stabilized. The search for adequate conceptual formulations of the principal's role is a significant and continuing task—one that has attracted the attention of both scholars and practitioners in recent years. Several factors appear to be prompting this continued search.[1]

First, school district practice reflects conflicting images of the appropriate functions of secondary school administrators in both executive and leadership aspects. Diversity of definition of the principal's role is exemplified in many ways: in the manner in which different principals spend their time; in the salience attached to their particular tasks and duties; in the expectations held for their participation in educational policy making and leadership; in the definitions of their responsibilities for improvement of teaching-learning opportunities; and in the scope of their responsibilities for structuring educational programs, for effecting staff improvement, for fostering student development, and for developing effective school management procedures.

This variation undoubtedly stems in part from the unstandardized situations in which administration occurs. In some school districts, the secondary school principal meets with the board of education and carries

1. The major propositions developed in this chapter were first presented in Stephen P. Hencley, "Functional Interrelationships Within Administrative Performance Systems," a paper presented at the Seventh Career Development Seminar of the University Council for Educational Administration, Michigan State University, November 11-14, 1962.

the responsibilities of a district superintendent. In large metropolitan centers, on the other hand, most principals may have few opportunities to participate in top-level policy making. Between these extremes are principals who function in medium-sized districts headed by school superintendents. In all three situations, however, expectations surrounding the principal's role and function differ. These expectations are conditioned by the number and competence of administrative personnel serving the district, by varying traditions and operating procedures, and by the organizational concepts that underlie the district's operations.

Diversity in school district practices is paralleled by a second significant factor. Striking differences exist in scholarly viewpoints concerning the appropriate roles and functions of school executives. During the past twenty years, the school administrator's job has been defined in at least four different ways,[2] and each definition has been instrumental in shaping existing concepts of the appropriate functions of administrators in the school setting.

One definition, the inclusive type, requires that the school executive assume responsibility for all tasks and duties for which administration and administrators may be held accountable. A second definition, the exclusive or restrictive type, seeks to separate administration from policy making and stresses the organizational maintenance function of the administrator.[3] Still another definition, the standardized or division-of-labor type, highlights the administrator's role in impersonalizing and standardizing administrative procedures through the development of job descriptions, the structuring of bureaucratic working patterns, and the formalization of organizational work flow procedures. A fourth definition, the integrative or relational type, directs attention to the administrator's role in the development, management, and maintenance of decision making with reference to (1) educational goals and purposes, (2) operations, and (3) interactions and adjustments within the organization and between the organization and its environment.[4] Different assumptions concerning the nature, emphasis, and purposes of both

2. Van Miller, "Four Definitions of Your Job," *Overview,* November 1960, pp. 60-61.

3. John Walton, *Administration and Policy Making in Education* (Baltimore, Md.: Johns Hopkins Press, 1959).

4. Daniel E. Griffiths, *Administrative Theory* (New York: Appleton-Century-Crofts, 1959), pp. 98-102.

administration and administrative function underlie each of these definitions. Models of administrative function based on these differing conceptions lead to strikingly divergent images of the salient features of administrative performance.

A POINT OF VIEW

The administrator of the modern secondary school faces an imposing array of tasks and responsibilities in fulfilling his role as a school executive and institutional leader. If he is to be successful in his position, he must have insight into the relative importance of different administrative functions. Indeed, the ability to separate the trivial from the crucial is a most important characteristic in successful administrative performance. If, however, clear conceptions of the significant dimensions of administrative performance are lacking, the multiplicity of tasks inherent in secondary school administration makes judicious allocations of time and energy extremely difficult.

First Major Premise

The rationale underlying the functional view of administration presented in this chapter is based upon a number of major and minor premises. First, the secondary school administrator functions not in isolation but as an important member of a total administrative system, encompassing a large number and variety of administrative functions. It also spans many types of positions—from the school superintendent to the classroom teacher. Effective performance in the principalship requires (1) basic familiarity with the total task of administration in the school setting; and (2) insight into the manner in which the functions of the principalship fit into, mesh with, and complement the total task of administration.

Allport has suggested that "system" may be defined as:

. . . any recognizably delimited aggregate of dynamic elements that are in some way interconnected and interdependent and that continue to operate together according to certain laws and in such a way as to produce some characteristic total effect. A system, in other words, is something that is concerned with some kind of activity and preserves a kind of integration and unity; and a particular system can be recognized as distinct from other systems to which, however, it may be dynamically related. Systems may be complex; they may be made up of interdependent subsystems, each of which, though less autonomous than the entire aggregate, is nevertheless fairly distinguishable in operation.[5]

A mature concept of administrative function at the secondary school level can best be achieved through (1) comprehensive consideration of the significant functions of school district administrative performance systems, and (2) intensive study of the relationship between the functions of secondary school administration and the functions of the total administrative performance system. In this process, attention must be directed to the functional emphasis of different positions encompassed by such systems, the context in which administrative functions are performed, the integrative relationships among positions and functions, and the processes required to guide interaction both within the system and between the system and its environment.

Second Major Premise

A second major premise underlying the rationale is that functions of administrative performance systems in the school setting may be encompassed along four major dimensions. The descriptive model of secondary school administration introduced in the first chapter foreshadowed the important role of secondary school administrators along each of these dimensions within the total administrative performance system.

Dimension I. *Development and legitimation of broad educational policies relating to the basic purposes and ends of education.* This dimension may be characterized as largely political in nature. Here, stress is placed upon the performance system's responsibility for active participation in the determination of the direction and emphasis of public education. Essential to effective functioning along this dimension is active involvement of the system in policy-structuring that seeks to define and shape the basic purposes and ends of the educational enterprise.

Dimension II. *Development and legitimation of operational policies*

5. Floyd H. Allport, *Theories of Perception and the Concept of Structure* (New York: John Wiley & Sons, 1955), p. 469. *See also* Paul Meadows, "Models, Systems and Science," *American Sociological Review,* Vol. 22, No. 1, February, 1957; Gordon Hearn, *Theory Building in Social Work* (Toronto: University of Toronto Press, 1958; Daniel E. Griffiths, "Some Assumptions Underlying the Use of Models in Research," in Jack A. Culbertson and Stephen P. Hencley (eds.), *Educational Research: New Perspectives* (Danville, Ill.: The Interstate Printers and Publishers, 1963).

that seek to implement broad educational policies. In this area the performance system translates broad legitimized statements of educational policy and purpose into specific operational policies in each of the task areas of administration: instruction and curriculum development, staff personnel, pupil personnel, finance and business management, school plant and services, school-community relations, and relations with local, state, and Federal agencies.

Dimension III. *Technical-managerial implementation of legitimized educational policies.* This dimension of administrative performance encompasses (*a*) the determination of specific functions necessary in each task area for the accomplishment of legitimized educational goals and purposes, (*b*) the allocation of functions to positions through a logical system of task division, and (*c*) the formalization and integration of organizational work flow and decision-making patterns.

Dimension IV. *Sophisticated utilization of administrative processes in all phases of administrative activity.* Skill in planning, decision making, communicating, organizing, directing change, appraising, and improving morale are competences that characterize effective school leaders. An integrated view of administrative performance indicates that competence in the use of these processes is required of administrators in many settings —both within the school organization and within the larger community.

DEVELOPING BROAD EDUCATIONAL POLICIES: FIRST DIMENSION OF PERFORMANCE

A basic assumption of the classical concept of administration has been that administration and policy making are separate, distinct functions. As early as 1900, Goodnow enunciated the proposition that government consists of two separate functions: politics and administration.[6] The viewpoint that policy making is outside the administrator's area of concern has, for many years, had wide currency in the literature and folklore of education. It is probably best exemplified in the oft-repeated axiom that "the board of education makes policy; the administrator implements policy."

The passive role of the administrator in developing and advocating

6. Frank J. Goodnow, *Politics and Administration* (New York: The Macmillan Co., 1900).

educational policy implied by the classical definition of administration has been sharply criticized in recent years.[7] The emerging viewpoint is that administrators can, and do, play a livelier and more active role in developing and advocating policy than a strict dichotomy between administration and policy-making would indicate. Narrow interpretations of administrative function which tend to place the administrator outside the realm of political activity in policy making have been openly questioned in both public administration and education. Price, in speaking of government administrators for example, has noted that ". . . the great failure in our political vision is our not seeing that the main function of the top career administrators is to help develop policy. If the career administrators above the level of the specialized bureaus do not provide strong support for their political superiors in the development of policy, our system of political responsibility suffers." [8]

In the school setting, both observation and evidence indicate that a complementary, team relationship exists between superintendents and boards of education in determination of educational policy and purpose. There appears to be "no real dichotomy of board and superintendent functions . . . the generally accepted notion that the board establishes policy and the superintendent administers the policy would seem to be an oversimplification of what is actually a rather complex relationship." [9] Political leadership in the board of education is usually determined by the roles and actions of participants who exercise influence in the deliberative stage of the decision-making process. Since influence is exercised *prior* to the decisional outcome, innovative ideas stemming from chief school officers have great impact in structuring alternatives for action.

Superintendents are generally involved in political decision making during board of education deliberations; moreover, they are in good positions to exercise influence in the policy-making process. Not only are

7. See, for example, Paul H. Appleby, *Policy and Administration* (University, Ala.: University of Alabama Press, 1949); Jack Culbertson, "Essay-Review: The School Administrator and Policy-Making Function," *School Review,* Spring, 1961, pp. 98-111; Philip Selznick, *Leadership in Administration* (Evanston, Ill.: Row, Peterson & Co., 1957); James G. Harlow, "Purpose Defining: The Central Function of the School Administrator," in Jack A. Culbertson and Stephen P. Hencley (eds.), *Preparing Administrators: New Perspectives* (Columbus, Ohio: University Council for Educational Administration, 1962), pp. 61-71.

8. Don K. Price, "Administrative Leadership," *Daedalus,* Fall, 1961, p. 8.

9. Daniel E. Griffiths, "Boards of Education and Their Superintendents," in *The Changing Role of the Chief School Officer* (Albany, N.Y.: Center for Field Services, State University of New York, College at Albany, 1962), p. 6.

superintendents active in the initiation of policy making, but board members usually look to superintendents to supply information, evidence, and advice to guide policy making. Thus, the difference between political and administrative decision making in the board of education setting may be conceived as a difference of degree rather than of kind.

Administrative performance systems face significant challenges and responsibilities if they are to function effectively in the development and legitimation of broad educational policies. Participation in policy-structuring processes demands perceptiveness concerning education's role in the total society; sensitivity to the important educational implications of broad social movements; competence in structuring educational policies based upon these implications; skill in advocating meaningful alternatives for implementing social purposes through education; and comprehension of the political context in which educational policy is structured.

Effective performance in this significant area of function requires more than fine attunement to the interrelationship between education and the broader culture. Effective performance also requires that administrative performance systems utilize the full administrative potential of both "generalists" and specialists in determination and legitimation of purpose.

The Principal and Broad Policy Development

All positions in the administrative performance system possess some responsibility for engaging in determination and legitimation of purpose, but major leadership responsibilities in this area fall primarily upon the superintendent and his "cabinet." In small and medium-sized school districts, secondary school principals are ordinarily members of administrative councils or cabinet structures which meet regularly to discuss policy questions. In large school districts, the cabinet structure usually includes various central-office personnel such as the directors of program, staff personnel, pupil personnel, business affairs, and research. Even in these situations, however, secondary school principals may play significant roles in influencing policy development in relation to vital educational issues.

An integrated view of administrative function indicates that secondary school administrators, as heads of operating units, must act in concert with other cabinet members to develop broad educational policies for consideration and legitimation by the board of education and the broader community. The role of the principal in this vital area is to assist, to advise, and to develop meaningful educational propositions for consideration by the administrative cabinet. Together with other members of the cabinet, the principal also accepts responsibility for the development and delineation of policy positions that may be (*a*) tested with community groups and opinion leaders, and (*b*) advocated for adoption by the board of education.

The rapid cultural changes and broad social movements discussed in Chapter 3 reinforce the viewpoint that members of administrative performance systems require sophistication not only in relating educational policy to social changes and movements, but also in determining ways in which education can implement the purposes of the broader culture. It is through policy development and legitimation that basic foundations are structured for making operational such concepts as "excellence in education" and "equal educational opportunity." It is in the same area of activity that significant decisions can be forged concerning the role of education in a society affected by population growth and mobility, metropolitanism, technology and cybernation, advances in science and new knowledge, and shifting national and world values.

Table 4-1 outlines functional interrelationships among members of an administrative performance system in the determination of broad educational policies. The interrelationships suggested may be clarified through brief discussion of one of the problem areas indicated. For example, changing occupational structures and the impact upon society of technology, science, automation, and cybernation have implications for adult education, vocational education, the retraining of the technologically unemployed, and the utilization of automated systems approaches to the total educational task. The superintendent and his cabinet (positions indicated by 2 and 3 in Table 4-1) have major roles in developing policies in such areas for consideration and legitimation by the board of education. Moreover, two-way communication with diverse individuals and groups (depicted by 4 and 5) is essential in this dynamic process.

The size of the administrative performance system shown in Table 4-1 is probably most appropriate to a city district. But the role suggested for the secondary school principal is not appreciably affected by school district size. In broad policy development his role is to assist and advise at the cabinet level, to structure meaningful educational propositions for cabinet consideration, and to maintain and foster open communication

Table 4-1. Suggested Interrelationships Among Positions in the Determination of Broad Educational Policies

Position	Relating educational policy to broad societal movements and determining ways in which education can implement the purposes of the broader culture
Superintendent	2
Secondary School Principal	3
Asst. Sec. School Prin.	5
Department Head	4
Elem. School Principal	3
Director of Program	3
Coord. of Adult Education	4
Coord. of Sec. Education	4
Coord. of Elem. Educ.	4
Instructional Supv. and/or Consultant	5
Dir. of Pupil Personnel	3
Coordinator of Guidance	4
Attendance Officer	
Dir. of Staff Personnel	3
Dir. of Research	3
Dir. of Business Affairs	3
Coord. of Bldgs. & Grounds	5
Coord. of Transport	5
Coord. of Cafeteria	4
Business Manager	5
Teachers	4
Community Leaders & Groups	5
Lay Advisory Boards	4
Board of Education	1

LEGEND

1 = Enact policy
2 = Advocate policy, consult, coordinate
3 = Assist supt. in determining policy to be advocated
4 = Advise on matters specifically submitted
5 = Provide exchange of views

Sample problem areas:

1. Equal educational opportunity
2. Excellence in education
3. Population growth and metropolitanism
4. Allocation of societal resources
5. Automation, science, technology
6. Changing occupational structure
7. Race relations
8. Conflicting world ideologies

with teachers and citizens in the continuous testing of educational propositions.

DEVELOPING OPERATIONAL POLICIES: SECOND DIMENSION OF PERFORMANCE

Following development and legitimation of broad educational policies, the administrative performance system may turn its attention to a second important dimension of administrative performance. Broad policies legitimated by the board of education must be translated into more specific, operational policies to guide function in each of the task areas of administration. Organizational decisions and agreements must be forged in relation to (*a*) the educational programs and instructional procedures that will contribute to the achievement of basic goals; (*b*) the pupil personnel, staff personnel, and finance and business policies that will facilitate goal achievement; (*c*) the environmental conditions that will be necessary for optimizing teaching-learning processes; (*d*) the policies that will guide school-community relations and interactions; (*e*) the emphasis that will be placed upon research in the improvement of knowledge and practice; and (*f*) the way in which the school organization will operate in relation to local, state, and Federal agencies. Moreover, effective administrative performance will also ensure that decisions are made and agreements are reached concerning the use of organizational means such as ETV, learning machines, packaged courses, team teaching, programmed instruction, and teacher aids.

In the development of operational policies the focus of the administrative performance system is basically intraorganizational. Primary concern is directed toward the development of intelligent guidelines to ensure that the available means, resources, and skills of the organization are marshaled toward achievement of purposes. Professional specializations of members of the performance system are extensively utilized in the development of guides to implement more general policies legitimated by the board of education. In developing operational policies the focus of the performance system is upon technological-managerial decision making rather than upon political decision making. As suggested in Figure 4-1, the decisions formulated are based primarily on *knowledge* rather than on *values*.

The functional interrelationships suggested in Table 4-2 for developing operational policies emphasize a team approach which utilizes the

Figure 4-1. Values and Knowledge in Decision Making

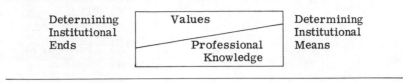

competence of both generalists and specialists. Both those who carry line authority and responsibility and those who possess technical knowledge and specialized competence take part in the process. The development of pupil personnel policies, for example, proceeds under the general direction and coordination of the superintendent of schools. But major responsibility for developing pupil personnel policies falls upon those line personnel who carry operating authority in relation to this dimension of function—the principal and the department heads—and those staff personnel who possess technical knowledge and specialized competence—the director of pupil personnel and the director of program. Other line and staff personnel (positions indicated by 4) carry moderate responsibility according to the extent to which their knowledge and competence are useful in policy determination. Still others (positions and groups depicted by 5 and 6) either play an advisory role or provide exchange of views as necessary.

In developing operational policies the administrative performance system communicates with community leaders, lay advisory groups, and other interested community groups. The views of individuals and groups from the community receive consideration and assessment during the process of policy formulation. Moreover, representatives from all levels of the school organization have opportunities to study and review initial policy statements. Suggestions for change or modification of policy statements are given careful consideration before the superintendent recommends their adoption and legitimation by the board of education.

The Principal's Role in Developing Operational Policies

Since operational policies have as their focus the marshaling of total organizational means and resources for optimizing teaching-learning opportunities, the principal, as head of an operating unit, plays an essential role. Table 4-2 indicates that the secondary school administrator has major responsibility for assisting in the development of operational poli-

Table 4-2. Suggested Interrelationships Among Positions in Developing Operational Policies

LEGEND

1 = Enact policy
2 = Advocate policy, consult, coordinate
3 = Major responsibility for policy development in this area
4 = Moderate responsibility for policy development in this area
5 = Advise on points specifically submitted
6 = Provide exchange of views

Developing operational policies	Superintendent	Secondary School Principal	Asst. Sec. School Prin.	Department Head	Elem. School Principal	Director of Program	Coord. of Adult Education	Coord. of Sec. Education	Coord. of Elem. Educ.	Instructional Supv. and/or Consultant	Dir. of Pupil Personnel	Coordinator of Guidance	Attendance Officer	Dir. of Staff Personnel	Dir. of Research	Dir. of Business Affairs	Coord. of Bldgs. & Grounds	Coord. of Transport	Coord. of Cafeteria	Business Manager	Teachers		Community Leaders & Groups	Lay Advisory Boards	Board of Education
1. Instruction and curriculum policies	2	3	6	5	3	3	3	3	3	4	3	5		4	4	4	6	6	5	5	4		6	6	1
2. Pupil personnel policies	2	3	4	5	3	3	4	4	4	5	3	6	5	4	4	4	6	6	5	6	4		6	6	1
3. Staff personnel policies	2	3	5	5	3	4	5	5	5	6	4	6		3	4	3	4	4	4	4	4		6	6	1
4. Finance and business policies	2	4	6	6	4	4	5	5	5	6	4	5		4	4	3	4	4	4	3	6		6	6	1
5. School plant and services policies	2	3	5		3	4	5	5	5	6	4	6		4	6	3	3	3	3	3	5		6	6	1
6. Community relations policies	2	3	5	5	3	3	4	4	4	6	3	5	5	3	3	3	4	4	4	4	5		6	6	1
7. Policies in relation to local, state, and federal agencies	2	3	6		3	3	5	5	5	6	3	5		3	4	3	5	5	5	3	6		6	6	1

cies in every task area of administration, excepting business and finance. Even there, the principal has some responsibility in policy development. Thus, the translation of broad policies into specific, operational policies may be viewed as a significant dimension of performance in the secondary school principalship. High levels of professional competence and insight are necessary for effective performance along this dimension.

TECHNICAL-MANAGERIAL IMPLEMENTATION: THIRD DIMENSION OF PERFORMANCE

Following development and legitimation of purpose-centered and operation-centered policies is a third dimension of performance in which the secondary school administrator plays a major role—the technical-managerial implementation of those policies. Three important facets of administrative performance are discernible along this dimension: (1) the identification of specific functions necessary to attain legitimized goals and purposes; (2) the allocation of functions to positions through rational task division; and (3) the structuring of functional interrelationships that result in integrated and formalized decision making and work flow patterns. Price has emphasized the importance of this dimension as follows: ". . . the administrator of the future, for all his concern for policy, can never forget the other aspect of his job, which is to organize and coordinate a complex and dynamic system to carry out policy decisions. . . ." [10] The three facets of administrative performance mentioned above are essential in the development of dynamic systems capable of implementing policy decisions.

In approaching this third task, members of administrative performance systems discover that (*a*) numerous purpose-derived functions are required and necessary in the school setting; (*b*) many of these functions are common in all school districts; (*c*) functions may be grouped conceptually into task areas such as those presented in Table 4-2; (*d*) functions are allocated to positions in a variety of ways in school districts; (*e*) different sets of interrelationships may be structured in relation to functions and positions; and (*f*) interrelationships are determined by accepted assumptions concerning the roles of various personnel in the system.

The development of the functional interrelationships shown in Table 4-3 was guided by several considerations. First, administrative functions

10. Price, *op. cit.,* p. 9.

Table 4-3.   Suggested Interrelationships Among Positions in the Technical Areas of Administration[1]

LEGEND

X = Work is done
1 = General supervision
2 = Direct supervision over work done
3 = Supervision & coordination
4 = Decision on points specifically submitted
5 = Person must be consulted
6 = Person must be notified
7 = Person may be called in for exchange of views

	Superintendent	Secondary School Prin.	Asst. Sec. School Prin.	Department Head	Elem. School Prin.	Director of Program	Coord. of Adult Educ.	Coord. of Sec. Educ.	Coord. of Elem. Educ.	Instructional Supv. and/or Consultant	Dir. of Pupil Personnel	Coord. of Guidance	Attendance Officer	Dir. of Staff Personnel	Dir. of Research	Dir. of Business Affairs	Coord., Bldgs. & Grounds	Coord. of Transport	Coord. of Cafeteria	Business Manager
A. Instruction and curriculum development																				
1. Revising curriculum content and organization	1	2	7	5	2	3	X	X	X	5	7	7								
2. Selecting curricular materials	1	2	7	5	2	3	X	X	X	X	7	7								
3. Relating curriculum to time, facilities, personnel	1	2	X	5	X	7	X	7	7	7						7	6		7	
4. Articulating elementary and secondary program	1	2	4	X	2	3	X	X	X	5										
5. Directing program for exceptional children	1	X	4	X	X	3		7	7	7	7	7								
6. Planning and directing remedial instruction	1	2	4	X	2	3	X	X	X	X	5	7								
7. Directing school testing program	1	2	4	X	2	3	X	X	X		5	4			7					
8. Assisting teachers in instructional improvement	1	2	4	4	2	3	X	X	X	X	7	6			5					

[1]See Daniel E. Griffiths, et al., Organizing Schools for Effective Education (Danville, Ill.: The Interstate Printers and Publishers, 1962), p. 320.

	C1	C2	C3	C4	C5	C6	C7	C8	C9	C10	C11	C12	C13	C14
9. Assisting in diagnosis of pupil learning difficulties	1	2	4	4	2	3	3	X	X	X	3	X	7	7
10. Directing adult education program	1	4					X						7	7
11. Coordinating use of instructional equipment	1	2	7	7	2	3	3	X	X	7	7	X	7	7
12. Directing research and experimentation	1	5	7	7	5	5	5	5	5	7	7	7	X	
B. Staff personnel														
1. Recruitment of professional staff personnel	2	5	7	7	5	5	7	7	7		5	X	7	3
2. Recruitment of nonprofessional staff personnel	2	5			5	7							5	5
3. Selection of professional staff personnel	2	5	7	7	5	5	7	7	7		5	X	7	3
4. Selection of nonprofessional staff personnel	2	5		5	5	7							5	5
5. Induction and orientation of professional staff personnel	1	X	3	3	X	3	X	X		3	3	X	4	3
6. Induction and orientation of nonprofessional staff personnel	1	3		3	3			X					2	2
7. Scheduling of professional staff personnel	1	2	X	5	X	3					X	6		
8. Scheduling of nonprofessional staff personnel	1	3			3						6		2	2
9. Supervision of professional staff personnel	1	X	7	3	X	3	3	X		3	7	X	2	X
10. Supervision of nonprofessional staff personnel	1	3		3	3						7		2	4
11. Evaluation, recommendation to board of promotion, and retention of professional staff personnel	X	X	7	7	X	5	7	7	7	5	5	5		

(cont.)

Table 4-3. Suggested Interrelationships Among Positions in the Technical Areas of Administration (cont.)

LEGEND
X = Work is done
1 = General supervision
2 = Direct supervision over work done
3 = Supervision & coordination
4 = Decision on points specifically submitted
5 = Person must be consulted
6 = Person must be notified
7 = Person may be called in for exchange of views

	Superintendent	Secondary School Prin.	Asst. Sec. School Prin.	Department Head	Elem. School Prin.	Director of Program	Coord. of Adult Educ.	Coord. of Sec. Educ.	Coord. of Elem. Educ.	Instructional Supv. and/or Consultant	Dir. of Pupil Personnel	Coord. of Guidance	Attendance Officer	Dir. of Staff Personnel	Dir. of Research	Dir. of Business Affairs	Coord. Bldgs. & Grounds	Coord. of Transport	Coord. of Cafeteria	Business Manager
12. Evaluation, recommendation to board of promotion, and retention of nonprofessional staff personnel	X	5			5									5		X	5	5	5	5
13. Maintaining staff personnel records	1	5	X		5	5					5			X		X				
14. Obtaining and scheduling substitute teachers	1	2	X	X	X															
15. In-service education of professional personnel	1	3	5	X	3	3	X	X	X	X	X	7		5						
16. In-service education of nonprofessional personnel	1							X	X	X				5		3		X	X	X
17. Directing research and experimentation	1	5			5	5					5			5	X	5	X	X	X	
C. Pupil personnel																				
1. Providing orientation for students	1	2	X	X	2		X	7	7		7	X								

	C1	C2	C3	C4	C5	C6	C7	C8	C9	C10	C11	C12	C13	C14	C15	C16	C17	C18	C19
2. Scheduling pupils	1	2	X	4	2	7	X	4	4	4	4		7	X					
3. Providing student counseling services	1	2	X	4	2								3	X					
4. Scheduling student health services	1	2	7	X	2	7		7	7				3						
5. Providing stud. placement & follow-up	1	2	7	7									3	X					
6. Maintaining indiv. stud. records	1	2	2	4	2	7	2	4	5	5									
7. Providing occupational & educational information services	1	2	X	7	7	7		7					3	X					
8. Assessing and interpreting student growth	1	2	X	X	2		2	4	4	4	5		3	X					
9. Dealing with pupil irregularities	1	2	X	X	X								7	4					
10. Applying extreme measures under dealing with pupil irregularities	X	4	5		4								7	7	6				
11. Directing and supervising activity programs	1	2	X	7	2	7		7	7										
12. Maintaining student accounting (attendance and census)	1	2	3		2	2								X				3	X
13. Directing the guidance program	1	2	7	7	2	3							X						
14. Directing research & experimentation	1	5	7	7	5	5						5				X			
D. Finance and business management																			
1. Construction of the budget	2	X	7	6	X	X	4	4	6		X	6	X	4	X	4	4	4	4
2. Control of the budget	X	6			6	6					6	6	6		1			5	
3. Administration of the budget	1														X				5
4. Debt service administration	1														2			2	X

(cont.)

Table 4-3. Suggested Interrelationships Among Positions in the Technical Areas of Administration (cont.)

LEGEND

X = Work is done
1 = General supervision
2 = Direct supervision over work done
3 = Supervision & coordination
4 = Decision on points specifically submitted
5 = Person must be consulted
6 = Person must be notified
7 = Person may be called in for exchange of views

	Superintendent	Secondary School Prin.	Asst. Sec. School Prin.	Department Head	Elem. School Prin.	Director of Program	Coord. of Adult Educ.	Coord. of Sec. Educ.	Coord. of Elem. Educ.	Instructional Supv. and/or Consultant	Dir. of Pupil Personnel	Coord. of Guidance	Attendance Officer	Dir. of Staff Personnel	Dir. of Research	Dir. of Business Affairs	Coord., Bldgs. & Grounds	Coord. of Transport	Coord. of Cafeteria	Business Manager
5. Administration of payroll	1	2	7		2											2				X
6. Supervising and auditing internal accounts	1															2				X
7. Administering insurance program	1															2				X
8. Determining specifications for equipment and supplies	1	2		X		5	5	5	5	5	5	X		5	5	2	X	X	X	X
9. Writing specifications for equipment and supplies	1															2	X	X	X	X
10. Purchasing equipment & supplies	1															2			X	X
11. Distributing equipment & supplies	1	6	3	X	6	3	X		X	X	3	6		6	3	2	3	3	3	X
12. Inventorying equipment & supplies	1	2	7	X	2	3	X	X	X	X	3	X		3		2	X	X	X	X
13. Administering programs such as NDEA	1	2	2	7	2	3		X	X	X		X				2				X
14. Directing research and experimentation	1	5	5		5										X	5				

E. School plant and services																				
1. Plant planning	1	X	7	5	X	5	7	5	5	5	5	7			7	X	5		X	7
2. Plant construction	1															3	2			
3. Plant operation & maintenance	1	3	7		3											2	X		7	
4. Grounds maintenance	1	3	7		3											2	X			
5. Scheduling bus operations	1	3	7		3											2		X		
6. Directing bus maintenance program	1															2		X		7
7. Directing plant safety program	1	3	7		3											2	X	X		
8. Directing transportation safety program	1	3	7		3											2	X	X		
9. Coordinating and directing school lunch program	1	2	5		2											3			X	
10. Directing research & experimentation	1	5			5										X	5	5	5	5	
F. School-community relations																				
1. Preparing reports and bulletins for community distribution	1	2	X	7	5	3	X	X	X	7	3	X		5	X	3	5	5	5	X
2. Conferring with parents and citizens	X	X	X	X	X	X	X	X	X	X	X	X	X	7	7	X	7	7	7	7
3. Developing and coordinating the program	2	X	7	7	X	X	7	7	7	7	X	7	7	X	7	X	7	7	7	7
4. Preparing releases for communications media	1	X	7	7	X	X	X	X	X	X	X	X	X	X	X		7	7	7	7
5. Improving means for reporting to parents on pupil progress	2	X	5	7	X	3		5	5	5	3	5			7					
6. Direction of program for use of school facilities by nonschool groups	1		5		5	X										3	X			5

included in the table were restricted to those common in most school districts. Second, the functions were grouped into task categories similar to those presented in Table 4-2. Third, a consistent method was sought for structuring interrelationships—one that could be utilized with different sets of assumptions concerning the appropriate roles of various positions. Fourth, the basic task of the administrative performance system in the technical areas of administration was defined as that of maintaining, facilitating, and improving educational opportunity. Fifth, stress was placed upon a team approach to administration—the necessity for extensive communication and cooperation among members of the system was recognized. Sixth, a decentralization pattern of operation was built in—the autonomy of building units was increased and the importance of the principal's role was emphasized. Finally, strong support was given to the concept of organization which places primary responsibility for maintaining and improving teaching-learning opportunity upon the operating line extending from the superintendent to principals to teachers.

Acceptance of this organizational concept lends support to the viewpoint that staff personnel possess authority of knowledge but not line authority, in relation to the school's basic mission. Thus the relationship of staff personnel to line personnel in the technical areas of administration is advisory, and becomes operative at two levels: (1) the central-office level where staff personnel advise the superintendent, and (2) the attendance-unit level where advisory relationships are establishd with principals and teachers. Moreover, this concept of organization recognizes that although superintendents have general responsibilities for supervising functions in the task areas, substantial responsibility for direct supervision over the work done is assumed by the building principals.

Interpretation of Table 4-3 may be facilitated through reference to the interrelationships shown for a specific function. One of the functions listed under the task area headed "Instruction and Curriculum Development" is that of revising curriculum content and organization. Table 4-3 indicates that major responsibility for this function is assigned to the coordinators of elementary, secondary, and adult education, with staff department supervision provided by the director of program. But general and direct supervision in relation to the incorporation of new or revised program content is exercised by members of the operating line—the superintendent and principals respectively.

The Principal's Role in Technical-Managerial Implementation

The secondary school principal has a demanding role in the technical-managerial aspects of administration. He must interact with many members of the administrative performance system. Moreover, he functions as a key decision maker in many technical tasks, and as a key link in significant work-flow patterns within the total configuration of tasks. As head of an important operating unit he requires sophistication in marshaling the total resources available in the organization for the continuous improvement of teaching-learning opportunities. His job is one of the most complex and challenging in the total administrative performance system.

In developing a comprehensive and consistent concept of the principal's role in the technical areas of administration, the reader is encouraged to give careful consideration to Table 4-3. As suggested in the table, effective performance in the technical areas requires both knowledge and skill relative to a wide spectrum of tasks necessary in the efficient operation of schools.

In instruction and curriculum development, for example, the principal exercises direct supervision over a wide range of tasks, encompassing the operation, revision, and evaluation of school programs. In relation to staff personnel, both professional and nonprofessional, he plays a significant role in recruitment, selection, orientation, supervision, evaluation, and research. Moreover, he is actively involved in in-service education and in obtaining and scheduling substitute teachers.

In tasks associated with pupil personnel, the principal has direct supervisory responsibilities over a wide variety of functions ranging from scheduling to guidance. As indicated in Table 4-3, he maintains close relationships with varied staff and line personnel in relation to these functions.

The involvement of the secondary school administrator is less intense in the area of finance and business management. But he performs significant tasks in budget construction, in determining specifications for and inventorying of supplies and equipment, and in administering programs such as those under the National Defense Education Act.

Participation in school plant planning is a major responsibility of the principal. Moreover, he exercises some degree of supervision over plant operation, plant and grounds maintenance, bus scheduling, safety programs, and the school lunch program.

The principal has important responsibilities in the area of school-community relations. Included among his tasks are: (1) the development and coordination of school-community relations programs, (2) the preparation of reports and bulletins for community distribution, (3) the preparation of releases for mass communications media, (4) participation in conferences and meetings with parents and citizens, and (5) improvement of procedures for reporting to parents on pupil progress.

Thus, many and varied tasks are necessary in the technical-managerial implementation of legitimated educational policies. Effective and efficient accomplishment of these tasks involves the combined effort of all members of the administrative performance system. The secondary school principal's role in this process is significant; only a competent and broadly prepared administrator can function adequately in such a position.

PROCESSES OF ADMINISTRATION: FOURTH DIMENSION OF PERFORMANCE

Fundamental to effective performance along each of the first three dimensions of administrative function is expert utilization of various administrative processes. As noted in Chapter 1, processes such as decision making, communicating, coordinating, organizing, directing change, appraising, and maintaining morale are characteristic behaviors of administrators in all organizations as they engage in the formulation and achievement of institutional purposes.

Sophisticated use of administrative processes is essential in the development, legitimation, and implementation of goal-centered and operation-centered policies. Moreover, process skills are basic in developing functional order in organizations, in unifying and formalizing work-flow patterns, and in maintaining and improving the organization-environment exchange system. As Figure 4-2 indicates, the administrative performance system is an open system which interacts and exchanges information with individuals and groups in many settings. Thus, process competences are required of administrators not only in the school setting but in varied settings in the community.

Experience and evidence indicate that there is some differentiation in the settings in which administrators employ process competences. Certain members of administrative performance systems use processes pre-

Figure 4-2. The Administrative Performance System
as an Open System

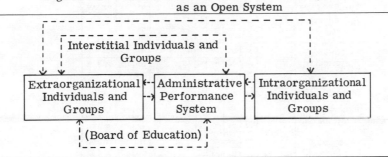

dominantly in a total school district context; others employ them primarily within an attendance unit context. In each of these settings, differences exist in the number, type, and complexity of the variables that must be encompassed and understood. The degree of sophistication required for effective performance depends substantially upon the nature and complexity of the variables characterizing each setting.

Ways in which processes are utilized in the administrative setting will be delineated in subsequent chapters. The aim here is to develop preliminary insights into various processes employed in administration and to indicate their importance to administrative action. It is evident, for example, that administrators must communicate with individuals, with small groups, and with large groups in both intraorganizational and extraorganizational settings. Moreover, they must influence goals and make decisions in both school and community contexts. In addition, they must direct attention to maintaining and improving morale if the organization is to function with optimum effectiveness. Finally, administrators must initiate and direct change for the continuous betterment of the educational enterprise. Thus, four important process competences required of administrators relate to decision making, communication, handling morale, and initiating and directing change. General judgments concerning demands facing members of administrative performance systems in these four process areas are delineated in Tables 4-4 through 4-7.

Administrative Processes in the Principal's Role

Table 4-4 indicates that most of the principal's communication activities occur within an attendance-unit context, although there are occasional demands in the principalship for two-person, small-group, large-group,

Table 4-4. Communication Demands for Selected Positions

LEGEND
1 = Major demand
2 = Moderate demand
3 = Occasional demand
4 = Rare demand

	Superintendent I*	Superintendent E†	Superintendent I	Sec. School Principal I	Sec. School Principal E	Elem. School Principal I	Elem. School Principal E	Director of Program I	Director of Program E	Instructional Supv. and Consultant I	Instructional Supv. and Consultant E	Dir. of Pupil Personnel I	Dir. of Pupil Personnel E	Dir. of Staff Personnel I	Dir. of Staff Personnel E	Director of Research I	Director of Research E	Director of Business Affairs I	Director of Business Affairs E
A. Total community-school district context‡																			
1. Two-person	1	1	1	3	3	3	3	1	3	3	4	2	2	1	3	2	4	2	3
2. Small-group	1	1	1	3	3	3	3	1	3	2	4	2	3	2	3	3	4	2	3
3. Large-group	1	1	1	3	3	3	4	2	2	3	3	3	3	2	3	4	4	2	3
4. Written	1	1	1	3	3	4	4	1	2	2	3	2	2	1	4	2	3	1	3
B. Attendance unit context**																			
1. Two-person	3	4	3	1	1	1	1	3	4	1	4	2	2	3	4	2	4	3	3
2. Small-group	3	4	3	1	1	1	1	3	4	2	4	3	3	3	4	2	4	3	3
3. Large-group	3	3	3	1	2	2	2	3	4	4	3	4	4	3	4	3	4	3	3
4. Written	2	3	1	1	2	2	2	3	4	3	4	2	2	2	4	2	4	2	4

* I = intraorganizational demands.
† E = extraorganizational demands.
‡ Refers to the total school district and its community environment.
** Refers to attendance units and their immediate community environments.

and written communication in the total community-school district context. In the attendance-unit context, the principal has major responsibilities for communicating with organizational and community individuals and groups. His communication activities relate to and encompass many areas of vital concern—including systemwide and building policies, operational procedures, and intraorganizational and extraorganizational problems of numerous kinds. Moreover, the principal must communicate in group decision-making activities, in handling problems of human relationships, in relating individual needs and organizational purposes, and in acting as school spokesman in many community settings.

General demands for critical and routine decision making in the principalship are depicted in Table 4-5. Demands within the attendance-unit context and the total community-school district context are postulated in relation to (1) individual decision making, (2) individual decision making with intragroup consultation, (3) individual decision making with extragroup consultation, (4) small-group decision making, and (5) large-group decision making.

In like manner, Tables 4-6 and 4-7 outline general demands upon the secondary school administrator for initiating and directing change and for maintaining and improving morale. Both of these process competencies are applicable in relation to individuals, to small groups, and to large groups.

Significant research in the social sciences is providing increasing quantities of relevant knowledge in relation to administrative processes.[11] Research in political science and public administration, for example, is continuing to shed light upon processes of decision making in both political and administrative contexts. Studies in various disciplines such as sociology and social psychology are providing needed understanding concerning processes of communication, morale, and change. Research on leader behavior and human relations is generating new knowledge about factors affecting organizational climate and the impact of various variables upon organizational effectiveness and efficiency.

In the process areas of administration, successful performance demands

11. See, for example, Ronald Lippitt, Jeanne Watson, and Bruce Westley, *The Dynamics of Planned Change* (New York: Harcourt, Brace & Co., 1958); Carl Hovland, Irving Janis, and Harold Kelley, *Communication and Persuasion* (New Haven, Conn.: Yale University Press, 1953); Herbert A. Simon, *Administrative Behavior* (New York: The Macmillan Co., 1959); and Morris Viteles, *Motivation and Morale in Industry* (New York: W. W. Norton & Co., 1953).

Table 4-5. Decision-making Demands for Selected Positions

LEGEND
1 = Major demand
2 = Moderate demand
3 = Occasional demand
4 = Rare demand

	Superintendent		Sec. School Principal		Elem. School Principal		Director of Program		Instructional Supv. and Consultant		Dir. of Pupil Personnel		Dir. of Staff Personnel		Director of Research		Director of Business Affairs	
	C*	R†	C	R	C	R	C	R	C	R	C	R	C	R	C	R	C	R
A. Total community-school district context ‡																		
1. Individual decision making	1	1	4	4	4	4	2	2	3	3	2	2	2	2	3	2	2	2
2. Individual decision making with intragroup consultation	1	1	3	3	4	4	1	2	3	3	2	2	2	2	4	3	2	1
3. Individual decision making with extragroup consultation	1	2	4	4	4	4	1	2	3	3	3	3	3	3	4	4	3	3
4. Small-group decision making	1	1	3	3	3	3	2	2	3	3	2	2	2	2	2	2	2	1
5. Large-group decision making	1	2	3	3	3	3	3	3	4	4	4	3	3	3	4	4	3	3
B. Attendance-unit context **																		
1. Individual decision making	3	3	1	1	1	1	3	4	3	3	4	3	3	3	4	4	3	3
2. Individual decision making with intragroup consultation	3	3	1	1	1	1	3	4	3	3	4	3	3	3	4	4	3	4
3. Individual decision making with extragroup consultation	3	3	2	2	2	1	4	4	4	4	4	4	4	4	4	4	4	4
4. Small-group decision making	3	3	2	2	1	1	3	4	4	3	3	3	3	3	3	3	3	3
5. Large-group decision making	3	3	3	3	3	1	4	4	4	4	4	4	4	4	4	4	4	4

* C = critical decision making (general purposes and objectives).

† R = routine decision making (specific operational objectives).

‡ Refers to total school district and its community environment.

**Refers to attendance units and their immediate community environments.

Table 4-6. Demands upon Selected Positions for Initiating and Directing Change

LEGEND
1 = Major demand
2 = Moderate demand
3 = Occasional demand
4 = Rare demand

	Superintendent		Sec. School Principal		Elem. School Principal		Director of Program		Instructional Supv. and Consultant		Dir. of Pupil Personnel		Dir. of Staff Personnel		Director of Research		Director of Business Affairs	
	I*	E†	I	E	I	E	I	E	I	E	I	E	I	E	I	E	I	E
A. Total community-school district context‡																		
1. Individual	1	1	3	3	3	3	1	3	3	4	2	3	3	3	2	4	2	3
2. Small-group	1	1	3	3	3	3	1	2	2	4	2	3	2	3	3	4	2	3
3. Large-group	1	1	4	4	4	4	2	3	3	4	3	4	3	3	4	4	2	3
B. Attendance unit context**																		
1. Individual	3	3	1	1	1	1	3	4	1	3	3	3	2	4	3	4	3	3
2. Small group	3	3	1	1	1	1	3	4	1	3	3	3	2	4	3	4	3	3
3. Large group	3	3	2	2	2	2	3	4	4	4	4	4	3	4	3	4	3	3

* I = intraorganizational demands.
† E = extraorganizational demands.
‡ Refers to the total school district and its community environment.
**Refers to attendance units and their immediate community environments.

Table 4-7. Demands upon Selected Positions for Maintaining and Improving Morale

LEGEND

1 = Major demand
2 = Moderate demand
3 = Occasional demand
4 = Rare demand

	Superintendent	Sec. School Principal	Elem. School Principal	Director of Program	Instructional Supv. and Consultant	Dir. of Pupil Personnel	Dir. of Staff Personnel	Director of Research	Director of Business Affairs
A. Total school district context*									
1. Individual	1	3	3	1	2	1	1	2	1
2. Small-group	1	3	3	1	3	2	2	3	1
3. Large-group	1	3	3	2	4	4	4	4	2
B. Attendance unit context†									
1. Individual	3	1	1	3	1	3	3	3	3
2. Small-group	3	1	1	3	2	3	3	3	3
3. Large-group	3	1	1	4	4	4	4	4	4

* Intraorganizational.
† Also intraorganizational.

not only knowledge but understanding of and insight into the influence of important variables in the organizational setting. One variable which exerts great impact upon institutional effectiveness and efficiency is the manner in which organizational subsystems operate and interact. It appears important that principals understand the impact upon goal achievement of each of the following subsystems identified by Stogdill:

1. The structure of positions which is given formal definition and sanction by the differentiation of function and status.
2. The operative role system which is defined by the different degrees of responsibility, authority, and delegation exhibited by the occupants of various positions.
3. The formal interaction system which tends to parallel the formal structure of positions but is subject to deviation in response to changing demands for coordination of individual performance and subgroup operations.
4. The norm system of the group and of its subgroups which, through sanction and prescription, defines acceptable conduct for group members.
5. The system of member performances which describes the operations of the group and changes in response to variations of the group task.
6. The system of informal interactions which brings together group members on the basis of propinquity, mutual liking, and similarity of interests.
7. The system of covert interactions, if present, which brings together persons who challenge the legitimacy of the operative role structure and differential sanctions associated with it.[12]

Other variables are equally important:

1. All administrative performance systems function in a milieu of power. Principals require competence in identifying and working with formal and informal power systems in both school and community settings.

2. Motivation toward action and accomplishment in organizations and communities is affected not only by prevailing value patterns but by important psychological, economic, political, and sociological factors and variables. Principals require sophistication in (a) identifying existing systems of belief and thought, and (b) utilizing available motivational bases to generate activity and support for the betterment of schools.

3. The leadership potential available in administrative performance

12. Ralph M. Stogdill, *Individual Behavior and Group Achievement* (New York: Oxford University Press, 1959), p. 147-148.

systems can significantly affect organizational effectiveness and efficiency. Principals must clearly define their leadership roles in policy formation and legitimation, in decision making, in initiating and directing change, in morale building, in conflict resolution, in building functional organizations and unified work-flow patterns, and in improving the organizational-environmental exchange system.

REFERENCES

Allport, Floyd H., *Theories of Perception and the Concept of Structure* (New York: John Wiley & Sons, 1955).

Appleby, Paul H., *Policy and Administration* (University, Ala.: University of Alabama Press, 1949).

Bailey, Stephen, *et al., Schoolmen and Politics* (Syracuse, N.Y.: Syracuse University Press, 1962).

Bertalanffy, Ludwig, and Rapoport, Anatol (eds.), *General Systems—Yearbook of the Society for the Advancement of General Systems Theory* (Ann Arbor, Mich.: Braun-Brumfield, 1956).

Cahill, Robert S., and Hencley, Stephen P., *The Politics of Education in the Local Community* (Danville, Ill.: The Interstate Printers and Publishers, Inc., 1964).

Culbertson, Jack A., and Hencley, Stephen P. (eds.), *Preparing Administrators: New Perspectives* (Columbus, Ohio: University Council for Educational Administration, 1962).

Griffiths, Daniel E. (ed.), *Behavioral Science and Educational Administration,* Sixty-Third Yearbook, Part II, National Society for the Study of Education (Chicago: University of Chicago Press, 1964).

Griffiths, Daniel E., *et al., Organizing Schools for Effective Education* (Danville, Ill.: The Interstate Printers and Publishers, 1962).

Harris, Ben M., *Supervisory Behavior in Education* (Englewood Cliffs, N.J.: Prentice-Hall, Inc., 1963).

Kimbrough, Ralph B., *Political Power and Educational Decision-Making* (Chicago: Rand McNally & Company, 1964).

Leu, Donald J., and Rudman, Herbert C., *Preparation Programs for School Administrators* (East Lansing, Mich.: Michigan State University, 1963).

Likert, Rensis, *New Patterns of Management* (New York: McGraw-Hill Book Co., 1961).

Lucio, William H., and McNeil, John D., *Supervision* (New York: McGraw-Hill Book Co., 1962).

Wengert, E. S., *et al., The Study of Administration* (Eugene, Ore.: School of Business Administration, University of Oregon, 1961).

Chapter 5
The Principal
as Leader

A N important characteristic distinguishes leader-statesmen from manager-executives in secondary school administration: the statesmen have accomplished the transition from administrative management to institutional leadership. For several reasons, secondary school administrators have experienced difficulty in making this important transition.

Often in the past the task of secondary school administration has been equated with organizational management and maintenance rather than with institutional leadership. As a consequence, from the time of the first "principal teachers" of an earlier era, many secondary school administrators have unwittingly and successfully projected a low-level image of their profession and its concerns. In many communities, the public image of men in these positions has become associated with competence in the management of facilities, equipment, and supplies; with the allocation of teaching functions; with the grading, promotion, guidance, and discipline of pupils; with the mechanics of schedule building, school bus operations, and PTA meetings; and with the promotion of successful basketball teams and junior proms.

Overemphasis on limited aspects of leadership has prevented many secondary school administrators from rising above technical-managerial roles necessary in "running the schools." As able and dedicated servants, many have done well what they were expected to do. Many have achieved satisfaction from dealing with executive details and "administrivia" and have found few avenues to circumvent the pressure of immediate problems in the secondary school setting. Administrators under such circumstances have long functioned as heads of school organizations; they have seldom served their profession as educational statesmen and institutional leaders.

Uncertainty among secondary school administrators about the appropriate model for their profession has been conditioned by two significant trends. The first has been the preoccupation of both professional educators and training institutions with educational means rather than educational ends. This emphasis has been reinforced in the past by the scientific management and human relations movements; the intensive study of organization; the emphasis on social roles and organization-individual interaction; the cult of the administrative process; the study in depth of communication, decision making, conflict, and morale; and the emphasis on efficiency. All of these focuses have been primarily concerned, not with organizational ends, but with organizational means and processes. Each movement has provided new knowledge and insights about the means for making organizations more productive and efficient. But altogether they have shed little light on institutional purposes or the unique role of institutional leadership.

Overemphasis on skills and techniques for building efficient administrative organizations has highlighted administrative preoccupation with the matching of available means to predetermined organizational ends. Primary stress has thus been placed upon *routine* decision-making skills required in organizational maintenance. The separation of ends and means has left undefined the important functions of institutional leadership: in effecting organizational change, in defining organizational goals and purposes, and in determining the basic character of the educational enterprise through critical choice making. Past emphases have produced many administrative managers but few institutional leaders for America's public schools.

A second trend that has influenced leadership in the school setting has been the eagerness of professional educators to accept evolving role models and leader images from other fields such as government, industry, and business. Several of these models have had major impact upon leader behavior in public education; others will undoubtedly continue to influence such behavior as the profession moves toward greater responsibility for institutional leadership.

IMAGES OF THE LEADER

Leader images in many societies are remarkably culture-bound and socially conditioned. In this country, several such images have emerged in the past sixty years. One of these was exemplified in the "scientific management" outlook of Frederick W. Taylor and associates at the turn of the century.[1] A second image, current from the 1920's to the late 1940's, was evident in the descriptions by Urwick, who stressed the leader's role in conceptualizing design and structure in formal organizations.[2] A third image, which ran somewhat counter to the first two, was projected by Mary Parker Follett and others who viewed leadership and administration as a science, an art, and an ethical practice.[3] Follett, Ordway Tead, Morris L. Cooke, and C. W. Valentine formed an early beginning for the work which was to culminate in the "social engineer" image of the leader set forth by the Harvard Group, which stressed the importance of human relations.[4] More recently, a view of the leader as a clinician has been popular.[5] Each of these points of view has affected conceptions of the role of leadership; each should be understood if one is to grasp the full significance of mature institutional leadership.

The Efficiency Expert

The image of the leader as an efficiency expert has had a marked effect upon leader behavior in administrative organizations in various fields. The image was given impetus as a result of the "machine model" thinking of the early exponents of scientific management such as Taylor, Gantt, and Gilbreth. The industrial culture of the early twentieth century—characterized by the Horatio Alger myth, Spencer's adaptation of Darwinism, the religious sanction of business, the "New Thought" movement, the concept of the entrepreneur as his own master—readily accepted the ideas of the scientific managers.

1. Frederick W. Taylor, *Principles of Scientific Management* (New York: Harper & Bros., 1911).
2. See L. Urwick, "Scientific Principles and Organization," address given at the Institute of Management, New York, N.Y., September 15, 1938.
3. Henry C. Metcalf and L. Urwick (eds.), *Dynamic Administration: The Collected Papers of Mary Parker Follett* (New York: Harper & Bros., 1940).
4. Elton Mayo, *The Human Problems of an Industrial Civilization* (Cambridge, Mass.: Graduate School of Business Administration, Harvard University, 1946).
5. W. C. Schutz, "The Interpersonal Underworld," *Harvard Business Review,* July-August, 1958, pp. 123-135.

The scientific managers viewed the worker as a machinelike production unit, another resource to be managed in the production process. Man was primarily an inert instrument; the function of the leader was to fit him scientifically to necessary tasks on the basis of a minute examination of his technical capacities.[6] Stress was placed on efficiency, time and motion studies, functional foremanship, and improved production rates. The Taylorian leader had few doubts about his mission in organization. His responsibility was to build a smoothly functioning organization; his prerogative was to fit men to jobs; his goal was efficiency. His means were scientific job analysis, authoritarian direction, incentive wages, and threats of dismissal.

The extent to which the philosophy of scientific management shaped the thinking of educational leaders early in this century was exemplified in Cubberley's statement:

Our schools are, in a sense, factories in which the raw products (children) are to be shaped and fashioned into products to meet the various demands of life. The specifications for manufacturing come from the demands of the twentieth-century civilization, and it is the business of the school to build its pupils according to the specifications laid down. This demands good tools, specialized machinery, continuous measurement of production to see if it is according to specifications, the elimination of waste in manufacture, and a large variety in the output.[7]

The impact of Taylorism on leadership functions in education was vividly illustrated in Spaulding's finding in Newton, Massachusetts, that "5.9 pupil recitations in Greek are of the same value as 23.8 pupil recitations in French," and in his remark that "the price must go down, or we shall invest in something else." [8] Although the operations of school personnel were less routinized than those in industry, certain efficiency concepts have persisted in schools to the present time, including fixed positions, interchangeability of personnel, and the patterning of organization to provide a reasonable division of labor.

The concept of leadership advocated by scientific managers pictured the job of the leader primarily as one of developing a smoothly operating

6. James G. March and Herbert A. Simon, *Organizations* (New York: John Wiley & Sons, 1958), p. 13.

7. Ellwood Cubberley, *Public School Administration* (Boston: Houghton Mifflin Co., 1916), p. 33.

8. Frank E. Spaulding, "The Application of the Principles of Scientific Management," National Education Association, *Journal of Addresses and Proceedings,* 1913.

school organization. This view largely ignored the psychological forces involved in human interaction, and the role of the school leader in the larger environment received little consideration.

The Organizational Engineer

An image of the leader current between 1920 and 1950 showed leaders to be, in large measure, organizational engineers competent to build rational formal organizations. The integration and application of organizational concepts—control, authority, coordination and responsibility, line and staff, unity of command, span of control, departmentalization, centralization and decentralization, and others—were held to be of primary importance in organizational leadership. Since formal organization was thought to be meaningless without reference to organizational form as conditioned by organizational purpose, the task of the leader was seen largely as that of scientifically defining the formal structure of the organization.

The building of geometric conceptions of organization—in which tasks and activities could be related to processes of authority and consent over specified time periods—became important leadership concerns. Leaders were urged to conceptualize and operationalize the necessary specialized functions to be performed in a manner that would facilitate both organizational purpose and control. Thus, Gulick stressed the importance of work division in organizations in terms of major purpose or function, process, clientele, and place.[9] The organization chart became an important medium for communicating the relationships that were to exist among leader and follower, line and staff, organization and department. Once the formal organization was set, the functions of the leader were encompassed by Gulick's famous administrative process formulation, POSDCORB: planning, organizing, staffing, directing, coordinating, reporting, and budgeting.

Even though Gulick acknowledged in his conclusion that from the "standpoint of organization" less than adequate attention had been given to "political life and leadership" the concept of the leader as an organizational engineer has had profound effect in education. Elaborate organizational charts in many high schools, intricate scheduling arrange-

9. Luther Gulick, "Notes on the Theory of Organization," in Luther Gulick and L. Urwick (eds.), *Papers on the Science of Administration* (New York: Institute of Public Administration, 1937), p. 1.

ments, line and staff functions, together with newer concerns such as effective ways to organize and implement teaching teams, large-group instructional patterns, and individualized instruction—all attest to the importance attached to this concept of leadership in education.

The limitations of leadership as organizational engineering are clearly evident, however, when the leader is called upon to build a structure that is *uniquely* tailored to facilitate and promote goal accomplishment in a *particular* organization. Organizations differ in their purposes, their methods, the people they serve, the competence of their employees, and the distinctiveness of their decision-making procedures. Uniform translation of organizational structures from one type of enterprise to another fails to accommodate these differences and loses sight of the need for organizational structure to permit adaptation in depth to unique organizational purposes. Moreover, the structure must be so tailored that it facilitates the acquisition of unique organizational values and promotes group loyalty, commitment, and solidarity in relation to such values. The building of a value-infused organization committed to organizational purposes requires more than the skills of organizational engineering: it requires the maturity and vision of institutional leadership.

The Social Engineer

The leader as social engineer is another role model that has had a pronounced effect upon the behavior patterns of public school administrators. This image gained wide acceptance in many fields during the depression of the 1930's and was given impetus by the findings of Mayo and Henderson in their studies of industrial fatigue. The work of the Harvard Group (Mayo,[10] Henderson, Roethlisberger,[11] Homans,[12] and Lombard), which began in 1927, enunciated the theory underlying the importance of human motivation, sentiment, and behavior in work situations and group processes. The work of others, including Chester Barnard,[13] was also notable in this area.

The importance of human relations in leadership was prominently established by the Harvard Group in studies which began in the Western

10. Elton Mayo, *The Social Problems of an Industrial Civilization* (Cambridge, Mass.: Graduate School of Business Administration, Harvard University, 1945).

11. See Mayo, *The Human Problems of an Industrial Civilization, op. cit.*

12. George C. Homans, *The Human Group* (New York: Harcourt, Brace & Co., 1950).

13. Chester I. Barnard, *The Functions of the Executive* (Cambridge, Mass.: Harvard University Press, 1938).

Electric Company's Hawthorne Plant. Among the group's important contributions that provided a foundation for the image of the leader as a social engineer were the following:

1. The Western Electric Studies revealed that a leader's interest in workers, together with personal interest in the workers' duties, resulted in better on-the-job performance. Changing physical working conditions did not in themselves make for appreciable difference in production output. But morale was improved and production increased when workers felt they were appreciated by management. This finding has come to be known as the "Hawthorne Effect."

2. Mayo and his colleagues refuted the rabble hypothesis and the current model of economic man. They found that economic motivations were subsidiary to the human desire for acceptance and recognition by friends and work associates. These important matters, they found, could not be resolved primarily by negotiating contracts. Human motivation, sentiment, and behavior were of primary importance.

3. The function and functioning of informal groups were found to be of primary importance in worker motivation: man's most important single drive was to stand well with his fellows. The studies increased awareness of the emotional, nonrational, and subconscious motivations of interpersonal behavior. In work situations where groups had little opportunity to form, symptoms such as turnover and absenteeism resulted. Any disregard of man's inclination to be continuously associated with his fellows led ordinarily to some form of defeat for organizational leadership.

4. Stress was placed upon communicating and counseling with employees regarding any changes affecting their welfare or duties. The studies undermined management's fallacious assumption that employees would accept its decisions as being in their interests while they were denied both a voice in the decisions and an understanding of them. The studies pointed up the necessity for change away from industrial feudalism toward an open society.

5. Goals were advocated for leader behavior on the basis of human relations findings. These included recommendations that leaders (*a*) develop respect for others, accept individual differences, sharpen sensitivity to the feelings of others, and recognize that kindness is not a weakness; and (*b*) be aware of the importance of a clinical approach to human relations problems.

The model of the leader as a social engineer has become widespread not only in education but in most other fields as well. The human relations movement added to the image of the leader an important dimension which was generally lacking in the images of the efficiency expert and the organizational engineer. As is generally true with exciting new movements, however, certain extremists were so struck with the significance of human relations principles that they went far afield in their concern for "democratic" leadership. Critics of this extreme element have pointed out that authority must still be exercised in organizations, that the function of leaders in organizations is to lead, that leaders are no less "democratic" if they assume leadership responsibilities, and that the important criterion in leadership is not "democracy" but rather the style, manner, and quality of leader behavior exemplified in positions of leadership.

The Clinician

Increased awareness of the emotional, nonrational and subconscious aspects of interpersonal behavior in organizations has led to a fourth image of the leader as a clinician. This view holds that the leader is constantly involved in human interaction. Consequently, it is necessary that he not only "understand the vast interpersonal underworld that operates beneath the overt, observable behavior" [14] but also have competence to deal with intragroup hostilities, dissatisfactions of organizational members, organizational power struggles, "problem" members in organizations, and hostility directed toward leadership. Schutz has summarized his theory of interpersonal relations as follows:

> There are three interpersonal need areas—inclusion, control, and affection—sufficient for the prediction of interpersonal behavior. Orientations which an individual acquires toward behavior in the areas are relatively invariant over time. Compatibility of two or more persons depends on (*a*) their ability to satisfy reciprocally each other's interpersonal needs; (*b*) their complementarity with respect to originating and receiving behavior in each need area; and (*c*) their similarity with respect to the amount of interchange they desire with other people in each need area. . . .
> Every interpersonal relation follows the same general developmental sequence. It starts with inclusion behavior, is followed by control behavior, and finally affection behavior. This cycle may recur. When the relation approaches termination, it reverses direction, and investment in the relation is withdrawn in the order affection, control, and inclusion.[15]

14. Schutz, *op. cit.,* p. 135.
15. William C. Schutz, "The FIRO Theory of Interpersonal Behavior," in Stephen P. Hencley (ed.), *Research in Educational Administration,* Report of Cooperative Research Project No. F-2 (Columbus, Ohio: University Council for Educational Administration, 1962), pp. 150-151.

Much importance is attached in some circles to a clinical orientation in leadership positions. For example, "sensitivity training workshops," [16] designed to put a keen edge on leaders, have greatly expanded in number since their inception at the National Training Laboratory in Group Development at Bethel, Maine. Not only have trained psychologists and psychiatrists begun to offer such training in more than a dozen universities, but corporations such as International Business Machines, Western Electric, and Standard Oil of New Jersey have operated experimental group training sessions. The swing toward the role model of the leader as clinician was accelerated, in some measure, by Moreno's and Lewin's studies of group dynamics and the sociometry of interpersonal relations. Their interests included the use of psychodrama and role playing to sensitize individuals to the way they were being viewed and accepted by others. This, of course, is also the objective of sensitivity training.

Proponents of sensitivity training have stated that participation in experimental groups sensitizes leaders to others' feelings and makes them aware of their own personality and behavioral defects. In addition, training sessions increase the insight of leaders into factors that motivate individual and group behavior, and they also improve competence in interpersonal interaction. Critics of the programs, on the other hand, have held that participation in such training programs leads to excessive introspection and self-criticism which may destroy the traits and personality characteristics that make leaders effective. Moreover, some critics have stated that individuals who are most in need of understanding their own undesirable behavioral characteristics are the very persons who profit least from this type of training.

As yet, the role model of the leader as a clinician has had less influence in education than other models that have been presented. There can be little doubt, however, that this leader image will have major impact in educational administration in the coming years.

STUDIES OF LEADER BEHAVIOR

The lively preoccupation of our culture with leadership has led to considerable speculation and study in relation to this phenomenon. Much

16. Also referred to as "T-group training," "awareness training," "laboratory training," and "diagnostic skill training." See, for instance, John H. Suchr, "Awareness Training for School People?" *Phi Delta Kappan,* Vol. XLIII, No. 6 (March, 1962), pp. 263-265.

of this work has been highly productive. New insights and understandings have emerged concerning the leader's role in affecting organizational achievement, reducing conflict and inefficiency in organizations, and maintaining effective and efficient work groups. Despite such advances, however, the banality and triviality of certain viewpoints on leadership have, at times, been sharply criticized. Peyre,[17] for instance, has noted that the reading of many volumes about leadership in this country is a dismal and ludicrous experience which is sufficient to convince all but the admirers of factual surveys and statistical data that "leaders are indeed mystery men, born in paradise or in some Devil's pit, but that they never must have become leaders through the study of books on management or of treatises on the making of higher executives." [18]

In spite of such criticisms, the study of leader behavior has provided practicing school administrators with valuable concepts and knowledge to enhance the impact of leadership in organizational settings. Research on leader behavior has been conducted in several fields: government, business, the armed forces, and education. Each field has contributed leadership concepts; each has helped to identify commonalities concerning the nature of leadership and its impact in human affairs.

A recent summary of attempts to identify community and public leaders concluded that leadership was being exercised by a variety of people in most communities: by those who held status positions, by members of community power structures, by community service volunteers, by latent leaders who held no office but who still influenced opinion, and by individuals who exercised initiative when unusual situations and circumstances arose in community life.[19] Floyd Hunter, who has used reputational techniques to study leaders and power figures in American cities, contends that leadership at the national government level is exercised by relatively few—fewer than 300—persons.[20] Others have estimated the figure to be nearer several thousand. Disagreements of this kind can be attributed primarily to varying definitions of leadership used by investigators and to differences in the methods of study employed.

17. Henri Peyre, "Excellence and Leadership: Has Western Europe Any Lessons for Us?" *Daedalus,* Vol. 90, No. 4, Fall, 1961, p. 629.

18. *Ibid.,* p. 629.

19. Wendell Bell, Richard J. Hill, and Charles R. Wright, *Public Leadership* (San Francisco: Chandler Publishing Co., 1961), Chapter II.

20. See Floyd Hunter, *Top Leadership, U.S.A.* (Chapel Hill, N.C.: University of North Carolina Press, 1959).

Traits and Situations

For years the study of leadership was concentrated on identification of the traits or personality characteristics that would distinguish leaders from nonleaders. Numerous studies have compared leaders and followers with respect to such traits as physical characteristics, personality, and intellectual qualities. Generally speaking, such studies have done little to advance knowledge about leadership; their primary weakness has been an overconcern with the static qualities of leaders. Little attempt has been directed toward description of the dynamic elements of the leadership process.

Criticisms of the trait approach have pointed out that such studies have not indicated the relative importance of different traits, that they have not proved various traits to be mutually exclusive, and that they have not differentiated between traits consistently necessary in leadership and traits essential merely for attaining positions of leadership. Moreover, conflicting studies have indicated that leaders have been successful and effective even though they have exhibited strikingly dissimilar traits.[21] Thus, Jennings has identified three types of leaders who bear little resemblance to one another: princes, who are motivated by their desire for power and dominance; heroes, who seek to serve high ideals and noble causes; and supermen, who emerge at various times from many walks of life.[22] In writing about the trait approach to leadership, Stogdill has indicated that individuals do not become leaders by virtue of a combination of traits. Nevertheless, he has cited certain research studies that tend to support the notion that leaders are characterized by good intelligence, dependability, social activity, scholarship, and status in the socioeconomic sphere.[23]

Recent studies have shed additional light on the relationship of personal variables to success in the leadership role. In attempting to distinguish between promotable and nonpromotable insurance underwriters, Malo found that personality variables such as intensity, conjunctivity, social ability, reality orientation, achievement drive, and superego orien-

21. See R. M. Stogdill, "Personal Factors Associated with Leadership: A Survey of the Literature," *Journal of Psychology,* January, 1948; and C. A. Weber and M. E. Weber, *Fundamentals of Educational Leadership* (New York: McGraw-Hill Book Co., 1955).

22. See Eugene E. Jennings, *An Anatomy of Leadership* (New York: Harper & Bros., 1960).

23. Stogdill, *op. cit.*

tation were judged by superiors to characterize promotable individuals.[24] Lipham used a number of Malo's instruments, together with interviews and the *Edwards Personal Preference Schedule,* to study personal variables and their relationship to the judged effectiveness of principals. He found that principals judged to be ineffective by superiors were deliberate in nature; satisfied with present status and achievement; preferred assisting children to working with teachers; depended on others for support; often showed strong emotion in charged situations; and showed preoccupation with speculative reasoning. Principals judged to be effective engaged in strong, purposeful activity; related well to people; sought success and higher-status positions; and felt secure in both home and work settings.[25] Another study reported by Boyce indicated that both the Aesthetic and Religious scales of the *Allport-Vernon-Lindzey Scale of Values* and the Abasement and Nurturance factors of the *Edwards Personal Preference Schedule* showed significant positive correlations with superiors' effectiveness ratings of subordinates.[26] While personal variables similar to those reported appear to be part of the competency pattern of successful leaders, it should be noted that many persons possessing such characteristics do not engage in purposeful leadership activity.

A second approach to the study of leadership has maintained that leadership is determined not by the characteristics of individuals but by the requirements of social situations. This view has held (1) that leadership is a product of relationships in social situations, and (2) that leaders in different situations may show dissimilar characteristics. Thus, leaders in one situation may not be leaders in other situations where circumstances and social factors are different. Although this view has found support, Andrews has noted that its general acceptance may lead to the conclusion that the study of leadership is at a dead end: generalization about leadership may be meaningless.[27]

The shortcomings of both the trait and the situationist approaches to the study of leadership are now generally recognized. Although studies are still being conducted from these earlier orientations, the study of

24. Albert H. Malo, "Personality Variables Related to Administrative Potential" (Doctor's thesis, University of Chicago, 1959), p. 185.

25. James M. Lipham, "Personal Variables of Effective Administrators," *Administrator's Notebook,* Vol. II, No. 1, September, 1960, pp. 1-4.

26. R. D. Boyce, "An Empirical Evaluation of Five Tests for Administrator Selection: The Composite Study" (Doctor's thesis, Stanford University, 1960).

27. John H. M. Andrews, "Recent Research on Leadership," *Canadian Education,* Vol. XIII, No. 4, September, 1958, pp. 15-24.

leadership has recently been directed into newer and more productive avenues.

Recent Emphasis in Leadership Theories

Despite differences in terminology, present-day theorists and researchers have reached remarkable agreement concerning two major dimensions of leader behavior. In many ways the two dimensions appear to encompass certain characteristics of leader images discussed earlier: the efficiency expert, the organization engineer, the social engineer, and the clinician. Barnard, for instance, noted the difference between organizational efficiency and organizational effectiveness several decades ago: an organization was effective if its common purposes were being achieved; it was efficient if individual motives were being satisfied and cooperation of organizational members was being elicited.[28]

The objectives of leaders in maintaining organizational efficiency and effectiveness have been described by Cartwright and Zander under rubrics that do not differ materially from Barnard's. These men have pointed out that most group objectives may be encompassed under two headings: (1) activities directed toward the attainment of stated group goals, and (2) activities directed toward maintaining or strengthening the work group. Examples cited by Cartwright and Zander which are indicative of member behaviors directed toward goal achievement are: "initiates action," "keeps members' attention on the goal," "clarifies the issue," "develops a procedural plan," "evaluates the quality of work done," and "makes expert information available." Behaviors exemplifying the group-maintenance function include: "keeps interpersonal relations pleasant," "arbitrates disputes," "provides encouragement," "gives the minority a chance to be heard," "stimulates self-direction," and "increases the interdependence among members."[29]

In like manner, Kahn and Katz have discussed two major modes of behavior among supervisors: some supervisors are production-oriented, others are employee-oriented.[30] Employee-oriented supervisors focus primarily on employee motivation, satisfaction of employee needs, and the building of employee morale. Production-oriented supervisors, on the

---

28. Barnard, *op. cit,* Chapter 7.
29. Dorwin Cartwright and Alvin Zander, *Group Dynamics: Research and Theory* (Evanston, Ill.: Row, Peterson, & Co., 1953), p. 541.
30. Robert L. Kahn and Daniel Katz, "Leadership Practices in Relation to Productivity and Morale" in Cartwright and Zander, *op. cit.,* pp. 554-570.

other hand, emphasize increased efficiency, greater production, and institutional goal attainment.

Investigators at the Personnel Research Board, Ohio State University, also identified two major dimensions of leader behavior:

1. *Initiating structure in interaction,* that is, the leader's behavior in relation to (*a*) outlining, clarifying, and delineating leader-follower relationships, and (*b*) establishing clear organizational patterns, communication channels, and procedures for accomplishing organizational tasks.

2. *Consideration,* that is, the leader's behavior in indicating friendship, respect, trust, and warmth in relationships between himself and group members.

The Ohio State group made a significant operational definition when it decided to use the concept "leader behavior" in preference to the concept of leadership. Leader behavior, in contrast with leadership, was subject to investigation because it could be described and subjected to content analysis. Behavioral data derived through observation, job analysis, R-A-D Scales, and the Leader Behavior Description Questionnaire (LBDQ) could be quantified for purposes of statistical analysis to provide new insights into the dimensions of behavior of officially designated leaders.

More recently, Getzels and Guba have indicated various styles of leader behavior derived from their study of administration as a social process. These men have stated that administration occurs, structurally, as a hierarchy of subordinate-superordinate relationships within a social system. Functionally, the administrative process consists of the allocation and integration of roles and facilities for the achievement of the goals of the system with reference to a broader cultural framework. Operationally, administration takes place in an interpersonal setting and is invariably concerned with social relationships.[31] Viewed in these terms, leader behavior in social systems is a function of the interaction of three classes of independent phenomena, as indicated in the model shown in Figure 5-1. The model points to three major modes of leader behavior: behavior that stresses nomothetic considerations, behavior that stresses idiographic considerations, and behavior that utilizes a judicious combination of the two.

Such theoretical models have become the bases for new conceptions and definitions of leadership which encompass the leader behavior di-

31. J. W. Getzels and E. G. Guba, "Social Behavior and the Administrative Process," *School Review,* Vol. LXV, No. 4, Winter, 1957, pp. 423-441.

Figure 5-1. Behavior in Social Systems:
The Getzels-Guba Model

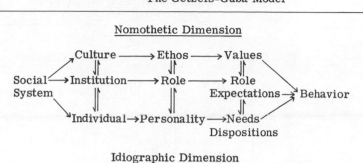

mensions discussed above. Generally speaking, new definitions of leadership encompass various combinations of the following: (1) the leader's ability to lead group members toward acceptance of common goals, (2) the leader's ability to initiate productive action in group situations, (3) the leader's ability to establish clear plans and work procedures, (4) the leader's ability to maintain warm relationships between himself and group members, (5) the leader's ability to obtain commitment and cooperation from group members, and (6) the leader's ability to effect change and to build value-infused organizations for the achievement of meaningful purposes. Thus, educational leadership has been defined as *"That action or behavior among individuals or groups which causes both the individual and the groups to move toward educational goals that are increasingly mutually acceptable to them."* [32] A second definition has stated that "leadership is a man's ability to take the initiative in social situations, to plan and organize action, and in so doing evoke cooperation." [33] Similar definitions of leadership are now current in most areas of study that have attempted to probe the nature of leader behavior in organizations.

GENERALIZATIONS ABOUT LEADER BEHAVIOR

Research based on theoretical formulations has contributed basic knowledge that can be of assistance to secondary school administrators who seek a better understanding of their own leadership roles. The fol-

32. John A. Ramseyer, "A Concept of Educational Leadership," *Leadership for Improving Instruction* (Washington, D.C.: Association for Supervision and Curriculum Development, National Education Association, 1960), p. 27.
33. Offices of Strategic Services Assessment Staff, *The Assessment of Men* (New York: Rinehart & Co., 1948), p. 301.

Figure 5-2. A Quadrant Scheme for Describing Leader
Behavior on the Initiating Structure and
Consideration Dimensions

C– S+ (IV)	C+ S+ (I)
C– S– (III)	C+ S– (II)

lowing generalizations about leadership are supported by research results drawn from various fields of study.

1. *Public school leaders exhibit different but characteristic leader behavior styles.* Figure 5-2 shows Halpin's quadrant scheme for describing the behavior of leaders in terms of the *initiating structure* and *consideration* dimension. Four distinct leader behavior styles were identified by Halpin in terms of these two dimensions: reference groups in his study perceived some leaders to be high on both dimensions; others were seen as low on both dimensions. Still others were seen as above average on one dimension but below average on the other.[34]

Leaders in Quadrant I, who were described as being high on both leader behavior dimensions, were perceived by reference groups to be highly effective. Conversely, leaders in Quadrant III were perceived as least effective: their "leadership" ordinarily led to organizational confusion. Leaders in Quadrant IV exhibited a number of the characteristics of the efficiency expert described in a previous section of this chapter. In their emphasis upon tasks and getting the job done, they treated people more like machines than human beings. The leaders in Quadrant II exhibited behavior similar to that of the extremists described under the social engineer image of leadership. Their emphasis upon "democratic" leadership and *consideration* led to ineffectiveness. Lacking *initiating structure,* they did not understand that the primary function of leaders in organizations is to lead. Halpin's study focused on superin-

34. Andrew W. Halpin, *The Leadership Behavior of School Superintendents,* Studies in School Administration, Monograph No. 6 (Chicago: Midwest Administration Center, University of Chicago, reprinted 1959).

tendents; Evenson's study replicated his work with a sample of high school principals, with parallel results.[35]

Similarly, Moser used the Getzels-Guba model to investigate super-intendent-principal relationships and interactions on the basis of three leader behavior styles. The *nomothetic* style emphasized goal accomplishment, rules and regulations, and the precedence of centralized authority over the needs of organizational members. Effective leader behavior was seen as that directed toward the achievement of school objectives. The *idiographic* style emphasized few rules and regulations, placed value on people as individuals, and was characterized by individualistic relationships between superior and subordinate. The *transactional* style made judicious use of both nomothetic and idiographic behavior as the occasion demanded.[36]

2. *Reference groups express conflicting expectations and preferences concerning leader behavior.* Halpin found that school boards preferred leader behavior oriented toward *initiating structure.* School staffs, on the other hand, preferred leaders who were perceived as being high on the *consideration* dimension.[37] A study of leader behavior in the Air Force also showed that superiors viewed *initiating structure* as fundamental to effective leader behavior.[38] Guetzkow also found that authoritarian leader behavior was "rejected by relatively many followers and accepted by relatively many superiors," while nonauthoritarian leader behavior was "accepted by relatively many followers and rejected by relatively many superiors." [39] In reporting a study that was conducted in a school district setting, Moser stated that the principal is subjected to different expectations from his superintendent and from his teachers, and that he behaves in one way with his superiors and in another with his subordinates. Moreover, the study indicated that superintendents preferred principals who were *transactional,* with some emphasis upon nomothetic

35. Warren L. Evenson, "Leader Behavior of High School Principals," *Bulletin of the National Association of Secondary-School Principals,* September, 1959, pp. 96-101.

36. Robert P. Moser, "The Leadership Patterns of School Superintendents and School Principals," *Administrator's Notebook,* Vol. VI, No. 1, September, 1957, pp. 1-4.

37. Halpin, *op. cit.,* p. 78.

38. Andrew W. Halpin, "The Leadership and Combat Performance of Airplane Commanders," *Journal of Abnormal and Social Psychology,* Vol. XLIX, No. 1, January, 1954, pp. 19-22.

39. Harold Guetzkow, *Groups, Leaders, and Men* (New Brunswick, N.J.: Carnegie Press, 1951), p. 171.

behavior.[40] Similarly, in a study of 77 school leaders and 1065 teachers, Seeman found that conflicting expectations of reference groups led to ambivalence among leaders in relation to (*a*) the status dimension, (*b*) the authority dimension, (*c*) the institutional dimension, and (*d*) the means-end dimension.[41]

Conflicting expectations for the behavior of school leaders are also evident among community groups. Hencley has reported wide divergences in such expectations among business groups, parent groups, and labor groups.[42] Similar conflicting expectations for the principal's role have been reported by Buffington [43] and Medsker.[44]

3. *Incongruence in expectations for leader behavior influences satisfaction, effectiveness, confidence in leadership, and attitudes toward the work situation.* In a study of teachers' attitudes and expectations, Moyer found that the more alike members of a teaching group are in terms of their attitudes toward leadership, the more alike they are in amount of satisfaction derived from working in the school situation.[45] Brown and Neitzel have reported a parallel finding: morale tended to suffer if there were disagreements among leaders and their reference groups in defining the leader's role.[46] Campbell, in studying role conflict among teachers, also found that (*a*) teachers whose wants and needs agreed with their principals' expectations expressed more confidence in the leadership of their principals; (*b*) teachers whose desires and needs approached their principals' expectations expressed significantly higher job satisfaction than did teachers whose desires were in conflict with their principals' definitions of their roles as teachers; and (*c*) when principals designated

40. Moser, *op. cit.,* pp. 1-4.

41. Melvin Seeman, "Role Conflict and Ambivalence in Leadership," *American Sociological Review,* Vol. XVIII, No. 4, August, 1953, pp. 373-380.

42. S. P. Hencley, "A Typology of Conflict Between School Superintendents and Their Reference Groups" (Ph.D. dissertation, Department of Education, University of Chicago, 1960).

43. Reed L. Buffington, "The Job of the Elementary School Principal as Viewed by Parents," *Dissertation Abstracts* (Ed.D. dissertation, Stanford University, 1954), Vol. 14, No. 6, pp. 943-944.

44. Leland L. Medsker, "The Job of the Elementary Principal as Viewed by Teachers," *Dissertation Abstracts* (Ed. D. dissertation, Stanford University, 1954), Vol. 16, No. 6, pp. 946-947.

45. Donald C. Moyer, "Teachers' Attitudes Toward Leadership as They Relate to Teacher Satisfaction" (Doctoral dissertation, University of Chicago, 1954).

46. C. G. Brown and Betty J. Neitzel, "Communication, Supervision, and Morale," *Journal of Applied Psychology,* Vol. XXXVI, No. 10, April, 1952, pp. 86-91.

the effectiveness of teachers, the effective teachers were those whose desires and needs were similar to the principals' expectations.[47]

Moser has also added support to these findings. Following his study of principal-superintendent relationships, he concluded that "high mutual ratings of effectiveness and confidence by superintendents and principals were accompanied by similarities in leadership style, feelings of security, general satisfaction with the relationships, desire to consult one another on important matters, and clear delineation of duties and authority for decision making." Conversely, when high mutual ratings were absent, the relationship was characterized by "confusion, lack of security, general dissatisfaction with the relationship, poorly defined duties, and poor delineation of authority for decision making." [48]

4. *Misperceptions and value differences interfere with the effectiveness of leaders in interpersonal relations.* Getzels has suggested that difficulties in interpersonal relationships arise not so much from complexities and differences in values that are in the open and understood as from complexities and differences that are underground and misunderstood.[49] Several studies appear to have corroborated this view. Sletten has reported that attitude and value differences account for many conflicts between school leaders and boards of education.[50] McPhee found that congruence in educational viewpoint between community respondents and schoolteachers was related to the degree of school support manifested by the citizens.[51] In examining the influence of values upon relationships between school leaders and boards of education, Abbott noted that these relationships are influenced not only by differences of viewpoint on basic issues but by accuracy or inaccuracy characterizing individual perceptions of others' positions in relation to these issues.[52]

5. *Leader behavior affects organizational achievement.* Stogdill's "mid-

47. Merton V. Campbell, "Self-Role Conflict Among Teachers and Its Relationship to Satisfaction, Effectiveness, and Confidence in Leadership" (Ph.D. dissertation, University of Chicago, 1958).

48. Moser, *op. cit.,* pp. 1-4.

49. J. W. Getzels, "Changing Values Challenge the Schools," *School Review,* Vol. LXV, No. 1, Spring, 1957, p. 1.

50. Vernon Sletten, "A Related Study of the Opinions of Montana School Board Members and Superintendents on Selected Board Policy Practices" (Doctoral dissertation, University of Oregon, 1954).

51. R. F. McPhee, "Individual Values, Educational Viewpoint, and Local School Approval," *Administrator's Notebook,* Vol. VII, No. 8, April, 1959.

52. Max G. Abbott, "Values and Value-Perceptions in Superintendent-School Board Relationships," *Administrator's Notebook,* Vol. IX, No. 4, December, 1960.

Figure 5-3. Stogdill's Theory of Organizational Achievement

Member Inputs	Mediating Variables		Group Outputs
Behavior	Formal Structure	Role Structure	Achievement
Performance	Function	Responsibility	Productivity
Interactions	Status	Authority	Morale
Expectations	Purpose	Operations	Integration
Group Structure and Operations			Effects

dle range" theory of organizational achievement has supported the view that organized groups are input-output systems that are maintained in unstable balance.[53] The components of his theory, as shown in Figure 5-3, indicate that group outputs are determined not only by member inputs but also by a number of mediating variables normally present in all organizations.[54]

In addition to the generalizations stated above, research studies on leadership in various fields lend support to the following propositions:

1. Although leader behavior evolves from group interaction, it may be entirely independent of the status or position of the person exercising leadership. Status enhances, but does not create, leadership potential. Moreover, most individuals possess some leadership capacity which may be released, under propitious circumstances, during group interaction.

2. Leader behavior is not dependent upon the static qualities or personal variables of individuals. Leaders have been effective and successful in different situations even though they have exhibited markedly dissimilar traits. Moreover, even though an individual exhibits leader behavior in some group situations, there is no guarantee that he will exhibit such behavior in all group situations.

3. Power and leadership are not synonymous. Leaders lead; they do not drive. The authoritarian use of power derived from status cannot be equated with leadership.

53. Ralph M. Stogdill, *Individual Behavior and Group Achievement* (New York: Oxford University Press, 1959).
54. *Ibid.*, p. 13.

4. Leader behavior is characterized by both the ability to initiate productive group action toward acceptable goals and the ability to maintain group cohesion, cooperation, and commitment.

5. Values play an important role in the leadership process. Effective leaders accurately perceive the value orientations of those with whom they interact and seek to modify values that appear inconsistent with organizational objectives.

INSTITUTIONAL LEADERSHIP

Leadership trends during the past fifty years have emphasized means and processes as the primary stock-in-trade of educational leaders. The importance of such trends cannot be denied. Means and processes are essential in educational leadership: leaders must understand decision making, utilize the administrative process, communicate skillfully, deal insightfully with conflict, build morale, and understand the bases of effective and efficient organizations. Such emphases, however, represent an inadequate foundation for institutional leadership. Facility in the use of means and processes marks efficiency experts and interpersonal leaders. Such competence forms only part of the image projected by educational statesmen.

The educational statesman is much more than an organizational manager, efficiency expert, and interpersonal leader. The statesman concerns himself with ends as well as means, with purposes as well as processes. He plays a responsible role in policy development as well as in policy implementation. Indeed, the distinguishing characteristic of educational statesmanship is most clearly evident in the realm of policy and purpose activity: institutional leaders actively seek not only to define and interpret the aims, goals, and roles of organizations but also to build cohesive, value-infused social structures that are impelled toward the achievement of institutional purposes. Institutional leadership thus encompasses and, at the same time, goes beyond means and processes, routine organizational maintenance, efficiency, and skills needed for interpersonal leadership. Most important, the educational leader must have a firm grasp of significant educational goals to be achieved in our time. Only then will research and new social theory be of maximum assistance to him as he chooses among means to attain ends.

There can be little doubt that some secondary school administrators have been kept from serving their field as professional leaders and educational statesmen because they have not understood that *the attainment of complete institutional leadership requires a political orientation. The primary concern of institutional leaders is policy; their profession is politics.* School leaders in a democracy are appointed because of their perceived capacity to make contributions to community and society through intelligent exercise of leadership responsibilities. To effect the transition from administrative management to institutional leadership, however, requires a deep understanding and broad conception of these responsibilities.

Responsibilities of Institutional Leaders

Chapter 4 presented a view of the tasks of secondary school administrators. As was indicated, many functions of administrators are directed toward organizational maintenance rather than institutional leadership. Such functions demand routine rather than critical decision making.

There are, however, numerous areas in which secondary school administrators must exercise institutional leadership. Generally speaking, these areas encompass *change*—in organizational values, goals, purposes, directions, and structures. In Selznick's words, "leadership creates and molds an organization embodying—in thought and feeling and habit —the value premises of policy." [55] The involved change requires not only intelligent leadership but also cooperative decision making and continuous interaction among many individuals and groups in a broadly defined school community. Institutional leadership will be demanded of secondary school administrators in each of the areas discussed below.

Development of Goals and Purposes

Despite their responsibilities in various areas of change, some secondary school administrators have exhibited a curious tendency to accept the myth that they can best serve education's interest by avoiding the public arena of politics. Thus, they have sometimes exhibited parochial and indifferent attitudes toward important political, social, and economic factors that have precipitated significant educational issues in our time.

In the controversy over the adequacy of American schools, in the concern for educational excellence, and in the emphasis on school programs to meet social needs, secondary school administrators have generally

55. Philip Selznick, *Leadership in Administration* (Evanston, Ill.: Row, Peterson & Co., 1957), p. 62.

been tardy in identifying problems and issues facing their profession. As a result, basic goals for education have been formulated and advanced by scientists, lawyers, and admirals. Failure to identify significant educational issues has placed the profession into the uncomfortable defensive position of having to react to outside pressure. Lack of professional initiative and foresight has led, at times, to a loss of public confidence; consequently, professional advice has often been bypassed on significant questions of educational policy and practice.

Despite the existence of outstanding leadership opportunities, secondary school administrators have been inactive in advocating policies or programs for the solution of critical professional problems; as a result they have neglected much of their responsibility for helping to guide educational decisions at the community and national level. Thus, the profession has found itself outside the mainstream of societal forces that initiate and guide social reform.

Secondary school administrators, superintendents, and other professional leaders have a joint responsibility for forging common agreements in relation to educational goals and purposes among citizens, professional teaching staffs, and boards of education. To do otherwise results in opportunistic reliance on the vagaries of public opinion rather than in professional approaches to the solution of public issues concerning education. Failure to assume responsibility for bringing well-considered educational proposals and programs to the attention of community and national decision-making groups is to miss the true function of institutional leadership. Three recommendations that appear particularly appropriate in this connection have been made by Keppel:

1. Educational administration . . . must feel a corporate sense of responsibility as a professional adviser on issues of public policy that affect education and on which education has an effect. Rather than make more difficult the present role conflicts of the school administrator in his local community, such a change will, in my opinion, make his local task easier. He will be seen as a participant in a larger movement, as a man of standing in a larger community. . . .

2. Educational administration, having reached this self-view, must relate itself to other aspects of public administration, and particularly to economic policy, programs of social reform, and foreign affairs. . . .

3. After having taken these two steps, school administration would be ready to become an active participant in the formulation and execution of national policy. Its statements would be heeded in the halls of Congress, in

the executive branch of the government, and in the judiciary. Even the fourth estate might be impressed.[56]

INCREASING TEACHING-LEARNING POTENTIAL. The image of principals as institutional leaders is incomplete without adequate conceptions of the role of leadership in improving teaching-learning potentials in schools. The leadership task in this area encompasses many dimensions:

1. The leader will provide opportunities for continuous clarification and redefinition of educational goals and aims to guide the instructional process toward worthy purposes accepted by both citizens and professional staff members.

2. The leader will strive to create equal educational opportunities for the large number of secondary school pupils with varying abilities who will enter high schools in the wake of the current population "explosion." As leader, the principal will develop with his staff the curricula and learning opportunities that will (*a*) ensure the acquisition of basic skills and knowledge among pupils, and (*b*) place value upon creativity in the use of knowledge and upon the development of critical judgments, fertile hypotheses, and reasoned conclusions. Moreover, the leader will facilitate the development of common values and shared purposes among staff members. He will understand that maximum effectiveness of the school organization will be attained when organizational and individual values reinforce one another, when all staff members reach fundamental agreement concerning the primary role and contribution of high schools in the educative process.

3. The leader will assume responsibility for reaching shared agreement on the potential contribution toward achievement of goals that may be made by each of the following: (*a*) new technological media such as ETV, language laboratories, teaching machines, and "systems" approaches to instruction; (*b*) new curricula and "packaged" courses in various instructional areas; (*c*) new staffing patterns, including team teaching and teacher aides and assistants; (*d*) new pupil deployment patterns, such as large-group teaching, individualized instruction, and seminar groups; and (*e*) new school building designs incorporating the latest innovations in flexibility and adaptability. Creative leadership will demand close scrutiny of many basic assumptions that have guided edu-

56. Francis Keppel, *Public Policy and School Administration* (Cambridge, Mass.: The New England School Development Council, 1961), pp. 21-22.

cational practices in the past. Among these are the notion that all teachers are fundamentally alike and should therefore perform similar instructional roles; the assumption that learning takes place only if classes are small; and the assumption that teachers must take responsibility not only for professional tasks involved in the teaching-learning process but for tasks of a clerical, custodial, and police nature. Intelligent leaders will assume responsibility for testing the validity of these and other "sacred cows" in education.[57]

4. The leader will facilitate the development of instructional effectiveness in the teaching staff. Effective instruction cannot be achieved without effective teachers. The leadership approach to instructional improvement is based on the premise that instruction can best be improved at the school building level with effective guidance from building administrators. Several barriers currently present stimulating challenges to creative leadership in this area. As Foster says: "For a long time we have defended the right of the teacher to work in isolation; we have reacted negatively to merit rating, to supervision (which some of us have scornfully termed 'snoopervision'), and to just about anything that smacks of the critical approach. We must get away from this and be willing to put our work on the line. This is a prerequisite for improvement." [58]

Leadership in instructional improvement becomes evident in (*a*) the nature of questions and hypotheses used to promote instructional improvement; (*b*) the encouragement of creativity, exploration, and experimentation in instruction; (*c*) the opportunities made available for the acquisition of new skills and the use of new resources in the teaching-learning process; and (*d*) the use of valid concepts for evaluating teaching effectiveness.[59] Leadership opportunities will be widely available in this area as principals assume responsibility for developing the in-service education of teachers in new instructional methods, new staff deployment patterns, and the use of new instructional media.

5. The leader will assume responsibilty for helping groups in the school community to comprehend the need for resources and services that facilitate instructional and learning effectiveness. With startling changes occurring in new media, new curricular aids, new buildings, and

57. See Lester W. Nelson, "New Ideas in Education," *Harvard Graduate School of Education Association Bulletin,* September, 1959.
58. Charles R. Foster, "Current Challenges to Educational Leadership," *Phi Delta Kappan,* Vol. XLIII, December, 1961, p. 107.
59. Ramseyer, *op. cit.,* p. 35.

other areas, it will be necessary for secondary school administrators to assure that the nature and meaning of such changes in relation to the teaching-learning process are fully understood and appreciated by citizens and the professional staff. The need for human resources that facilitate change must also be communicated: better teachers in classrooms will be necessary; assistance from expert resource persons to assist teachers in becoming more effective must be provided; and specialized assistance will be needed in structuring fruitful instructional hypotheses that can be tested and implemented in secondary schools.

6. The leader will foster an organizational climate that encourages the full professional development of all staff members. In working toward this goal, the secondary school administrator will (*a*) encourage leadership potentialities among staff members, (*b*) provide avenues for the optimum realization of staff propensities toward experimentation and creativity, (*c*) shield creative staff members from unwarranted criticism, and (*d*) encourage rather than censure staff members who request assistance in remedying professional weaknesses.

7. The leader will not only value new ideas but will also be receptive to research aimed at finding new avenues to improved practice. The testing of questions in the form of hypotheses will be encouraged in the continuous search for improved curricular organization, better methods for deploying staff and students, more efficient teaching methods, effective utilization of new media, and general improvement of teaching-learning opportunities.

In all ways possible, the leader will seek to build a productive organization where goals and purposes are jointly formulated and mutually accepted, where common values prevail, where organizational roles and relationships are cooperatively defined, where communication is facilitated, where destructive conflict is minimized, and where role achievement and role satisfaction are optimized.

REFERENCES

Association for Supervision and Curriculum Development, *Leadership for Improving Instruction, 1960 Yearbook* (Washington, D.C.: the Association, 1960).

Bass, Bernard M., *Leadership, Psychology, and Organizational Behavior* (New York: Harper & Bros., 1960).

Jennings, Eugene E., *An Anatomy of Leadership* (New York: Harper & Bros., 1960).

Leu, Donald, and Rudman, Herbert, *Preparation Programs for School Administrators* (East Lansing, Mich.: College of Education, Michigan State University, 1963).

Likert, Rensis, *New Patterns of Management* (New York: McGraw-Hill Book Co., 1961).

Moore, Hollis A., *Studies in School Administration* (Washington, D.C.: American Association of School Administrators, 1957).

National Society for the Study of Education, *Behavioral Science and Educational Administration, Sixty-third Yearbook, Part II* (Chicago: University of Chicago Press, 1964).

Selznick, Philip, *Leadership in Administration* (Evanston, Ill.: Row, Peterson & Co., 1957).

Stogdill, Ralph M., *Individual Behavior and Group Achievement* (New York: Oxford University Press, 1959).

Tannenbaum, Robert, Wechsler, Irving R., and Massarick, Fred, *Leadership and Organization* (New York: McGraw-Hill Book Co., 1961).

Chapter 6
Government for
Youth Education

TWO fundamental concerns dominate the public interest in secondary education and shape the administrator's role in matters of educational policy. One centers upon the purposes of secondary education and includes consideration of the kinds of education needed for American youth. The other centers upon the form of the institution needed to provide the education required—its structure, functions, controls, and support. The relationship of these two topics makes up a major portion of the presentation of Chapter 2. In this and the succeeding chapter, attention is brought to bear upon the latter topic—the nature of educational government and the organization of the secondary school.

The common schools, of which the secondary schools form a major part, are agencies of government. They are established and operated within a governmental structure especially created for public education, which is, in turn, encompassed within the framework of general government. The structure is cumbersome and complex; the processes are intricate and generally not well understood. The system suffers most of the defects found in our branches of state and local government. Yet even the severest critics recognize its many advantages and almost unlimited potential strength.

The secondary school administrator encounters the operations of government from two directions. From a purely administrative point of view, all activities of the secondary school must be conducted within the bounds of legally authorized policies and practices. The enactments of local, state, and national governments create a framework of legal authority for the organization and operation of the local school. This framework is never complete, however; nor are its existing parts static.

Changing circumstances constantly reveal the need to alter, clarify, or add to the legal framework to permit adaptations within schools. Thus the administrator has the opportunity to participate in evolving the legal framework instead of merely working within a fixed structure. He must accept and work within the limits provided at the same time he studies and calls attention to needed changes in the policies and structures which govern secondary schools.

POLITICAL THEORY AND EDUCATIONAL GOVERNMENT

Political theorists view the various bodies of law in the United States as formal expressions of the values and ideals of the American people. Constitutional provisions, laws, court decisions, and officially enacted rules and regulations create the framework for organizing and operating educational institutions according to the will of the people. Hamilton and Mort have called these legal formulations a "conceptual design" for education.[1] They observe that such legal formulations embody purposes, procedures, and required or prohibited practices in a reasonably consistent system. The degree of consistency remains a matter of debate, but this is not the crucial point. The nature of the legal process not only gives liberal opportunity for the citizen to concern himself with education but also guarantees his right to participate in its development. Because of this fact the role of the professional in the development of education is a delicate one, and knowledge of educational government becomes important to educational improvement.

There is no mysticism in the American concept of the state. Certain fundamental principles apply universally and have particular meaning to the manner in which education is provided. These principles may be briefly summarized as follows:

1. The origin of all authority of government rests upon popular consent.

2. Actions of public officials must conform to the enactments of officially constituted public bodies and are subject to review.

3. Certain fundamental freedoms protect the individual from the state. These freedoms are beyond the authority of either public officials or political majorities.

4. Education is a public function and is to be provided equally to all at public expense.

1. Robert Hamilton and Paul Mort, *The Law and Public Education* (Brooklyn, N.Y.: The Foundation Press, 1941), Chapter I.

5. Plenary power over education rests with each state legislature subject only to the restraints of the federal Constitution and the respective state constitution.

6. Public tax funds are to be used for the support of public education and for no form of nonpublic education.

These few basic principles underlie the development of public education in this country. They reveal significant aspects of what might be termed the political theory of democratic government as practiced in the United States. They are found most explicitly perhaps in federal and state constitutional provisions and in judicial proceedings.

Constitutional Provisions

Constitutional provisions describe general structures of government, areas and extent of governmental authority, relationship of the citizen to the state, and relationships of the various parts of the government. As the fundamental law, the federal Constitution contains provisions having implications for education which may not be transcended by Congress, by state constitutions, or by state legislatures. Within the framework of the Constitution each state constitution contains provisions applicable to that particular state.

THE FEDERAL CONSTITUTION. Although education is not mentioned in the federal Constitution, Sections 8 and 10 of Article I and the First, Tenth, and Fourteenth Amendments hold particular significance for the conduct of education. The nature of these provisions and their implications are given here in brief form.

Sections 8 and 10 of Article I are the "general welfare" and "obligation to contracts" clauses, respectively. Section 8 provides the authority for practically all efforts of the federal government to foster and support education. Section 10, although invoked in other areas, has been the basis of legitimizing private education.

The Tenth Amendment reserves to the respective states all powers not specifically enumerated in the Constitution. This provision is responsible for the establishment of education as a function of the individual states. It created a principle basic to the organization of public education in the United States without mentioning the word "education." [2]

2. For an elaboration of this point, see Lindley J. Stiles, Lloyd E. McCleary, and Roy Turnbaugh, *Secondary Education in the United States* (New York: Harcourt, Brace & World, 1962), pp. 34-35.

The First and Fourteenth Amendments are usually companion clauses invoked in most of the federal litigation directly concerned with public education, primarily cases arising in secondary schools. The "fundamental freedoms" and "due process" clauses protect the citizen against the state and all of its agencies. As stated in a famous opinion written by Justice Jackson:

They [boards of education and school officials] have, of course, important, delicate, and highly discretionary functions, but none that they may not perform within the limits of the Bill of Rights. That they are educating the young for citizenship is reason for scrupulous protection of constitutional freedoms of the individual, if we are not to strangle the free mind at its source and teach youth to discount important principles of our government as mere platitudes. . . .[3]

All cases reaching the Supreme Court of the United States concerning religious practices, racial discrimination, and the rights of parents and students have been judged upon either the First or Fourteenth Amendments or both taken together.

STATE CONSTITUTIONAL PROVISIONS. Every state admitted to the Union under the Constitution has been required by the Congress to include in its state constitution a clause pertaining to the establishment of public education. At this writing all states have constitutional provisions in some form charging the legislatures to erect and maintain uniform and efficient systems of public education. The extent to which this clause will be modified in the fourteen states maintaining segregated schools is as yet unclear.

Only one county (Prince Edward County, Virginia) of the fourteen southern states has attempted to abandon its public schools completely. In the fall of 1961, a United States District Court ordered county officials to reopen the schools. The opinion of Judge Lewis reads: "[county schools] may not be closed to avoid the effect of the law of the land . . . while the Commonwealth of Virginia permits other public schools to remain open at the expense of the taxpayers." Although a system of scholarships at public expense is operating in Prince Edward County to permit white children to attend segregated "private schools" at public expense, litigation is still in process to carry out the intent of the desegregation court order. The final effects of the 1954 segregation order of

3. *Minorsville School District* v. *Gobitis,* 310 U.S. 586 (1940). The reader is encouraged to consult the full text of this important decision.

the United States Supreme Court will not be determined for many years to come, but it is doubtful that the states will abandon this important responsibility.

Many states have gone further than the general provision indicated above. Notably, these provisions pertain to financing education: (1) They establish a permanent school fund. (2) They earmark certain taxes partially or wholly for the support of education. (3) They set limits upon the rate of taxation to be levied for education. (4) They limit use of educational funds strictly to the support of public education.

It may be seen from item 3, above, that constitutional provisions may be limiting in nature as well as conducive to adequate education. In states where definite tax limits are set, it is illegal for citizens to support education at a rate higher than the fixed limit, even if every citizen of a given district wishes to do so.

From the general clause, noted in the opening paragraph of this section, state constitutions unanimously reserved plenary power—full and final legislative authority—in matters of education to the state legislatures.[4] This power places the ultimate legal control of education in the hands of the state—contrary to a widely held belief that such power is in the local school district. A fundamental principle of our political theory, sometimes not well understood, underlies this arrangement.

The conception of the meaning and powers of the state under which the federal Constitution was drawn holds each state to be sovereign unto itself. The Tenth Amendment is unequivocal on this point. The state may use all means, except where it is restrained by provisions of the federal Constitution, to assure its own preservation. Education is the most powerful means the state may use to guarantee its future. The education provided by the state, therefore, is considered to be primarily for the benefit of the state and secondarily for the benefit of the individual. In terms of political theory, education is neither a charitable nor a philanthropic venture.

Judicial Decisions

Courts at times are influential in directing the course of public education. Several important court decisions are noted in previous sections of this chapter. Certain features of judicial practice should be pointed out

4. This power is restricted only by constitutional provisions as interpreted by the courts.

at the outset. First, courts do not rule on the legality of a certain practice on their own initiative. Judicial decisions result only when the legality of a given practice is contested and presented to a proper court following prescribed procedures. Further, all cases are judged upon specified principles of law stemming from explicit constitutional provisions, statutes, or established legal precedents. Courts are to judge the legality and "reasonableness" of a law, not its wisdom. Finally, judicial decisions have the effect of law; many have established legal precedent with far more powerful effect than most laws.

Federal courts, particularly the Supreme Court of the United States, deal with very few cases involving public education—and these never pertain to education per se since education is not a matter subject to federal jurisdiction. However, the few cases decided by the Supreme Court—28 during the period 1925 to 1963—have considerable importance for public education. These decisions include: clarifying the rights of nonpublic schools, denying use of school facilities and school authority to provide religious instruction, a 1962 ruling to outlaw public prayer as a prescribed school practice, confirming the freedom of pupils from compulsory participation in formal patriotic ceremonies (in this case the flag salute), and the now famous 1954 decision that schools segregated by race are inherently unequal and unlawful. Each of these decisions has basically altered some specific practice or course of action and touched off new state legislation.

Often public reaction to these decisions has been emotional and intemperate—for example, the press and radio reactions to the "antiprayer decision" of 1962. Too frequently the public has not been properly informed of the reasoning behind these rulings and of the protection of fundamental freedoms they accord. A quotation from the majority opinion which declared unconstitutional the compulsory flag salute illustrates this point:

The case is made difficult not because the principles of its decision are obscure but because the flag involved is our own. Nevertheless, we apply the limitations of the Constitution with no fear that freedom to be intellectually and spiritually diverse or even contrary will disintegrate the social organization. To believe that patriotism will not flourish if patriotic ceremonies are voluntary and spontaneous instead of compulsory routine is to make an unflattering estimate of the appeal of our institutions to free minds ... freedom to differ is not limited to things that do not matter much. . . . the test of its substance is the right to differ as to things that touch the heart of the existing order.

If there is any fixed star in our constitutional constellation, it is that no official, high or petty, can prescribe what shall be orthodox in politics, nationalism, religion, or other matters of opinion. . . . If there are any circumstances which permit an exception, they do not now occur to us.

We think the action of the local authorities in compelling the flag salute and pledge transcribe constitutional limitations and invade the sphere of intellect and spirit which it is the purpose of the First Amendment of our Constitution to reserve from all official control.[5]

From this brief portion of the Supreme Court opinion the reader can gain some insight into the care with which the issue was examined and the crucial point identified upon which the case was decided. Although the Supreme Court has always been reluctant to accept cases involving education, the influence of all federal courts in matters of education is likely to be increased greatly by present civil rights, religious, and patriotic concerns involving education now being pressed at the national level.

Actions of state courts in cases involving education are both voluminous and varied. These courts deal directly with all matters of education properly brought before them. Authorities in the field of school law have failed to distinguish an area of educational activity which has not produced litigation in state courts.[6] Attention has been given to matters ranging from the right to teach the "cosmic cloud" theory of the origin of the earth in secondary school classrooms to the point beyond the front door of the home at which the conduct of the pupils becomes the responsibility of the school.

State constitutional provisions and laws cannot be written to include the details necessary to cover every contingency of their application, to make perfectly clear the intent of their writers, or to account for future conditions under which the law must be applied. Experience has demonstrated the wisdom of writing laws which establish major policies and directives, define limits to the authority of officials, and omit details which might require frequent changes or limit flexibility of execution. Yet, whether laws are written in detail or as general policies, their intent,

5. *Minorsville School District* v. *Gobitis, op. cit.*
6. The reader may wish to consult the works of Newton Edwards, Paul Mort, Madaline K. Remmlein, and Robert Hamilton, among others.

reasonableness, or proper interpretation seems almost certain to be questioned at some point. Any party involved in this kind of disagreement has access to the courts.

STRUCTURE OF EDUCATIONAL GOVERNMENT

Educational policies are made and implemented in the governmental process. The quality of decisions and the effectiveness of their execution depend not only upon the knowledge of problems and the wisdom to create solutions but upon the governmental machinery used. Needs of secondary education often seem to be thwarted by deficiencies in the structure and operation of government.

Structure in government implies defined purposes; specified authority; orderly arrangement of tasks and responsibilities; and procedures for policy making, execution, and review. The structure of educational government is built in accord with the basic principles of the nation's political theory as expressed in the federal Constitution and the constitutions of the fifty states, and as interpreted by the courts. It is explicitly described by laws, administrative rules and regulations, and established practices. These taken together form the legal framework for secondary education referred to in the opening section of this chapter.

Educational government is structured on the basis of function and authority into four distinct levels—federal, state, intermediate, and local. Each of these entities is considered in the remainder of this section.

Federal Level of Educational Government

Federal participation in public education is extensive. In 1958-1959, the last year for which official figures are available, a total of $2,412,-136,000 was expended. Of this amount, more than $964,500,000 was spent directly upon elementary and secondary school programs and projects. The specific programs, their legal basis, and the governmental structures through which all educational activities of the federal government are administered cannot be given here in detail. These activities are scattered through nine departments and five separate agencies, listed in Table 6-1.

Federal laws establishing programs of education are based upon Article I, Section 8, of the Constitution—the general welfare clause. Albert Munse and E. P. McLoone of the U.S. Office of Education have

Table 6-1. Federal Assistance for Educational Programs,
1958-1959

Agency	Amount (in 1,000 of $)
Department of Health, Education, and Welfare	$737,864
Department of Agriculture	383,556
Department of Commerce	3,493
Department of Defense	300,877
Department of the Interior	113,577
Department of Justice	1,416
Department of Labor	10,941
Department of State	57,811
Department of the Treasury	5,212
Veterans Administration	602,036
Atomic Energy Commission	51,047
Canal Zone	5,019
District of Columbia	7,742
National Science Foundation	122,820
Others	8,725
Total	$2,412,136

SOURCE: Adapted from Clayton D. Hutchins, A. R. Munse, Edna D.
Booker, Federal Funds for Education, 1956-1957 and
1957-1958, Bulletin 1961, No. 14 (Washington D.C.: U.S.
Government Printing Office, 1961), pp. 14-17.

summarized the purposes for which federal funds are used in the support
of education:

1. To encourage and support programs of education or services in the
   schools that are essential or beneficial to the national welfare and
   security.
2. To contribute to or provide for education where there is a federal
   responsibility or obligation.
3. To provide educational and training services essential to the national
   defense but which are not separate responsibilities of any local, community, state, or segment of the population.
4. To assist students, selected on the basis of tests and recommendations,
   to receive scholarships for advanced training that will serve the national
   welfare.
5. To assist the economically developing areas of the world and to improve international relationships through the exchange of information,
   students, teachers, professors, technicians, and leaders with other
   countries.
6. To maintain efficient governmental services and increase the effectiveness of the federal service through programs of education.

7. To promote the general welfare of the nation through research in the physical, biological, and social sciences that will develop new areas of learning and prepare more specialists with competencies in these fields.[7]

From the list of purposes and the data in Table 6-1, the wide range of federal interest and involvement in public education is readily apparent. In the light of current debate over the matter of general aid to public schools, it is worth noting that the principle of federal support has been amply tested in the courts and that no grounds seem to exist to challenge its legality.

CHANNELS OF FEDERAL AID TO LOCAL SCHOOLS. In all cases of support to local schools, federal laws have respected the established structures of operation within the states. In general, each state prepares a plan, outlining its proposed use of funds, the state's contribution, and the means of administration and control. If the plan is approved by the responsible federal agency, the funds are released to the state. In most cases, federal agencies retain the right to audit accounts involving federal funds.

Two recent federal activities involving secondary schools may serve to illustrate the structures employed. The National Defense Education Act of 1958, under which more than one billion dollars has been expended on fourteen programs, provides in one program for local schools to purchase needed science equipment with federal funds. Each state participating in the program designates the state agency, usually the state office of public instruction, to establish procedures, criteria, and other regulations. This agency receives, reviews, and processes applications for purchases of equipment from local schools, and it receives and disburses federal funds to those schools it approves.

On July 1, 1962, the Federal Vocational Training Program was begun. Under this program 435 million dollars were appropriated to train about one-half million technologically unemployed. Out-of-school, unemployed youths of sixteen to nineteen years of age are being trained under a special provision of this act. Public high schools and other existing facilities are being used. The U.S. Department of Health, Education, and Welfare administers the program for teen-age youth. Planning committees in local communities, working through the state offices of vocational

7. Albert R. Munse and E. P. McLoone, *Public School Finance Programs of the United States, 1957-1958,* Misc. Bulletin No. 33 (Washington, D.C.: U.S. Government Printing Office, 1960), p. 22.

education or employment security, prepare and complete arrangements for local training programs. Although candidates for training are screened by the U.S. Employment Service, financial and administrative procedures conform to traditional federal-state relationships.

UNITED STATES OFFICE OF EDUCATION (USOE). Of the numerous federal agencies that have responsibilities for education, the United States Office of Education is the only federal agency whose complete concern is with education. According to its own report, its interests encompass "all aspects of the country's educational system with its many areas of subject matter, levels of instruction, and types of schools." [8] The general functions of the USOE have remained unaltered for the almost one hundred years of its existence. They include: (1) developing cooperative relationships with agencies interested in the promotion of education; (2) providing leadership and consultative and informational services in dealing with problems and conditions of education; (3) engaging in and stimulating study and research in all phases of education; (4) publishing research findings, studies, and reports; and (5) acting as the official agency in programs of education involving the United Nations and foreign nations. Under this last function the USOE has become a principal source of information for cultural, economic, and scientific cooperation with foreign nations, and it directly administers student exchanges and technical assistance programs. From time to time, additional specific tasks have been assigned to the USOE by an act of Congress or by executive order.

A division of the United States Department of Health, Education and Welfare, the USOE has representation in the Cabinet through the Secretary of that department. Headed by a Commissioner who is appointed by the President with the approval of the Senate, it is organized (see Figure 6-1) into the Office of the Commissioner, four planning "branches" attached directly to the Office of the Commissioner, and three operational bureaus. A deputy commissioner shares administrative and policy development functions with the commissioner, and an assistant commissioner has been assigned responsibility for special projects. Each unit's assigned function is indicated by its title in Figure 6-1.

8. U.S. Office of Education, *Progress of Public Education in the United States of America,* Summary Report, OE-10005 (Washington, D.C.: U.S. Government Printing Office, 1960), p. 4.

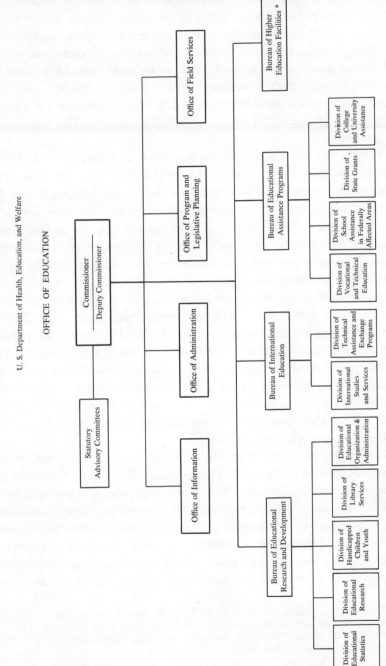

Figure 6-1: Organization of the United States Office of Education, 1964

U. S. Department of Health, Education, and Welfare

OFFICE OF EDUCATION

* To Take Effect Upon Enactment of the Fiscal Year 1965 Appropriation Act

The USOE has no direct organizational or administrative relationship with any local public school. Many of its services, however, can be of considerable value to the local school. These include regular conferences, programs, reports, and publications as well as limited, direct consulting and library services, visual aids, and information relating to specific questions handled through correspondence. Research bulletins, the Annual Report, and the periodical *School Life* may be obtained for a small charge and can provide a source of information of USOE services to the local school.

FEDERAL ROLE IN EDUCATION CONTROVERSIAL. Concern for and participation in public education at the federal level are very real. The contributions, particularly to secondary and higher education, can be predicted with confidence to rise significantly within the next few decades. The particular form these contributions will take, the governmental structures that will be employed, and the alterations of relationships between federal, state, and local levels that will result are, at this point, matters for speculation only.

International relationships, economic factors, population (mobility, concentration, and age distribution), technological and scientific demands, unemployment, delinquency, and school dropouts all present problems to which education holds the key to satisfactory solutions. The conditions out of which these problems arise are national in scope. This logic produces a powerful argument for the reconstruction of educational government at the national level to provide a more comprehensive, better-coordinated, and more sharply directed assault upon educational problems than is presently possible.

Some argue that such steps can be taken through traditional procedures and point to the National Defense Education Act of 1958 and the Vocational Training Act of 1962. Some argue for a separate cabinet post for education, the development of a national planning commission, and substantial federal financial support.[9] Decisions concerning the role of the federal government in public education are political in nature. A wide range of interests and issues, many noneducational, immediately appear when educational programs are presented to Congress. These

9. See Paul R. Hanna, "Proposed—A National Planning Commission for Curriculum Research and Development," *Phi Delta Kappan,* May, 1961, pp. 331-338; and Harold W. Stoke, "National Necessity and Educational Policy," *Phi Delta Kappan,* April, 1959, pp. 266-269.

include concern about federal control, states' rights, support for parochial schools, racial segregation, and general opposition to increased federal expenditures in any field. Thus, any major proposals for change at the national level will probably produce controversy far beyond debate over the educational issues involved.

State Level of Educational Government

Control of the organization and administration of public education and the general supervision of nonpublic education reside with the governments of the fifty states. The political theory underlying this condition, as set down in constitutional form, has been outlined in previous sections of this chapter. Within this political framework, two widely held doctrines have strongly influenced state structures of educational government. First, education is best served when control over it is kept, insofar as possible, from partisan political influence. Second, control over policy decisions in educational matters is to be retained in the hands of the citizenry.

Whatever other considerations are taken into account by state legislatures in designing a structure for public education, the two doctrines noted above are the most persistently and widely held. There seems to be no other means to rationalize certain unique features of governmental structure for education as created by most states. These features, representing important contributions to governmental structure, include:

1. Treatment of public education as a separate governmental function with its own set of laws and derived rules and regulations.
2. Use of boards of education for establishing educational policy at the state, intermediate, and local levels.
3. A chief state school officer who is not directly subordinate to the governor or to any other single state political officer.
4. A decentralized organization for public education with local districts as independent or semi-independent units of government.[10]

The features of educational government, noted above, and the two doctrines of political philosophy which gave rise to them seem to be

10. In twenty-nine states all local school districts are independent units of government. In five states there are no independent districts; here, schools are administered within the structure of general government—either local, county, or, in the case of Hawaii, state. In sixteen states a mixed situation exists, with some independent and some dependent districts.

more widely supported within the corps of public educators than outside of it. Increasing demand for uniform national policies for public education is indicated in a previous passage. Effort to minimize, if not terminate, "local control" of public education is much discussed. At the same time, some observers—even political scientists who are partisans of public education—question the separation of educational government from general government. Concerning this latter point, Phillip Monypenny, a noted political scientist, objects to "a compartmentalized system which tends to separate general political leadership from leadership on educational issues." He foresees a major problem of support developing because of this condition, and he justifies his position with the observation "that their [public schools'] isolation from general political issues may make it difficult for them to get support for the enormous demands on income and manpower which they will be making in the future." [11]

The major structures of educational government at the state level are state boards of education, the office of the chief state school officer, and state departments of education. The present status of these units is given below. In the light of current educational needs and issues, they are likely to become increasingly important centers of attention and controversy.

STATE BOARDS OF EDUCATION. Some type of state board of education exists in all states. Forty-six of the fifty states have boards that exercise general policy-making functions for public education at the elementary and secondary levels. In the remaining four states—Illinois, Michigan, North Dakota, and Wisconsin—boards exist only to fulfill the requirements of the federal program for vocational education.

There is considerable variation from state to state in size of state boards; methods of selection of members; terms of office; board relationships with the legislature, governor, and chief state school officer; and in assigned responsibilities. Current status and trends relating to these characteristics are indicated in Figure 6-2. In 1927, Ellwood Cubberley presented a list of recommendations for the establishment of state boards of education. His recommendations reveal prophetic insight, for they represent in every detail the practice now accepted as best. Cub-

11. Phillip Monypenny, "A Political Analysis of Structures for Educational Policy Making," in William P. McLure and Van Miller (eds.), *Government of Public Education for Adequate Policy Making* (Urbana, Ill.: Bureau of Educational Research, University of Illinois, 1960), p. 20.

Figure 6-2. Current Status and Trends Relating to
Characteristics of State Boards of Education

Characteristic	Current Status	Trend
Number*	46 states have boards	Boards added by 6 states since 1945
Method of selection	34 states—appointment by governor 10 states—popular election 1 state—convention 1 state—election by legislature	Movement to select boards by popular election Special qualifications rarely prescribed by law
Term of office	3 to 13 years	Current opinion in favor of the practice of 6-to-9-year terms
Relationship to elected officials	16 states provide ex officio membership in addition to the chief school officer	States moving to eliminate ex officio membership, particularly governors; in 22 states, the chief school officer a board member
Authority		Movement toward specifically defined responsibilities and limitations of authority

*Boards that have responsibilities for elementary and secondary education and whose powers are not restricted to one specific area such as vocational education.

berley's list of recommendations is presented here as a conclusion to this section, indicating that a state board should:

1. Be a lay board representing the people.
2. Be neither too small nor too large, with seven as the optimum size.
3. Be appointed or elected for relatively long and overlapping terms.
4. Be appointed by a governor who does not have opportunity to change the entire character of the board during one term.
5. Be appointed solely on the basis of ability to serve the people without reference to race, creed, occupation, party and residence.
6. Be elected by the people if this is preferred to appointment.
7. Be removed only by action of the governor and then only for such causes as immorality, malfeasance, and gross incompetence.

8. Be without *ex officio* members, even the governor.
9. Be organized so that the state superintendent is not a member of the board.
10. Be paid an honorarium instead of a per diem allotment (or salary).
11. Be such as to consider as its most important function the appointment of a state superintendent.
12. Be organized in such a way that the subordinate officials of the state department are selected only on the recommendations of the superintendent.
13. Be empowered to make its own rules and regulations.
14. Be organized so that there is a clear distinction between the legislative and executive function.[12]

CHIEF STATE SCHOOL OFFICER. A position of chief school officer is provided by each of the fifty states and carries the title of "commissioner of education" or "superintendent of public instruction." The chief state school officer fills the major administrative post for public education at the state level. Since education is an essential state function and is treated as a distinct form of government and since the office was pioneered by such distinguished men as Horace Mann and Henry Barnard, it should be both a strategic and a venerated position. Yet, in all fairness, it must be pointed out that this position has not fulfilled the leadership function for education that might be reasonably expected from it.

The causes are not difficult to find, nor are they easily remedied. First, the office is elective in twenty-four of the fifty states. In these states few, if any, professional requirements are necessary for qualifications to candidacy. In five of the remaining twenty-six states, appointment is in the hands of the governor. Second, the decentralized structure for public education and the strong orientation to "local control" have moved legislatures to place little leadership responsibility and few resources in the office. Third, as with the United States Commissioner of Education, the traditional concept of leadership by this office has been exercised through the maintenance of informational services, collection of statistics, performance of clerical functions, and service as nominal spokesman to the public. This combination of structural conditions has tended to restrict the number of professionally competent men to fill the office. With tenure subject to popular election, little authority to direct change, and low salary—the average salary of a state superintendent

12. Ellwood P. Cubberley, *State School Administration* (Boston: Houghton Mifflin Co., 1927), pp. 290-294.

has been about half that of a superintendent in a medium-sized city—
the lack of aggressive, consistent leadership is not surprising. Despite
this unpromising picture, a movement is under way to strengthen the
position of the chief state school officer and his department.

Since 1945, changes paralleling those concerning state boards of education (see Figure 6-2) have been undertaken to strengthen the position
of chief state school officer. With the increase in state boards, the chief
state school officer is becoming an appointed official, responsive to the
board and usually appointed by it. This is the case in twenty-one of the
twenty-six states that now have general, policy-making boards of education. These boards have tended to select more competent professional
executives than those under an elective system. Legislatures have responded by providing the means to undertake developmental projects,
research studies, and services and to enlarge supervisory and consultant
help to local schools. It is symptomatic of the improved stature of chief
state school officers that the average salary for this office has almost
doubled during the past ten-year period.

STATE DEPARTMENTS OF EDUCATION. A state department of education exists in each state as the executive branch of educational government at the state level. The state board of education, or the legislature
in a state that does not have a board, determines educational policies.
The chief state school officer through the state department of education
executes these policies. Into the present decade, policy development for
education at the state level has been largely restricted to the establishment of minimum standards and the encouragement of local initiative.
Under these conditions, the functions of state departments have been
primarily inspectorial and exhortative. Their structures have reflected
this state of affairs.

In 1960, the number of personnel in a state department of education
averaged about 400. Although more than double the 1950 figure, this
number was responsible for the administration of a state system averag-
ing more than 700 local school districts. Typically, the state departments
were occupied with accrediting schools; certifying teachers; handling
disbursement and accounting of state funds for public education; collecting statistics; preparing educational materials; approving texts, films, and
instructional materials; providing services to the legislatures and state
boards; reviewing requests for deviations from state requirements; administering special federal and state programs such as vocational edu-

cation; inspecting school buildings; and rendering consultant services —to name only some of the major duties.

As late as 1961, Henry Brickell conducted a study of the State Education Department of the State of New York. Although one of the best-supported and best-staffed departments in the nation, it was described by Brickell as: "too *small* for the job it is attempting. In its efforts to supervise or to help almost 900 public school systems through direct contact, the Department is spreading its resources far too thin. It assumes that it is performing functions which it cannot perform; it promises aid which it cannot give." [13] The major question to be answered during the 1960's is whether state departments can be restructured to lead educational improvement. There are encouraging signs.

State departments of education are powerful agencies. Even the most "locally oriented" school systems look for encouragement and direction to the state office. Few local districts, even those wealthy enough to be financially independent of the state department, will initiate or fail to initiate programs and practices contrary to state department policy. Thus the "stimulus effect" of state departments is itself a significant factor. State departments are now apparently eager to encourage innovation and change.

State departments are taking initiative in new educational developments. In Maryland, New York, Illinois, and California, to name concrete examples, major projects are under way in educational television and in programs for the gifted and the handicapped, for team teaching, and for improved science and mathematics instruction. Financed and administered through state departments of education, these projects link research, field testing, and aid to local schools as a means of rapid effective improvement of education.

State departments are reorganizing to assume leadership responsibilities. Symptomatic of this trend is the Brickell study noted above. Though the report was highly critical of the leadership function of the New York State Department of Education, it was energetically supported by Commissioner James Allen and his staff. There is every indication that this study and others like it will become a basis for continuous effort of state departments to improve their leadership capability.

Resources are being made available to permit increased state activity.

13. Henry M. Brickell, *Organizing New York State for Educational Change* (Albany, N.Y.: State Education Department, 1961), p. 43.

State appropriations for public education in 1960 reached the 7 billion dollar level. Such an enormous expenditure of state funds has brought with it a concomitant demand that education be improved. Leadership both for the reorganization of public schools into efficient districts and for improved quality of instruction is being placed in the state departments.

State departments occupy a position of great potential strength. Developments now under way provide conditions for fundamental changes in the structure and role of these agencies in matters of public education. The extent to which state departments restructure themselves to participate actively in the improvement of local educational programs will largely determine their future effectiveness.

Intermediate Units of Educational Government

The term "intermediate district" came into general use after World War II to designate an element of educational government interposed between state and local units. In twenty-seven states, the county is the basis of a type of intermediate district—five states having county boards of education, all twenty-seven having county superintendents of schools. In thirteen southern states, the county system is employed with the exception that it is not an intermediate district. Here, the local school district is organized on a countywide basis, the county superintendent being the local school officer. Four states—Alaska, Delaware, Hawaii, and Nevada—provide no intermediate educational unit. To further complicate description, the New England states plus New York have supervisory unions or districts. In these states, the county is not a strong unit of government, and the supervisory district is not coterminous with county boundaries. These intermediate units might best be described as confederations of local districts.

Structurally, the intermediate district encompasses a small group of local districts. Dawson and Reeves define it as "an area comprising two or more basic administrative units and having a board, or officer, or both responsible for performing stipulated services for the basic administrative units or for supervising their administrative or educational functions." [14] In most states, the intermediate district is primarily an administrative

14. Howard Dawson and Floyd Reeves, *Your School District* (Washington, D.C.: Department of Rural Education, National Education Association, 1958), p. 52.

rather than a policy-making agency. Authorities generally believe that this unit has become archaic as an element of educational government and that both its structure and function require reappraisal.

Because of the strong local character of school organization, the intermediate district typically is left with few resources to promote education and little authority to influence the direction of its development. It has no direct control over personnel, program development, services, or financial support in local schools, except through enforcement of minimum standards prescribed by the state or delegated to it by consent of its local districts. The result is that intermediate district officers spend considerable time with "laggard" local districts and little time leading educational advancement.

The major question in considering the adequacy, or even the necessity, of the intermediate district hinges upon the purposes to be assigned to it. If the intermediate district is to be a subdivision or regional office of the state department, one kind of structure is needed. Should this become clearly established as the central need, present units are much too small geographically and are not appropriately staffed. In such a case, the intermediate unit would become merely an administrative arm of the state department and would not function as a distinct level of educational government. If the intermediate district is to provide educational services that a single district cannot better provide on its own, a different kind of structure is needed.

Size of the "service-type" intermediate district should be based upon pupil population rather than upon predetermined political boundaries such as those of a county. An area containing a school age population of 10,000 or more has a pupil population with sufficient needs for special services and requires a teaching staff large enough to support a strong central office. If the geographic area necessary to include an enrollment of about 10,000 pupils is compact enough to be administered by a single local district, there is no need for intermediate district organization. However, so long as the organization of public schools remains "community-centered" and vast areas of the nation are sparsely settled, the intermediate district is a necessity.

A strong case for the service-type intermediate district can be made when local districts cannot justify adequate provision for at least the following:

1. Special teachers, as, for example, in art, music, and homemaking, as well as in academic areas.
2. Consultant services and facilities, such as those provided for reading, speech, and science.
3. Facilities for technical-vocational preparation.
4. Library and audiovisual services, including a professional library.
5. Special instructors for the gifted and the handicapped.
6. Health services of a nurse and oral hygienist.
7. Pupil personnel services, including guidance and counseling, testing, and psychological and psychiatric treatment.
8. Supervision, in-service training, and curriculum leadership for teachers.
9. Record keeping, analysis, and reporting in the areas of pupil personnel, teacher personnel, and business management.

Within each state, consultant services are usually available from state departments or from universities to conduct studies of local needs in these areas. Surveys can aid in determining the kinds and amounts of services required and the possibilities of local districts to provide them. Where local resources are inadequate, local districts should be reorganized or an intermediate district structure studied.

Local School Districts

The local school district is the basic structural unit in educational government. It is both a political subdivision of the state and an administrative unit of education. The legal status of the school district is that of a quasi-municipal corporation especially chartered by the state to provide education within a defined geographic area. The term "quasi-municipal corporation" means simply that the school district operates "as if" it were a municipality such as a town or city, except that its activity is limited to the educational function.

In almost all local school districts, authority for the operation of the district is placed in the hands of a locally elected lay board of education. In certain large cities, such as Chicago, the board is appointed by the mayor with the consent of the city council; in a few rural districts, authority is vested in a single elected trustee. School boards in all states function as agents of the state legislature. Whatever actions they may wish to take must be expressly granted or clearly implied by state law as necessary to the effective conduct of the district's affairs.

Although the municipality and the school district often have coterminous boundaries, each is a separate corporate structure with its own function or functions to perform. In all but sixteen states, local school districts are completely independent of any municipal control. In eleven of these sixteen states, some local districts are independent, and some are dependent for specific decisions upon state departments or local municipal governments. The most frequent form of control exercised over dependent school districts is the approval of district budgets and tax rates by municipal councils.

ADEQUACY OF LOCAL DISTRICTS. The relationship of structure to educational program may be brought into sharp focus by consideration of the status of local districts. Standards of adequacy may be attained from two approaches: first, by describing features or characteristics of program which may be *assumed* to enhance educational opportunity; second, by measurements of achievement of students educated under specified conditions. Both of these approaches have been attempted with reference to the factor of enrollment size in local school districts.

From a number of previous studies, the National Commission on School District Reorganization of the National Education Association concluded that a district should have an enrollment of at least 10,000 to 12,000 pupils in grades K–12. This enrollment base contains the number of pupils needed to form special classes, provide services, and justify the necessary specialized staff and supervisory personnel of a comprehensive program.[15] Many authorities, including the National Commission, recommend local districts of approximately 6000 enrollment when "service-type" intermediate districts are employed, and under absolute minimum conditions a district of 1500 enrollment. James Conant, after completing a study of the comprehensive high school in 1959, recommended a size that would guarantee a minimum graduating class of 100. His recommendation also supports the absolute minimum size of a school district as 1500 pupils.

Obviously, recommended sizes of districts as given here are arbitrary figures based upon the best judgment of authorities. This represents the first approach to relating size of district to adequacy of educational program. In this case, authorities specify the characteristics and program features they judge to be essential and then find the sizes of districts in

15. National Commission on School District Reorganization, *Your School District* (Washington, D.C.: the Commission, National Education Association, 1948).

which their definition of "adequate programs" actually exist. There remains the question of whether districts, if reorganized to attain recommended size, tend to add program features judged necessary to adequate education. C. O. Fitzwater, as early as 1953, conducted a survey of 522 reorganized districts. He found that important additions to programs were made by reorganized districts and that the larger districts showed the greater number of changes. Later studies bear out these findings, although no studies found by the authors equated changes to the range of enrollment noted above.

The second approach, that of measuring the achievement of pupils in various-sized school districts, again supports the case for the larger district. Representative of a large body of studies is the one conducted by Leonard Felt that included nearly 80 percent of the pupils in Iowa high schools in 1959.[16] Felt found a direct relationship between school size and pupil achievement. The difference in mean achievement of students in the largest and smallest high schools exceeded one full year of schooling in favor of the large high school as measured by the *Iowa Test of Educational Development*. Since in this study a small school was defined as one with an enrollment below 100 students and a large school as one with more than 200 students, it seems reasonable to assume even greater differences in achievement to the advantage of large schools as defined by Conant's criterion.

The impact upon state legislatures of studies of the kind described above is revealed by a dramatic nationwide movement to reorganize local school districts. This trend is revealed in Table 6-2. Reorganization is

Table 6-2. School Districts in the United States, 1948-1962, by Total Number, One-Teacher Districts, and Nonoperating Districts

Districts	1948	1958	1960	1962
Total	100,946	48,043	42,457	35,330
One-Teacher (elementary)	74,823	25,979	23,870*	21,010*
Nonoperating	17,131	6,607	6,005*	5,280*

*Estimates

SOURCE: National Education Association, Research Division.

16. Leonard Felt, "Relationship Between Pupil Achievement and High School Size" (Iowa City, Iowa: State University of Iowa, mimeographed, 1960).

presented, almost always, as a step to make local districts more efficient. And yet sufficient evidence is available to show that reorganization leads to greater rather than less expenditure for education. It is clear that the reorganization movement represents a major effort to structure local districts in order to make the improvement of educational programs possible.

Adequacy of Local Districts and Quality of Educational Programs

Table 6-3 indicates the estimated 1963-1964 distribution of the public school enrollment according to the size of the district in which education is provided. In 1963-64 approximately 35 percent of the public school enrollment of the nation would be found in 2 percent of the school districts. These pupils are attending schools in districts that are judged to be of sufficient size. They *might* receive the quality of education expected by those who established the enrollment criteria noted above. An additional 16 percent of the public school pupils of the nation *might,* according to the criteria, be provided quality education if they attend schools organized within adequate intermediate districts. Approximately 42 percent attend schools that meet minimum enrollment criteria.

Table 6-3. Estimated Distribution of Total Public School Enrollment by Size of Local School District, 1963

No. Pupils Enrolled	Percent of School Districts in U.S.	Percent of Total Public School Pupils
12,000 or more	2	35
6000-11,999	3	16
3000-5999	5	18
1500-2999	8	24
1500 or less	77	7
None	5	—*

*This line represents constituted local districts that are not operating schools. The numbers of pupils in these districts are not available, but they would not likely number .5 percent of the total public school enrollment in the country.

SOURCE: Estimated by the authors from data of the Census of Governments of the U.S. Census Bureau and the Biennal Surveys of the U.S. Office of Education. Percentage figures given in the table have been derived from projections and rounded.

Although size is used most frequently as the basic dimension by which to study the adequacy of local district structure, it is not the only means available. Other approaches have employed studies of financial support, program characteristics, and types and qualifications of professional staff.[17] In any case, the importance of structure to excellence of education has been amply demonstrated by research. Although the presence of particular structural features does not guarantee excellence of educational opportunities for children and youth, there is sufficient evidence for the conclusion that excellence is impossible to attain without adequate structures for the conduct of education.

POLICY DEVELOPMENT AND PROFESSIONAL INVOLVEMENT

Governmental decision on whether to authorize new programs, modify or eliminate old ones, or establish levels of support, represents public policy. All educational policy in the United States is either formally approved by public bodies or subject to review by them. The general legal framework for decision making and the four levels of government with authority to make policy decisions have been described in an earlier section of this chapter. Formal authorization of policy is, however, the final rather than the initial step of an extended and complex process. The process may be simply defined as the phase of political action undertaken to determine what educational values are to be implemented by government.

Since all major questions of policy and support for public education are politically determined, the question immediately follows as to what is appropriate professional activity in the policy development process. Harold McNally and Harry Passow have examined present political controversy in an attempt to identify public expectations for education. They conclude that a struggle for the control of public education is now under way and that the professional educator seems uncertain of the role he is to play in it.[18]

It is ironic that little professional study has been directed toward the formulation of educational goals and programs as political phenomena.

17. The reader may wish to consult the writings of Paul Mort, Edgar Morphet, and William McLure.
18. Harold J. McNally and Harry Passow, *Improving the Quality of Public School Programs* (New York: Teachers College, Bureau of Publications, Columbia University, 1960).

Secondary schools, more than any other phase of American education, face perplexing and controversial issues in the realm of public policy. Whether secondary school administrators will be able to define their professional roles in the policy-making process and develop the knowledge and skills to participate effectively is a question that can only be answered in the future.

Process of Policy Making

Structures, procedures, and legal prescriptions precedent to action are well known. Events, activities, and other *antecedents* to policy making have not been subjected to as systematic research, although promising studies have been made.[19] The major phases of the process may be seen from Figure 6-3. Changes in educational policy (I) derive from (II) basic social forces that have been (III) studied and debated and from which (IV) formal expressions of policy result. The process, to be understood, must be viewed as a continuous effort to realize certain values through political action. The professional educator, if he is to realize educational values, cannot restrict his activity to formal, legal expressions of policy alone (IV of Figure 6-3).

Leadership Roles in Policy Development

The complexity of education and of educational government, regardless of the level of structure, implies that various leadership roles are required. For descriptive purposes they are referred to as (1) intellectual leaders, (2) consent builders, (3) bureaucratic organizers, and (4) political energizers. Few significant educational advances requiring formal policy decision would likely be possible without the contribution of each type. Stephen Bailey and his associates conducted an extensive study of educational policy development in eight eastern states and confirmed this multiple-leadership theory.[20]

According to the descriptions of the Bailey study, the four leadership types and their functions are:

19. For one proposed formulation, see Lloyd E. McCleary, "Intra-organizational Administrative Problems," in B. J. Chandler, Lindley J. Stiles, and John I. Kitsuse (eds.), *Education in Urban Society* (New York: Dodd, Mead & Co., 1962), Chapter X.

20. Stephen Bailey *et al., Schoolmen and Politics* (Syracuse, N.Y.: Syracuse University Press, 1962).

Figure 6-3. The Process of Policy Making in Education

I

Educational policy
results from. . . .

II

Basic social,
economic, poli-
tical, and techno-
logical forces,
often national and
worldwide in scope,
which produce. . . . .

III

Political activity
extralegal in
nature. Many
groups debate
and seek infor-
mation, and
school leaders
exert influence.
These activities,
usually inter-
related at local,
state, and
national levels,
culminate in. . . .

IV

Formal, legal
expression of
policy which
represents the
value choices
of influentials
who participated
in the process.

SOURCE: William P. McLure and Van Miller (eds.), <u>Government of Public Education for Adequate Policy Making</u> (Urbana, Ill.: Bureau of Educational Research, University of Illinois, 1960), p. 73.

1. *Intellectual leaders,* who translate inchoate public needs into specific policy proposals. They function to study and elaborate needs; survey existing laws, policies, and practices; formulate general goals; study and recommend courses of action. Intellectual leaders may discontinue their participation at the point of making recommendations; frequently, however, they continue to revise and study as deliberation proceeds.

2. *Consent builders,* who work at the grass roots to educate within

their groups. They mobilize interest and effort, build communication between and within groups, and provide sustained energy to accomplish their purposes.

3. *Bureaucratic organizers,* who work within the government structure to keep proposals "reality-oriented." They can contribute needed information relating to political and legal procedures, finance, and statistics bearing upon governmental action in the areas of concern.

4. *Political energizers,* who work within the political apparatus to sponsor and support needed proposals. They build educational policy proposals into acceptable political frameworks. They build the political climate within which the other types of leadership may function.

Although other types of leadership may emerge, both logical analysis and empirical study bear out the necessity of at least the four types enumerated above. Professional educators have been identified in each of the four categories.

Professional Involvement in Policy Development

The fact of differentiated leadership in policy development seems clearly established. This condition raises the possibility that school administrators might participate in various leadership roles relating to policy development. The arena of primary leadership activity of the secondary school principal might very well be restricted to the roles of intellectual leader and consent builder from the list above. In any case, however, the needs of public education are not likely to become known or adequately met without persistent professional attention.

The ethics of professional involvement in policy development, whatever specific role is undertaken, must be carefully considered. The proposition that education should be kept out of politics may be a myth, and the politics of education may not be entirely understood; but certain principles seem undeniably clear. Education cannot exist without public support—both economic and moral. This support rests squarely upon the demonstrated ability of professional educators to improve educational services. The influence of the professional will increase in proportion to his ability to contribute expert knowledge to the development of educational policy. This expertise will not be effective without a knowledge of the process of policy development and the skills associated with the leadership roles needed.

From the presentation of Chapter 4, the reader may be better able to understand the need for professional involvement in general policy development as necessary to his direct role in building compatible operational policies for a particular school. Chapter 7 contains an examination of principles relating to the organization of secondary schools and their relationship to other units of educational organization.

REFERENCES

American Association of School Administrators, *Educational Administration in a Changing Community, Thirty-seventh Yearbook* (Washington, D.C.: the Association, 1959).

Bailey, Stephen, *et al., Schoolmen and Politics* (Syracuse, N.Y.: Syracuse University Press, 1962).

Brickell, Henry M., *Organizing New York State for Educational Change* (Albany, N.Y.: University of the State of New York, 1961).

Burkhead, Jesse, *Public School Finance: Economics and Politics* (Syracuse, N.Y.: Syracuse University Press, 1964).

Cahill, Robert S., and Hencley, Stephen P., *The Politics of Education* (Danville, Illinois: The Interstate Printers and Publishers, Inc., 1964).

Chandler, B. J., Stiles, Lindley J., and Kitsuse, John I. (eds.), *Education in Urban Society* (New York: Dodd, Mead & Co., 1962).

Kimbrough, Ralph B., *Political Power and Educational Decision-Making* (Chicago, Rand McNally & Co., 1964).

McLure, William P., and Miller, Van (eds.), *Government of Public Education for Adequate Policy Making* (Urbana, Ill.: Bureau of Educational Research, University of Illinois, 1960).

Polsby, Nelson W., *Community Power and Political Theory* (New Haven, Conn.: Yale University Press, 1963).

Reeves, Charles E., *School Boards: Their Status and Functions* (Englewood Cliffs, N.J.: Prentice-Hall, 1954).

Walton, John, *Administration and Policy Making in Education* (Baltimore, Md.: Johns Hopkins Press, 1959).

Chapter 7
Organization and the
Secondary School

THE basis of organization in public education is the individual school—the building unit. Except in a very few large city systems where significant aspects of organization have been removed from his purview, the major responsibility for organization rests with the school principal. District-level planning and activities can at best only facilitate the continuous development of consistent organizational design within each school. The crucial administrative function relating to organization is welding an increasingly divergent team of specialists into a functioning unit at the point at which institutional purposes are translated into operational practice.

Certain elements are primary to sound organization. These include well-conceived purposes and priorities, clearly defined responsibilities and relationships, stimulating and satisfying climate, and a continuously developing design of operation—all oriented to practical considerations of staff, facilities, and resources. Each seems to be an essential administrative concern relating to effectiveness and efficiency in organization. A review of standard texts in educational administration reveals only slight attention to this important area of administrative concern. Yet problems of organization in schools are growing rapidly with their increasing size, mounting complexity of programs, and a resulting increase in specialization of staff.

Functional interrelationships of positions within school district organization, presented in Chapter 4, represent an effort by the authors to present a clear definition of administration tasks and their assignment to positions within the total administrative structure. This scheme can be used both as a model for study and as a means for analysis of existing administrative structures in actual school settings. The legal framework, presented in Chapter 6, is an attempt to give perspective—a general frame of reference—for the study of internal organization. In this chapter the presentation is focused upon those concepts and points of view that seem most fruitful to an understanding of the internal organization of secondary schools.

ORGANIZATION AND ADMINISTRATION

The close relationship of administration to organization has kept some authors from differentiating clearly between the two. Often lists of principles are given which imply that organization is the totality of administration. Two basic notions may reveal the relationship between the two concepts and serve to clarify the ways in which the term "organization" will be employed in the remainder of this chapter.

Administration as Organizational Activity

Organization refers to a social institution—a factory, a football team, a business, a school—structured in such a way that individuals understand their relationships to other members and can contribute their talents to accomplish the tasks required to fulfill that institution's purposes. If individuals contribute their talents and give up a part of their autonomy to fulfill institutional purposes, they must see values to themselves in such activities and see organizational purposes as worthwhile. This attitude is essential to cooperative endeavor of any kind. At least in complex institutions of modern society, surrendering of individual autonomy to create some authority is necessary. To achieve the coordinated effort needed, administrative processes are required. Although encompassing much more (see Chapters 1 and 5 particularly), administration relating to organization may be characterized as the art and science of *coordination within organization*.

Organization, in the sense just described, encompasses administration. Administration is only one of the specialties within organization—it is not superimposed on organization, nor is it separated from it. Organization, then, is a definable entity—it has limits; it is composed of subentities; and it possesses properties that may be measured and described. This is the first of the two notions about organization mentioned in the opening paragraph of this section.

Administration as Responsibility for Organization

Administration is one of the specialties within organization; it differs, however, in certain important ways from other subentities of organization. Administration is the function of overseeing the activity of all the specialties and of determining the extent and timing of their contribution to the organizational effort. The role of administration is, in what may seem to be a contradiction of terms, the specialty of generalization. Professor Van Miller has coined the term "perceptive generalist" to apply to administrators. Brooks Adams, as early as 1913, referred to administration as "the power of organizing a series of relations between numerous special interests, with all of which no single man can be intimately acquainted. . . . yet administration or generalization is not only the faculty upon which social stability rests, but is probably the highest faculty of the human mind." [1]

The second important notion in explaining the relationship of organization and administration follows from the paragraph above: administration, while a part of organization, is that part responsible for creating, developing, and controlling it. In this sense, administration is in legitimate control of organization and must see that organization is adequate to the tasks assigned to it.

THREE VIEWS OF ORGANIZATION

Study and theorizing about organization, particularly about organization within what is termed "large-scale enterprise," has been an absorbing interest of political science and public administration since the 1890's. Beginning in the 1920's, industrial and social psychology, management, sociology, and, after mid-1950, education became stimulated by new findings and resultant improvement of knowledge in this field. In turn, government, industry, and business were deeply affected; there are some signs that educational administration may respond to its own wave of study of organization.

Although often employing common terminology ("task," "process," "authority," "coordination," "line and staff," for example), and related at certain points, the various approaches to the study of organization have not followed a single orientation. Rather, within the general move-

1. Brooks Adams, *The Theory of Social Revolutions* (New York: The Macmillan Co., 1913) p. 19.

ment, at least four reasonably distinct orientations have occurred. For the interested reader they are noted here very briefly:

First, an organized effort had a broad social-philosophical orientation, drawing together and adapting from early works a general formulation of organization in which administration was treated as based equally upon art, science, and ethics. From its beginning with the writings of Mary Parker Follett in the 1920's, this emphasis has been carried into the present by the works of Peter Drucker and others.

Second, an attempt was made to restrict the study of organization to that of the analysis of formal structure and design. Sometimes referred to as "scientific management," this movement largely terminated with the work of L. Urwick.

Third, an almost antithetical position to that of scientific management turned the study of organization to features of human relations. This emphasis began strongly with the "Hawthorne Studies" of Mayo, Roethlisberger, and Dickson, and it has continued.

Fourth, current interest seems to be directed toward the development of general scientific formulations. Represented by Likert's *New Patterns of Management,* this approach employs "systems analysis" and "operations research," briefly described in Chapter 4 of this work. In the field of education, the work of Daniel Griffiths is most notable in formulating logico-hypothetical propositions centered upon organization as patterns structured for decision-making activity.

Each of the emphases has made significant contributions to the study of educational organization, but thorough review of each is beyond the scope of this chapter. Rather, the authors believe that three points of view relative to organization can be developed to reveal fundamental distinctions in current views of organization and practice in secondary administration. The statements contained in the three views below are paraphrases of actual statements of secondary school principals given to the authors. They serve to reveal differing views presently employed in practice, and they offer a means of orienting the reader to the problems posed by organization.

ORGANIZATION AS A FORMAL, INSTITUTIONAL ENTITY

Many school administrators take the view that organization is constructed apart from the people who compose it. In effect, a general design of relationships is drawn up, and positions are identified. Organization members are to fulfill the tasks assigned to those positions and abide by the relationships set up for them. In this view, organization has an independent identity and an existence of its own—thus one speaks of "the school" or "the institution." One principal wrote, "The school is bigger than all of us; it requires us to live up to its fine traditions and calls out the best that is in each of us."

Authority must be respected, for it is exercised with the benefit of the school in mind and ultimately, therefore, to the benefit of those who are members of it. Individuals are expected to be dedicated and loyal in serving the organization.

The administration must be careful to reflect the values and traditions of the school, to harmonize conflicts, and to restore damage. The organization has a life cycle with periods of growth and decline. The administration must work to nurture growth and act to prevent decline.

Purposes must be reviewed from time to time and adjusted to serve social needs. Fundamental values remain the same, but require reinterpretation and reapplication to changing conditions.

Organization as Human Relations

To speak of organization as having independent status apart from those who are its members is a delusion. The school is composed of people; and purposes and values are always *someone's* purposes and values.

It is important to get organization members together—teachers, administrators, and students—because this is the only way to develop shared notions about what is important. Every major issue should be discussed frankly and openly. But organization members should not be brought together only when problems occur; they should interact regularly under various circumstances, in friendly social settings as well as in work, and as frequently as it is practical to do so.

The crux of attaining high efficiency is to have high morale. To obtain high morale, individuals must get personal satisfaction from their work. Thus, organizational goals must "grow" out of the interests and abilities of the staff. When new skills are called for, they must be learned by the staff; or new members with those skills must be added.

Administrators cannot "govern" an organization. Administrators can only lead and influence out of the quality of their own ideas and demonstrated competence. The best administrators constantly seek for leadership within the staff and encourage it to arise wherever it occurs.

Organization as Structured Interrelationships

Organization is composed basically of personal interrelationships of staff. Some relationships have prescribed or formal aspects and are required by the demands of the work situation; some relationships are informal and spontaneous; some relationships have both formal and informal components. All are necessary to sound organization, and where they seem to be out of balance or inadequate, measures must be taken either to provide or to develop them.

Person-to-person relationships, then, form the structure of organization. They serve as the communication links for control, coordination, and development. Properties of these relationships—pattern, frequency, stability in time, content of communications, determinants, and the resulting psychological climate—represent what is meant by organization.

The legitimate role of administration is to structure the working relationships of organization members on a functional basis; that is, to use the authority vested in administration to establish work patterns to accomplish purposes. A general structure of authority and responsibility is essential to stability. Each organizational function must be specified and assigned, however, so that it may be analyzed and altered without drastically overhauling the total structure.

Although the three views are somewhat incomplete and were reconstructed by the authors, they seem to reveal positions held by practicing secondary school administrators. They represent ways in which administrators are trying to make sense out of the complex forces with which they deal. One would be relatively safe in assuming that administrators do interpret organizational problems in these terms and attempt to make judgments in light of the position they hold.

Perhaps the reader has already identified one of the three views that might represent the nucleus of his own position. In any case, the individual who is to perform as an administrator will, of necessity, develop some more or less consistent way of viewing organization. His particular view will determine what he believes represents the reality of the situations he confronts, and it will become a pattern to which he will attempt to shape conditions as he believes they ought to be. With this in mind, the authors will attempt, in the remainder of the chapter, to define some of the properties of organization in order that the reader may become more aware of his own point of view, its strengths, and weaknesses, and how it might be improved.

NATURE OF ORGANIZATION

Activity which requires cooperative effort establishes the need for organization. Order and stability in society, in general, depend upon whether sufficient talent, resources, and authority can be brought together to form organizations that can perform the functions needed. Robert Dubin notes that "the organizations of society institutionalize power and are the means for carrying out the ordered and regular daily activities of society. Within organizations, the activities of the members and the functionaries must be directed in systems of cooperation and coordination. These coordinating functions are grounded in authority. . . ." [2]

Organizations—particularly those (such as a school) that serve vital social functions—are closely tied to socially approved activities and ways of doing things. One might aptly apply the expression "culture-bound" to them. The social welfare requires that schools develop strong, stable organization. An enumeration of conditions essential to organizational stability follows:

1. Purposes are defined and the tasks necessary to accomplish them are specified.
2. Authority for direction and control is assigned and power sufficient to enforce authority is available.
3. Tasks are assigned to positions so that responsibility is fixed and a division of work is arranged.
4. A system of communications is created to coordinate activities within and between all parts of the organization.
5. Leadership is developed so that proper relationships are maintained and continuous assessment and improvement of operations occur.
6. Consideration is given to insure high individual motivation. Individuals find challenging work, satisfying relationships, and conditions adequate to encourage high output of individual effort.

In addition to listing essential conditions of organization, clarification of the meaning of the term is in order. First, organization refers to the design or plan rather than to the operation itself. For example, referring to the task aspect of organization, the specification of tasks means their identification and assignment, not the orders and directions issued or the work performed. In the case of authority, it refers to the specification of those in the organization who have certain authority, not to the actual exercise of authority.

Second, organization is a means to an end; it is not a purpose in itself. When organization takes place, it merely puts people in a position to perform; it does not guarantee the quality of performance. Third, organization is a continuous task of those who compose it. Changes in conditions, purposes, personalities, and resources require adjustments of the plan—organization is dynamic. At any given time, however, the structure should be stable. Except for minor day-to-day adjustments of

2. Robert Dubin, *Human Relations in Administration* (Englewood Cliffs, N.J.: Prentice-Hall, 1951), pp. 229-230.

plans, any radical changes usually must be "phased in" to avoid confusion and a resultant lowering of individuals' ability to carry out their responsibilities.

Fallacies in Administrative Thought Relating to Organization

Of the comments solicited from practicing secondary school principals (some were paraphrased in the previous section), a certain number represented what the authors judged to be fallacious views of organization. This set of comments seemed to fall into distinct groupings revealing three fallacies: organization by personality, organization by the whole staff, and organization by traditional practice.

ORGANIZATION BY PERSONALITY. Some principals believe that "good people" make the organization. If good people are selected they will "shake down" the job, dig in, and get the work done that needs doing. It is unclear whether "good people" refers to competent and knowledgeable people, compatible people, willing and hard-working people, or some other variety.

Herbert Simon, a noted student of industrial management, has found the same view in his field and responded to it in this way:

Personality! Truly a magical slogan to charm away the problems that our intellectual tools don't handle. . . . And if organization is inessential, if all we need is the man, why do we insist on creating a position for the man? Why not let each create his own position, appropriate to his personal abilities and qualities? Why does the boss have to be called the boss before his creative energies can be amplified by the organization? And, finally, if we have to give a man some measure of authority before his personal qualities can be transformed into effective influence, in what ways may his effectiveness depend on the manner in which others are organized around him? [3]

ORGANIZATION BY THE WHOLE STAFF. Several principals in the sample expressed the view that the best way to organize a school was "by handling each problem as it arises." The administrator tries to avoid making decisions by leaving it up to the staff. These administrators referred frequently to "the team," and felt that the principal functioned best when he did not "tip his hand," but let everyone have his say in deciding how problems would be handled.

3. Herbert A. Simon, *Administrative Behavior* (New York: The Macmillan Co., 1959), p. 15.

Griffiths calls this "administration by the gang." He describes a visit to such a school district: ". . . a typical day would find the superintendent calling in all the administrative staff members, whatever their assigned function might be, and saying: 'We have a little problem here—how should we handle it?' His query would provoke feverish effort on behalf of the whole staff until they felt the issue was handled adequately. No person felt or assumed an individual responsibility for anything other than the strictly routine." [4]

The guise of democratic organization seems to prevail in such a setting. Yet the freedom lost to each individual to assume responsibility and take direct and independent action, the frustration and waste of staff time, and the possibilities for subtle manipulation go a long way toward defeating democratic action. Defined authority and the development of explicit policy to guide decision making and action seem to be more clearly related to democratic practices.

ORGANIZATION BY TRADITIONAL PRACTICE. A small number of the principals sampled expressed a distaste for those who "tinkered with" organization. They indicated that once the line of authority was established the best procedure was to insist upon adherence to it. One simple structure drawn up on a chart should take care of all the organization a school required. New activities should be assigned to the traditional structure. These responses included the fear of "developing too many chiefs," of creating "top-heavy administration," of massing simple procedures into complex, tangled machinery. Finally, some of these comments revealed an impatience with those who espouse a need for such positions as guidance director, curriculum coordinator, master teacher, and administrative assistant, and questioned the tendency to depart from simple, traditional organizational patterns.

There is reason to be critical of new departures, whether in organization or in other areas of administrative concern, but a "closed-mind" attitude prevents the possibility of improvement. The reticence to add positions to a structure, if such additions hold little promise of improving the effectiveness of instruction or services, is commendable. Unless organizational problems are analyzed in a rational manner, altering lines of authority and responsibility or adding ill-defined positions is likely to represent "tinkering," "tangling the machinery," and "developing too

4. Daniel Griffiths *et al., Organizing Schools for Effective Education* (Danville, Ill.: The Interstate Printers and Publishers. 1962), p. 16.

many chiefs." But reactions such as these might easily represent a rationalization for the avoidance of consideration of organization. New and important specializations are developing which can contribute greatly to the improvement of secondary school programs. Increased specialization is bound to require organizational planning and adjustments; to ignore this fact leads to restricted opportunity for improvement and to the possibility of drastic reorganization at a later date.

These three fallacies and others like them often are symptoms of either lack of knowledge of organization and understanding of its importance or lack of courage to examine organizational requirements and make needed changes. If these comments are valid descriptions of the attitudes of secondary school principals—as the authors believe they are—improvement in knowledge and understanding of this area of administration is called for.

Three Dimensions of Organization: Purpose-Task, Structure, Climate

The principal and other administrative personnel of the secondary school exercise leadership within two interrelated spheres of activity—the internal organizational sphere and the external organizational sphere. The style and consistency of leadership will depend upon the particular image of leadership (see Chapter 5) held by the administrator and the skill with which he fulfills the leadership role. Regardless of the manner in which the administrator attempts to exert leadership, his effectiveness with organizational concerns will depend partially upon his understanding of the basic concepts of organization.

Three primary features of organization are: purpose-task, structure, and climate. Identification and analysis of concepts and processes relating to purposes, structure, and climate should aid in understanding organization—how it functions, how its problems may be diagnosed, and how its effectiveness may be assessed and improved.

PURPOSE-TASK DIMENSION OF ORGANIZATION

The study of organization cannot be separated from the concern for purpose. Many authorities view the continuous process of identification, interpretation, and adaptation of purposes to be the most important—and most neglected—task of secondary school administrators. Those who accept this point of view believe that the most significant contribution the principal can make is to translate the objectives of the school from the vague, exhortative language common to education into a language by which the effectiveness of each school organization can be measured.

Statements of purposes in general terms are useful for delineating broad functions schools are to serve. They are not, however, useful guides for directing organizational accomplishment; nor are they useful criteria by which to assess the effectiveness of organizational units within a school. To clarify this problem in organizational terms it is helpful to employ two separate terms—purpose and task.

Purposes project the outcomes which are to be produced by the separate, but interrelated, activities carried out within the school. Thus purposes constitute the mission assigned to the school and validated by regulations and policies of governing agencies *external to the school itself*.[5]

Tasks are the specific activities identified by those *within the organization* as the necessary means to accomplish the assigned purposes. Tasks might be thought of as the organizational interpretation of purposes *at a particular time*. A specific example might make clear the distinction between the two terms as they are employed here.

A universally accepted purpose of secondary education is education for citizenship. The board of education of a district known to the authors set up a lay-professional study committee to clarify the meaning of this purpose for the school district. The board adopted the committee's recommendation which contained the statement that the program of the school should "include the study of the political ideology, the economic theory, and the historical development of the communist movement." The principals of the high school and the two junior high schools appointed a joint committee to assess the program in operation and prepare recommendations for changes to include "content, suggested learning activities and materials, time allotments, sequence of treatment, their assignment within the social studies program of the junior and senior high schools, and suggestions for evaluation of the changes recommended."

Without extending the description to include the dynamics of what took place or the administrative process of review and implementation, the distinction should be clear between purposes—as the mission as-

5. The process is described in Chapter 6.

signed to the school—and tasks—as the specification of purposes and their assignment to segments of the organization.

Characteristics of the purpose-task dimension of organization may be summarized:

1. Purposes are the means of defining the school's total responsibility.
2. Purposes are determined primarily on the basis of value criteria rather than scientific criteria. Therefore, public consensus is involved, and purposes are sanctioned, either explicitly or implicitly, by public authority.
3. Tasks, as differing from purposes, are defined primarily on the basis of technical knowledge. Thus, tasks are primarily a professional responsibility. Prescription of tasks by boards of education, legislatures, and other lay bodies, besides infringing on the moral rights of the teaching profession, leads to organizational inflexibility and ultimately reduces efficiency and effectiveness.
4. Tasks are the means of organizing to realize purposes most efficiently. They permit the structuring of organization through the rational division of work and fixing of responsibility.
5. Task definition and assignment to organization provide the only valid means for directing organizational activity and evaluating effectiveness in terms of purposes.
6. Tasks may change without a change in purposes. Changes in technology, in student body, in knowledge, or from a host of other sources may call for a redefinition of tasks. Tasks must be subject to continuous review in the light of operational experience.

Administrative decisions relating to tasks—their priorities, allocation of staff and resources to accomplish them, processes to be employed, and modes of relating compatible tasks and separating conflicting ones —contribute to the structuring of organization. Primary tasks are not, however, the only basis of structure for school organization. Some parts of structure are required to develop and assess tasks, some to articulate organizational needs and activities to its patrons (citizens) and to related organizations, and some to provide for the maintenance of the organization itself. A purely task-based model of organization is almost universal in educational organization. The systems model, described in Chapter 4, encompasses a task dimension and is compatible with the treatment followed in this chapter. Organizations other than education have employed task, process, and service-based models.[6]

6. See Paul Meadows, "Models, Systems, and Science," *American Sociological Review,* Vol. XII, No. 1, 1957, pp. 3-9; and Talcott Parsons, "A Sociological Approach to the Theory of Organization," *Administrative Science Quarterly,* Vol. 1, No. 1, 1956, pp. 63-85.

STRUCTURE OF ORGANIZATION

All organizations have identity in terms of location and time, clientele being served, tasks to be accomplished, and processes to be initiated and maintained. Members of organizations must arrange their work within requirements imposed principally by these four conditions. The manner in which this is done creates persistent, regularized activities and relationships that are characteristic of each organization. This *patterning* of the relationships of people within organization is its structure.

Basic patterns of relationships are prescribed or required by those placed in authority. Other patterns are developed by organizational members themselves as they go about their work. Prescribed relationships are referred to as the formal structure; those that seem just to develop are referred to as the informal structure. This distinction, though useful in analysis, is an oversimplification, for almost all prescribed relationships develop informal components and informal relationships frequently become incorporated into the formal structure.

Design of Structure

In designing structure, the administrator is caught between the need to project an ideal plan—one which represents relationships as they ought to be, or would be if human factors could be ruled out—and a plan which represents competences and relationships as he believes them to exist. Both approaches seem to be needed. Sound planning requires that the administration study and develop idealized structures while specifying for operational practice the most effective structure possible under existing conditions. For both purposes, certain basic elements form the design.

Every organization is composed of two integrally related parts. One is made up of the work groups that perform the operations for which the organization exists. In a school this would be the teachers, counselors, and other personnel who work directly with youth. The other part is made up of the administration and staff who direct, supervise, and service the work groups. In a production organization, such as a factory, the distinction is quite sharp. In a school or a hospital where professional workers have a high degree of autonomy and where the same individuals perform both kinds of functions, this distinction, though important, is less clear and is often overlooked and confused.

Administrative Component of Organizational Structure

That part of the structure serving administrative and service functions is often mistakenly thought to represent the total prescribed structure of organization. It does represent positions in the organization according to their *authority relationships*. The basic elements of this part of formal structure are given below:

1. *Position.* Each person in the organization occupies a formally defined position. In secondary schools these include: student, teacher, supervisor, department chairman, director, manager, coordinator, administrative assistant, assistant principal, principal, and perhaps others. The position is defined both by the duties assigned to the person who occupies it and by the expectations established for the manner in which the duties are to be performed.

2. *Authority hierarchy.* Positions are related according to the authority assigned to them. The resulting hierarchy of positions indicates the order of authority relationships throughout the organization. There is general agreement that each position from the bottom level to the top should be placed in a single line of authority to the next higher position. The number of subordinate positions assigned to any position of higher authority is called the *span of control*. Effect of a hierarchical structure is to create *levels of authority*. In Figure 7-1, three levels of authority are shown, and in this case, the span of control of the principal is ten.

Figure 7-1. Illustration of Position Hierarchy in a Secondary School

```
                              Principal
          ┌───────────────────────┼───────────────────────┐
8 Department Chairmen    Director of Guidance     Assistant Principal
          │                       │                        │
      Teachers                Counselors            Main-Office Staff
```

3. *Line and staff positions.* Line positions are those in which general administrative authority is assigned in direct flow from top to bottom. Line organization defines the decision-making structure, routes of appeal, and official communications channels for reporting information and issuing of directives. Staff positions represent specialties which are necessary to the proper function of a particular line position; they might include, for example, a director of testing and research, a curriculum

coordinator, or an administrative assistant. Staff members may perform a service, coordinate an activity, or advise; they do not make decisions or direct line personnel.

The pattern of the administrative component of organizational structure is universally depicted by the organization chart. The organization chart (Figure 7-2), though often abused and overused, is a helpful instrument for designing administrative structure for planning reorganization. It can serve as a general guide for orienting staff. If the administrator uses it operationally, he may well keep in mind the comments of L. Urwich concerning slavish adherence to authority structure as prescribed by the organization chart: ". . . it [the organization chart] is concerned with authority and, provided the authority is recognized and no attempt is made to evade or to supersede it, there is ample room for avoiding in matters of action the childish practices of going upstairs one step at a time or running up one ladder and down another." [7]

Figure 7-2 is indeed representative of a complex structure. It is, as a matter of fact, a somewhat simplified version of an actual chart of a secondary school organization. It can be used to illustrate each of the points raised in this section. The chart reveals positions, authority hierarchy, and line and staff relationships. One can also note that it deals only with administrative and service staff relationships and not with the structure of work groups. To illustrate the "double assignments" of personnel between work group and administrative positions in professional organizations, the director of research and the supervisor of buildings and grounds were half-time teachers in the school from which this chart was taken. Also, the director of television and the director of adult education served as department chairmen, and the director of summer school was a division principal. In addition, all department chairmen held some teaching assignment.

AUTHORITY HIERARCHY: SKELETAL STRUCTURE. The hierarchy of authority relationships depicted by the organization chart is a "barebones" picture of the organizational structure. It is the skeletal structure of essential administrative processes of:

Decision making. The chart pinpoints authority and responsibility for the effective functioning of each unit and the total organization.

7. L. Urwich, *The Elements of Administration* (New York: Harper & Bros., 1943), p. 46.

Figure 7-2. Organization Chart of a Complex Secondary School Structure

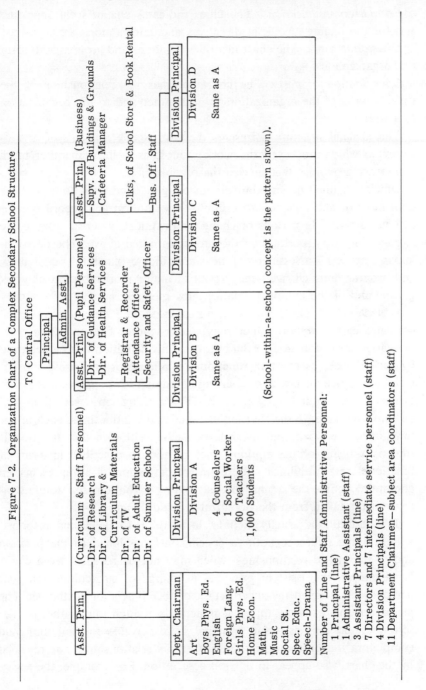

Formal communications. The chart indicates channels for reporting and for the issuing of official directives and information.

Division of work. The chart identifies positions and groupings to form the organization.

Coordination of parts. The chart specifies the relationships of the various parts of the organization to each other and to the organization as a whole.

This skeletal structure represents the more stable elements of organization to which are keyed the work groups, as well as all other more temporary groupings that service the organization.

Official channels under relatively unchanging conditions do little more than monitor and regulate work flow—they confirm and record organizational activity. In periods of change, adjustment, or crisis, they come strongly into play, performing the processes noted above. The decision-making process—assessment of new conditions, planning, reassigning, and programming change—may result in major reorganization of work groups and of the authority relationships themselves.

FUNCTIONAL RELATIONSHIPS: JOB DESCRIPTION. To fill out the skeletal structure of the authority hierarchy, most schools further define positions in terms of functional relationships. This definition can be achieved by such devices as charting functional relationships and using job descriptions. Since the device of charting functional relationships was rather extensively illustrated in Chapter 4, the one using job descriptions will be employed here. In the charting of functional relationships, each major function is identified, and the role of each position in that function is shown. In using job descriptions, each position is described in terms of functional responsibilities and relationships. Figure 7-3 represents an attempt to outline the actual job descriptions of the four top administrative officers taken from the organization chart, Figure 7-2.

Job descriptions usually include, in addition to functional responsibilities, some reference both to specific tasks assigned to the position and to prescribed relationships which may not be revealed by a chart. For example, the assistant principal in charge of curriculum and staff personnel is assigned the specific task of recommending textbooks. The procedure for textbook approval is actually written out in the job description, and this assistant principal is responsible for initiating and completing the procedure outlined. Certain relationships, not revealed by the chart, also appear in this job description. For example, the assist-

Figure 7-3.   Outline of Job Descriptions of Four Administrative Officers Shown in the Organization Chart, Figure 7-2

Principal

Maintain general supervision of the school

Coordinate work of the assistant principals

Evaluate effectiveness of the total organization

Establish policies, procedures, and other matters not specifically assigned to a subunit

Create work groups to study and recommend revisions in program and services

Transmit all proposals, questions of policy, and reports of operation to the superintendent

Assistant Principal (Business)

Maintain general supervision of buildings, grounds, and property of the school

Maintain records and make reports of all bus. affairs of the school in accord with district policy

Recruit & recommend employment of nonacademic personnel & supervise their work

Consult with other school officers on use and maintenance of offices and class-rooms

Approve use of space by outside groups

Establish financial records & procedures relating to all student activity funds

Receive, store, & distribute all books, supplies, & materials

Coordinate with appropriate officers involvement of professional personnel in purchasing, property control and use, budgeting, etc.

Assistant Principal (Pupil Personnel)

Direct a complete program of pupil ser-vices to include health, safety, guidance, testing, psychological, and social work services

Work with dir. of guidance and division principals to organize and implement the guidance and counseling program

Supervise admission of pupils, develop-ment of records and follow-up

Develop all pupil records required by the school, central office, & the state

Direct development of the master sched-ule & procedures for scheduling & assigning pupils to classes

Organize, with cooperation of officer of staff personnel, the work of teachers and counselors relating to pupil welfare

Conduct program of in-service training of the guidance staff

Consult with dir. of guidance & division principals on all matters of policy relating to pupil personnel

Assistant Principal (Curriculum and Staff Personnel)

Direct continuous study of instruction

Administer a program of in-service training

Supervise curriculum development with the aid of a curriculum committee

Oversee supervision and evaluation of teachers by dept. chairman and division principals

Direct the preparation of curriculum guides, courses of study, & other instructional materials; recommend textbooks

Investigate methods and problems of learning with teaching and guidance personnel

Recommend major changes in the instructional program to the principal

Cooperate with officer in charge of pupil personnel to prepare course offering and master schedule

Work with central-office personnel on program articulation with other schools ant principal is to consult with division principals as well as department chairmen in evaluating teachers. He is also to involve guidance personnel in the study of learning problems.

Thus, job descriptions put some meat on the bare bones of the organization skeleton. They are frequently of help in the analysis of organizational problems. When prepared by the staff members themselves, they may reveal differing perceptions about what each job should entail. And, as in Chapter 4, when each function is taken separately and analyzed, differences can be located and resolved.

Work Groups Structure

Work groups form the second major component of organization. As with the administrative component, the *patterning* of relationships within and between work groups gives structure to the organization. Work groups may be formed and keyed into any part of the authority hierarchy. At the operational level, they are teacher teams, subject specialists, whole departments, grade-level groupings of teachers and counselors, or a number of other arrangements. At higher levels in the hierarchy, they may be planning committees, study groups, production units preparing materials, action research teams, or one of a number of kinds of groups performing deliberative and consultative functions.

SERVICE-TYPE WORK GROUPS. Work groups may be loosely identified as either operational or service. Operational work groups are production units; they perform duties and functions that have been specified by policies and procedures. Service work groups aid in the decision-making process, coordination of operational work groups, planning and evaluation functions, and programming change. Figure 7-4 is a chart showing permanent work groups that have been created within the structure shown in the organization chart, Figure 7-2. The composition of the administrative cabinet, curriculum, and guidance committees is given in order to show how these work groups are keyed to the authority hierarchy by their membership.

Work groups of the service type seem to be most useful when their function is clearly specified. For more permanent groups, as shown in Figure 7-4, a policy statement—quite analogous to the job description —is most often used. For *ad hoc* groups, a concise "charge" to the group is adequate for this purpose. In addition to the functions served by such groups, they are defined in the following ways:

Figure 7-4. Formal Work Groups Within the Organization Charted in Figure 7-2

Administrative Cabinet
{ Principal
Assistant Principals
Administrative Assistant
Others as needed

Faculty Groups
Staff Welfare
Program Comm.
Faculty meetings
Professional days
Hospitality Comm.
Reps. to PTA Council
Reps. to Professional Organizations

Dept. Chairmen ↔ Division Principals →
Guidance Comm.
Prin., ex officio
Asst. Prin. (Pupil Personnel)
Dir. of Guidance
Division Principals
Dir. of Research
1 Social Worker
4 Counselors
2 Dept. Chairmen
2 Teachers

Group Guidance Comm.
Advanced Placement Comm.
Job Placement Comm.
College Planning Comm.

Pupil Orientation Comm.
Activities Comm.
Awards Comm.
Commencement Comm.
Student Welfare

Curriculum Comm. ↔ Dept. Chairmen ↔ Division Principals
Prin., ex officio
Asst. Prin. (curriculum)
Dept. Chairman
2 Division Principals
Dir. of Research
Dir. of Guidance
8 Teachers
2 Counselors

Talented Youth Comm.
Underachiever Study Group
Summer School Comm.

Subject Area Committees
Grade-Level Committees

Teacher, Counselor, Staff: Work Groups in Instruction, Guidance, Activities, and Pupil Services

Basis of membership—appointed, elected, occupants of particular positions, mixed bases of selection.

Tenure—*ad hoc,* permanent, on-call, or self-constituting.

Type of result requested—recommendation, decision, report of study or investigation, materials prepared.

OPERATIONAL WORK GROUPS. Traditional practice in the structuring of teaching and guidance personnel is to treat individuals atomistically. That is, positions are defined as though each position is isolated operationally and is standardized in terms of work demands. For example, all teachers are to instruct four or five classes each day of nearly equal size. Except for subject specialty, all positions are assigned with little regard for other individual competences. The assumption is made that a given teacher or counselor is equally capable of filling any position in his special field.[8]

In the traditional pattern, teachers are assigned to classes according to (1) a vertical dimension by teaching specialty, as, for example, English, mathematics, foreign language; and (2) a horizontal dimension by grade level. Groupings for in-service training, curriculum planning, and the like are universally based upon this pattern. In the conduct of instruction, however, teachers are treated as autonomous and are scheduled individually.

Several factors make rigid adherence to traditional practice seem unwise:

1. As teachers become better trained, special competences appear within subject area specializations; in English, for example, some teachers become especially skilled in creative writing, speech, literature, drama, and the like. These competences are not likely to be most effectively used in the traditional classroom arrangements.
2. When subjects are taught in isolation, important relationships between subjects may be overlooked, as, for example, in mathematics and science; art, literature, and history; music and drama; or science and technical vocational studies.
3. Inexperienced teachers do not profit from association in the classroom with experienced teachers.
4. Many menial tasks within the classroom are repeated over and over, wasting the time of professional personnel.

8. This practice has been questioned most persistently by the Commission on Staff Utilization of the National Association of Secondary-School Principals. See the writings of J. Lloyd Trump.

5. Students are likely to learn more efficiently if class sizes and environments can be altered to fit the learning task.
6. New technological devices are available for instruction which are not used most effectively in standard-sized classes of twenty-five to thirty students.
7. Types of learning, such as independent study, creative expression, and problem-solving activities, require equipment and space which are difficult to arrange in the traditional classroom.

During the past decade, many secondary schools have attempted to structure work groups of teachers to alleviate the conditions noted above. Although the new patterns have not been the subject of definitive research, the large number of secondary schools that have tried various groupings have accepted them as established practice in structuring work groups of teachers.

Work groups tend to take the following forms:

1. An experienced teacher is paired with one or more inexperienced teachers. Classes are pooled and exchanged, and instruction is largely planned by the experienced teacher.
2. Two or more teachers cooperate to plan instruction, pool, and exchange classes. One teacher may take primary responsibility for a language laboratory, science or art laboratory, or a resource materials center while the others conduct instruction. Three or four teachers may group classes for certain presentations, each teacher taking charge during the periods when his particular specialty or area of interest is being studied.
3. Teacher aides, readers, or other paraprofessional personnel are assigned to one or more teachers.
4. Teacher teams are organized in one of the following patterns:
   a. Master teacher, one to three teachers, and an aide, with all teachers representing specialties within a single subject area. In the teaching of English, for example, one teacher may be a specialist in literature, one in speech, one in composition, and one in reading techniques.
   b. Master teacher, two to four teachers, and some teachers of differing subject fields. For example, one mathematics teacher may be added to a science team, or one foreign language teacher added to a team of English teachers.
   c. Teacher, intern or probationary teacher, paraprofessional, and/or a teacher aide.

The team concept seems to be the most flexible in the use of new devices such as closed-circuit television, language laboratories, and independent study centers. It is the most easily adapted to the large-group, small-discussion-group, and independent-study patterning of instruction.

Where the size of school permits a sufficiently large guidance staff, various work patterns have also emerged. Pairs and even teams of counselors are used in group guidance activities and in group counseling. The counselor-intern has become a recognized pattern; and teams of two to four counselors and a social worker are being used in a few large schools. This latter pattern is the one employed by the school in the illustration given in Figures 7-2, 7-3, and 7-4.

Informal and Formal Relationships: Total Pattern of Structure

Beginning with the famed "Hawthorne Studies," [9] a large number of investigations have probed the nature of individual participation in groups. George Homans, in *The Human Group,* reviews five significant studies to document the existence of informal relationships within groups as having significant effects upon formal relationships. Not only do formal relationships seem always to have an informal component—aspects that are not prescribed by formal authority—but within the structure of formal relationships, informal patterns develop that have an identity of their own.

In a school organization, where professional knowledge and judgment are essential to success, professional personnel have considerable freedom to develop their own working relationships. Relationships, determined by the staff itself, become structured into regular, persistent patterns of operation. This structure is often as permanent and regularized as that which is prescribed.[10]

Informal patterns become so stable and resistant to change that they persist even though the formal structure is changed. McCleary conducted an investigation in which the total structure of work-oriented relationships was identified. W. W. Charters repeated the study the next school year, using the same instruments, and found that the pattern of structure had remained almost intact even though one third of the staff had changed.

Charters became interested in a follow-up of the McCleary study because he was curious about how seriously a large staff turnover disrupted the structure of peronal relationships. He writes:

9. F. J. Roethlisberger and William J. Dickson, *Management and the Worker* (Cambridge, Mass.: Harvard University Press, 1938).

10. L. E. McCleary, beginning in 1956, has documented this phenomenon empirically in a number of studies of school staffs.

When we charted the networks of contacts among teaching positions in the high school (as in a sociometric diagram), we were astonished to find that it looked almost the same as the one from the previous spring. The new English teacher assumed roughly the same pattern of contacts as the teacher who left during the summer; the new principal assumed roughly the same pattern of contacts as the former principal, and so on. We derived a measure showing the degree of similarity in the network of contacts between spring and fall—the score could range from zero to 100, with 100 indicating complete identity in contacts. The stability index, as we called it, was 82 for this high school.[11]

The structure of a school organization, composed of both formal and informal relationships, seems to be a very stable element that persists even though individuals are replaced.

The close relationship of informal and formal patterns of relationships is shown by the McCleary series of investigations in that he identified for study the "work-oriented" patterns regardless of their origin. The informal and the formal interact upon each other, and both have significance for organization—whether they are prescribed and required or whether they result from individual choices. Each person-to-person relationship, in addition to adding up to the total structure of an organization, is important in many other ways. First, person-to-person contacts function as a communication network for the organization. Second, person-to-person interactions yield the opinions and attitudes about the work of the school, standards of performance, expectations concerning member behavior, and the like. Third, most creative innovations and suggestions are likely to be raised and tried out informally rather than presented as proposals through formal channels. Most authorities agree that if all ideas, questions, and disagreements normally worked out in face-to-face contacts had to be channeled through the hierarchy of authority the administrative staff would be swamped with formal communications and organization could not function.

ORGANIZATIONAL CLIMATE

Most individuals who are members of an organization become quite sensitive to the climate of their particular groups and of the organization as a whole. They sense the climate in terms of their perceptions of the prevalent attitudes and the psychological qualities of their relationships.

11. W. W. Charters, unpublished research report (St. Louis, Mo.: Washington University, May, 1958).

The terms "morale," "feelings," "atmosphere," "friendliness" or "hostility," "consideration," and "informality" are all used in describing generalized perceptions of climate.

Organization, both in its tasks and the structure it provides for accomplishing them, creates a set of conditions to which individuals must adjust. Each person brings into an organization his own set of needs. From the individual's point of view, organizations provide the opportunities for meeting his needs and aspirations. The accommodation, or lack of it, between these two sets of needs and goals—individual and organizational—generates climate. Out of this point of view can be drawn the assumption that tasks, structure, and climate will determine the kinds and extent of individual participation and that, in turn, individual participation will tend to affect each of these three elements of organization.

Relationship of Climate to Task and Structure

Andrew Halpin, in examining the bases of successful organization, posits two essential features which he terms "group achievement" and "group maintenance." [12] He reasons that no organization can continue to exist unless it can arrange the work of its members to maintain itself as an organization and, at the same time, achieve the purposes for which it was created. He defines these two categories as:

1. Group achievement: measured in respect to how well the group accomplishes the group task.
2. Group maintenance: measured by the extent to which the group remains intact as a group; gauged in respect to "morale," "cooperation" among group members in working with one another, and other indices of job satisfaction.[13]

Cartwright and Zander describe these same two categories as follows:

It appears that most, or perhaps all, group objectives can be subsumed under one of two headings: (*a*) the achievement of some specific group goals, or (*b*) the maintenance or strengthening of the group itself. Examples of members' behaviors that serve functions of goal achievement are "initiates action," "keeps members' attention on the goal," "clarifies the issue," "develops a procedural plan," "evaluates the quality of the work done," and "makes

12. Andrew Halpin, "A Paradigm for Research on Administrator Behavior," in Roald Campbell and Russell Gregg (eds.), *Administrative Behavior in Education* (New York: Harper & Bros., 1957), pp. 169-171.

13. *Ibid.,* p. 169.

expert information available." Examples of behaviors that serve functions of group maintenance are: "keeps interpersonal relations pleasant," "arbitrates disputes," "provides encouragement," "gives the minority a chance to be heard," "stimulates self-direction," and "increases the interdependence among members." [14]

It seems reasonably clear that defining tasks and developing patterns of organization in themselves are insufficient to sound organizational performance. Mutual trust, respect, and warmth of relationships are also required, between individuals and between and within subgroupings, if an organization is to function efficiently.

Halpin carried this rationale into studies of the leadership behavior of school administrators. He employed a factor analysis procedure and could identify only two significant dimensions of leader behavior. These two dimensions were "initiating structure" and "consideration." His report includes this statement:

Initially, in the search for a solution to the analysis, a number of "blind" rotations of the axes were made, but to no avail. In each instance only a single large general factor emerged. This factor probably reflected merely a general, vague evaluation, and contained a sizeable but undefined halo effect. Since the various blind factors proved futile, we posited the initiating structure and the consideration dimensions of leader behavior. When the axes were then rotated in respect to these posited dimensions, the empirical data were found to fit the hypothesis.[15]

Halpin's consideration dimension encompasses all of the leadership activity that influences the climate of organization.

DETERMINANTS OF CLIMATE. Climate is largely attitudinal; it is the qualitative aspect of the interpersonal relationships within organization. Thus, it depends upon the individual's perceptions of his work and his status, other members, and the total organization. These perceptions are largely determined by the individual's participation in the organization; they depend upon the cumulative behavior that conditions the working relationships of individuals.

A number of investigations have been made into the determinants of

14. Dorwin Cartwright and Alvin Zander, *Group Dynamics: Research and Theory* (Evanston, Ill.: Row, Peterson & Co., 1953), p. 541.
15. Andrew W. Halpin, *The Leadership Behavior of School Superintendents,* Studies in School Administration, Monograph No. 6 (Chicago: Midwest Administration Center, University of Chicago, reprinted, 1959), p. 4.

organizational climate. Frequently they have been limited to measures of individual satisfaction with the array of activities required by the work situation. One study, however, seems to offer a much broader approach to the problem. The study began as an investigation of faculty morale as a concern of the school principal. As the study proceeded, it became apparent that school principals were concerned with a number of variables when they referred to "morale." The concept of climate was substituted.

The study identified eight dimensions of organizational activity as determinants of a school's climate. These are:

1. *Disengagement* refers to the teachers' tendency to be "not with it." This dimension describes a group that is "going through the motions," a group that is "not in gear" with respect to the task at hand. In short, this subtest focuses upon the teachers' behavior in a task-oriented situation.

2. *Hindrance* refers to the teachers' feeling that the principal burdens them with routine duties, committee demands, and other requirements which the teachers construe as unnecessary busywork. The teachers perceive the principal as hindering rather than facilitating their work.

3. *Esprit* refers to "morale." The teachers feel that their social needs are being satisfied, and that they are, at the same time, enjoying a sense of accomplishment in their job.

4. *Intimacy* refers to the teachers' enjoyment of friendly social relations with each other. This dimension describes a social-needs satisfaction which is not necessarily associated with task accomplishment.

5. *Aloofness* refers to behavior by the principal which is characterized as formal and impersonal. He "goes by the book" and prefers to be guided by rules and policies rather than to deal with the teachers in an informal, face-to-face situation. His behavior, in brief, is universalistic rather than particularistic; nomothetic rather than idiosyncratic. To maintain this style, he keeps himself—at least, "emotionally"—at a distance from his staff.

6. *Production emphasis* refers to behavior by the principal which is characterized by close supervision of the staff. He is highly directive, and plays the role of a "straw boss." His communication tends to go in only one direction, and he is not sensitive to feedback from the staff.

7. *Thrust* refers to behavior by the principal which is characterized by his evident effort in trying to "move the organization." "Thrust" behavior is marked not by close supervision but by the principal's attempt to motivate the teachers through the example which he personally sets. Apparently, because he does not ask the teachers to give of themselves any more than he willingly gives of himself, his behavior, though starkly task-oriented, is nonetheless viewed favorably by the teachers.

8. *Consideration* refers to behavior by the principal which is characterized

by an inclination to treat the teachers "humanly," to try to do a little something extra for them in human terms.[16]

This approach is not prescriptive; that is, it does not provide specific principles to be followed to attain a climate conducive to efficiency. Rather, it identifies the areas of behavior that contribute to climate and recognizes the complexity of the determinants of it. These dimensions might serve the administrator as a means of making his own analysis of climate more systematic.

REFERENCES

Abbott, Max G., *et al., Administrative Organization in Education* (Chicago: Midwest Administration Center, University of Chicago, 1958).

Council for Administrative Leadership, *The Administrative Organization of the Modern Junior High School* (Albany, N.Y.: New York Teachers Association, 1959).

Griffiths, Daniel, *et al., Organizing Schools for Effective Education* (Danville, Ill.: The Interstate Printers and Publishers, 1962).

Halpin, Andrew W. (ed.), *Administrative Theory in Education* (Chicago: Midwest Administration Center, University of Chicago, 1958).

March, James G., and Simon, Herbert, *Organization* (New York: John Wiley & Sons, 1958).

Prestwood, Elwood L., *The High School Principal and Staff Work Together* (New York: Teachers College, Bureau of Publications, Columbia University, 1957).

Simon, Herbert, A., *Administrative Behavior* (New York: The Macmillan Co., 1959).

16. Andrew W. Halpin and Don B. Croft, *The Organizational Climate of Schools* (Washington, D.C.: U.S. Office of Education, July, 1962), pp. 40-41.

Part III
Educational Program: Student and Staff Personnel

Chapter 8
Educational
Program

E ACH school achieves identity in terms of the manner in which it carries out its program. Determinants of each program's content originate far beyond the confines of the school. They are produced—as indicated in previous chapters—through current social, economic, and political forces; through traditional conceptions of schooling; through relationships with other agencies and institutions; through the backgrounds of teachers and students; and in a host of other ways. Deliberate program design is required to achieve organized, coherent, and effective education out of this welter of influences.

In periods when forces affecting education are relatively stable, basic sets of beliefs become established through research and practice. These beliefs—about what should be taught, how it should be taught, which students should take which subjects, and the like—provide a model to guide the schools.[1] Practice is closely aligned to the model. It becomes the "natural order" of things, and few questions are raised about basic premises underlying modular practice. New ideas or radical departures are easily ignored because they don't fit into the established schema—they are not too useful. Normal practice gets written into the laws, regulations, textbooks, and accrediting standards. These then become criteria for judging practice; and a consistent, though "closed," system results.[2]

1. Refer to Chapter 2 for an examination of the concept of the comprehensive school as the model for secondary education.
2. For an interesting and valuable account of this phenomenon in the field of science, see Thomas S. Kuhn, *The Structure of Scientific Revolutions* (Chicago, Ill.: University of Chicago Press, 1952).

Secondary education—encompassing both junior and senior high schools—is now well into a period in which certain premises basic to its established model are being challenged. Brought about by new demands upon education and altered emphases in learning theory and theory of knowledge, practices are being evolved that do not fit established conceptions neatly. New practices, reviewed in Chapter 3, are symptomatic of shifts in objectives, instructional methods, organization and selection of content, and areas of instruction. These shifts require new schema for ordering and rationalizing educational programs for the secondary schools. Unless adequate designs are constructed, the internal continuity and integration of programs will suffer; articulation between programs will be reduced; and confusion over materials, teacher competences, and curriculum development will result.

Programs of secondary education are built upon discrete fields of knowledge. The curriculum side of the program encompasses such concerns as which programs are to be employed and for what specific instructional purposes; how they are to be organized and related; and numerous other questions directly related to instruction. Extending beyond curriculum concerns are such matters as modes of instruction, assessment of student needs and student growth, and facilities and arrangements to stimulate readiness and enhance, reinforce, and round out a student's education. Finally, the development of institutional purposes and a rationale that fits the pieces together is required to give meaning and direction to the total program and interpret it to students, staff, and public.

The principal is expected to lead the development of program formulation and implementation. He is in a unique position to assess the influences of the youth-serving agencies of the community—including the family. As he works upon program development in the school, he must not limit himself to formal education, narrowly conceived. He needs to relate the educational program of the school to the total life of the students it serves.

ELEMENTS OF EDUCATIONAL PROGRAM

The program of a school represents the total influence system that establishes the learning environment for students. Particular professional staffs may go about ordering their school's program more or less systematically, by focusing upon certain elements rather than others, or perhaps by letting each teacher or department tend to its own area of concern with little coordination or over-all direction. Certain program elements, however, represent distinct features of educational programs as they are identified and organized by secondary schools. These include purposes and objectives, the curriculum, modes of instruction, student learnings, and a system of evaluation. Figure 8-1 is a chart identifying these program elements.

An examination of Figure 8-1 is likely to raise a question in the reader's mind concerning the meaning of curriculum. The various, often unclear, definitions of curriculum are well known. The authors do not equate the total educational program with curriculum as some authorities would. Rather, the curriculum is here conceived as *content* organized into subjects of instruction or planned learning experiences for students. Students are exposed to the curriculum in certain ways by teaching. Properly conceived and executed, modes of instruction will involve students with the curriculum so that desired learnings will result (see Figure 8-1). The system of evaluation is a part of the total program—at times it is a part of the instructional process itself; but a system of evaluation, adequately planned, permits assessment of any program element.

The rubrics used to label program elements may be altered, but this formulation seems to accommodate any curriculum theory and to describe current practice satisfactorily. In the remainder of this chapter, certain program elements are examined in detail, with particular regard to current curriculum proposals.

EDUCATIONAL PURPOSES

Basic to an adequate conception of program are a consideration of educational purposes and the development of specific objectives to guide instruction. Broad educational purposes are essential to delineate the role of the school from that of other community agencies and to establish the scope of the educational program. Within these purposes, specific learning objectives are necessary to fix responsibility for instruction and provide an adequate base for evaluation.

Martin Mayer, among others of those pressing for novel approaches,

Figure 8-1. Elements of Educational Program

Sources of Purposes	Curriculum	Modes of Instruction	Learning Products	Evaluation System
Societal demands	Content and modes of inquiry	Operational	Manipulative skills	Pupil performance
Cultural heritage	Facts	Verbal presentation	Intellectual operations	Teacher judgment
Fields of knowledge	Concepts	Discovery and intuition	Fund of knowledge	Self-evaluation
Individual needs, motivations, potentials	Principles and generalizations	Problem solving	Cognitive structures	Follow-up studies
Specific objectives	Laws, norms, rules	Situational	Value systems	
	Attitudes and values	Independent study		
	Subjects and planned learning experiences	Group learning		
		Activity and project instruction		

derides concern on the part of teachers about the aims of education.[3] The authors take exception to this view. Different classroom activities had better serve different objectives, and both teachers and administrators had better know what they are. The destruction of the theory of formal discipline and its replacement by the pragmatic axioms of immediacy and utility present a historical illustration of what can happen to such central school subjects as Latin, Greek, and mathematics. There were no convincing answers to the question "Why?" and these subjects gave way to others that had convincing advocates.

Purposes embody value preferences about what the immature need to know. Properly studied, they provide criteria for developing the curriculum and the control of what youth actually learn. Purposes always provide a view of the ends schooling is to achieve; curriculum and instruction provide the means.

Basic Functions of Education

Regardless of changing emphases, purposes of education derive from four basic functions of education. Formal education, to exist, must provide an education that conveys at least a modicum of each of the following elements: (1) development of the individual—personal, emotional, and aesthetic aspects of life; (2) modes of thought and techniques of inquiry—disciplined intellect; (3) transmission of the cultural heritage —civic and moral values; and (4) promotion of vital societal needs contributing to economic, social, and political well-being—the realm of technics.

These four aspects—personal, intellectual, civic-moral, and technical —appear to be timeless. Each society in each age alters educational content and reorders educational emphasis. Yet, whenever educational institutions fail to interpret properly and fulfill effectively these functions, the institution is replaced, or serious cultural disintegration results.[4] In the brief history of the United States the Latin grammar school and the academy were discarded, in turn; the high school, which followed,

3. Martin Mayer, *The Schools* (New York: Harper & Row, 1961), pp. 471-472.
4. For one provocative analysis by a cultural anthropologist, see Anthony F. C. Wallace, "Schools in Revolutionary and Conservative Societies," in Frederick C. Gruber (ed.), *Anthropology and Education* (Philadelphia: University of Pennsylvania Press, 1961), pp. 25-54.

Figure 8-2. Priorities of Education During Major Phases
of Cultural Change

Moral	Technic	Moral	Intellect
Intellect	Personal	Technic	Technic
Technic	Moral	Personal	Moral
Personal	Intellect	Intellect	Personal

Revolutionary Phase	Conservative Phase	Reactionary Phase	Transactional Phase

was once dramatically transformed and is currently undergoing a second transformation.

Cultural anthropologists view societal demands upon schools in terms of cyclical processes of cultural change. They posit the major phases to be revolution, conservatism, and reaction.[5] According to this theory, the priorities accorded the four basic functions of education vary depending upon the phase of cultural change. Figure 8-2 gives the authors' adaptation of this anthropological formulation. The present phase of development is classified as transactional. The impetus to cultural change is primarily a scientific-technological revolution and secondarily a social one. The long-term changes toward centralization of government, business, and industry; breakup of traditional community patterns; increased population mobility and urbanization; and the resultant shift from middle-class to affluent values seem to provide argument for this arrangement of priorities among basic educational functions.

There is some empirical evidence to support the anthropological views of educational functions and their close relationship to cultural change. Lawrence Downey conducted an extensive investigation into the task of public education. From a careful review of an array of statements concerning educational purposes by both critics and advocates of public education, Downey classified purposes into a conceptual framework— see Table 8-1. By the use of a unique Q-sort technique, he asked subjects to order the sixteen items into a sequence from least to most important, revealing individual preferences. Data from each subject permitted analysis in terms of preferences by groups according to such factors as age, sex, occupation, region of the country, and religious affiliation.

5. *Ibid.,* p. 25.

Table 8-1. Dimensions of the Task of Public Education—
A Conceptual Framework

A. Intellectual Dimensions

1. Possession of knowledge: a fund of information concepts
2. Communication of knowledge: skill to acquire and transmit
3. Creation of knowledge: Discrimination and imagination
4. Desire for knowledge: a love of learning

B. Social Dimensions

5. Man-to-man relationships: cooperation
6. Man-to-state relationships: civic rights and duties
7. Man-to-country relationships: loyalty and patriotism
8. Man-to-world relationships: interrelationships of peoples

C. Personal Dimensions

9. Physical: bodily health and development
10. Emotional: mental health and stability
11. Ethical: moral integrity
12. Aesthetic: cultural and leisure pursuits

D. Productive Dimensions

13. Vocational selection: information and guidance
14. Vocational preparation: training and placement
15. Home and family: homemaking, do-it-yourself, marriage
16. Consumer: personal buying, selling, investment

SOURCE: Lawrence Downey, The Task of Public Education
(Chicago: Midwest Administration Center, University
of Chicago, 1960).

Downey's findings, based upon the total responses, are given in Table 8-2. With the caution that these results reflect an opinion poll, they convey several points of interest. The first phase of the Downey study (see Table 8-1) broke down quite naturally into four areas clearly revealing the four basic functions of education. His tabulation of responses (see Table 8-2) bears out the ordering of priorities as proposed by the authors. Similar studies based upon smaller populations and limited to single geographic regions have tended to confirm Downey's findings.

The authors suggest that both scholarly study and empirical investigation support a belief in the four basic functions of education as pro-

Table 8-2. The Task of Public Education

The Public School

I. Primary Task: to teach and train in

1. Intellectual skills—means of acquiring and communicating knowledge
2. Creativity and discrimination—applying facts and imagination to problems
3. A desire for knowledge
4. A fund of information about

—man	—his cultural heritage
—his work world	—his ancestors and neighbors
—his physical world	—his civic responsibilities

II. Secondary Task: to supplement home and community by

1. Fostering social competence in

   —man-to-man relationships
   —civic responsibilities
   —patriotism

2. Providing an environment and instruction for personal well-being in

   —physical health
   —emotional stability
   —moral integrity
   —aesthetic appreciation

The Home and the Educative Community

I. Primary Task: to take leadership in developing

1. Physical health	4. Aesthetic appreciation
2. Emotional stability	5. Social skill
3. Moral integrity	6. Civic competence

7. Consumer skill   9. Home and family living
8. Patriotism   10. Occupational preparation

II. Secondary Task: to supplement and reinforce the school in
     its primary tasks

SOURCE: Lawrence Downey, The Task of Public Education, Chicago:
        Midwest Administration Center, University of Chicago, 1960).

posed above. They further suggest that these basic functions can serve as a broad perspective within which to develop and validate educational purposes to guide program planning.

Educational Purposes as Social Policy and Professional Responsibility

Educational purposes, properly understood, are a reflection of social policy. Whether within the school, the local community, or through professional activities of a broader nature, there is a constant effort to redefine and interpret the purposes of secondary education. This is not idle labor for there is a constant interaction of social forces that have import for school programs. No matter how much the academician would like to keep the schools isolated from social conditions and focused upon purely intellectual pursuits, he cannot ignore the educational implications in race relations, crime, unemployment, national security, traffic safety, and a host of other conditions.

Professor Phillip Monypenny, a political scientist, observes:

... in considering any school enterprise one must view its outcomes as being multiple and the stakes involved in its existence as far outrunning matters ordinarily discussed as educational philosophy or administration. No matter how much school people try to go about their business in an orderly, systematic way of tending their own back yard, what they do is of interest to far more people than those who occupy roles of either students or parents of students.[6]

Various groups from the local community to the national community must be viewed as supporting groups of the schools. Sets of values, with

6. Phillip Monypenny, "A Political Analysis of Structures for Educational Policy Making," in William P. McLure and Van Miller (eds.), *Government of Public Education for Adequate Policy Making* (Urbana, Ill.: Bureau of Educational Research, University of Illinois, 1960), pp. 16-17.

a distribution of population around them, find expression in terms of educational purposes—through formal, governmental policies if necessary. Under these circumstances, the secondary school administrator is expected to relate the program of the school to broad trends, issues, and problems and to understand the possibilities of education in meeting them.

Educational Purposes and Program Planning

General purposes, specified by Downey (Table 8-1), function in program planning at the local level in several ways. First, they provide a reference for assessment of local programs. Through such a set of purposes, judgments can be made about the relative emphasis of instruction, order of priorities, and scope of the local program. Second, they provide one means of marking out areas within which specific objectives can be identified to guide curriculum design. Third, they can serve to orient the professional staff by providing a base for the rationale of the program.

Formulations of purposes can serve as both orientation and criteria of assessment. Whether or not such statements are functional seems to depend upon the leadership in the local school—particularly in regard to the extent of commitment to them and the degree to which they are stressed in the planning and assessment phases of program development. No empirical evidence is available on this point, but an acquaintance with program development at the local school level indicates wide variation in levels of sophistication with which schools treat purposes. In schools where program improvement is seriously undertaken, a consideration of purposes is typically a primary concern.

DEVELOPMENTS IN CURRICULUM

The construction of a curriculum depends upon principles, value considerations, and theory relating to: (1) purposes, (2) nature and uses of knowledge, and (3) concept of learning. These three elements are interrelated—one cannot be separated easily from the others even for intellectual analysis. Furthermore, current practice has tended to be eclectic, incorporating features that are inconsistent, if not contradictory, within the same program. The organization of the curriculum into traditional subjects, taught within a time schedule of equivalent class periods and by standardized modes of instruction, has tended to mask fundamental curriculum issues. In the remainder of this chapter an examination of issues in curriculum and instruction is undertaken, and a fresh approach to curriculum design—one that shows promise of resolving major issues—is described.

Historical Perspective

A study of the history of the curriculum movement from the turn of the century to the present is a rewarding, though devious and extensive, effort. In 1890, fewer than 8 percent of all youth were in attendance in high school. Since a common education was to be achieved in eight years, the seventh and eighth years of schooling were devoted to intensive review and extension of elementary study. By 1920, more than 35 percent of all youth were attending high school—although two-thirds of this number would not graduate. During this thirty-year period, child labor laws, trade union activity, and numerous social pressures brought demands for a curriculum that would prepare youth for the social conditions they would face. There was an obvious need for a broadened, multipurpose curriculum.

In 1893, the report of the Committee of Ten, chaired by Harvard President Eliot, strongly supported a six-year secondary school based upon English, science, mathematics, and languages. Other national committees also tackled the problem, but the National Education Association (NEA) Commission on Reorganization of Secondary Education capped the effort to frame an acceptable statement of purposes with its famous Seven Cardinal Principles of 1918. Its recommendations included (1) a two-year junior high school composed of "exploratory" programs geared to the abilities of all youth, and (2) a series of curriculums in the high school devoted to industrial arts, agriculture, commercial subjects, household arts, and fine arts.

The result of the Commission's report was to produce a series of separate curriculums—which in the larger cities became completely separate schools—of academic, vocational, commercial, fine and performing arts, and general studies. The curriculum in general studies was for youth without the talents, ability, interests, or economic support required of the other programs. Under this scheme, the standard subjects required for college admission defined a "liberal" education, and later these became the "constant" portion of the curriculum or common education. Constants were to provide a general education, while electives were available for specialization and individualization. Without acceptable definitions, no distinctions have been made between a common or required education and a general education; nor has the balance required between general and specialized education been satisfactorily resolved.

With education in the elementary school devoted to the tool subjects, in junior high to "exploration" and "transition," and in senior high to general and specialized education, each school—even each "curriculum" within the school—tended to go its separate way. Three approaches to this problem evolved and are still in use. First, separate curriculums have tended to be eliminated and replaced by course sequences. Under this arrangement, students may change their fields of specialization or take some work in what would otherwise be completely separate curriculums. Programs of study may be developed out of the course offering so that each student, in effect, follows his own program of study. Summer schools and other special arrangements permit students to increase the number of subjects studied. Second, the junior high schools—and to a very limited extent senior high schools—have attempted to integrate or correlate subjects through core, fused, or broad field approaches. Third, curriculum development involving joint planning by the professional staffs within and between schools results in integrated courses of study by subject field. This latter device is typically referred to as curriculum articulation.

IMPACT OF THE MASSES. Without an adequate conception of general education and without a solution to the dropout problem, junior and senior high schools, from the 1890's into the present period, have been receiving dramatically larger portions of youth to educate. Traditional, textbook-oriented subjects have remained central in the curriculum. The curriculum solutions have been to decrease the number of required courses; increase the offerings of vocational, commercial, homemaking, and related subjects; and employ "ability grouping" practices within academic subjects. Two counter movements to the so-called separate subject curriculum developed after the 1918 report of the Commission on Reorganization of Secondary Education.

One effort focused upon building social and political cohesion. In 1952, the Education Policies Commission of the NEA asserted, "In the secondary school, no responsibility is so great as that of teaching the principles of the democratic way of life." [7] This approach to general edu-

7. Educational Policies Commission, National Education Association, *Education for All American Youth: A Further Look* (Washington, D.C.: the Association, 1952), p. 7.

cation encompassed the concept of the community school, with education "directly concerned with improving all aspects of living in the community." [8] It was largely an outgrowth of John Dewey's insistence upon the social uses of intelligence and his theoretical and experimental approach to a curriculum based upon the common vocations. Dewey's method of problem solving was used to combine the concept of the community school with a curriculum composed of the "real life" problems of youth. This movement waned rapidly as social mobility, mass communications, and mass production destroyed the social values attendant to the small, local community.

A second movement, often termed "life adjustment education," received formal recognition with the Prosser Resolution in 1945.[9] It incorporates a series of attempts to reform the sterile, narrowly conceived subject curriculum to include common learnings, needs of youth, and citizenship education. Focusing primarily upon immediate needs—sometimes called developmental tasks—of youth, life adjustment education employs a core of common learnings as the central content of general education. To quote directly from the United States Office of Education publication: "Life adjustment education programs are evaluated in terms of each pupil's educational progress evidenced by skills, habits, attitudes, understandings, and appreciations. Through these he works out his participation in individual, family, work, community, and civic activities rather than in terms of ability to master abstract concepts in logically organized subject matter courses." [10]

Whether or not a block-time core program is employed, studies such as English, social studies, mathematics, and science are to be reorganized in terms of immediate, social problems. Objectives of a general science course illustrate the influence of this point of view:

1. Functional information or facts about matters such as: our universe: earth, moon, stars, weather, and climate.
2. Functional concepts, such as: all life has evolved from simpler forms.
3. Functional understanding of principles, such as: energy can be changed from one form to another.
4. Instrumental skills, such as: ability to perform simple manipulatory activities with science equipment.

8. Paul R. Hanna and Robert A. Naslund, "The Community School Defined," in *Fifty-second Yearbook of the National Society for the Study of Education,* Part I (Chicago, Ill.: University of Chicago Press, 1953), p. 52.

9. Cited in U.S. Office of Education, *Education for Life Adjustment* (Washington, D.C.: Federal Security Agency, 1948), pp. 1-3.

10. *Ibid.*

5. Problem-solving skills, such as: ability to sense a problem and define the problem.
6. Attitudes, such as: open-mindedness, willingness to consider new facts.
7. Appreciations, such as: appreciation of the contributions of scientists.
8. Interests, such as: interest in some phase of science as a recreational activity or hobby.[11]

The test of content is functionality—its usefulness and immediacy—whether one can directly observe if the learner has attained it.[12]

Reaction to the principles of immediacy, functionalism, and utility as primary criteria for selection of content of a general education was swift and bitter. Arthur E. Bestor led the attack in *Educational Wastelands* (1953) and *Restoration of Learning* (1954). Both titles were descriptive of the traditionalists' view of the then current educational emphasis. The issues were never sharply drawn, and although debate began between a few academicians and educators, it remained acrimonious and largely unproductive. The extreme position of the life adjustment movement faded as it normally would have. A general education remained —wedded to aims and content reminiscent of the old academy of the post-Colonial period. Bestor and his cohorts insisted that the academic curriculum was good for all time and for all students—with suitable modifications. The suitable modifications were never explored by the extreme traditionalists.

COMPREHENSIVE SCHOOLS REDEFINED. James Conant clarified the model upon which junior and senior high schools were to design programs. After a series of surveys Dr. Conant set forth criteria for programs in *The American High School Today* (1959) and *Education in the Junior High School Years* (1960). Conant subscribed to the concept of the comprehensive school at both junior and senior high school levels, recognized the value of local control with modifications, and recommended approaches to increase the challenge of school work. His recommendations follow:

11. Victor H. Noll, "The Objectives of Science Instruction," in *Science Education in American Schools, Forty-sixth Yearbook of the National Society for the Study of Education,* Part I (Chicago: University of Chicago Press, 1947), pp. 28-29.

12. For a current treatment, see William H. Lucio and John D. McNeil, *Supervision: A Synthesis of Thought and Action* (New York: McGraw-Hill Book Co., 1962), especially Chapter 12, "A Rationale for Curriculum Development," pp. 241-273.

JUNIOR HIGH SCHOOL PROGRAM CRITERIA [13]

1. The following subjects should be required of all pupils in grades 7 and 8: English (including heavy emphasis on reading skills and composition), social studies (including emphasis on history and geography), mathematics (except as noted in Item 2), and science.

2. A small fraction of pupils should start algebra (or one of the new brands of mathematics) in grade 8. Some, if not all, pupils should start the study of a modern foreign language on a conversational basis with a bilingual teacher in grade 7.

3. Instruction in the basic skills begun in the elementary school should be continued as long as pupils can gain from the instruction. This statement applies to reading and arithmetic. Pupils with average ability should read at or above grade level; superior pupils considerably above grade level. By the end of grade 9, even the poorest readers (except the mentally retarded) should read at least at the sixth-grade level.

4. Group activities which have particular relevance for early adolescents should be part of the total program. These include musical and dramatic activities, assembly and homeroom programs, interest clubs, intramural athletics, and student council.

5. Provisions should be made to assure a smooth transition for the young adolescent from the elementary school to the secondary school. [Authors' note: Conant recommends a combination of block-time and departmentalized schedule to meet this recommendation.]

6. The daily class schedule should be sufficiently flexible to avoid the necessity for pupils to make choices between, for example, science and foreign languages.

7. Instruction should be organized to provide intellectual challenge for the whole range of abilities found in a school.

8. A full-time specialist, or the equivalent, in guidance and testing should be available for every 250-300 pupils in grades 7 and 8.

9. Meaningful homework is profitable in grades 7, 8, and 9; drudgery, however, is not meaningful homework. Teachers and principals should develop careful procedures to assure coordination of homework assignments between teachers of different subjects. High standards should be maintained in academic courses in grades 7, 8, and 9 because of the mastery of basic skills.

10. In the ninth grade, the curriculum should provide for the usual sequential elective program as well as the continuation of the required courses in general education.

11. Satisfactory instruction requires that the following facilities be available for pupils in grades 7 and 8: (1) a well-stocked library (see

13. James B. Conant, *Education in the Junior High School Years* (New York: McGraw-Hill Book Co., 1960), pp. 16-37.

Standards for School Library Programs, American Library Association, 1960); (2) a gymnasium with locker rooms and showers; (3) specially equipped home economics rooms for girls and industrial arts rooms for boys; (4) an auditorium or assembly space for at least half of the student body; (5) cafeteria space for at least one-third of the student body.

12, 13, and 14. These recommendations refer to systemwide provisions for coordination and articulation, supervision, professional staff and teacher load, and the leadership role of the principal.

SENIOR HIGH SCHOOL PROGRAM CRITERIA [14]

A. Adequacy of general education for all as judged by
  1. Offerings in English, American literature, and composition
  2. Social studies including American history
  3. Ability grouping in required courses
B. Adequacy of nonacademic elective program as judged by
  4. The vocational programs for boys and commercial programs for girls
  5. Opportunities for supervised work experience
  6. Special provisions for very slow readers
C. Special arrangements for the academically talented students
  7. Special provisions for challenging the highly gifted
  8. Special instruction in developing reading skills
  9. Summer sessions from which able students may profit
  10. Individualized programs (absence of tracks or rigid programs)
  11. School day organized into seven or more instructional periods
D. Other features
  12. Adequacy of the guidance service
  13. Student morale
  14. Well-organized homerooms
  15. The success of the school in promoting an understanding between students with widely different academic abilities and vocational goals (effective social interaction among students)

Dr. Conant's recommendations were widely circulated and discussed. His major contribution was to crystallize the best of current practice. Unlike most scholarly critics who feel free to make pronouncements about public education, Dr. Conant made systematic surveys and observations of practice. He tempered his recommendations in terms of attainable conditions, and he gave freely of his time to listen to practical problems faced by schools and to present extensions of his views. In a

14. James B. Conant, *The American High School Today* (New York: McGraw-Hill, Book Co., 1959), pp. 10-11.

subsequent work, he investigated the need for diversity among schools by contrasting conditions in slum and suburban schools in the metropolitan areas of the nation.[15]

Secondary Education: an Unresolved Issue

Dr. Conant's work, though a valuable contribution, has resolved none of the basic issues. He has clearly marked out the specifications of a quality program in terms of current practice. He has not provided a rationale for curriculum—what is to be studied and for what purposes; nor has he specified the kind of education needed for the future and the grounds upon which continuous appraisal can be made. In short, his recommendations have provided a set of temporary norms for practice. If followed blindly, they will become standards as rigid as any now in existence and will require another equally rigorous effort to establish a competing set to meet new conditions in the near future. If tempered by reason and followed by serious study, they may provide a base from which constructive changes can be made.

The question of what is a needed and defensible education at the secondary levels, what is its content, and how it might be organized for instruction remains. The observation made by John Dewey in 1936 is as appropriate today. He wrote, "The problem as to the direction in which we shall seek for order and clarity in education has now become the most important question facing education and educators today." [16] The main stress of the traditional curriculum is upon civic-moral and intellectual values. It is not a mass concept—it aims at selecting and training the few. Secondary education according to this view is not a *terminus ad quem* but a *terminus a quo*—a significant part of its function is to sift out and turn away the unfit and begin intensive scholarly study. Bestor and the other traditionalists are very clear on this point.

Wherever the European tradition is followed in education, the United States included, the content has been rooted in the seven liberal arts—the trivium and the quadrivium. The technics and aspects of the personal dimensions, referred to in an earlier section of this chapter, are to have no place in secondary education. The commentary of Socrates regarding the shoemaker is final and conclusive—any vocational or per-

15. James B. Conant, *Slums and Suburbs* (New York: McGraw-Hill Book Co., 1962).
16. John Dewey, "Rationality in Education," *The Social Frontier,* December, 1936.

sonal activity that contains no general notions of theoretical importance is unsuitable for formal education. Traditional secondary education is antivocational; any inclusion of such matters is anti-intellectual.

Traditional education through the turn of the century was correct and wise. Until the 1920's, when the United States became the exception, nations were not sufficiently wealthy to release youth from the production of basic economic needs and to provide facilities of formal education. Only within the past ten years has it become recognized that education is a *precondition* of economic progress rather than its result (see Chapter 2). The training of elites as the primary function of secondary education has given ground rapidly since the 1918 report of the Commission on Reorganization of Secondary Education. And yet the overwhelming majority of secondary schools—particularly, but not only, in their college preparatory programs—have never been, and are not now, progressive in curriculum content or methods.

Modification of the Traditional Curriculum

Even though traditional theory remains vigorous—and in many ways an obstacle to curriculum reform—the curriculum of secondary education has undergone significant modification. The subject offering has been broadened to give prominence to the study of science. Vocational, agricultural, commercial, homemaking, and purely personal interest subjects—including such subjects as photography, crafts, and creative writing—have been given a place, though a secondary one, in modern school programs. These latter developments have been piecemeal modifications, however, not encompassed within a consistent theoretical position. They have, in effect, been tacked onto the existing structure. This, in large part, is a source of friction and competition within professional staffs and often a matter of public debate over the "frill subjects."

The only grounds for legitimacy and respectability of these subjects are that they are demanded by the conditions of modern living. President Eliot of Harvard University at his 1869 inauguration championed the cause of subjects representing the personal and technical dimensions of education by stating that any established subject was worth studying. This kind of curriculum justification is not in the realm of theory. It establishes a norm that persists as long as popular demand and the influence of the norm-creating agency wish to sustain it.

Traditional subjects have themselves undergone fundamental modification. Without rejecting the Platonic, or at best Aristotelian, rationalism the universities have maintained the theory of the liberal arts. Yet these subjects are now being worked out in terms of other theories of knowledge and other psychologies of learning. The problem-solving method epitomized in John Dewey's *How We Think* created major shifts away from didactic teaching—that is, away from syllogistic and deductive reasoning. Meanwhile, connectionist and Gestalt psychologies completely undercut the formal-discipline psychology of the rationalists.

Within traditional subjects the content has become problem- or topic-centered with the use of the "teaching unit" approach. Wherever possible, students are confronted with real and contemporary problems. Learning by doing is a key concept, for students are expected to be able to apply what they learn in terms of specific situations. There is considerable value in these assertions, but they are not entirely correct. The significant point, however, is that an unbearable burden is placed upon an outmoded and fragmented curriculum structure by the impact of science, the overwhelming amounts of new knowledge, the necessity to educate the masses more fully, the demands for specialization, and the conditions of mass society.

NEW DEPARTURES: CURRICULUM AND INSTRUCTION

The present mass of large-scale curriculum projects gives evidence of a keen interest in reshaping parts of the curriculum. The prototype of this effort is the Physical Science Study Committee (PSSC). In this project, scientists and educators worked together to update the teaching of physics. If this had been the extent of their effort, however, the work of this group would be of little note. Although several features of the project were revolutionary—including the mechanisms for rapid implementation in the schools—two aspects are significant here. First, the content was rigorously selected to organize and relate only the most basic aspects of physics. Second, the materials were designed to provide for an imaginative blend of didactic, problem-solving, and discovery modes of teaching.

These two features are particularly interesting. In fact, they are an important key to an understanding of new curriculum developments. The real innovations in curriculum are not technological—teaching machines, television, and the like; nor are they new content, per se—revolutionary ideas, concepts, and values. Rather, the revolutionary and new elements in secondary education are the grounds upon which subjects are organized and the psychological principles that underlie teaching.

The teaching machine may serve to illustrate the point. The major contribution of this device is the detailed, systematic way in which the learner is led to understand the internal logic of the content to be learned. Comprehension is tested point by point, so the pupil is never taken beyond any point of confusion. He is never "lost" as is so often the case in traditional textbook study. The result, according to the noted educational psychologist, Lee J. Cronbach, is:

Now the writing [of texts] is so lucid and well structured that the reader cannot escape the meaning even when it is presented in ordinary text form with the blanks filled in. Activity-and-reinforcement is most needed when lessons are nonsense, and becomes less and less necessary as presentations become clearer. If I am right, the machine will be relegated to its proper role as a proving ground for text material in draft form and as a laboratory instrument helping us toward a science of clarity.[17]

The contributions of the new curriculum developments focus upon the internal logic—the structure of what is to be learned and the means of achieving more efficient learning.

Nature of Subjects and the Structure of Knowledge

Although the point is argued by some, subjects of instruction do not have existential status. They are human creations and depend upon the means by which knowledge is organized for use. "Use" must be interpreted broadly, for knowledge may be employed for understanding, for appreciation, and in other ways than for direct application to immediate problems. There could not have been a course in physics called "mechanics" until Newton's famous *Principia* appeared, nor a course in electricity until Faraday and Kelvin demonstrated how it could be dealt with understandably, logically, and consistently. Fields of knowledge become established as facts are correlated, concepts developed, and as theoretical propositions that explain their relationships are tested and confirmed.

17. Lee J. Cronbach, *Issues Current in Educational Psychology,* a paper prepared for the Social Science Research Council Conference on Mathematical Learning, May, 1962, pp. 15-16.

Harry Broudy, noted educational philosopher, has defined a subject as containing the following elements:

1. A set of entities or units that are described or defined. In chemistry, for example, there are atoms, molecules, elements, compounds. In history there are events. . . . These entities are sometimes called "constructs" because they are logically constructed by the scientist.
2. These entities are related to each other in some fashion. In history events are related by cause and effect or in chronological order. . . . In chemistry the units combine, break up, and recombine according to laws.
3. There are facts or data. That is to say, there are statements that are taken as proved or proved sufficiently to spare them any further questioning.
4. There are hypotheses that purport to account for certain facts, e.g., the migration of birds at various seasons, the origin of galaxies, the causes of some diseases, and the nature of light energy, which have not been accepted as being beyond controversy.
5. There are well-established hypotheses that are accepted by the leaders of the discipline as being warranted on evidence already adduced for them.
6. Each discipline has its own method of investigation.[18]

Major new curriculum projects have aimed to describe the structure of the particular subject so as to incorporate the elements as Broudy has enumerated them. In addition, they have attempted, with some singular successes, to select the most powerful concepts in terms of both generality and potential productivity of new knowledge. The purpose is to get the learner to understand the network of propositions supporting a given field of knowledge and to know it as a system, itself constantly being reorganized, in order to account for ever new experience. Mathematics and science are particularly fruitful fields for this type of curriculum reconstruction, and in these fields the effort to move from teaching the products of inquiry to inquiry itself is most promising.

Emphasis upon Intellectual Learning

George Stoddard throughout *The Meaning of Intelligence* (1944) seems to be cautioning the pragmatists that the individual learns by thinking about what he is doing or about to do, not just "by doing." Rather than active learning for the sake of activity—often a means of

18. Harry S. Broudy, *Building a Philosophy of Education* (Englewood Cliffs, N.J.: Prentice-Hall, 1961), p. 323.

manipulating students to learn prearranged solutions, the emphasis in new curriculum proposals is to convey habits of thinking and ways of gathering and looking at data that will make factual knowledge more intelligible. The test of the value of this kind of instruction is not so much what factual knowledge is gained but what intellectual habits are developed and how rapidly and easily the student learns later on.

The concept of readiness has, perhaps, received most attention. The tendency has been to believe that biological maturation limited the immature in what he could learn at a given age. Research, particularly that of Piaget and Inhelder, indicates that there are fewer and less rigid limits than the doctrine of readiness would imply. Complex mathematical concepts have been taught to first- and second-grade children; reading has been taught to three- and four-year-olds, and there are numerous other examples of the negation of the readiness principle. Brownell, Moser and other psychologists have restated the concept of readiness as merely the "ability to take on new skills or ideas, that and nothing more." Readiness, then, is determined more by the level of development of concepts and ways of organizing information than by physical and neurological maturation. This implies a sequential curriculum in which the content is rigorously selected to exhibit a logically and intuitively consistent schema for learning.

New approaches, as promising as they are, raise many more questions than they solve. First, within subjects there is no clear understanding of the proper placement of materials—how early a given concept can be learned or when a given concept should be learned in terms of sequence. Second, the emphasis upon structure to the exclusion of practical topics is almost certain to produce its own brand of educational failure and result in a reaction. Third, the proper conditions for didactic, discovery, and problem-solving learning are far from clear. Professor Beberman of the University of Illinois Committee on Mathematics (UICM) has long advocated that students discover mathematical constructs before they are verbalized for classroom analysis—the verbalization of rules is the end product of this type of teaching and not the initial activity as in the traditional teacher-presentation method. Others, including David Ausubel of the same institution, strongly disagree and support the concept of verbal learning.[19]

19. David P. Ausubel, "In Defense of Verbal Learning," *Educational Theory,* Vol. XI, No. 1, January, 1961, pp. 15-25.

OVER-ALL CURRICULUM DESIGN

The new curriculum approaches seem to be most appropriate in the areas of science and mathematics. Although some interesting developments have been reported in the teaching of English, social studies, and foreign languages, they are far less dramatic. The approach to curriculum reform through separate subjects is, itself, not a sufficient solution to major curriculum problems. What is needed is a design by which schools can achieve organized, coherent, and effective patterns of instruction. The central curriculum issue is whether or not the traditional subjects are the ones that are needed. If the alteration of content is desirable, perhaps the modes of organizing the curriculum are just as important. Traditional subject patterns are related not only to the level of knowledge of a past period but to outmoded cultural patterns.

Herbert Spencer, who fostered the first attempts to insert science into curriculum, was the first to press seriously for a radical reorganization of knowledge into new subjects for the purpose of instruction. He cut across the traditional organization of material and proposed new ways of structuring subjects—a new curriculum design. Spencer was compelled to his new design when he raised the philosophical question, "What knowledge is of most worth?" Today, this is not just a philosophical question; it is pedagogically important.

Curriculum Design: A Proposal

The need for a new "grand design" for secondary education has been clear for at least three decades. Throughout this chapter the shortcomings of the traditional design have been examined. There remains to be presented the proposal of a design for secondary education that offers the possibility of resolving major curriculum issues. One that deserves particular attention has been proposed by Harry S. Broudy. It is briefly summarized in this section.[20]

Professor Broudy bases his proposal for an educational program upon the demands of mass society, the relationship of general education to specialized education, the uses of schooling, and the scheme for the classification of all knowledge developed by Joseph T. Tykociner. A basic

20. The authors are indebted to Professors Broudy, B. O. Smith, and Joseph Burnett for permitting the study of a draft manuscript of a book devoted to the development of a theory of curriculum supporting this design. Readers may also wish to consult Broudy, *op. cit.,* Chapters 12 and 13.

point of departure entails examination of the ways school learnings are to be used to attain self-fulfillment in modern, mass society. Each individual can use what he learns in the following ways:

1. *Unconsciously*—out of habit and conditioning one learns to respond in certain ways without awareness of how or where a given response was attained.

2. *Associatively*—by automatic response, as one learns and employs the multiplication tables; conscious overlearning is essential because a perfect recall is necessary to successful use.

3. *Replicatively*—an operation is repeated as learned. Complex skills, even attitudes, are learned and invoked when the individual sees the elements common or similar to circumstances previously learned. Present teaching methodology is aimed primarily at achieving this type of learning by the use of real-life situations and problems.

4. *Applicatively*—the handling of unstructured problems and situations not amenable to handling by the simple recall of past learning. Here, key principles and general concepts give clues to the missing or unfamiliar elements. Once such a problem is solved, the next case elicits a response that is replicative.

5. *Interpretively*—when a situation must be organized first in order to be dealt with effectively, knowledge is employed interpretively. It is the means of achieving a perspective, an orientation, in order to decide the specific knowledge to be applied.

According to Broudy, the specialist uses knowledge replicatively, and occasionally applicatively. His field of knowledge is narrow and deep. Within his narrow field of interest he has to have access to a large amount of knowledge and skills and has to learn the types and categories of problems he is going to encounter. This is true of the surgeon, auto mechanic, and schoolteacher. All need a sound general education both to attain perspectives of their own specialty and to function fully as individuals in a society of specialists. General education entails the mastery of concepts and principles of the widest generality that can serve to provide the individual with cognitive and valuative maps. Such mental maps permit the easy identification and classification of problems and situations and provide the means for deciding the level of attack upon them.

With this theory of the uses of schooling, Broudy proceeds to classify knowledge into a curriculum design for the attainment of a general education within grades 7 to 12. Six areas of study are proposed (see Figure 8-3); these are:

Figure 8-3. Curriculum of Common Studies, Grades 7-12

Grade or Difficulty Level

	Grade 7	Grade 8	Grade 9	Grade 10	Grade 11	Grade 12
AREA I	Symbolic tools: language of ordinary discourse language of quantity language of the arts					
II	Basic areas of knowledge: e.g., physics, chemistry, biology					
III	Developmental studies: evolution of cosmos and man evolution of groups and institutions evolution of culture and mankind					
IV	Selected societal problems					
V	Exemplars of literature, art, philosophy					
VI	Individual problems: guidance and counseling					

SOURCE: Derived from Harry S. Broudy, <u>Building a Philosophy of Education</u> (Englewood Cliffs, N.J.: Prentice-Hall, 1961), Chapter 13.

I. *Symbolic tools*—the use of symbol systems of language, quantity, poetry, art, and music. The test of achievement is that of facility —of correct and easy use.

II. *Basic areas of knowledge*—a small number of precise, logically ordered disciplines, as, for example, mathematics, physics, chemistry, and biology. Each field should be reduced to a minimum of central concepts studied rigorously over a long period of time.

The test of achievement is mastery and application to the problems of the field.

III. *Developmental studies*—the evolution of cosmos and man, groups and social institutions, culture and mankind. The object is to attain perspective, not to master subject matter. The methodology would be thematic. The test of achievement is the attainment of perspective.

IV. *Selected societal problems*—perfection of the arts of deliberation; not knowledges and skills, but strategies.

V. *Exemplars of literature, art, and philosophy*—develop values and discrimination, seek what might be termed "taste." Study relating to the development of literature or art would be organized under the subject "developmental studies."

VI. *Individual problems*—guidance and counseling; the study of one's own problems and the skills and knowledge for meeting them.

The mechanical details of organizing these subjects and of scheduling them within the restrictions of current secondary school practice have been examined by Professor Broudy and his associates. The proposal is that these subjects shall make up the entire instructional program and that all other specialized subjects and currently required studies, including physical education, shall be organized as activities. The schema of a school program presented in an earlier section of this chapter would make this theoretically feasible.

The Educational Leader and Curriculum Development

The authors have presented the formulation of curriculum in the preceding section as a theoretically sound approach to the problem and one that may stir the reader to probe deeper into the study of curriculum—particularly the premises that underlie traditional practice and new proposals. The authors have accepted the view throughout this book that educational administrators are, by necessity, pragmatists. They must operate within a complex of forces to bring educational programs into being and work continuously to improve them. Curriculum, modes of instruction, and all other features of a school, within the purview of its administrator, comprise institutional phenomena. Fruitful inquiry rests upon an institutional analysis of the particular determinants of curriculum at a particular time (see Chapter 2 and the introduction to this chapter).

One must ask how and why new materials are introduced into the curriculum and old materials rearranged or discarded. Since the form a curriculum takes in a particular school is determined as much by the individuals involved as by the philosophy or theory accepted in its general formulation by most of them, the administrator needs to be able to distinguish between theories of curriculum and those aspects of curriculum that are determined by social forces. This is not to pay lip service to theory. On the contrary, there is a major point of issue between the public school administrators and others who see educational programs as entirely rationally derived. The latter point to the undue concentration of the administrator upon the institutionalized aspects of curriculum to the neglect of a theoretical analysis of the positions taken. Perhaps the type of treatment given in this chapter can provide a basis for a more compatible arrangement between theory and practice.

REFERENCES

Association for Supervision and Curriculum Development, *New Insights and the Curriculum* (Washington, D.C.: the Association, 1963).

Ausubel, David P., *Learning by Discovery: Rationale and Mystique* (Urbana, Ill.: Bureau of Educational Research, University of Illinois, 1961).

———, "In Defense of Verbal Learning," *Educational Theory,* Vol. XI, No. 1, January, 1961.

Broudy, Harry S., *Building a Philosophy of Education* (Englewood Cliffs, N.J.: Prentice-Hall, 1961).

Broudy, Harry S., Smith, B. Othanel, and Burnett, Joe R., *Democracy and Excellence in American Secondary Education* (Chicago: Rand McNally & Co., 1964).

Bruner, Jerome S., *The Process of Education* (Cambridge, Mass.: Harvard University Press, 1960).

Fraser, Dorothy (ed.), *Current Curriculum Studies in Academic Subjects* (Washington, D.C.: National Education Association, 1962).

Heath, Robert W. (ed.), *New Curricula* (New York: Harper & Row, 1964).

Hendrix, Gertrude, "Learning by Discovery," *The Mathematics Teacher,* Vol. LIV, No. 5, May, 1961.

Inhelder, Bärbel, and Piaget, Jean, *The Growth of Logical Thinking: From Childhood to Adolescence,* translated by Anne Parsons and Stanley Milgram (New York: Basic Books, 1958).

Mayer, Martin, *The Schools* (New York: Harper & Bros., 1961).

Thayer, V. T., *The Role of the School in American Society* (New York: Dodd, Mead & Co., 1960).

Chapter 9
Extending
Educational
Opportunity

THE administrative function, broadly conceived, is that of insuring an appropriate education to each individual—appropriate in terms of both curriculum and instruction. If the latter were the only concern, the problem would be complex, to be sure, but reasonably manageable. Instruction involves pedagogical questions. To deal with these, the profession furnishes technical knowledge and methods of inquiry and evaluation. The curriculum problem, however, is another matter. Here, the dominant questions are not resolved primarily in terms of specialized knowledge and empirical evidence. Questions in the realm of curriculum —those concerning what is to be taught and for what purposes—call largely for answers in terms of value preferences. For example, should vocational training be provided in the junior and senior high school? If so, which vocations are to be studied? And which students—if not all —are to study them? Should a student talented in art or music be given specialized study at the expense of other subjects?

The questions posed refer to the area of studies usually termed "specialized" or "elective," rather than "common" or "required." There are similar questions that apply with equal force to the area of common studies when one considers the special needs of the academically talented or the slow learner. Also, parallel questions must be raised in considering the handicapped or in providing educationally valuable student activities. In fact, like questions occur in whatever areas the school wishes to extend educational opportunity beyond a standard, single curriculum pattern.

It is worthwhile to note that in almost all other countries the kinds of considerations attendant to the extension of educational opportunity are not within the province of local educational leaders. The central educational authority prepares an outline of study and enforces its teaching through inspection, control of textbooks and instructional materials, and by examinations. Local professional participation in curriculum matters is limited both by central control of the curriculum itself and, where some latitude is permitted, by allocation of resources from the central authority. Under these conditions, local professional responsibility is largely limited to pedagogical matters.

Wherever diversity is valued and the development of human potential is recognized to be the ultimate aim of education, professional leaders seek means to extend educational opportunity beyond normal curriculum provisions. Fortunately, in the public schools of the United States, the expectations are that all youth are to be served, not by a uniform curriculum for all, but by curricular provisions that meet individual needs. Under these conditions the primary impediments to special provisions are likely to be lack of local leadership and lack of resources. Symptoms of these lacks are the persistent efforts at federal and state levels to extend vocational training, programs for the academically able and the handicapped, and aid for the study of the problems of the dropout. Although these efforts have been initiated by other motives, many administrators have been able to prevent them from overbalancing the local program in any one direction. Where this has been done, the net effect is to extend educational opportunities for the individual.

SPECIAL PROVISIONS TO MEET INDIVIDUAL STUDENT NEEDS

Success in extending educational opportunity to any significant degree depends heavily upon the skill and interest of the professional staff. Awareness throughout the staff—among teachers, guidance workers, and administrators—of student potentials and deficiencies is a necessary step. Special provisions cannot be effectively utilized without staff cooperation both in the initial planning and design of programs and in their successful implementation. Leadership by the administration is also essential, for little can be accomplished until the means are made available to study student needs and to experiment with various approaches for meeting them.

Determining Need for Special Provisions

Many basic procedural changes in schools reflect attempts to gear for continuous and systematic study of student needs. In order to facilitate broadened program provisions, alterations are being made in procedures for classification and assignment of students, pupil accounting systems, and the evaluation and reporting of student progress designed for narrowly conceived academic purposes.

One major influence has resulted from the development of professionally staffed, student personnel programs. Here the emphasis upon understanding the individual and aiding him to identify and meet his own problems has had a favorable effect. Personnel services, operating to help the student make the most of schooling, have in the process aided the school in the identification of student needs and in the assessment of its program.

Much of the information about students that previously was unavailable or could not be collected systematically is now being routinely recorded, collated, and studied. Devices now in regular use in many schools include, for example, standard testing programs, interview schedules, personality and interest inventories, case studies, anecdotal reports, sociometric measures, special diagnostic and intelligence tests, teacher behavioral records, and follow-up studies.

A planned system for identification of student needs should yield data relating to:

1. Individual potentials—in academic pursuits, areas requiring specialized talents as in music and the arts, and human relations and leadership.

2. Specialized interests—by the time of admission to junior high school many areas of interest have become established; these will result in selected effort with resulting further development of specialization; or, if contrary to the school program, they will contribute to further loss in level of achievement relative to other students.

3. Achievement—assessment of development in mental, social, physical, and educational growth.

4. Deficiencies and handicaps—identification of learning problems,

deficiencies in skills, emotional and social problems affecting adjustment, mental retardation, physical handicaps—particularly those relating to sight, hearing, speech, orthopedic, and psychomotor impairment.

Identification of student needs is, of course, only an initial step in adequate program development. Diagnosis, classification, determination of the extent of incidence, and the design and trial of special provisions are steps which must also be completed. Most special provisions require planned procedures for the identification of needs and the assignment of students. In programs for the talented, as an example, careful observation by teachers is usually an important part of identification in addition to standard testing and actual student performance.

Types of Special Provisions

Special provisions may be classified into four general types: individualization of instruction, remedial and corrective aid, facilitative studies, and differentiated programs. Each type requires special administrative planning and decisions, and elements of each are likely to be found in both junior and senior high schools. The exceptions occur most frequently in schools that are small and poorly supported, or in schools that consciously restrict enrollment by maintaining a limited program. The four types of special provisions are examined here, with illustrations and with indications of the distinctions between them in terms of administrative concerns.

INDIVIDUALIZATION OF INSTRUCTION. Individualization is the oldest and most common type of special provision. Within regular classrooms teachers attempt to treat differing needs in numerous ways. They group students, for example, employ project work, use different sets of texts, and provide choices of work for students. Such standard practices can now, however, be considerably extended even within the traditional classroom. Among the new possibilities are the use of programmed texts; "contract" methods, whereby students work through planned sequences of topics at their own rate; television; and even computer-programmed learning. In addition, other arrangements can greatly increase the individual teacher's potential to supply this type of special provision—as with the use of teacher teams, paraprofessionals, and project rooms. The point should be obvious that even in traditional patterns individualization to any significant extent requires in-service training of staff, special facilities and materials, and allocation of time to staff for detailed preparation, as well as encouragement, support, and close supervision by the administration.

Other provisions for individualized instruction depend directly upon the administrator. He must make basic decisions—hopefully, out of careful study and local experimentation—in the provision and use of material resource centers, language laboratory and project centers, teacher teams, educational television, learning machines, and project courses such as PSSC (Physical Science Study Committee) physics or UICM (University of Illinois Committee on Mathematics) mathematics. He is also responsible for certain special provisions for individualization which are nothing more than administrative devices. Scheduling students into tracks or levels, acceleration, and enrichment plans—particularly those providing extra periods and flexible periods—are basically administrative plans attempting to increase the efficiency of the school to provide for student differences. The effectiveness of such plans requires the involvement of the professional staff, of course, as there is little reason to employ the plan unless significant changes in instruction are involved.

REMEDIAL AND CORRECTIVE AID. Within even the smallest secondary school population, learning difficulties and deficiencies occur. Only in carefully selected student populations can such conditions be minimized, and they can only be eliminated completely by a weeding-out process of failing and rejecting students. Reading seems to be the most widespread problem demanding special remedial procedures. Whether it is the most widespread or merely the most readily detected because it is the skill most crucial to textbook learning is not clear. Deficiencies that result in learning blocks in arithmetic may be just as extensive; following closely are difficulties requiring psychological therapy and speech therapy. These four major categories and others, including lack of adequate study habits, deficiencies due to temporary health problems, and those caused by deep-rooted cultural deprivation and long-standing nutritional deficiencies—now showing up in major proportions in the large cities—are some of the more prevalent.

In almost all cases detection occurs because of educational failure. Even in such medical cases as brain tumor, the first symptoms are sometimes sighted by the observant teacher or counselor. Whatever the problem, however, proper diagnosis is essential in all cases, and usually treatment, on an individual basis, by skilled specialists is necessary. The degree of incidence and the means necessary to provide adequate treatment make all but the common types of remedial and corrective aid difficult to provide within a single school. Remedial reading teachers, teachers of study skills, and speech and psychological therapists are found in large and increasing numbers in the secondary schools. Often school districts of moderate size are able to provide such aid on a cooperative basis with other social agencies, through joint efforts with other school districts, or through an intermediate district organization.

The primary concerns are early detection, adequate diagnosis, and some means of referral. Here again, the administrator is called upon to provide the organizational structure to facilitate such arrangements. In-service training of teachers and development of both planned procedures and adequate relationships with referral agencies—either within the school or outside it—require administrative attention.

FACILITATIVE STUDIES. A third type of special provision refers to the extension of the instructional program into areas beyond traditional academic practice. This type is best labeled "facilitative" in terms of provisions for additional opportunities to individual students. These provisions include instruction in personal typing, speech and drama, developmental reading, and creative writing outside of normal course work in English; special seminar work in science or the humanities, also outside of normal course work; and various special-interest studies such as modern dance, music composition, and photography. Typically, these studies are noncredit or are taken in addition to the traditional Carnegie-unit requirements at both junior and senior high school levels. Other extensions are made in the category of student activities, including subject-centered clubs, publications, student government, and skill development in physical education.

The kinds of activities noted in this category are facilitative of individual development. They contribute to the fuller accomplishment of educational objectives, and frequently they can be shown to contribute directly to improved performance in formal study. Teachers find this area of study one in which they can maintain their own specialized interests and develop satisfying relationships with students. Unfortunately, the facilitative studies are often viewed as frills. They are the first to be cut under the pressure of increased enrollments and tightened budgets. For this reason, teachers often are imposed upon to contribute their own time and energy to the staffing of these studies.

Administrative concerns relating to facilitative studies typically center upon the management tasks of staff assignment, space and time scheduling, and budget. The low priority accorded these studies and their special requirements seem to force management considerations above other considerations. Under such circumstances these provisions grow unplanned and seldom are revised or dropped as needs change. The danger of overextension of students, unbalanced offerings, and imposition upon staff is present unless frequent assessment is made of student needs and adequacy of the total program.

DIFFERENTIATED PROGRAMS. Major provisions for instruction within the secondary schools now entail the use of discrete programs designed to serve specified groups of youth. Traditional programs have had to be differentiated and tailored to fit more directly the needs of certain types of students. Among the most common are vocational programs; special education of the handicapped; and programs for the gifted or talented, the slow learner, and the underachiever. The program of student activities must also be placed in this category. Although it is typically not differentiated as serving an identifiable group of students, it must—for purposes of program planning and program design—be considered as a legitimate educational program differentiated from formal instruction and the curriculum.

The provisions of such special programs as those noted above are based upon assumptions that have been derived from practice and tested to some extent by controlled research. Excepting student activities, a major assumption is that certain characteristics possessed by students present conditions for instruction that may be handled most adequately by grouping and special treatment. A second assumption is that the curriculum, as well as instruction, should be different for these groups. Therefore, somewhat different curriculum prescriptions, different modes of instruction, and different materials are employed, in addition to the mere application of such administrative devices as grouping and scheduling.

As a category of special provisions, differentiated programs are so labeled because each provision, even for aspects of administration, must be treated more or less as a distinct program. Many of these are large in terms of enrollments and staff, and serious efforts are made to meet student needs fully through the use of fundamentally different instructional arrangements. In such cases, special administrative personnel are also employed to facilitate staffing, supervision, research and evaluation, and management requirements. In the remainder of this chapter, each of the types of special provisions that typically are treated as differentiated programs in the schools are examined in terms of program considerations.

HANDICAPPED YOUTH

Public attitudes have been a dominant influence in the provisions made for the education of handicapped youth. Two basic motivations seem to underlie current interest in supporting special educational provisions for the handicapped through the secondary school years. First is the humanitarian belief that each individual has a fundamental right to self-realization supported to the fullest by public resources. Second is a growing understanding that the handicapped can contribute to society provided they are given the opportunity to develop their capabilities. The shift to this view from one of providing minimum care and maintenance was caused by a complex of social forces. Primary among them, however, was the development of educational facilities and methodologies for the deaf, blind, and crippled. Later psychological, sociological, and rehabilitation studies supported the notion that investment in the education of the handicapped paid handsome personal and social dividends.

Public schools have been slow to respond wholeheartedly in the effort to make available adequate provisions for the handicapped. Small, locally oriented school districts still frequently take the provincial view that the numbers of the handicapped are insufficient to make special provisions feasible and that cooperative programs with neighboring school districts are unacceptable. In such districts, the handicapped are placed in regular classes "to provide something" until they can be released. Specialists in education of the handicapped refer to this practice as the "parking lot concept," and they seek a serious appraisal of the incidence of handicaps among youth and the educational possibilities for them.

Pioneering work in the education of the handicapped has been carried by state-supported residence schools, hospitals with special interests in children and youth, bureaus or divisions of special education within state departments, and universities. The status of research at the university level is illustrated by the award of the Kennedy Foundation given in 1963 to Professor Samuel Kirk of the University of Illinois. The award for research and leadership, which ranks with the Nobel prizes both in prestige and funds, was given to Professor Kirk for his work as director of the University's Institute for Research on Exceptional Children and as chairman of the Department of Special Education of the College of Education.

Local school district efforts to provide for certain types of handicapped youth began in earnest approximately thirty years ago as states began to provide funds to reimburse local districts for the extra costs of special provisions. By 1960, all states supported special provisions for one or more types of handicapped youth. The types of handicaps and the incidence excepted in the general school age population are given in Table 9-1. The classifications given are accepted generally as ones for which specially trained personnel are prepared, state support is made available, and tested materials and technics are in use in public schools. It should be noted, however, that the percentages of incidence given in Table 9-1 are only rough estimates. Improved methods of detection and

Table 9-1. Estimate of the Number of Handicapped Children
and Youth, with Estimates of the Number of
Teachers Needed, by Area, in 1961

Type	Incidence (Percentage)	Estimated No. of Pupils* (1961)	Teacher-Pupil Ratio† Recommended	Estimated No. of Teachers Needed
Blind	0.02	9,189	1:10	919
Partially seeing	0.2	91,890	1:18	5,105
Deaf	0.07	34,459	1:10	3,446
Hard-of-hearing	0.5	229,725	1:35	6,564
Speech-impaired	3.5	1,608,075	1:100	16,081
Crippled	1.0	459,450	1:15	30,630
Special health problems	1.0	459,450	1:20	22,973
Socially and emotionally maladjusted	2.0	918,900	1:20	45,945
Mentally retarded	2.3	1,056,735	1:15	70,449
Totals	10.6	4,867,873	--	202,112

*Based on an estimated 45,945,000 children five to seventeen years of age in the United States in 1961.
†Based on an analysis of state laws and regulations, as well as consultation with specialists.

SOURCE: U.S Office of Education, "Preliminary Estimate of the Number of Special Education Teachers Needed in 1961, by Area of Exceptionality " (Washington, D.C.: U.S. Department of Health, Education, and Welfare, mimeographed, 1960).

diagnosis may reveal much larger handicapped populations, and larger percentages of youth in school attendance may increase the percentages of those who are handicapped. One might expect that at least 10 percent of the students of a given school population have one or more handicaps sufficiently serious to require special treatment.

Handicapped youth in the school present three types of problems. First, some treatment to maintain or to overcome the handicap is necessary. Second, the handicap itself imposes certain adjustment problems to which teachers and counselors must be alert. Third, adaptations of both curriculum and instruction are essential to successful achievement. All authorities tend to agree that the fundamental aims of education are the same for the handicapped as for normal youth. A major consideration recommended is that handicapped youth—even the mentally retarded—participate in some normal classroom study and in the usual student activities whenever they can do so successfully. It is this concern for normal development in the handicapped that is largely responsible for provisions being made for them in the public schools.

The principal means of organizing and grouping the handicapped in the public schools is the special class. A class size of fifteen is generally regarded as maximum for the mentally retarded, while groups of two to six are normal for the speech impaired, the deaf and hard of hearing, the visually handicapped, and the socially maladjusted. The diagnosis may indicate individual treatment initially, with gradual introduction to a selected group, and finally some normal school participation.

Provisions have come to be varied. In many cities, special teachers instruct crippled youth in their homes and use telephone and radio devices to work with youth between visits. In Portland, Oregon, two-way radios have been employed between the regular classrooms and homebound high school youth. In Evanston, Illinois, an extensive physical therapy program for the orthopedically handicapped and special equipment for the blind have been set up in one school. Visiting counselors from the secondary schools work with individuals and small groups of maladjusted youth in homes and in various community facilities. Large cities, such as Chicago and New York, provide instruction and counseling to maladjusted youth in a special division of the city jail. The special classroom in the school, then, is not the only device for providing special education for the handicapped—provisions are limited only by the imagination and the conditions of the situation, and it is likely that they will become more varied as more technological devices come into use.

A major concept guiding those who work with skill and insight with the handicapped is that of individualization. Perhaps nowhere else in the entire educational scheme does the concept of individual needs have such paramount value—it is one aspect of a program for the handicapped that cannot be slighted by the administrator without impairing the effectiveness of instruction. An acceptance of this concept along with the principles implied in the paragraphs above will almost certainly bring administrative problems in terms of the relationships of a special program to that of the rest of the school. Administrative actions to meet anticipated problems include:

1. Initial study sufficient to clarify purposes; identification and admission procedures; services to be provided; staff facilities and materials needed; and relationships to community agencies and to the regular program of the school.
2. Adequate communications within the faculty as well as with the public to insure an understanding of the programs being undertaken.
3. Early identification of the individuals to be given special treatment; preparation of students prior to admission; and collection of data necessary for evaluation.
4. Preparation of the student body for the acceptance of the handicapped; its involvement, if appropriate, with some aspects of the program.
5. Preparation of regular teachers, counselors, and other staff members who will be directly involved with handicapped students and their parents.
6. Provision for regular communications about developments and changes in arrangements.
7. Provision for total staff involvement in policy making and in assessment of the program.

PROVISIONS FOR THE GIFTED

In contrast to the ideal of developing each individual to his fullest potential as a strong motivating force behind provisions for the handicapped, little of significance was done for the gifted until fears were aroused over the loss of talent to society. Lewis Terman, Leta S. Hollingworth, and others had established irrefutable evidence during the 1920's of the efficacy of early identification and rapid educational development of gifted youth.[1] But the argument for educational programs

1. See Leta S. Hollingworth, *Gifted Children: Their Nature and Nurture* (New York: The Macmillan Co., 1926); and Lewis M. Terman *et al., The Promise of Youth, Genetic Studies of Youth,* Vol. III (Stanford, Calif.: Stanford University Press, 1930).

tailored to the needs of the gifted made little headway in public schools until the mid-1950's. Then, educational leaders of the stature of Ralph W. Tyler, Director of the Center for Advanced Study in the Behavioral Sciences, Stanford, California, began to recognize the importance of such programs in social terms. Tyler wrote: "It becomes quite clear that the greatest threat to the continuation of modern civilization is the neglect of human potential. Failure to identify individuals with talent, to motivate them to develop their abilities, and to provide the education that they require would result in *the most serious damage society could suffer* [italics added]." [2]

The need to maintain the nation's vast technology and to power it with the basic sciences, coupled with the demands of national security for extremely skilled manpower, brought quick response. The National Defense Education Act of 1958 provided over one billion dollars to aid public schools during the first four years of its operation. During the same period heightened competition for college admission increased the public interest in intellectual aspects of secondary school programs to the benefit of those who sought support for special programs in the secondary schools. In 1960, the National Education Association made a survey of secondary schools to determine steps taken to provide special programs for the gifted. Eight out of every ten schools surveyed reported some special provision. The results by size of district are given in Table 9-2. Both junior and senior high schools appear to be making special provisions for the gifted in about equal proportions.

Table 9-2. Special Programs for the Gifted by Size of
School District, 1960

Size of District	Junior High School	Senior High School
500,000 and over	100.0%	100.0%
100,000-499,999	93.7	96.5
30,000- 99,999	91.3	93.7
10,000- 29,999	84.2	82.6
5,000- 9,999	65.9	66.4
2,500- 4,999	55.9	57.9
All districts	76.8	76.7

SOURCE: NEA Research Bulletin, May, 1960, p. 47.

2. Ralph W. Tyler, "Meeting the Challenge of the Gifted," *Elementary School Journal,* November, 1957, pp. 75-76.

Types of special provisions are of interest as well. In the same survey, the National Education Association collected information concerning the types of special provisions being developed. These results are given in Table 9-3. Although enrichment was the device most frequently reported, a program of separate classes in combination with some other form was reported by a total of 44.2 percent of all senior high schools.

Table 9-3. Types of Special Provisions for the Gifted
Reported by Senior High Schools in 1960

Type of Special Provision	Percent of Schools Reporting
Enrichment in heterogeneous classes only	24.7%
Separate classes only (ability grouping)	9.8
Acceleration	1.3
All of the provisions above	10.5
Separate classes and enrichment	21.4
Separate classes and acceleration	2.5
Enrichment and acceleration	6.5
Total school districts with special provisions	76.7

SOURCE: NEA Research Bulletin, May, 1960, p. 48.

The apparent lack of interest in forms of acceleration is particularly notable since the weight of research evidence is strongly in favor of acceleration.[3] Increases in state-supported programs for the gifted—particularly in such states as New York, Illinois, Maryland, and California—and special efforts being made by local districts support the conclusion that the number of special programs for the gifted has further increased and is likely to continue to increase.

The data reveal a major movement throughout the public schools to provide differentiated programs for the gifted. With public support, secondary schools have adopted the policy that the greater the ability possessed by the student the sounder is the investment of educational resources. The objection that special provisions for the gifted are a waste has largely been silenced. Still, there is honest concern, well taken, about the total effect of rigid grouping patterns—which fail to meet the need for youth of all abilities and background to communicate and interact together in learning situations—and the rapid adoption of relatively untested procedures. Deliberate assessment of desired outcomes from

3. See Lindley J. Stiles, Lloyd E. McCleary, and Roy Turnbaugh, *Secondary Education in the United States* (New York: Harcourt, Brace & World, 1962), pp. 405-406.

procedural arrangements—as listed in Table 9-3—and from changed instruction should be understood before special provisions are attempted and while they are under way.

As with other types of special provisions, those for the gifted require the use of procedures for identifying students and assigning them. At this point, the question of the meaning of "giftedness" arises. The factor of general intelligence is accepted as a major component of many special abilities and appears to be essential to high achievement in all fields. Measures of general intelligence through use of individual and standard tests are universally recommended as a first step. Although some cautions must be used in the interpretation of standard test scores and their application in selection, a score above the second standard deviation on properly constructed national norms should mark off the top 2 to 4 percent of the population. (This is a score of 132 on the Stanford-Binet scale.) A score above the first standard deviation should mark off the upper 20 percent. (This is a score of 116 on the Stanford-Binet scale.) In large schools, the use of scores near these points should yield sufficient numbers of students to form instructional groups even after further steps in selection are taken.

Intelligence alone is not an adequate index of potential. Special abilities and interests, personal motivation and adjustment, and other factors weigh heavily in future productivity. Scores on achievement tests combined with measures of general intelligence seem to provide the most effective prediction of future achievement. In one study conducted with 1400 junior high school students, Pegnato and Birch found that this procedure identified 97 percent of the gifted students when checked against Stanford-Binet intelligence test scores.[4] Schools marks, teacher judgments, peer nominations, and other methods are in use. Results of research lead to the conclusion that these latter procedures might best be employed after initial screening to locate special abilities, assess progress, determine specific assignments for individual students, and provide data for planning instruction.

Specialized abilities in group leadership, mechanics, the arts, and other areas of nonacademic accomplishment may not be readily identified by standard tests, grades, or even teacher judgments. Typically, special opportunities must be provided in which the student is instructed and required to perform—this is particularly true in the arts and in

4. C. W. Pegnato and J. W. Birch, "Locating Gifted Children in Junior High Schools: A Comparison of Methods," *Exceptional Children,* March, 1959.

physical and mechanical areas. If abilities in these areas are to be identified and developed, schools must be prepared to use staff and facilities to permit varied types of opportunities for performance and observation. Schools incorporating both academic and nonacademic types of special provisions might well identify the areas in which they are prepared to make provisions available and the specific abilities to be developed in each area before attempting to design procedures for identification.

Administrative devices for providing for the gifted include enrichment in depth within established course work, lateral enrichment (provision of additional studies apart from normal class work), ability grouping by "multiple track" plans or "flexible grouping," acceleration, and project plans. In themselves, they may entail no substantial changes from normal instructional and curricular offering. They are valuable devices, however, when coupled with new and stimulating materials and with challenging instruction. These devices can be arranged into numerous patterns and varied in ways to permit unusual opportunities for improved education of all students.

Wherever serious efforts are made to extend opportunities for the gifted, administrative attention must be directed to the planning of instruction, as well as to the organizational patterns in which it is to take place. Stiles and his colleagues summarize the kind of instructional practice to be sought in programs for the gifted when they write:

The general approach of the teacher will fit well with new practice if he can establish in his students a breadth of understanding of a particular field sufficient to provide the orientation for study in depth of significant aspects of that field; stimulate sensitivity to problems and the intellectual tools of problem solving; seek out learning activities to extend classroom study and promote independent scholarship; and stress creativity, problem solving, and critical thinking as outcomes more essential than conformity to fixed rules and procedures.[5]

Whatever administrative steps are taken, they are to facilitate this kind of learning to its greatest extent.

VOCATIONAL PREPARATION

Gainful employment and economic self-sufficiency for each individual have been immediate educational goals of the public secondary schools since the turn of the century. Until that time the assumption was that

5. Stiles, McCleary, and Turnbaugh, *op. cit.,* pp. 409-410.

high school graduates would enter college for training in the professions and other youth would obtain on-the-job training, particularly through the apprenticeship system. This assumption proved untenable as a high school education became a terminal goal of all youth and as the apprenticeship system of vocational training proved unworkable for modern technology.

Until after World War I, industry in the United States depended heavily upon the immigration of skilled technicians from foreign countries. Not until World War II did dangerous manpower shortages require a reexamination of the whole concept of vocational education. Both economic and social considerations seem finally to be merged in broad planning to meet the vocational needs of individuals and the nation. It is now clear that carefully designed vocational programs are required for the achievement of full employment and sustained prosperity, the acceleration of economic growth, and increased opportunities for all citizens to share in the national wealth.

Two major components characterize programs of vocational education in the public schools. The first deals with the implications of vocational preparation for general education. Vocational preparation is dealt with obliquely in the elementary schools, but at the junior high school level it becomes a major consideration. Here, a concrete beginning must be made in preparing youth to make knowledgeable choices about future occupational goals, to develop understandings of basic economic conditions, and to receive exploratory experiences in the world of work. With occupational information, aptitude testing, and vocational counseling, these aspects of general education need to be continued into the high school years.

The second component of vocational education deals with specialized training in vocational fields and requires the planning and resources of a differentiated program, described earlier in this chapter. This aspect of vocational education is typically conducted in high schools. It is designed to meet the employment objectives of those who are about to enter the work force and, in many cases, for those already employed who require further training. Federal and state financial aid is now provided to support occupational training in the areas of agriculture, distribution and sale of consumer goods, skilled trades, manufacturing, service, practical nursing and other health fields, office jobs, technical work supporting that of engineers and scientists, and homemaking. In

1961, more than 3,850,000 students were served by vocational programs in secondary schools, and the schools were reimbursed with federal and state funds to the amount of $206,100,000.

The strong role of federal and state agencies is particularly important in maintaining realistic programs—geared to regional and national trends and to the latest technical knowledge. The role of local, state, and federal agencies in planning as set down by the U.S. Office of Education is as follows:

The role of the state and local school system is to establish and operate programs based primarily on local needs, although state and national needs are also considered in such developments; to meet or exceed the standards outlined in state plans; and to qualify for acceptance of state and federal aid for approved programs.

The role of the federal government in the cooperative undertaking is to encourage the states to establish and expand needed vocational education programs; to provide financial aid and stimulation; to suggest desirable policies and standards for state acceptance; and to provide for research, publications, conferences, visits, and other types of assistance and leadership that will help the states in developing programs. The role of the states is to identify their own training needs; to establish their own standards, policies, and patterns of training with due consideration to their needs and financial abilities; to provide qualified state leadership, supervision, teacher training, and vocational guidance services; to provide appropriate state financial assistance within the limits established by state legislation; and to disburse federal funds in conformity with the provisions of state plans.[6]

The kind of planning implied by the USOE statement has served to gear training to occupational needs while, at the same time, maintaining the ideal of individual freedom of vocational choice.

Technical education is the most recent concern of those planning programs in the vocational field. It is designed to prepare highly specialized technicians to give direct and indirect assistance to professional scientists and engineers. This is the area of most serious shortage and the vocational area of most rapid increase of demand. The technical fields include electronics, electricity, instrumentation, petroleum processing, aeronautics, industrial chemistry, optics, materials testing, mechanical design, and civil highway construction. Here the disciplines of mathematics, chemistry, physics, and biology are essential to adequate prepara-

6. U.S. Office of Education, *Progress of Public Education in the United States of America, 1961-1962* (Washington, D.C.: U.S. Department of Health, Education, and Welfare, 1962), pp. 10-12.

tion, along with specialized training in shops and laboratories, and on-the-job experience. These programs require a full twelve years of public school study plus an additional two years beyond high school.

The demand for trained technicians to staff important research, engineering, laboratory, and industrial positions has spurred the development of the junior college and the community college as extensions of secondary schooling. Highly skilled, technically trained manpower is a rich community resource and an area of opportunity for the individual who may not wish or be able to complete full professional training at the university level.

Program planning for vocational education at both junior and senior high school levels presents numerous problems. Specialized training in the vocational fields must be oriented to immediate application; yet this is the type of learning that is subject to rapid obsolescence. The vocational areas selected must meet an identified need in the employment market; yet gearing job training to local conditions may not best serve the interests or the eventual employment opportunities of a mobile population. Facilities are expensive and rapidly become outdated. In addition, instructors and supervisors who have an adequate foundation of knowledge, technical experience, and ability to teach are in scarce supply. Finally, the scope and sequence of instruction, its placement in the total program, and maintenance of balance between general and special education are complex factors that must be examined and continuously assessed if vocational training is truly to contribute to education.

STUDENT ACTIVITIES

The contribution of student activities to the education of youth is perhaps the most questionable feature of secondary education. Some types of student activities have been openly attacked by educators of the stature of James Conant. Perhaps this attitude has been caused by some of the reasons behind the growth of student activities into a separate, differentiated program of the school. For example, activities are often openly encouraged for such purposes as supplying public entertainment, gaining community favor for the school, or using students to perform services needed in the maintenance of the school. All too frequently the educational values provided by activities are doubtful or nonexistent.

Few would question the power of student activities to attract and hold students' loyalty, to command their time and talents, and to motivate them to unusual effort. What is questioned is whether or not these activities serve educational purposes. Three criteria can be applied to an assessment of a particular activity. First, does the activity grow from and enhance the instructional or guidance programs of the school? Second, does the activity contribute to a balanced offering of learning activities for students? Third, does the activity provide opportunities for students to learn and practice skills, values, and attitudes recognized as appropriate educational goals for youth?

Despite unfavorable attitudes toward student activities in general, many of them do make an obvious and substantial contribution to secondary education. Those most directly related to formal study are subject-centered clubs, honor societies, special-interest groups, student government, and school publications—these are, or can be, direct extensions and applications of classroom study. In the areas of personal-social development, activities foster healthy heterosexual adjustment, improve human relations skills, develop leadership, and provide recreational and social interests. Activities may make their most significant contribution through the improvement of the group life of the school. In this area they provide an avenue for student-faculty participation in cooperative planning and work, build student interest and enthusiasm for the total school program, and provide the means by which students may contribute to their own well-being. Whether or not student activities accomplish these ends depends to a great extent upon the care with which they are planned and supervised.

The extensive and varied nature of student activities may be seen from a list of categories of activities devised for a study of student participation in Illinois high schools. The list includes these categories:

Academic	Music
Art	Publications
Assembly	Character building
Interscholastic athletics	Community service
Intramural athletics	School service
Class organization	Social
Subject clubs	Student government
Hobby clubs	Others
Debate, drama, speech	

This list has been used in surveys of numerous high schools, and responses usually reveal several specific activities within each category for each school.

Since the general administration of the activity program—its planning, supervision, and assessment—is the responsibility of the principal, an enumeration of critical points of concern are in order. These include:

1. Maintenance of student-centered rather than teacher-centered activities. Too often high school bands, drama groups, and the like are identified more with the teacher and his demands than with the students for whom they exist.

2. Continuous check on student participation to identify those who over-participate or who do not participate at all. In addition to the extent of participation, attention might be given to determining whether or not certain groups of students are dominating activities and whether or not activities are open to all without such undesirable practices as hazing, blackballing, and the like.

3. Study of student interests to locate areas in which needed activities might best be encouraged and those that might best be terminated.

4. Development of student–staff–parent cooperative planning and assessment of activities and recommendations concerning policies governing them.

5. Determination of costs of activities to students and implications of such data.

6. Investigation of community facilities and services offered by community agencies; identification of common areas of interest for possible cooperative planning.

7. Assessment and correction of problems related to conduct of activities, as, for example, competition for student talent, adequacy of staff involvement in supervision and control, and adequacy of funds, supplies, and equipment.

8. Development of schoolwide policies relating to such items as use of facilities, formation of activities, handling of funds, and time limits for practices and for late night affairs.

9. Encouragement of activities to provide opportunities for students to take responsibility, exercise leadership, test ideas, pursue special interests, and experience satisfying social relationships in the accomplishment of worthwhile projects.

The principal must play a strategic role in student activities if they are to become and remain a legitimate educational feature of junior and senior high schools.

OTHER SPECIAL PROVISIONS

In most secondary schools, significant proportions of students require programs for which the normal range of educational materials, the kinds of facilities, the training backgrounds of teachers, and the usual grouping and administrative arrangements do not provide meaningful learning situations. Almost all public schools, except the very small (enrollments below 350-400), that attempt to enroll all youth will find students who require broad types of special provisions already examined in this chapter. In addition, some schools, because of particular circumstances, may find groups of students whose needs require other types of special provisions.

Throughout the United States numerous secondary schools make special provisions for the exceptionally talented, the slow learners who are not mentally handicapped, the culturally deprived, those who do not speak English or for whom English is a second language, the underachievers at all levels of intelligence, and many others. In most cases, special provisions may be simply the use of an additional teacher to facilitate English study; in other cases, the numbers of students, the nature of the educational problem, and the extent to which instruction is to be provided may require what the authors have defined as a differentiated program.

Wherever student needs call for special provisions, the stages involved in sound planning remain the same: detection and identification of the students involved, diagnosis of specific learning needs, preparation of a planned approach, experimentation with types of treatment, and assessment of results. The administrator must anticipate requirements for special staff, facilities, and materials. Where teachers, counselors, and supervisors with specialized knowledge and skills are required, they must either be developed within the existing staff or added to it. Finally, few special provisions will succeed without wide faculty, student, and parent cooperation. Care in educating these groups to new educational needs and opportunities is a necessary part of program development. In the case of handicaps and deficiencies, the ultimate goal is to bring students to the point of resuming normal patterns of study.

REFERENCES

Conner, Leo E., *Administration of Special Education Programs* (New York: Teachers College, Bureau of Publications, Columbia University, 1961).

Gallagher, James J., *Analysis of Research on the Education of Gifted Children* (Springfield, Ill.: Office of the Superintendent of Public Instruction, 1960).

Getzels, Jacob W., and Jackson, Philip W., *Creativity and Intelligence* (New York: John Wiley & Sons, 1962).

McLure, William P., *Vocational and Technical Education in Illinois* (Urbana, Ill.: Bureau of Educational Research, University of Illinois, 1960).

President's Committee on Youth Employment, *The Challenge of Jobless Youth* (Washington, D.C.: U.S. Government Printing Office, 1963).

Roucek, Joseph S., (ed.), *The Unusual Child* (New York: Philosophical Library, 1962).

Stiles, Lindley J., McCleary, Lloyd E., and Turnbaugh, Roy, *Secondary Education in the United States* (New York: Harcourt, Brace & World, 1962).

U.S. Department of Labor, *Manpower: Challenge of the 1960's* (Washington, D.C.: U.S. Government Printing Office, 1961).

VanTil, William, Vars, Gordon F., and Lounsbury, John H., *Modern Education for the Junior High School Years* (New York: The Bobbs-Merrill Co., 1961).

Waetjin, Walter B. (ed.), *New Dimensions in Learning* (Washington, D.C.: Association for Supervision and Curriculum Development, 1962).

Chapter 10
Student Personnel

AMERICAN public schools have written large the principles of an education appropriate for all youth and the development of each individual to his fullest potential—in personal-social, civic-moral, and technical dimensions as well as the purely intellectual. Though major strides have been made to fulfill these principles, the statistics tell us that all is not well. One third of all court cases in this country involve juvenile delinquency; one third of all youth fail to complete a secondary education; 40 percent of all young men examined for military service are rejected because of illiteracy or for physical or psychological reasons. Similarly, there is ample evidence of serious unmet problems among the youth who are retained—perhaps "kept" is a better word— in the secondary schools.

The personnel function in the secondary schools has become a point of focus both for gearing education to the needs of youth and for aiding youth to profit more fully from schooling. By and large, the scope of a personnel program depends upon the philosophy of the school system and its staff concerning the role of the school. If secondary education in a given school is chiefly concerned with the able and the motivated, personnel services will reflect this attitude. Those with deficiencies, maladjustments, handicaps, or divergent interests will be treated as worrisome problems and shunted about within the school's program. Where the school expects and accepts the full range of talents, interests, personal and social problems, handicaps, and deficiencies, the professional staff is likely to be augmented with appropriate personnel specialists, actively studying its student body and revising and improving its total school program.

The changing American culture has brought about and extended the need for student personnel services. Its impact has been greater upon this area of secondary education than upon any other facet of the school's program. Until after World War II in the vast majority of schools, the only staff members giving a significant fraction of their time to student personnel matters were attendance officers, school nurses, and deans or assistant principals in charge of discipline. Only in the major cities had a very few social workers, teacher counselors, testing specialists, and an occasional school psychologist made their appearance. The scene has drastically changed during the postwar years, however, as the need for student personnel services for *all* youth has become evident.

YOUTH IN AMERICAN SOCIETY

A review of the dramatic changes in American culture and social patterns that have significance for the school seems unnecessary here, except for a brief allusion to the changed and changing status of youth. The concept of the individual, particularly the preadolescent and adolescent, as represented in attitudes toward youth and his relationships to adults is particularly important.

Shifts in occupational demands, family patterns, urbanization, and mass communications all influence adult attitudes toward youth and the conditions under which adults and youth relate to each other. Although ethnic groups, regional environmental conditions, and other factors produce what might be viewed as distinct subcultures where youth are particularly valued and accepted, children and youth seem to have become a significant social problem themselves. Certain attitudes and conditions relative to the treatment of youth have emerged and can be identified. These include:

1. Youth can no longer make a significant contribution to the economic well-being of the family. This is especially true as compared with their role in the rural American family of a few decades ago.

2. Youth are often used by parents as status symbols and alter egos. Parents' college mania, preoccupation with having their children do what "they didn't get to do," or outright rejection of their children are symptoms of this condition. Often the parents suffer deep humiliation over the "shortcomings" or "failures" of their children; failures frequently turn out to be the adults' expectations, unacceptable or unattainable to the child.

3. Adult patterns of living have forced youth to create a culture of their own. The need for status and the loss of a definable role have led youth to structure an "adolescent world" with their own values and norms, language, dress, manners, and amusements. In the large cities, housing and work patterns—particularly where broken homes exist and/or mothers work—have forced youth into gang associations. In the well-to-do suburbs, a comparable phenomenon exists, but on a grander scale, with the active encouragement of adults. Night clubs for teenagers patterned on adult standards are a recent invention. The effect is to foster conditions in which adolescents play at being adults even through the early years of marriage.

4. Closed occupational opportunities and the need to pursue an extended period of education have fostered attitudes of irresponsibility and sometimes of hopelessness. Unable to earn immediate material rewards, youth often convey the notion that society owes them the trappings of the good life. Recent surveys indicate that as many as half of all couples receive substantial financial support from their parents during the first years of marriage. A significant number of married university students receive all of their financial support from parents.

5. Within the secondary schools, little but lip service is being paid to the encouragement of youth to accept responsibility and, particularly, to exercise initiative. A recent study by Getzels and Jackson, for example, reveals that teachers choose and reward the intelligent, conforming students above those who are curious, creative, and questioning. And yet the same teachers rate these latter factors high on a scale of attributes desired and encouraged.[1]

6. Few experiences—except, perhaps, artificially fashioned social, athletic, and intellectual ones—are available to permit youth to test their own capacities. Real accomplishment is required to develop feelings of self-confidence, adequacy, and acceptance. Opportunities to participate and contribute to the adult world are lacking or largely undeveloped in the large cities and the suburbs that now contain over 75 percent of all youth.

To these conditions must be added at least three general and pervading forces that have direct, though subtle effects upon youth. These are:

1. The status of marriage and family life has been changing swiftly

1. Jacob Getzels and Philip Jackson, *Creativity and Intelligence* (New York: John Wiley & Sons, 1962), pp. 30-31.

to fewer children per family, higher percentages of divorces—and, incidentally, higher rates of remarriage, and an increasing number of working mothers. The significant point to be made is that the family seems to be becoming less and less important as other areas of social life become more institutionalized. One may well ponder the question—as sociologists, anthropologists, and psychologists have not done to any fruitful extent—What are the effects upon the developing personality as the family, and the individual along with it, become less important?

2. Rapid transition into a mass society has been examined in Chapter 8. The amorphous and faceless corporation, community, and government have been amply described in the professional and popular literature. Major institutions—including the federal government, organized religion, and giant corporations—have not only lost sight of the meaning of individual freedom and integrity within their own organizations but do not seem to value it in the schools. These organizations tend to view the schools as instruments to propagate their particular values and programs. The National Defense Education Act of 1958 is an interesting case in point. This legislation, though having some admirable qualities, was motivated to channel high school and college students into scientific and technological careers at a time of serious shortage of talent in many fields. There was no interest on the part of government in enhancing individual freedom of choice.

3. A lengthened period of education—resulting both from compulsory education laws and from indirect social pressures—poses problems for school and student personnel workers. "Unachieving" and "unmotivated" have become labels on a par with "delinquent." Compulsory education, even the pressures to study only academic subjects, are not new to secondary schools. What is new are the numbers, the diversity of interests and potentials, and the variety of problems being brought into the secondary schools. The unmet needs of youth can no longer be hidden by dispersing problem youth throughout regular classes conducted in traditional ways. The hard fact is that deviant youth must be identified and studied so that suitable educational programs can be designed to meet their needs and capacities.

The conditions listed above, to the degree they are present in a given community, are likely to create serious stress even in the normal pre-adolescent and adolescent. The extent to which schools are aware of and responsive to the effects of these conditions upon the personal, moral, social, and intellectual development of youth depends heavily upon the adequacy of the student personnel program.

What is needed is a positive point of view concerning the individual youth and his aspirations. Within the adult world two major influences for understanding, bolstering, and supporting the individual are religion and psychoanalysis. This is an interesting observation in view of the philosophical and deistic beliefs basic to this nation's origin—as expressed by John Locke, Adam Smith, Thomas Jefferson, Thomas Paine, Benjamin Franklin, and others. It is also interesting in view of the basic opposition between religion and psychoanalysis. Nonetheless, each projects a startlingly similar view of the individual. Religion generally presents man as sinful, as carrying from birth a burden of guilt put there by his ancestors. Psychoanalysis, as posited by Freud—and still surprisingly influential in the training of the psychologist, psychiatrist, and counselor—reveals man as endowed with unwholesome and destructive instincts which he constantly struggles to suppress. Each sees the individual as distressed, unhappy, and inherently weak.

A contemporary movement in psychology, already of proven use to school psychologists and counselors, projects a more healthy view of the individual and seems to be compatible with attempts at positive understanding of all youth, both normal and disturbed. Termed "ego psychology," it emphasizes normal development—a concept that would have troubled a competent psychologist of a decade ago.[2] Carl Rogers, noted psychologist, expresses the aim of this group:

> . . . we can choose to use the behavioral sciences in ways which will free, not control; which will bring about constructive variability, not conformity; which will develop creativity, not contentment; which will facilitate each person in his self-directed process of learning; which will aid individuals, groups, and even the concept of science to become self-transcending in freshly adaptive ways of meeting life and its problems.[3]

From this orientation the teacher and the professional personnel worker have a common meeting ground. Both need to have a view of the indi-

2. For a valuable treatment of this point of view, see Association for Supervision and Curriculum Development, *Perceiving, Behaving, Becoming, 1962 Yearbook* (Washington, D.C.: the Association, 1962).

3. Carl R. Rogers, "The Place of the Person in the New World of the Behavioral Sciences," *Personnel and Guidance Journal*, Vol. 39, No. 6, February, 1961, pp. 442-451.

vidual as a whole person with purpose in life, with potentials to be developed, and for whom values are important.

STUDENT PERSONNEL SERVICES

Four types of professional personnel are employed in the public schools. They are: instruction, service, administration, and student personnel. The category of instruction, of course, includes those whose major responsibility is teaching, whether classroom, group, tutorial, remedial, homebound, or a variety of others. The category of administration includes those who direct, control, supervise, and oversee other personnel in the operation of the school or its subdivisions. The service category includes workers in library, resource or study centers, and language laboratories; technicians; and other specialized workers not primarily involved in a teaching or student personnel function. The final category, that of student personnel, includes those specialists whose responsibilities include guidance and counseling; psychological and health examination, prescription, and treatment; and representation of the student to the school and to other proper authorities, as, for example, social workers, juvenile officers, and the like.

To identify the four categories of professional personnel is not to imply that their functions are separate and mutually exclusive. Each function facilitates the others and could not operate in isolation. The teacher, for example, is essential to student personnel services; without his active participation no such program could be successful. There is, however, need for specialized work that a teacher—even with the requisite knowledge and skills—would be unable to perform adequately without sacrificing the teaching function.

Because of the interdependence of the four functions the lines between them are not sharply drawn. Some authors refer to special education as a student personnel function rather than a teaching function. There is some debate about whether discipline, as handled by a dean of boys or dean of girls, is a pupil personnel or an administrative function. In practice, some professional staff members are assigned one function as a primary responsibility and one or more of the other functions as secondary—as in teacher-counselor positions. Only where the performance of one function impairs the performance of another does a serious problem result. The point to be made is that each major function requires specification if it is to be organized, staffed, and executed effectively.

Specialists in the area of student personnel services are the professional personnel most recently added to school staffs. The use of the term "pupil personnel" or "student personnel" came into wide acceptance after a 1951 report of the U.S. Office of Education.[4] This report summarizes a conference on guidance activities. The conference was devoted to identification of services and processes focusing directly upon the development of the pupil as a person. The need to coordinate student personnel activities around the guidance and counseling function became clear, and the term "guidance services" was dropped in favor of the more inclusive term "student personnel."

The first six principles set forth in the conference report provide the framework for current practice:

1. Pupil personnel services are most effectively administered when their organization is structured to meet the individual needs of pupils.
2. The success of the pupil personnel program in a school system is directly correlated with the vision and perseverance of the administrative officers.
3. In the process of focusing attention upon the development of the pupil, emphasis should be given to the preparation of teachers and administrators to use pupil personnel services appropriately.
4. Pupil personnel services will operate best when the specialist in one area has enough understanding and appreciation of the work of specialists in the other areas to be able to recognize the appropriateness of referrals and relationships.
5. All individuals who operate in school guidance should have familiarity with classroom procedures and appreciation of classroom problems. In turn, the classroom teacher should have an understanding of pupil personnel services.
6. Effective coordination of pupil personnel services may be secured either by placing such services within a single administrative unit and/or by establishing adequate coordination among various individuals responsible for segments of the program as long as policies and relationships are clearly defined.[5]

Item 6, above, is particularly important in any attempt to specify staff and activities comprising a student personnel program. This is at-

4. U.S. Office of Education, *Pupil Services in the Elementary and Secondary Schools,* Circular No. 235 (Washington, D.C.: U.S. Government Printing Office, 1951).

5. *Ibid.,* p. 12.

tempted in Table 10-1, although it must be made clear that practice has not become standardized to the point that functions, staff positions, and activities are consistent from school to school. Whether the services of a social worker, psychologist, or psychiatrist are provided depends heavily upon the philosophy of the school toward personnel services, the size of the school, and, frequently, whether or not specialized personnel are available. Most large junior and senior high schools in major cities and suburban areas do perform the functions indicated in Table 10-1 and do employ many, if not most, of the personnel indicated.

DEVELOPMENT OF A STUDENT PERSONNEL PROGRAM

An obvious fact of educational life, readily apparent to the competent principal, is that the provision of staff and the definition and assignment of tasks do not make a program. A further ingredient, often summed up in the word "teamwork," is required. The principal can perform the administrative work of providing student personnel services; but unless he can *lead* in developing the insight and vision required, no true program can exist.

The term "teamwork" is not sufficient to identify the moving force behind program development. It begins within the staff from a common understanding of what is being attempted, from acceptance of the plan by the individuals involved, and from a desire to cooperate to accomplish it. As communication develops, coordinated effort increases. Out of this kind of climate, attitudes evolve that not only aid in facing problems and misunderstandings but facilitate further improvements. Students and parents—the benefactors of school services—can then be involved more deeply than otherwise would be possible, both in more effective use of the school and in improvement of the school itself.

Although the leadership of the principal is important in other areas, it is often particularly crucial to the program of student personnel services. This is true not just because of the recency of this development or even because of the rapid changes taking place in this field. It is true primarily because of three factors: (1) Student personnel is a sensitive area, touching problems over which there can be intense emotional feeling; (2) There are many misconceptions and honest disagreements over certain issues; and (3) The area of personnel service cuts across many activities, and the problem of definition and coordination is difficult.

Table 10-1. Student Personnel Services

Function	Staff Position	Typical Activity
Custodial	Assistant principal in charge of attendance and discipline, deans of boys and of girls	Conduct admission interviews and make assignments, generally supervise student body, follow through on all referral cases, conduct parental conferences May oversee total guidance program
	Attendance officer	Check addresses of new students, check students not in attendance, etc.
	Juvenile officer	Investigate, represent students to community agencies, oversee general student welfare at activities, etc.
Health	Physician, dentist	Make examinations, give emergency treatment, advise preventive medical practice, make referrals
	Nurse, dental technician	Give emergency treatment, clear students returning to school from illness, maintain records, carry out prescribed medical practices
Counseling, guidance, psychological services	Director of guidance, assistant principal, or deans	Administer all phases of pupil personnel, coordinate functions, assign and supervise staff, plan budgets, etc.
	Teacher counselor, counselor	Conduct preadmission conferences and orientation, give individual and group guidance counseling, consider general student welfare and assessment, handle parent conferences
	Social worker	Conduct casework, make referrals to psychologists and/or psychiatrists, represent student to outside agency such as court or welfare service, make home visits
	Psychologist, psychiatrist	Do casework on referral, consult, participate in staff conferences, do individual testing, give therapy
Testing and research	Coordinator or director, psychometrician	Conduct testing program, do individual testing on referral, collate data and research, aid in curriculum development
Records	Central records clerk	Supervise records room, maintain cumulative records
Job placement and follow-up	Coordinator or director of placement and/or follow-up	Operate placement service and follow-up study, work with those who use these data in evaluating school program
Student activities	Coordinator of student activities	Plan, supervise, evaluate student activities dealing with student personal-social development

In preparing for this chapter, the authors surveyed over one hundred junior and senior high school principals throughout the country. The survey was a questionnaire designed to obtain an inventory of problems faced by secondary school principals in the area of student personnel. The schools selected varied widely in size and types of communities. The results of the survey did not lend themselves to statistical treatment because of the size of the sample and the instrumentation; however, the list of problems was surprisingly similar among the various kinds of schools. In order of incidence, the problems of all the principals as reported were:

1. Discipline
2. Providing guidance and counseling
3. Dropouts
4. Poor attendance
5. Student-teacher relationships
6. Student activities
7. Changing enrollments: both size and composition of student body
8. Slow learner
9. College admissions
10. Pupil reporting

Comments indicated that principals were becoming deeply involved in these problems, that they did not feel they had sufficient professional help in the student personnel area, and that the problems were causing repercussions throughout the total school program and were affecting staff morale.

For the principal who wishes to solve rather than live with the kinds of problems reported above, an appropriate beginning seems to lie in the way the program is conceived by the principal himself. He must come to see that services are needed beyond mere classroom instruction and a few student activities. Personnel services, within the framework listed in Table 10-1, must be viewed as being related—concerned with helping youth to a clearer and more certain understanding of himself and others, and of the possibilities in the situations he faces.

The principal must come to accept—and communicate through his leadership—a point of view akin to that expressed by Dugald Arbuckle:

It [student personnel work] is a point of view which holds high respect for the rights and the freedoms of the individual. It holds to the freedom of choice for the child, and it believes that the school is for the benefit of the child, just as the state is for the benefit of the free citizen. It implies an understanding of human behavior and a concern with differences only so that an individual may be understood more fully. . . . it is a profession not a job.[6]

Certain principles can be recommended to the administrator in developing pupil personnel services and making them fully effective:

1. Set up routines for the handling of student information, referrals, and consultation between teachers and counselors.
2. Staff the program with individuals highly trained in guidance, counseling, and testing. Where teacher-counselors are employed, a few highly trained individuals are strongly recommended.
3. Keep turnover to a minimum. A satisfactory program requires the development of individual relationships through the faculty, a process that takes years.
4. Spread knowledge and skills in the field of personnel services throughout the staff by in-service activities, committee work, case conferences, and other devices that increase channels of communication.

STUDENT PERSONNEL: RELATIONSHIPS AND ISSUES

Throughout Chapters 4 and 5 organizational functions, the relationships of individuals, and the interrelationships of both were stressed. These same concepts apply with equal force in a consideration of student personnel. Perhaps most difficult to achieve in this area is understanding of guidance and counseling functions, the role of the counselor and of the teacher, and functional relationships of student personnel services with the instructional and administrative phases of the school's program.

Guidance and Counseling

Throughout the field of student personnel there is considerable interest in developing a distinction between the terms "guidance" and "counseling." "Guidance" connotes some positive external direction. The student is guided when he is told about the rules of the school and that he is expected to obey them, or when he is directed to take certain tests. These and a host of other requirements and expectations are established "in the student's interest." At base, however, "guidance" seems to be concerned with action considered necessary in order that the school fulfill its responsibility to society. Thus, when such actions are

6. Dugald S. Arbuckle, *Pupil Personnel Services in American Schools* (Boston: Allyn and Bacon, 1962), p. 88.

prescribed the individual is being guided, even though he may be permitted a choice of when and how he will satisfy them.

"Counseling," on the other hand, refers to those activities that are conducted only in terms of the individual's interest, and *he* decides what action, if any, is to be taken. There is abundant evidence to indicate that attitudes and values are not likely to be changed by exhortation or even by objective, intellectual analysis. What the individual student needs is a confidential, accepting relationship with someone who understands and with whom he can review his problems, express emotions, and puzzle out solutions. Under these conditions the counselor can suggest; but, if he is to maintain the counseling relationship, he must always communicate to the student that the decisions are his own.

At least three levels of guidance and counseling seem to be advocated. First, guidance is a normal activity of teachers, teacher-counselors, counselors, and administrators. Although the range of activities of each type of professional may be limited by other functions of his position, all *can* perform important guidance activities. The restrictions upon the value of guidance performed by each position will depend upon the personalities of the individuals themselves and upon their primary functions. All teachers can and should be guidance-oriented; some can perform no true guidance functions because of their personal orientations. Administrators could perform valuable guidance functions; some cannot because owing to the nature of their responsibilities, they must limit their contacts with students.

A second level of guidance and counseling is the counseling done by the professional faculty member—whether teacher, teacher-counselor, or counselor. Many teachers—and we trust, most counselors—do possess the attributes, interests, and training to establish a counseling relationship with students. This kind of relationship is important to the healthy development of *all* youth. The school should make a serious attempt to see that every student has access to one professional staff member with whom he can establish counseling rapport.

A third level of guidance and counseling is professional counseling. As the teacher-counselor works with students, he should have access to a skilled therapist. This type of counselor may be a psychiatrically trained social worker, a trained psychological counselor, or a psychiatrist. He should operate with the teacher-counselors on a consulting and referral basis, working with individuals who have been identified as having unusual emotional problems. In many cases the teacher-counselor can continue to counsel the "client" under the direction of the professionally trained counselor. At other times the teacher-counselor may refer the case to the professionally trained counselor. Mental illness is a fact of modern life—perhaps more in need of attention than physical illness, since over one-half of all hospital beds in the nation are occupied by mental cases. As in therapy for physical ills, the most successful results accrue from early detection and treatment; the most desired action is prevention.

The absence of clear understanding of the essential distinction between guidance and counseling has led to misuse and misassignment of the counselor in the public schools and to mismanagement of entire student personnel programs. Counselors' positions are frequently structured so that they actually work as record clerks, substitute teachers, disciplinarians, and study hall supervisors. Often, when they are permitted to counsel, they are expected to serve as school sleuths and stool pigeons.[7] Unfortunately, the terms "guidance" and "guidance program" are still used almost exclusively, even in the professional literature, to encompass the counseling function.

Teaching, Guidance and Counseling, and Administration: Roles and Functions

If the definitions of student personnel work presented here—particularly guidance and counseling—are accepted, some restrictions upon the roles of teacher, counselor, and administrator become apparent. At the same time, certain issues relating to student personnel can be perceived more clearly. In a very real sense the school is a prime socializing agency. To the administrator and the teacher this implies a structured approach to youth. It includes predetermined goals, measurement and judgment of whether or not expectations are being met, and manipulation of the situations involving the student.

Competent teachers and administrators are aware that if instruction is to "take," the student must become involved, see the efficacy of what-

7. See James L. Hoyt, "Problems in a Guidance Program," *Bulletin of the National Association of Secondary-School Principals,* Vol. 43, 1959, pp. 55-57; Florence Purcell, "Counseling Assignments and Efficiency," *Vocational Guidance Quarterly,* Vol. 5, No. 3, 1957, pp. 111-113; and C. C. Stewart, "A Bill of Rights for School Counselors," *Personnel and Guidance Journal,* Vol. 37, No. 7, 1959, pp. 500-503.

ever is imposed—perhaps establish many of the standards himself, and accept them as the conditions of his work. The curriculum is imposed, albeit nicely and with understanding. The teacher and the administrator can be "student-centered" in their approach to youth, but sooner or later they will be tested as each youth seeks to discover the limits of his freedom. When this occurs—whether in a learning situation, in relation to school rules, or merely in the adult-youth relationship—the fork in the road is reached. At this point, the teacher and the administrators usually must demand conformity, and the basic difference in their roles and that of the counselor becomes clarified.

The teacher and the administrator must work with groups. They are, however, prone to become too much involved with the teaching process and too little concerned with the learning process. Imposition of standards, evaluation in terms of relatively fixed criteria, and frequent activity as judge and evaluator have little relationship to learning. Yet this aspect of the roles of the teacher and administrator is ascendant. An astute foreign educator on a second visit to American schools observed to the authors that he was constantly impressed by the spontaneity and creative responsiveness of American youth, but that he saw a difference between the first and second visits. This difference, as he termed it, was the apparent grim determination on the part of administrators and teachers to *make* students learn.

The manner in which youth perceive the teacher and the administrator is perhaps the important limiting factor in establishing a counseling relationship. Most students do believe, and accept, the authority positions of both teacher and administrator. They have been conditioned to it, sometimes in a most unhealthy manner. Whatever attitudes they have developed will be transferred to all individuals whom they view to have authority positions. Williamson is one of the many writers in the student personnel field who have identified this problem. He believes that most resistant students even identify the counselor as an authority figure and have difficulty because of it. He writes: ". . . a counselor dealing with a misbehaving individual, by means of the counseling attitudes, relationships, and techniques, is still viewed as a representative of authority. But it is true that by using these techniques he may be transformed into a symbol of benign authority." [8]

8. D. G. Williamson, "Counseling in Developing Self-Confidence," *Personnel and Guidance Journal,* Vol. 34, No. 7, 1956, p. 401.

The counseling relationship must be voluntary and confidential to be effective. How this is to be accomplished in the definition of the counselor's role is itself an issue. Perhaps the most controversial area is that of student discipline. Williamson comments further that discipline must be separated from counseling—"First, because a disciplinary relationship is nonvoluntary . . . and, second, because discipline is nonconfidential." [9] Jensen conducted a study in the Phoenix, Arizona, secondary schools in which he surveyed students who had talked to counselors about problems. He reports that deans of boys and deans of girls received few student choices as counselors because they were known to be responsible for school discipline. [10] Other writers take a variety of views. Some feel that the counselor can function properly if he withdraws from taking authoritative action with the student when he is in the counseling role. [11]

If the counselor cannot be completely separated from identification as an authority figure, there is evidence that he should be separated from the direct exercise of authority. Norman Gilbert, in a study in Illinois schools, found some startling differences in the attitudes of students toward counselors who assumed disciplinary functions as opposed to those who did not. Students counseled by counselors who did not have responsibilities for discipline were strongly favored by students as most helpful. They described their relationships with these counselors as being more like an ideal counseling relationship than those reported by students whose counselors had disciplinary responsibility. [12]

There seem to be important differences in the roles of counselors and of other professional personnel dealing directly with youth. These differences stem largely from the functions they perform. Whether or not the administrator works with his staff to understand and cooperate with this type of student personnel function will largely determine whether it can be performed effectively within a given school.

9. *Ibid.*, p. 400.

10. Ralph E. Jensen, "Student Feeling About Counseling Help," *Personnel and Guidance Journal,* Vol. 33, No. 9, 1955, p. 503.

11. Leona Tyler, *The Work of the Counselor* (New York: Appleton-Century-Crofts, 1954), p. 247.

12. Norman Gilbert, *A Comparison of Students' Perceptions of Counseling Relationships Among Schools in Which Counselor Duties Differ* (Lithographed report of doctoral dissertation, University of Illinois, 1962).

EXTENDING STUDENT PERSONNEL SERVICES

A full range of services, as depicted in Table 10-1, may be neither feasible nor appropriate in a given school or in a given community. The type of personnel services will depend upon the nature of the student body, the nature of the school, and the community agencies available to serve youth. There seems to be ample justification for the development of a core of trained professional staff in guidance, counseling, and testing. From this base, studies of the student body can proceed on a sound basis, and preparation can be made for needed extensions of student personnel services.

Some of the more promising developments in the study of needed personnel services, their design and trial, are now occurring in the major cities of the nation. After long years of neglect, schools are making a concerted effort to find solutions to youth problems in the large city. In one of the most promising developments, the school systems of fourteen major cities have formed a group to make a large-scale attack upon the full range of youth problems. Begun in 1956, the group was incorporated in 1961 as the Research Council of the Great Cities Program for School Improvement. This organization is fostering projects toward the solution of problems through a research-oriented approach. Activities can be categorized into the following areas: training of professional personnel; student services, including guidance, counseling, and social work; work with parents and the family; and work with community agencies.

The projects under way include the following features:

1. Home visits by a teacher or counselor (in Philadelphia, by a "community coordinator"). The visits are exploratory and are not associated with legal enforcement.
2. Reading clinics.
3. Academic and recreational summer schools.
4. Training of teachers in identification of talent and potential delinquency, and in the use of new materials.
5. Improvement of guidance function through the use of sociometric instruments, diaries, time budgets, autobiographies, and projection tests to aid in understanding student problems and views.
6. Improvement in medical and dental services.
7. Use of mentors to supply adult contact to dropouts and youth from broken homes.

8. Exploration of youth problems and the development of cooperative projects with the following agencies: National Conference of Christians and Jews, settlement houses, church youth centers, neighborhood improvement associations, Junior League, YMCA, YWCA, boys' clubs, public park and recreation departments.
9. Improvement of physical conditions of schools and neighborhood areas.
10. Social casework.
11. Work-study program—Minneapolis stresses part-time work for fourteen- and fifteen-year-olds.
12. Provision of books and periodicals in the home.
13. Home teaching by volunteers.
14. Tutoring service.
15. Preparation and tryout of new text materials that stress the urban setting; Negro, native-white American, and Latin-American characters; and reading levels appropriate to the large city student population.
16. Design of special-purpose schools, including residential schools with psychiatric treatment facilities.
17. Community job surveys and placement services.
18. Provision of psychological services to parents and students.
19. Use of the homeroom concept as a base for guidance.[13]

Although these activities are not yet fully developed, the school systems involved report a number of indications of improvement. The evidence includes: fewer dropouts, better job retention, improved progress in reading and arithmetic skills, fewer emotional and disciplinary problems, more rapid integration of deviants into regular classwork, improved parental cooperation, greater use of school facilities (including libraries), and improved school-community relationships.

The list of student personnel activities initiated within the brief period of the project's existence shows the emphases being placed upon these services. Further, an effort appears to be under way generally throughout the secondary schools to extend and improve student personnel services. Whereas the projects listed above represent extensions of student personnel services, another emphasis is in the use of these services and professional personnel in the improvement of other facets of the school program.

Increasing use of personnel services is being made particularly in the areas of curriculum planning, evaluation and research, and parent-school

13. From an unpublished paper by Henry Graf.

relations. Alert administrators are relating curriculum planning more closely to student needs. Through the testing program and the assessment of student strengths and weaknesses by counselors, groups of students can be identified for special attention. This use of student personnel services has not only improved the procedures for grouping students, but has also made more effective the use of special teachers in areas such as remedial reading, speech correction, and the like.

Student personnel staff are frequently directly involved in planned parent conferences, home visits, and participation on lay-professional committees. Within the school, guidance workers serve on curriculum committees, aid in planning and evaluating project work, meet with teachers on case conferences, serve on teaching teams, work with student activities, and contribute in a variety of other ways. By these means student personnel staff provide important professional knowledge and skills throughout the total school program.

REFERENCES

Allinsmith, Wesley, and Goethals, George W., *The Role of the Schools in Mental Health* (New York: Basic Books, 1962).

Arbuckle, Dugald S., *Pupil Personnel Services in American Schools* (Boston: 'Allyn and Bacon, 1962).

Association for Supervision and Curriculum Development, *Perceiving, Behaving, Becoming, 1962 Yearbook* (Washington, D.C.: the Association, 1962).

Combs, Arthur W., and Snygg, Donald, *Individual Behavior: A Perceptual Approach to Behavior* (New York: Harper & Bros., rev. ed., 1959).

Humphreys, J. Anthony, Traxler, Arthur E., and North, Robert E., *Guidance Services* (Chicago: Science Research Associates, 1960).

Johnson, Walter F., Stafflre, Buford, and Edelfelt, Roy A., *Pupil Personnel and Guidance Services* (New York: McGraw-Hill Book Co., 1961).

Maslow, Abraham H. (ed.), *New Knowledge in Human Values* (New York: Harper & Bros., 1959).

————, *Toward a Psychology of Being* (Princeton, N.J.: D. Van Nostrand Co., 1963).

Rosecrance, Francis C., and Hayden, Velma, *School Guidance and Personnel Services* (Boston: Allyn and Bacon, 1960).

White, Mary Alice, and Harris, Myron W., *The School Psychologist* (New York: Harper & Bros., 1961).

Wrenn, C. G., *The Counselor in a Changing World* (Washington, D.C.: American Personnel & Guidance Association, 1962).

Chapter 11
Educational
Improvement

CONCERN for excellence in American education is relatively recent as a movement. Only during the last decade have schools self-consciously directed critical interest to matters of quality—and only after social change, international tension, and vigorous criticism had precipitated social controversy concerning the aims, substance, and process of education.

For some years before and after World War II, criteria guiding educational improvement in the United States were largely quantitative in character. The road to school improvement was seen as one of improving educational breadth and supplying still larger quantities of what already existed. Stress was placed upon providing greater numbers of teachers, course offerings, buildings, books, equipment, instructional materials, and transportation facilities. Coupled with this orientation were sporadic efforts to improve practice on the basis of existing knowledge and known educational and institutional models. Serious efforts to structure quality educational programs on the basis of concentrated, programmatic research were rare: during the 1950's less than 0.1 percent of the resources of the educational enterprise were devoted to research.

QUANTITATIVE EMPHASES: CONTRIBUTING FACTORS

Several factors contributed to the quantitative orientation, among them the challenge of numbers in the wake of the "population explosion." The urgency of problems associated with constructing schools, securing teachers, raising money, and attending to a host of related educational problems consumed the time and energy of both school administrators and boards of education. The schools and their leaders were caught in an avalanche of numbers which threatened to swamp the facilities, resources, and capabilities of the educational enterprise. Maintaining the universality of educational opportunities was a mammoth problem requiring constant attention to quantitative questions.

The lack of clear mandates from society in relation to educational purposes also encouraged quantitative approaches to educational improvement. Social cleavages and conflicting values made difficult the assessment of desired educational directions. As a result, the salient goals of many schools appeared to reflect a desire to be all things to all people. For many years public education appeared to be adrift in a strong tide of unresolved values such as those suggested by Getzels and Jackson:

Beside the current goal of sociability and frictionless interpersonal relations stands the traditional work-success ethic with its focus on sustained labor and its rewards. Beside the relatively hedonistic present-time orientation of our culture with its exhortation to "Buy now—pay later" stands our belief in future-time orientation and the associated values of self-denial and conservation ("A penny saved is a penny earned"). Beside our current adulation of "the group" with its demands for consensus and conformity stands our belief in the integrity of the individual and his need for independence and autonomy. Beside our acceptance of relativistic moral attitudes with the accompanying emphasis on adaptability and change stands our belief in moral commitment and devotion to an ideal.[1]

Institutionalization in the schools was another major factor leading to quantitative approaches. Both elementary and secondary schools had developed formalized patterns of instruction and operation which reflected the characteristics of institutionalized bureaucracy. Strong movements for educational change were largely absent—the emphasis was upon perfecting old educational models rather than upon pioneering new ones. It was simpler in most instances to expand what already existed than to change institutionalized patterns. Clark's characterization of the schools "as the most unchanging institution in our society, with the possible exception of the church"[2] was a not inaccurate description of the state of affairs in many school districts.

The combined force of such factors tended to have serious conse-

1. Jacob W. Getzels and Philip W. Jackson, *Creativity and Intelligence* (New York: John Wiley & Sons, 1962), pp. 158-159.
2. David L. Clark, "Educational Research: A National Perspective," in Jack A. Culbertson and Stephen P. Hencley (eds.), *Educational Research: New Perspectives* (Danville, Ill.: The Interstate Printers and Publishers, 1963), p. 8.

quences for schools. Adaptive changes required in the educational enterprise to meet challenges other than those associated with growth and numbers were generally slow in coming. Although the development and expansion of science, automation, technology, new knowledge, revised occupational patterns, and new modes of living were everywhere evident, the schools appeared preoccupied with extending educational opportunity on the basis of existing educational programs and models. Whether or not these programs and models were anachronistic in the emerging space age was a question which failed to evoke widespread concern.

The change in orientation from quantity to quality is proceeding in American education today. It is, however, far from complete. Major problems and obstacles will prevent sweeping improvement, and consequently only broken-front approaches to quality education will be possible in many school districts. The shortage of outstanding teachers is a serious handicap that may continue for one or two decades. Institutionalization and the growth of enrollments will continue to present problems. Financial problems will also continue. Moreover, the lack of competent people to plan, initiate, and implement improvements will be felt in many places where the primary orientation has been survival rather than effectiveness, and quantity rather than quality.

The slowness with which schools use new knowledge to guide practice will also present problems. Many of today's educational concepts are not really "new"; indeed, some are more than thirty years old. Emphases upon creativity, self-directed learning, reflective thinking, scientific verification, intuitive discovery, independent study, laboratory techniques, and teacher-pupil planning were established in the theory and research of professional educators early in the 1930's.[3] However, schools and scholars have only recently begun to reanalyze them in critical fashion.

CONFRONTING EMERGING CHALLENGES

The root of present concern for educational improvement runs deeper than the fashionable pursuit of educational patterns aimed at producing greater numbers of scientists and intellectual leaders. Of greater moment than the education of the academically talented are problems concerning the nature, extent, and focus of educational preparation for the mass of young people who will lend stability to the social system in coming

3. See, for example, C. H. Judd *et al., Education as Cultivation of the Higher Mental Processes* (New York: The Macmillan Co., 1936).

decades. Many unanswered questions exist in relation to (1) the nature of future adult tasks facing today's learners, and (2) the scope of intellectual, social, occupational, and attitudinal preparation necessary for productive living in coming years.

The nature of the emerging social system is difficult to visualize. Enough is already known, however, to lend support to Alfred North Whitehead's remark concerning "the vicious assumption that each generation will substantially live among conditions governing the lives of its fathers, and will transmit those conditions to mold with equal force the lives of its children." [4] As Whitehead has indicated, our era is *"the first period of history for which this assumption is false."* [5] Predictions indicate that we have already entered the era in which the professional, the highly trained technician, and the skilled craftsman will be of unprecedented importance. Changing occupational patterns will generate successive impacts throughout the structure of society. In large organizations the present work of middle management will be programmed; operational researchers and organizational analysis will be highly prized; recentralization will be common; and normal lines of advancement will be drastically curtailed.[6] There have also been predictions that routine blue-collar and white-collar tasks will be almost depleted by cybernation in twenty years; that citizens, though better educated, will lack comprehension of a cybernated world; and that the interplay between an expanded science and the problems of government will be only dimly understood—even by college graduates.[7]

Michael's description of possible future developments is fraught with implications as to the magnitude of the task facing public education:

There will be a small, almost separate, society of people in rapport with the advanced computers. These cybernaticians will have established a relationship with their machines that cannot be shared by the average man any more than the average man today can understand the problems of molecular biology, nuclear physics, or neuropsychiatry. Indeed, many scholars will not have the capacity to share their knowledge or feeling about this new man-machine relationship. . . .

4. As quoted in Norman Cousins, *Modern Man Is Obsolete* (New York: The Viking Press, 1945), p. 16.
5. *Ibid.,* italics added.
6. Harold J. Leavitt and Thomas L. Whisler, "Management in the 1980's," *Harvard Business Review,* November-December, 1958, pp. 41-48.
7. Donald N. Michael, *Cybernation: The Silent Conquest* (Santa Barbara, Calif.: Center for the Study of Democratic Institutions, 1962), p. 44.

Some of the remaining population will be productively engaged in human-to-human or human-to-machine activities requiring judgment and a high level of intelligence and training. But the rest, whose innate intelligence or training is not of the highest, what will they do? We can foresee a nation with a large portion of its people doing, directly or indirectly, the endless public tasks that the welfare state needs and that the government will not allow to be cybernated because of the serious unemployment that would result. . . .[8]

Such predictions are startling—even to a society that has entered the space age. They present a somewhat pessimistic prognosis of the future of science-based societal developments. Moreover, they indicate the need for coping with a myth widely held in our society—that the growth of science is automatically translatable into great social benefits. This myth, as Hollomon has indicated:

. . . says that science converts itself into social values through some magic. Actually, there is no magic; there is not even an automatic quality to the process. The activity which puts science to use to meet society's needs requires a special environment of its own, not entirely but very largely independent of the environment of science. And there must be people with a special education and a particular outlook, and institutions which encourage invention, innovation, and the diffusion of technology. . . .[9]

The improvement of education to meet future societal needs is a critical problem facing leaders of the educational enterprise. The task will require penetrating insight into the nature of secondary schools as social institutions; deep understanding of the nature and purposes of the evolving society to be served and improved; knowledge of the theoretical bases upon which educational programs may be structured; appreciation of the strategies of inquiry undergirding educational programs; familiarity with a broad range of teaching-learning and organizational processes and alternatives; sophistication in determining the optimum contributions to be made to teaching-learning processes by professionals, organizational arrangements, technologies, and new media; and greatly expanded financial support.

8. *Ibid.,* pp. 44-45.
9. J. Herbert Hollomon, "The Brain Mines of Tomorrow," *Saturday Review,* May 4, 1963, p. 46.

TOWARD QUALITY: FINANCIAL SUPPORT

Quality education will not be achieved through tinkering with the status quo; it will require greatly expanded public investments in the educational enterprise. At the present time, property taxes are the primary source of support for schools. Although such taxes may have been adequate in an agrarian society, they are not only inadequate but unduly restrictive and inelastic for meeting educational needs in a rapidly growing industrial economy. Financial support generated through property taxes—coupled in some states with limited nonproperty taxes—is insufficient to deal with current quantitative problems such as rising enrollments, teacher shortages, physical plant and site replacements and additions, restricted curricular offerings, and limited programs for the range of talents and abilities represented in school populations.

Although the national average of school expenditures per pupil per day has increased steadily from $1.43 in 1952-1953 to $2.43 in 1962-1963, inflation during the same period has tended to cancel out the apparent gain. Moreover, the range in expenditures per pupil among the states has always been great; in 1962-1963, these expenditures varied from $230 per pupil to $645 per pupil (see Table 11-1). Since expenditure per pupil is one of the best indicators of the quality of education offered, it is apparent that wide disparities exist among the states in terms of educational opportunities available to learners.

Table 11-1. Distribution of School Expenditures Per Pupil, 1962-1963

Expenditures	Number of States
$200-249	2
$250-299	7
$300-349	5
$350-399	9
$400-449	10
$450-499	8
$500-549	6
$550-599	1
$600 and over	2

SOURCE: National Educational Association, Research Division, Estimates of School Statistics, 1962-1963, Research Report 1962-R13 (Washington, D.C.: the Association, 1962).

A report of the Research Council of the Great Cities Program for School Improvement has indicated the general inadequacy of fiscal support for education:

The great cities, like other communities throughout the nation, are investing too little of their economic resources in education. There is serious question as to whether enough citizens are taking careful stock of the crucial importance of education to their well-being. Too many people are giving education a low priority among the things they value in our society. As a consequence too few persons feel impelled to take action through their representatives in government to secure adequate fiscal policies to remedy the situation.[10]

Attainment of the following fiscal policies recommended by the Research Council would undoubtedly pave the way for vigorous movement toward quality in education in most school districts in the United States:

1. The fiscal support of public education should be a responsibility shared by all citizens and all levels of government.
2. The state program for financial support should recognize the complex needs of . . . school systems, but the determination of the needs should be the responsibility of the local boards of education.
3. The measure of the local school district's ability to contribute to the support of education should be in terms of the total burden of local government cost borne by the local tax base.
4. Local boards of education should be free from unreasonable restrictions in the administration of fiscal affairs, from undue controls by other governmental agencies, and from cumbersome legal procedures at state and local levels which thwart effective expression of citizens.
5. The fiscal procedures for adequate school support should provide the school districts with the direct access to taxes which can be administered best locally and indirect access to those which can be administered at the state level.
6. The state fiscal plan should include objective procedures to provide adequate funds for operating expenses and capital outlay and debt service payments.
7. The federal government should participate in the support of education when the national interest requires it and when local and state resources are insufficient to provide an acceptable educational program.

10. Report to the Board of Directors of the Great Cities Program for School Improvement, *Fiscal Policies to Meet the Needs of the Great City School Systems in America* (Chicago: Research Council of the Great Cities Program for School Improvement, 1963).

8. The level of financial support of public education should be kept responsive to the fluctuations of inflation and deflation in the price structure of the economy.[11]

The review of cost-quality relationships by the Committee on Tax Education and School Finance of the National Education Association has indicated the important role of adequate financing in fulfilling the goal of quality education in school districts. Some of the important conclusions of the Committee were:

1. Pupils on the average make higher scores on tests in the three R's in elementary schools and in the academic subjects in high schools in high-expenditure as compared with low-expenditure school systems.
2. Communities spending more per pupil generally get educational programs which take better account of the needs of society and the findings of psychological research on how children learn best. The scope of these school programs includes objectives ranging from excellent teaching of the three R's to such fundamental behavior patterns as good citizenship and the ability to think.
3. The ultimate, or point of diminishing returns, in educational quality has apparently not been reached in even the highest-expenditure school districts.
4. The effect of an intelligent long-range program of adequate financial support in a school system is cumulative and, therefore, especially powerful in its effect on quality. Also, low expenditure, if continued, will greatly reduce quality.
5. States which make superior provision for the financing of schools rank substantially higher than low-expenditure states in educational achievement and in earning power.[12]

Public support for policies oriented toward greatly expanded investments in education would enhance both the ability and readiness of educators and boards of education to embark upon concerted drives to improve educational quality. Without such policies, the push to define, operationalize, and implement quality programs may continue to be largely dependent upon the existing interests, motivations, and resources of institutions, agencies, and organizations external to school districts.

Significant strides toward educational improvement are possible today. New avenues to improvement have been opened up through the impact

11. *Ibid.*
12. Committee on Tax Education and School Finance, National Education Association, *Does Better Education Cost More?* (Washington, D.C.: The Association, 1959), pp. 21-37.

of technological applications to teaching-learning processes, through new patterns of staff organization and utilization, through fresh approaches to reorganization of knowledge in various content fields, through efforts aimed at the individualization of instruction, and through the availability of entire new curricula. Realization of the full potential for educational improvement will require enlightened school leadership, commitment to change, and extensive experimentation and research. It will also require adequate financing. The task of improvement can best proceed where it is liberated from an entrenched atmosphere of financial scarcity.

Until the educational needs of an evolving society are more fully understood; until increased sources of support are available from local, state, and Federal governments; until adequate equalized support becomes available for capital outlays, operating costs, and debt service charges; and until education is more universally viewed as an investment rather than a cost, it may be difficult to attain the goal of excellence in secondary education. Without adequate resources, the majority of school districts will be limited to tinkering approaches to quality—with a resultant minimal return.

TOWARD QUALITY: CURRICULUM AND LEARNING THEORY

The work of Piaget, Inhelder, Bruner, Luria,[13] and others has been instrumental not only in directing attention to essential weaknesses in current episodic curricula in schools but also in providing impetus to a major reconstruction of knowledge in various subject fields for instructional purposes. The emphasis on the reorganization of content is evident in recent filmed courses in several subject areas, in several new mathematics programs, in the Physical Science Study Committee's "packaged" course in physics, in the foreign language project at Wayne State University, in the Biological Sciences Curriculum Study at the University of Colorado, and in other movements.

The formulation of new structures of knowledge and the incorporation of the strategies of inquiry of various disciplines into secondary school curricula break sharply with several traditions that have dominated American education for several decades. The accelerated trend toward

13. A. R. Luria, "The Role of Language in the Formation of Temporary Connections," in B. Simon (ed), *Psychology in the Soviet Union* (Stanford, Calif.: Stanford University Press, 1957), pp. 115-129.

intuitive discovery, reflective thinking, scientific verification, concept formation, and cognitive and symbolic processes indicates a renewed interest in the intellectual aims of education. This interest contrasts sharply with former emphases such as study and analysis of the aptitudes, the emotional problems, and the educational weaknesses of learners.

The development of structures of knowledge, the structuring of various strategies of inquiry, and the continuing experimentation with programmed learning are presently generating new insights into learning processes. Current research is challenging learning principles that have long been in vogue in secondary education. According to Cronbach, each of the following principles of learning is open to some dispute in light of new research evidence:

1. Learning occurs through active practice.
2. Pupils should not try tasks where they are unlikely to succeed.
3. Transfer of learned responses is to be expected only if the later stimulus is much like that on which the person was trained.
4. A response that leads to a desired goal will be easier taught than one motivated by external incentives and compulsions.
5. Learning is shown to be "meaningful" if the pupil can use his knowledge in new situations, particularly concrete situations.
6. Factual learning or learning that is not clearly understood is quickly forgotten.
7. A well-understood verbal generalization is remembered, and aids in adaptation to new conditions.[14]

Current emphases and research directions are resulting in reformulations of learning principles that have guided teaching-learning practices in secondary education since the early 1940's.

The new curricula's emphasis upon increased understanding of the structures and operations of knowledge systems and strategies of inquiry is also shifting attention away from episodic curricula. The trend is toward more systematic analysis of the important elements of knowledge structures in relation to primitive terms, defined terms, formation rules, transformation rules, postulates, and theorems. Since all organized bodies of knowledge possess unique language systems, or *model* languages, the learner who seeks to master knowledge systems should progress success-

14. Lee J. Cronbach, "Issues Current in Educational Psychology," a paper prepared for the Social Science Research Council Conference on Mathematical Learning, mimeographed, May 4-6, 1962.

fully through each of the following stages of competence and under-standing:

1. *Primitive terms*—terms which are undefined in the model language but which are necessary to develop the knowledge system.

2. *Defined terms*—terms which are derived from and equivalent to various combinations of primitive terms.

3. *Formation and transformation rules*—the language of logic and/or mathematics utilized in working with empirical and conceptual constructs.

4. *Postulates*—statements of units and objects, their properties, and their interrelationships; that is, sets of propositions which make it possible to deduce all true statements in the knowledge system.

5. *Theorems*—the statements deducible from the postulates.

Systematic analyses of knowledge structures will have important implications—not only for teaching-learning processes, but also for programming. Such analyses will ultimately reveal the logical organization or framework of different subject fields and will lead to the development of appropriate teaching-learning strategies for laying a foundation of understanding. The defined terms, the postulates, and the formation and transformation rules will not only indicate the minimum essential concepts undergirding the knowledge system but will also provide new insights into both the processes which govern knowledge growth and the means by which conceptual systems are extended and changed.

The important work of reordering knowledge for teaching-learning purposes is under way. As this important task proceeds, it promises to usher in new levels of quality in secondary education—in terms of improved curricula and better understandings of learning processes and in the re-emphasis of intellectual aims.

TOWARD QUALITY: TECHNOLOGY AND THE REORGANIZATION OF TEACHING AND LEARNING

The integration of mass instructional technologies, individual instructional technologies, programmed learning, and conventional and team instructional patterns is opening unique avenues to excellence in secondary school programs. As yet, most experimentation with the technologies in secondary education has proceeded without the emphasis on instructional *systems* which the future promises to bring. Schools have used television, learning laboratories, self-instructional devices, massed filmed systems, and instructional packages—together with organizational arrangements such as team teaching—without extensive consideration of how these technologies and organizational arrangements might be welded into effective systems of instruction.

As the principles of instructional system design are formulated in coming years, the possibilities for integrated systems approaches to teaching and learning will present greatly expanded opportunities for excellence in instructional and learning tasks. The CLASS facility described in Chapter 3, with its emphasis on the use of computers, programmed instruction, data processing, and the storage, retrieval, and display of information in the teaching-learning task, is an example of future trends.

As progress is made in identifying the appropriate roles of mass data presentation, individual and small-group automated teaching, human interaction, individual study, creative periods, and other elements of possible importance to teaching-learning processes, the movement toward the development of integrated instructional systems will be greatly accelerated. The "black-box" concept of instructional systems shown in Figure 11-1 illustrates some of the elements that will require study and

Figure 11-1. The "Black-Box" Concept of Instructional Systems

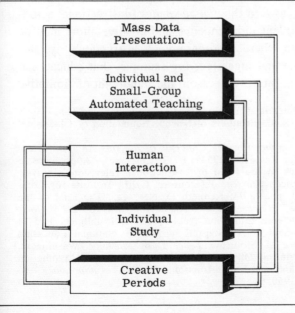

Mass Data Presentation	Lectures, film, television, tapes, etc.
Individual and Small-Group Automated Teaching	Self-instructional devices; teaching machines, viewers, listening units, etc.
Human Interaction	Teacher-student, group, sociodrama, etc.
Individual Study	Study periods, library, etc.
Creative Periods	Painting, composing, problem solving, etc.

consideration in the development of systems approaches. Finn, in discussing the black-box concept, has noted the complexity of problems and decisions facing the designers of systems approaches:

... assuming a clear understanding of objectives and content and further assuming that we had sufficient knowledge about these processes, such a system might be applied to an instructional problem.

Information concerning the nature of the students, the specific objectives and content, etc., would be supplied the teacher-designer. Decisions would be made as to which "black-box" to insert into the system at which point and which subsystem to trade off with another in the interests of the students, the facilities, the cost, etc. At this point an instructional system would have been designed.[15]

Systems approaches to the use of instructional media and the components of man-machine systems have been extensively described by Miller, Carpenter, Norberg, Stolurow, and Finn.[16] Possibilities for the use of systems approaches encompass not only various subject areas but also administration and testing. The development of systems will undoubtedly lead to tighter organizational arrangements in schools and to greater teacher dependence upon district- and state-level instructional planning—especially if stratovision, computer-based machines, and closed-circuit television are incorporated. Thus, the teacher's classroom role may shift extensively toward the *management* of instructional activities. Opportunities for student independence and creative effort may be more difficult to maintain where preprogrammed instructional systems are extensively used. Dale has suggested, for example, that educational activities may be viewed in future years from the standpoint of "imitative

15. James P. Finn, "A Potential for Educational Revolution?" in *Tomorrow's Teaching* (Oklahoma City, Okla.: Frontiers of Science Foundation of Oklahoma, Inc., 1961), p. 45.

16. See Robert B. Miller, *Some Working Concepts of Systems Analysis* (Pittsburgh: American Institute for Research, 1954); C. R. Carpenter, "Approaches to Promising Areas of Research in the Field of Instructional Television," in *New Teaching Aids for the American Classroom* (Stanford, Calif.: Institute for Communication Research, 1960), pp. 73-94; Kenneth D. Norberg, "The First of the Title VII Reports—A Review," *Research Abstracts and Analytical Review of Completed Projects,* National Defense Education Act, Title VII, Installment I, 5-14 (Washington, D.C.: Department of Audiovisual Instruction, National Education Association, 1961); Lawrence M. Stolurow, *Teaching by Machine* (Washington, D.C.: U.S. Government Printing Office, 1961); James P. Finn, "Automation and Education: III, Technology and the Instructional Process," *Audiovisual Communication Review,* Winter 1960, pp. 5-26.

reaction" and "creative interaction"—both of which appear necessary in the total program.[17] The former may be preprogrammed. The latter, however, calls for independent, self-programmed learning. Little is known at present about the balance required between creative learning and the use of instructional systems. Proposals such as Ramo's, for an electronic system of total teaching where machines would perform the entire teaching task,[18] tend to point up the urgency of finding answers to such questions.

TOWARD QUALITY: EXCELLENCE IN TEACHING

Although adequate financial support, continuous development of curriculum and learning theory, utilization of technological advances, and sound reorganization of teaching-learning processes are all essential foundations in the movement toward quality, it is necessary to anchor these foundations upon an able and enlightened teaching profession. Improvement of professional standards in teaching will require critical assessment and upgrading of existing aims, patterns, and practices in the selection, preparation, and utilization of secondary school teachers.

A task of considerable importance will be that of image definition— the delineation of standards for intellectual, scholarly, and personal characteristics required in teaching. Redefinition of standards appears necessary in relation to (1) the level of intellectual ability required in the teaching force; (2) the scholarly, professional, and personal qualifications necessary for optimum performance; (3) the working environment and salary levels necessary to attract capable individuals; and (4) the design of training programs to incorporate broad liberal preparation and to stress high levels of competence in appropriate strategies of inquiry.

Several factors have inhibited the development of general excellence in teaching. Requirements for entry into teacher training programs have been characterized by mediocrity. As a result, large numbers of able young people have rejected teaching as a career. Stiles has indicated that "the teaching profession has limped along content to admit almost any-

17. Edgar Dale, "No Room for Amateurs," *Audiovisual Instruction,* May, 1961, pp. 190-192.
18. Simon Ramo, "A New Technique in Education," in Arthur A. Lumsdaine and Robert Glaser (eds.), *Teaching Machines and Programmed Learning: A Source Book* (Washington, D.C.: Department of Audiovisual Instruction, National Education Association, 1960), pp. 367-381.

one, including rejects from other professional fields." [19] Concentrations of students characterized by low ability, poor motivation, and doubtful potential have not been uncommon in teacher training programs.

The quality of programs for prospective teachers has been another inhibiting factor. Few programs have stressed either the need for acquiring substantial bodies of organized knowledge or the need for high levels of competence in processes of intellectual inquiry. Thus, they have tended to be intellectually uninspiring. Moreover, institutions of higher learning have seldom involved their ablest scholars in the preparation of teachers. The implications of such shortcomings have been highlighted by Chase:

How can we expect to produce stimulating teachers of history unless they are taught by historians of the first rank and inducted by them into the study and criticism of the sources of historical knowledge and the art and science of historical interpretation? Where shall we find teachers who will introduce our children and youth to the great ideas and the noble expressions of ideas in literature, unless scholars who understand the uses and abuses of the art of criticism and retain a fresh and spontaneous enthusiasm for great works participate in the education of teachers? Where will our teachers acquire the ability to develop in their pupils mastery of foreign languages, unless they themselves are taught by those thoroughly at home in the particular languages and the cultures of which they are a part? How shall we produce creative teachers of science, unless their education includes contact with genuinely creative scientists and provides the excitement of participating in the discovery of new truths? [20]

Still other factors have inhibited excellence in teaching. Important among these are the low esteem in which teaching is held by the public and the inadequate economic returns associated with the profession. The National Education Association has estimated that in 1962 the annual starting salary of male teachers with a B.A. was $4800. In the same year, male graduates in engineering were paid an average beginning salary of $6648, while in accounting and sales the averages were $5856 and $5616 respectively.[21] The average annual salaries of all classroom teachers in 1961-1962, in comparison with other selected professional

19. Lindley J. Stiles, "Revolution in Instruction," in B. J. Chandler, Lindley J. Stiles, and John I. Kitsuse (eds.), *Education in Urban Society* (New York: Dodd, Mead & Co., 1962), p. 169.

20. Francis S. Chase, "Universality Versus Excellence," in *Education Looks Ahead* (Chicago: Scott, Foresman & Co., 1960), p. 36.

21. *NEA Research Bulletin,* "Economic Rewards of Teaching," May, 1963, pp. 45-49.

occupations, also indicated that teaching offered substantially smaller economic returns than most other professions. While the estimated average salary of all teachers in 1961-1962 was $5515, the average salaries of other professionals in private industry were as follows: accountants, $6924; auditors, $6412; attorneys, $10,032; chemists, $7453; engineers, $8147.[22]

The results of several studies have indicated that standards of selection, preparation, and reward in the teaching profession have a direct bearing upon the quality of education available in school districts. Improvements in the quality of teaching personnel result in increased educational achievement among students. Bloom has indicated that "a number of different indicators (salary level, professional interests and qualifications, etc.) all appear to be related to student achievement and grade standards. . . . The quality of the output (student achievement) is highly related to the quality of the teachers." [23]

Commitment to Excellence

The movement toward quality in education through excellence in teaching will require commitments of various kinds:

1. *Commitment to raising general standards for entry into teaching.* These standards should match those required for entry into other recognized professions. The time is ripe for dispelling the myth that almost anyone can become a teacher. Excellence in teaching demands intellectual, scholarly, and personal characteristics of the highest order.

2. *Commitment to careful screening and rigorous selection of candidates who meet basic standards for entry into preparation programs.* Teaching requires intellectual curiosity, motivation, a desire to master pertinent fields of knowledge, and ability to work productively with both children and adults. Such characteristics are not universally distributed among candidates seeking entry into teaching. Sophisticated selection procedures are essential. Those who are to guide the pursuit of knowledge at the secondary school level require outstanding ability in the analysis of evidence, in the exercise of the critical faculties, in the formulation of sound judgments, and in the projection of reasoned conclusions.

22. *Ibid.*, pp. 45-49.
23. Benjamin S. Bloom, "Quality Control in Education," in *Tomorrow's Teaching, op. cit.*, p. 57.

3. *Commitment to rigorous preparation programs.* The foundations of teaching excellence reside in broad liberal approaches to preparation, in solidly based and intellectually challenging programs that stress mastery of organized fields of knowledge, in learning environments that require intimate acquaintance with the strategies of inquiry, and in preparation procedures that develop pedagogical competence. The goal of excellence in teaching will require reformulation and reorientation of preparation programs in terms of intellectual rigor, curricular content and focus, and involvement of outstanding scholars in teacher preparation.

4. *Commitment to in-service improvement of professional competences.* Optimum returns from teaching-learning activities require not only intelligent organization of the specialized abilities of teachers but continuous opportunity for the development of these abilities. The development of teaching and scholarly competences is as appropriate in the school district as it is in the university. Leaders in secondary schools have unique opportunities for extending the in-service development of teaching staffs; their roles in promoting instructional excellence are delineated in Chapters 5 and 12.

5. *Commitment to appropriate rewards for excellence in teaching.* Two types of rewards appear essential. One is financial, the other attitudinal. If excellence is to be fostered in teaching, outstanding prospects for the profession should perceive that service in education is both highly valued and adequately rewarded. The valuing of scholarly pursuits should be made evident not only through monetary support but through attitudinal support within the profession and the larger society.

TOWARD QUALITY: INCREASED RESEARCH

As indicated earlier in this chapter, the support—attitudinal and financial—accorded research in education has not always presented a happy picture. Despite the stellar role that research has played in many of the movements toward quality in education, support for these research endeavors has usually come from sources other than local, state, or national educational agencies. Although the Cooperative Research Program of the U.S. Office of Education and the National Defense Education Act have supported educational research, Clark has indicated the inadequacy of these sources:

The sum total of such support has been paltry in quantitative terms. . . . The relative emphasis placed on research in education at the federal level can be seen in gross terms by noting that in 1958 the expenditure for research and development in the U.S. Office of Education was equivalent to approximately 1 percent of that allocated to research and development in the Public Health Service and was less than that provided in agencies such as the Forest Service, Commercial Fisheries, or the Bureau of Sport Fisheries and Wildlife.[24]

If educational practice is to be solidly based, educational research appears mandatory. Educational improvement will require heightened and sustained attention to increased financial and attitudinal support for research; development of facilities for storing and retrieving knowledge; greater attention to training research workers; and more emphasis upon field testing, demonstrating, and disseminating research findings.[25]

IMPLICATIONS FOR ADMINISTRATION

The task of educational administrators in effecting widespread educational transformations and in guiding the educational enterprise toward quality is formidable. Achievement of excellence in secondary education will require movement along many fronts, and the expert guidance of enlightened educational leaders will be a *sine qua non* in the total task. The quality of administrative leadership available and the depth of insight used in approaching educational problems will, in large measure, determine the extent to which excellence can be approximated in secondary schools.

REFERENCES

Burkhead, Jesse, *Public School Finance* (Syracuse, N.Y.: Syracuse University Press, 1964).

Chandler, B. J., Stiles, Lindley J., and Kitsuse, John I. (eds.), *Education in Urban Society* (New York: Dodd, Mead & Co., 1962).

Committee on Tax Education and School Finance, National Education Association, *Does Better Education Cost More?* (Washington, D.C.: the Association, 1959).

Conant, James B., *The Education of American Teachers* (New York: McGraw-Hill Book Co., 1963).

24. Clark, *op. cit.,* p. 15.
25. *Ibid.,* p. 10.

Getzels, Jacob W., and Jackson, Philip W., *Creativity and Intelligence* (New York: John Wiley & Sons, 1962).

Groves, Harold M., *Education and Economic Growth* (Washington, D.C.: Committee on Educational Finance, National Education Association, 1961).

Harcleroad, Fred, "Theoretical Formulations in Audiovisual Communications," *Review of Educational Research*, Vol. XXXII, No. 2, April 1962.

Michael, Donald N., *Cybernation: The Silent Conquest* (Santa Barbara, Calif.: Center for the Study of Democratic Institutions, 1962).

Norton, John K., *Changing Demands on Education and Their Fiscal Implications* (Washington, D.C.: National Committee for Support of the Public Schools, 1963).

Stolurow, Lawrence M., *Teaching by Machine,* Cooperative Research Monograph No. 6 (Washington, D.C.: U.S. Government Printing Office, 1961).

Chapter 12
Staff Personnel

FEW areas in secondary school administration offer greater opportunities for general school improvement than those associated with personnel selection, orientation, development, and coordination. Quality in educational programs is obviously dependent not only upon intelligent and viable program conceptions but also upon competent and motivated professional personnel. Without effective, able personnel, the most carefully conceptualized and precisely planned educational programs may fail.

The significance of staff competence and motivation in program implementation is prompting many secondary school principals to seek greater responsibility for personnel selection, development, and coordination. Fortunately, the era in school administration characterized by strict central-office determination of personnel needs, assignments, and required developmental activities is tending to disappear in American education. Although principals in very small and very large school districts have, at times, been inactive in important staffing functions, others have shouldered great responsibilities in this area. In many medium-sized school districts, principals carry full responsibility not only for selecting and nominating teacher candidates, but for organizing viable programs and procedures for personnel coordination, development, and improvement.

The trend toward greater involvement of secondary school administrators in personnel administration is destined to continue for several reasons. First, continuous redefinition of the principal's role has led to inclusion of responsibility for program development and instructional leadership; responsibility for maintaining, facilitating, and improving educational opportunities; responsibility for marshaling total organizational resources for the continuous improvement of teaching and learning. As recognized leaders in important operating units, secondary school principals in many districts are becoming partners of central-office personnel in building effective instructional resources to serve varied educational requirements.

Second, school leadership and management are becoming increasingly complex both in terms of the number and diversity of school personnel requiring coordination and in terms of the variety of community groups and interests exerting influence upon general school policies, administration, and instruction. Accelerated social change, increased internal differentiation of line and staff functions, and the growing size of secondary schools are all adding significant new dimensions to the task of secondary school administration.

In all probability, few areas of administrative responsibility will tax the abilities and skills of secondary school principals as much as those associated with personnel improvement and administration. Since it is axiomatic that principals share responsibilty for both the success and the failure of professional personnel, improved administrative competence in recruiting and selecting capable staff members, in providing avenues for continuous staff development, and in designing organizational procedures that facilitate the attainment of legitimized educational goals and purposes is crucial.

ORGANIZATIONAL SURVIVAL AND EFFECTIVENESS

The secondary school, as an organization, operates as an open social system with multifunctional characteristics. Two major subtypes of system models are particularly relevant to secondary school administrators in the consideration of personnel improvement and coordination. These are the *survival* model and the *effectiveness* model.

The survival model seeks to delineate minimal conditions that must be met in order to keep the organization, as a system, in existence. Every relationship specified in such a model is a *necessary* condition for the existence of the organization; removal of any one causes the system to cease operation. Caplow has suggested three of these conditions: "no organization can continue to exist unless it reaches a minimal level in the performance of its objective functions, reduces spontaneous conflict below the level which is distributive, and provides sufficient satisfaction to individual members so that membership will be continued." [1] A more inclusive list would include the following:

1. Some method of member identification to distinguish organizational members from those outside the organization.
2. Some means for acquiring and replacing human, financial, and material resources.
3. Some system for allocating and distributing resources, tasks, messages, authority, and responsibility.
4. Some means for evoking effort among organizational members toward organizational task accomplishment.
5. Some method for patterning and coordinating individual efforts.

Several analyses of organization, including the Barnard-Simon theory of organizational motivation and equilibrium, are based upon the survival model. Basic premises underlying such concepts of organization are that systems will continue in existence only so long as (1) they can acquire and replace human and other resources, and (2) they can induce sufficient member participation for organizational survival. Several of the necessary conditions for organizational survival are met in the schools primarily through administrative and institutional activities associated with personnel selection, orientation, development, and coordination. Tasks related to these areas are therefore of singular importance to administrators of secondary schools.

A major reason for requiring optimum administrative performance in these tasks is that schools, as societal institutions, are particularly susceptible to survival model operation—they often experience difficulty in meeting the minimal conditions for organizational existence. Limiting factors such as teacher shortages, teacher turnover, minimum certification requirements, program lacks, and inadequate personnel development and coordination procedures are barriers which, at times, preclude operations beyond survival levels.

Despite such handicaps, the legitimate goal of secondary school administrators requires movement beyond survival levels toward a second subtype of the system model, the *effectiveness* model. The administrator's greatest concern is to structure consistent models of social units which are both capable of, and effective in, the achievement of organizational

1. Theodore Caplow, "The Criteria of Organizational Success," *Social Forces,* Vol. 32, No. 1, 1953, p. 4.

goals. Such an approach requires delineation of those patterns of inter-relationships among the parts of the system and allocation of means within the unique framework of particular organizations which will lead to optimum effectiveness in goal achievement.

A marked difference characterizes secondary school administrators who accept survival models as the basis for organizational operation and those who seek to structure effectiveness models. The administrator whose orientation is organizational survival will, as Simon has suggested, satisfice rather than optimize.[2] In considering sets of functional alternatives in organization, satisficing behavior ordinarily leads not to the selection of the best possible alternative, but to the selection of any one that meets the requirements for organizational survival. In terms of the effectiveness model, however, these same sets of alternatives have different values. Some are more functional than others; choices must be made in terms of the relative effectiveness of each for organizational purposes.

IMPROVEMENT: INSTITUTIONAL AND INDIVIDUAL DIMENSIONS

Integration of the requirements of the institution with the needs and demands of individual staff members poses a significant problem to the secondary school administrator. Institutional improvement requires administrative attention to the accomplishment of organizational purposes and goals, that is, to the promotion of organizational *effectiveness*. At the same time, the individual dimension of organization demands satisfaction of individual needs and desires so that the organization may be *efficient* as well as effective. Developing an appropriate "blend" of effectiveness and efficiency is a primary task in secondary school administration.

In considering the problems of effectiveness and efficiency in organizations, the secondary school administrator would do well to reflect upon the useful distinctions Chase has drawn between satisfaction, morale, motivation, work, and achievement:

... satisfaction grows out of a sense of achievement and of being valued in the organization; it is a result of past experiences and typically is uppermost in a state of rest between activities. Morale is compounded from a commit-

2. Herbert A. Simon, *Administrative Behavior* (New York: The Macmillan Co., 1959), pp. xxv-xxvi.

ment to common purposes and a sense of unfulfillment or challenge and is powerfully influenced by the expectation (grounded in past experience) of satisfying future achievement. Motivation springs from interaction between the ready organism (individual or group) and the external situation, and is the trigger which releases energy for work. Work is behavior directed toward organizational goals and, when performed under favorable conditions, results in achievement. Achievement in organization terms is the attainment of, or progress toward, goals; but for the individual in the organization it is the feeling of a task well done or of a substantial contribution to goal achievement.[3]

Effectiveness: The Institutional Dimension

An organization's effectiveness is determined by its capacity and ability to achieve desired ends and goals. If the secondary school is to operate beyond survival levels, the administrator's role in identifying and analyzing factors that promote organizational effectiveness is critical. Previous chapters have directed attention to several basic dimensions of administrative performance which tend to enhance organizational effectiveness. Among these were:

1. The development and legitimation of broad educational policies relating to the basic purposes and ends of education.
2. The development and legitimation of operational policies to implement broad policy statements.
3. Technical-managerial implementation of legitimized policies through:
   a. Suitable role definitions and job descriptions.
   b. Logical task division.
   c. Formalized and integrated decision making, communication, and workflow patterns.
   d. Clearly defined authority and responsibility relationships within the framework of sound, stable organization.
4. Leadership in the structuring and maintenance of proper relationships to facilitate continuous assessment and improvement of operations.
5. Sophisticated use of administrative processes in all phases of organizational activity.

The fostering of effectiveness in the secondary school requires administrative commitment coupled with a clear sense of purpose. It demands

3. Francis S. Chase, "The Administrator as Implementor of the Goals of Education for Our Time," in Roald F. Campbell and James M. Lipham (eds.), *Administrative Theory as a Guide to Action* (Chicago: Midwest Administration Center, University of Chicago, 1960), p. 194.

the mobilization of every organizational resource toward achievement of purpose. It calls for the patterning of necessary interrelationships among parts of the system. It requires intelligent and purposive allocation of means. Above all, it demands capable and dedicated personnel —committed to the aims and goals of the school organization and motivated toward the accomplishment of individual and shared tasks.

In terms of staff improvement, "effectiveness" is a measure of congruence between staff behavior and institutional expectations. The Getzels-Guba model, introduced in Chapter 5 and delineated here more fully in Figure 12-1, shows effectiveness to be related to the normative or *nomothetic* dimensions of organization.[4] Thus, the closer the role behavior to institutional expectations, the greater the effectiveness of role incumbents. The model clarifies the unique task of the secondary school administrator in promoting staff improvement; his concern is to seek successively closer approximations between organizational expectations and individual behavior.

Since the salient functions of institutional expectations are to guide, to limit, and to circumscribe personnel behavior in ways that optimize organizational goal achievement, the essential purpose of those expectations is to set standards for desired behavior and to inhibit behaviors which detract from effectiveness. The building of successively closer

Figure 12-1. The Expanded Getzels-Guba Model

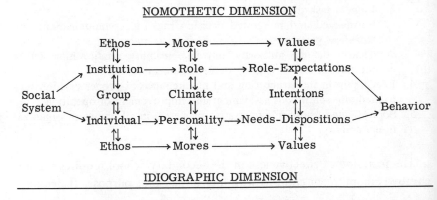

NOMOTHETIC DIMENSION

IDIOGRAPHIC DIMENSION

4. For an expanded discussion of the relevance of this model to administration, see Robert E. Sweitzer, "An Assessment of Two Theoretical Frameworks," in Jack A. Culbertson and Stephen P. Hencley (eds.), *Educational Research: New Perspectives* (Danville, Ill.: The Interstate Printers and Publishers, 1963), pp. 199-232.

approximations between organizational expectations and individual behavior requires clear role definitions, continuous clarification of role requirements, emphasis upon organizational goal achievement, control of the activities of all staff members, and coordination of the efforts of organizational members toward accomplishment of purpose.

Efficiency: The Individual Dimension

If every organizational member identified completely with organizational aims and purposes, found absolute compatibility between his needs and his assigned organizational role, felt highly motivated toward the accomplishment of organizational tasks, and perceived complete congruence between his own goals and those of the system, the administrator's task in building an effective secondary school organization would be relatively simple. Such an ideal state is rarely found in secondary schools, however. Argyris [5] and others have pointed out that incongruence between the needs of organizational members and the requirements of formal institutions is a frequent phenomenon. Such incongruence results in frustration, failure, tension, conflict, and hostility. The demands of task specialization in hierarchical structures may lead to dependence, submissiveness, and leader-centeredness—all of which are inimical to organizational efficiency. Especially is this true when school personnel have little control over instruction, participate mainly in decisions characterized by short-term perspective, are given little opportunity to perfect latent abilities, and are expected to perform as passive subordinates.

In terms of the individual, efficiency may be defined as congruence between behavior and individual needs. When congruence exists, the individual's behavior is both natural and satisfying. Goals are attained through *efficient* behavior with minimum demands upon psychic energy. Thus, efficiency denotes the absence of conflict, tension, frustration, and anxiety in an individual's behavior in organization. Absolute efficiency in organization, however, is rare. Guba and Bidwell have noted that:

... There will always be a gap between expectations and needs in any real situation, for even the attempt to structure expectations congruent with the needs of one role incumbent will produce results at least partially unsuitable for another incumbent. As a result, the administrator is always faced with the task of maintaining a balance between effectiveness and efficiency. The prob-

5. Chris Argyris, *Personality and Organization* (New York: Harper & Bros., 1957).

lem is to determine the extent to which effectiveness will be maximized at the expense of efficiency, or vice versa. Clearly, it is through this effectiveness-efficiency relationship that the problem of staff motivation (expectation-needs congruence) can be approached.[6]

Figure 12-2 clarifies the interrelationships existing in organizations among effectiveness, efficiency, and a third organizational phenomenon, satisfaction. The basic interrelationships among these three important phenomena in organizations may be summarized as follows:

1. Effectiveness refers to congruence between expectations for behavior (role) and actual behavior.
2. Efficiency refers to congruence between an individual's needs and his behavior.
3. Satisfaction refers to congruence between expectations and needs.
4. A person in a given role may be effective yet inefficient; efficient yet ineffective; and satisfied while both ineffective and inefficient.[7]

It appears important to emphasize the fallacy of complete administrative reliance upon either the effectiveness or the efficiency dimension in working toward personnel improvement. An appropriate blend of these dimensions is necessary in moving organizations toward legitimate goals. Although the secondary school administrator who is concerned entirely with effectiveness may be viewed by subordinates as an autocratic "pusher," effectiveness is a necessary condition in organizations that operate beyond survival levels. At the same time, the administrator who places undue stress upon efficiency needs to bear in mind that high morale, though it may be valuable, is not sufficient to generate high achievement. These two important dimensions of organization require a judicious "mix." Situations and conditions vary in secondary schools;

Figure 12-2. Interrelationships Among Effectiveness, Efficiency, and Satisfaction

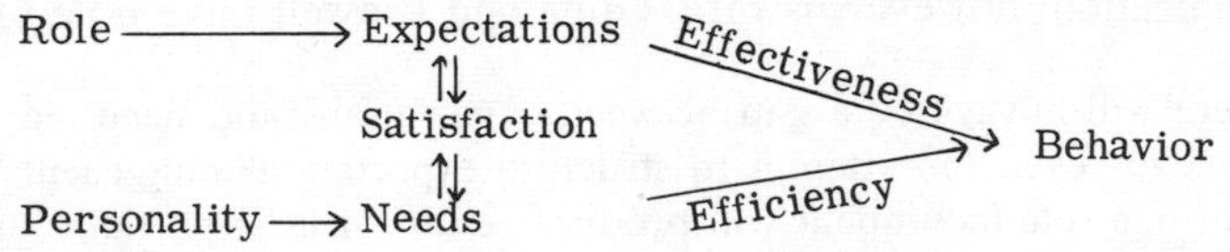

6. Egon G. Guba and Charles E. Bidwell, *Administrative Relationships* (Chicago: Midwest Administration Center, University of Chicago, 1957), p. 9.
7. *Ibid.*, p. 8.

different approaches to maximizing effectiveness and efficiency are necessary. The ability to exercise mature judgment in determining organizational needs in relation to effectiveness and efficiency is a salient characteristic of outstanding practitioners in secondary school administration.

SELECTING PERSONNEL

A most important avenue to potential organizational effectiveness lies in careful and sustained administrative effort to improve the criteria and procedures for staff selection. Perfunctory selection procedures often lead to concentrations of incompetent personnel who hamper, if they do not actually preclude, improved organizational performance. For this reason, a high degree of selectivity is essential in filling every position in the secondary school. One of the greatest contributions to organizational effectiveness the administrator in the secondary school can make is to ensure that selection procedures and criteria lead to the selection of quality personnel.

Ideally, the selection of a candidate to fill a position in a school is the culmination of a prolonged screening process. "Haste makes waste" is nowhere more true than in personnel selection. It is an important part of the principal's responsibility to develop adequate and logical procedures for assessing staff needs, for establishing criteria for placements and additions to the staff, and for engaging in cooperative effort with other staff members to determine the personal and professional qualifications of required personnel. The principal should either seek responsibility for these functions or establish avenues for close cooperation with the central-staff person in charge of staff personnel.

There are several important steps in the establishment of a screening process. Each contributes to the over-all effectiveness of selection:

1. *Developing accurate role definitions.* It is important to have clear conceptions of the expectations attached to every vacant position. The responsibilities of prospective job incumbents should be clearly defined and made available in the form of written job specifications. Both faculty and community expectations should be reflected in these specifications. Moreover, expectations concerning the directions of expected growth should be clearly formulated and discussed with prospective candidates. Thus, role definitions should encompass both initial and possible future contributions expected of prospective personnel. A clear indication of

where the vacant position fits into the total configuration of positions is also necessary.

2. *Establishing selection standards.* The written job description should offer important clues to selection standards. Factors that require consideration in the development of selection standards include (*a*) age, (*b*) health, (*c*) education, (*d*) work experience, (*e*) aims, (*f*) intelligence, (*g*) appearance, (*h*) general knowledge, (*i*) communication skills, (*j*) motivations, (*k*) interests, (*l*) professional knowledge and abilities, (*m*) attitudes and values, (*n*) mental health, and (*o*) general suitability for work with students, faculty, and community members. Since many of these factors are difficult to assess, agreement should be reached among those responsible for selection concerning types of evidence to be considered in relation to each factor.

3. *Identifying promising candidates.* Consideration should be given to outstanding candidates both from within and outside the school system. Lists of candidates showing unusual promise can often be generated through (*a*) reviewing the district's file of previous applications, (*b*) visiting and interviewing candidates from other school districts, (*c*) contacting professors who are in close touch with school personnel in a number of districts, and (*d*) visiting university campuses to interview prospective candidates and to acquaint teacher placement officers with special personnel needs.

4. *Gathering required information.* Each applicant for a position should submit university transcripts, recent credentials, and letters of recommendation. Evaluation of performance should be requested from past employers, if not offered by the candidate. Moreover, the district's biographical information schedule should be completed by all applicants. Candidates who appear most promising on the basis of the above types of evidence should be requested to appear for personal interviews.

5. *Evaluating prospective candidates.* Arrangements should be structured for individual and group interviews to assess each candidate's potentiality. Every effort should be made during the evaluation process to gain accurate assessments of the candidate's ability to fulfill role expectations and to ensure that such expectations do not run counter to the applicant's needs and motivations. It is far better to discover any serious limitations of this nature during the selection process than to expend a large amount of organizational time and resources in corrective measures following the hiring of a candidate.

Wherever possible, the use of trained interviewers, performance tests, written tests, and rating scales should be incorporated into the selection procedure. Following appraisal of all available evidence on each candidate, the applicant best suited for the position should be selected. The superintendent should be notified so that he may recommend the candidate for appointment by the board of education. Unsuccessful candidates should receive notification of this appointment.

ORIENTING PERSONNEL

Although the election of candidates to fill vacant positions fulfills an important requirement for organizational survival, the act of election, in reality, brings an organization only to the zero point in terms of organizational effectiveness. The better the candidate selected, however, the greater the potential for movement toward organizational effectiveness. Much remains to be done following selection to assure a meaningful adjustment between the individual and the organization. The orientation of new staff members is one of the first activities to be undertaken.

Orientation requires sensitive planning and careful execution. It is during the orientation period that new staff members gather their first impressions concerning the school's policies, objectives, leadership, and methods of operation. Moreover, it is at this time that initial acquaintance is made with colleagues and with the community's inhabitants, characteristics, agencies, and services. Since first impressions are often lasting, every effort should be expended during orientation to assure that new staff members gain correct understandings of the many facets of school and community life.

During orientation new staff members first become acquainted with the philosophy and purposes underlying the school operations. The aims of the educational enterprise require clarification during this period— as do long-range and short-term educational goals toward which the district is striving. Opportunities for making meaningful contributions toward goal accomplishment within the framework of school organization require careful delineation. Since the aims, goals, and purposes of school organizations are of an evolving nature, clear definition is required of avenues available to new personnel for participation in determining the desired ends of the educational enterprise.

Special attention should be directed to acquainting new staff members with opportunities offered by the school system for both professional improvement and service. Brief descriptions should be made available of current and projected activities encompassed by study councils, workshops, special projects, advanced study groups, and professional associations. New staff members should be encouraged to become acquainted with the activities of such professional bodies and to formulate plans for continuing professional improvement.

Above all, attention should be given to the delineation of ways in which performance expectations for various positions contribute to goal accomplishment in the institution. Indications should also be given of the types of assistance available for the improvement of professional performance: consultants, in-service activities, source materials, and others.

The induction and orientation of new staff members are major responsibilities of the secondary school principal. Worthwhile activities during this period can be extremely helpful in laying proper foundations for the continuing task of personnel development. The sharpened perceptions and heightened understandings engendered concerning school district goals, aspirations, expectations, operations, and procedures can be of outstanding value in facilitating the new staff member's initial adaptation to the school organization.

IN-SERVICE IMPROVEMENT

In-service improvement of the professional performance of teachers is a significant aspect of administrative responsibility in the secondary schools. The over-all task is not one to be approached in superficial fashion. It requires clarity of purpose and direction, extensive knowledge and skill, deep professional commitment, and penetrating insight into the capabilities and potentialities of both organizations and professional personnel.

The experience of secondary school administrators indicates that many barriers may need to be surmounted if in-service programs are to become important and productive avenues to school improvement and effectiveness. Teacher apathy and resistance to change are often major obstacles, as are heavy teaching schedules, extracurricular assignments, staff disharmony, lack of financial resources, teacher turnover, teacher-administrator conflict, unprofessional attitudes, or general unrest in the school and community. Despite such obstacles, the outstanding individual and organizational benefits that may accrue from carefully conceptualized in-service activities make this area of organizational endeavor worthy of the best efforts of secondary school administrators.

Characteristics and Objectives of In-Service Programs

Varying objectives and characteristics are exhibited by in-service training programs. Certain of these appear to be salient in terms of the aims and goals of secondary education.

1. *The program should be aimed at improving professional performance.* Increased teacher competence should be sought in relation to understanding of the learning process, mastery of subject matter, ability to identify and reach important teaching-learning objectives, insight into teaching methods and learning experiences required in competent classroom performance, and effectiveness in working with both students and faculty members toward cooperative achievement of organizational goals.

2. *The program should be characterized by an atmosphere of inquiry.* Professional involvement in questioning the validity of established practices and procedures and in promoting increasingly sophisticated approaches to both self-evaluation and program evaluation should be distinguishing characteristics of in-service programs. Many important areas worthy of professional inquiry exist in all school systems. Among these are: (*a*) the teacher's role as mediator between students and the world of ideas, knowledge, and desirable attitudes; (*b*) the validity of accepted educational aims and goals; (*c*) the assessment of educational innovations such as ETV, team teaching, pupil deployment patterns, and technological media; (*d*) the identification of dimensions of teacher effectiveness in terms of skills, knowledge, creativity, and competence in directing learning processes; (*e*) the study of patterns of effective behavior in relation to co-workers, the classroom, and the community; (*f*) the exploration of means for providing for individual differences among pupils; and (*g*) the assessment of new avenues for utilizing community resources and for enlisting the cooperation of community members.

3. *The program should seek active engagement with worthwhile problems in an atmosphere of freedom and psychological safety.* The administrator's role in providing an appropriate, anxiety-free climate is most important to the success of in-service programs. This means neither the

abdication of responsibility nor the assumption of a laissez-faire attitude, however. The secondary school administrator has important leadership responsibilities in:

 a. Leading his staff in the identification of important barriers blocking improvement.

 b. Suggesting fruitful ways in which problems might be approached and/or studied.

 c. Participating with individuals and groups in designing guidelines for problem solution.

 d. Allocating necessary organizational resources (time, consultants, source material, equipment, finances) to further work of staff members on problems of educational significance.

 e. Assisting staff personnel toward maximum growth in terms of skills, information, values, and processes that may be derived from in-service opportunities.

 f. Interpreting and evaluating in-service experience of staff members.

 g. Supporting the efforts of staff personnel motivated toward inquiry and the improvement of professional performance.

 h. Fostering exchanges among professional personnel.

The range in problem activity appears fully as important as the significance of problems undertaken for study. Although it is customary in school districts to emphasize different problem areas at different times, care should be taken to provide staff members with opportunities for engagement covering a broad spectrum. The objective should be to provide growth experiences on a broad front rather than to stress the vertical accumulation of experience in any single problem area.

 4. *The program should make provision for both individual and group activities.* Teachers should have opportunities to plan programs of independent study, to initiate proposals for inquiry and research, to experiment with pupil deployment patterns, to test new teaching methods, to plan visits and travel, and to make use of available new technologies. Moreover, resources for self-improvement in the form of books, periodicals, professional journals, films, pamphlets, and other materials should be plentiful and accessible. Compatibility with program objectives should be a constant guide in the formulation of independent, individual programs for self-improvement.

 Often, the principal's responsibility for supervising teaching affords opportunities for encouraging self-improvement programs for individual teachers. Diagnosis of deficiencies in teaching may suggest fruitful avenues for ameliorating handicaps and for enhancing instructional potential through the use of specialists or other teachers to improve teaching performance.

The structuring of independent programs for self-improvement should not preclude the teacher's participation in group activities aimed at improvement. It is the administrator's responsibility to ensure that both types of activity receive recognition and sanction and that both may progress concurrently. Opportunity for participation in study councils, special group projects, workshops, and other group activities should be made available to all staff members. Growth in behavioral effectiveness as a result of group activity is fully as important as the substantive learnings and conclusions derived through group effort.

5. *The program should encompass opportunities for formal instruction.* Two possibilities are open to administrators of secondary schools in incorporating formal instruction into programs of in-service training. Competent consultants and instructional specialists may be called in to assist school personnel to move to new levels of understanding and performance. The important function of outside specialists is not to solve the problems of school staffs but rather to delineate difficulties, bring new perspectives, and suggest heuristic approaches that will assist the staff in seeking its own solutions to problems.

Opportunities for formal instruction beyond the confines of the local school or school system should also be encouraged. Many activities are available whose aims are consistent with the accepted objectives of improvement programs undertaken in local schools. Attendance at worthwhile conferences, workshops, professional meetings, and university lecture series can be of material assistance in extending the professional horizons and competences of staff personnel.

6. *Although the program should encompass both, the creative, experimental aspects of goal seeking should take precedence over the study of subject matter or the routine preparation of curriculum guides and aids.* Probably nothing will deaden enthusiasm for in-service programs so much as ill-conceived projects based upon mundane trivia. The emphasis should be upon meaningful growth in a creative, experimental atmosphere where value is placed upon formulation and testing of hypotheses that are important to staff members. The in-service program should stress the "releasing" rather than the control functions of administration. It should normally exclude purely administrative matters or activities designed to generate acceptance of the status quo.

7. *The program should not be structured through administrative edict and should avoid the implication that it is tied to a plan or system of salary adjustment.* Since the development of desirable teacher attitudes is a prime objective of the administrator, mandatory aspects of in-service programs should be minimized. Mandated in-service activities are usually seen as extra chores foisted upon teachers by administrators; the resentment generated is often sufficient to ensure low-level motivation, enthusiasm, and participation.

8. *The program should encompass procedures for evaluation.* The evaluation methods adopted should be of such nature that they result in reliable, valid measures of individual and group achievement in terms of agreed-upon objectives. Opportunities should be made available to each teacher for independent self-evaluation of professional behavior. In addition, formal rating scales, follow-up studies, records of proceedings, and behavioral evidences of change may all be introduced into the evaluation process as the need for these devices is perceived and accepted by program participants. Premature introduction of evaluation procedures, together with unwise use of evaluative data, may destroy the atmosphere of freedom and psychological safety that is essential to group security and to initial success in group work.

EFFECTING CHANGE

Although a scientifically based technology of social management has yet to emerge in administration, the secondary school administrator who is concerned with guiding change may draw upon a wealth of research in planning his strategies and actions. Guiding change in school organizations is a delicate process. To "change," per se, is threatening. The process of change often affects deep-rooted values. In guiding change, the administrator must be prepared to cope with the emotional reactions which change may engender and to avoid being branded as a calculating, designing, manipulator. He must remember at all times that the negative implications of "manipulation" are contrary to the basic values of egalitarian cultures.

The role of agents of change, however, frequently involves manipulative processes. As Cunningham has noted, manipulative processes employed by agents of change encompass:

. . . the assessment of circumstances, the planned arrangement of people, of conditions, of resources, and of events which will lead to the attainment of socially acceptable objectives for a school system. Manipulation, after all, may involve strategy, not cunning; intelligence, not deception; statesmanship, not demagoguery; discretion, not duplicity; premeditation, not impulsiveness." [8]

Thus, *diagnosis* of existing patterns of organizational behavior and *intervention* to effect modifications in these patterns become important dimensions of the administrator's role.[9]

The secondary school administrator's responsibility for effective intervention in organizational processes (in modifying purposes, curricula, work-flow patterns, resource allocation, personnel behavior, decision-making procedures, and the like) requires sophisticated understanding of the dynamics of group change. Although the results of research based upon change in small groups are not completely translatable to school situations, they provide school administrators with important clues concerning strategies and tactics involved in processes of change. The works of Lippitt, Watson, and Westley,[10] Bennis, Benne, and Chin,[11] Coffey and Golden,[12] and Ginzberg and Reilly,[13] are important sources for secondary school administrators who wish to effect change. Using these sources, together with relevant findings from a number of studies of change, the authors offer the following generalizations as important in the initiation and control of change processes within school organizations.

1. *Group membership exerts strong influence upon member behavior —either toward change or toward maintenance of the status quo.* When change becomes necessary in school organizations, it is usually effected through group processes. Groups in school organizations can be effective instruments of change; they can also be instrumental in resisting change. Thus sensitivity to group processes and to the intervention role of agents

8. Luvern L. Cunningham, "Viewing Change in School Organizations," *Administrator's Notebook,* Vol. XI, No. 1, September, 1962, p. 2.

9. *Ibid.,* p. 3.

10. Ronald Lippitt, Jeanne Watson, and Bruce Westley, *The Dynamics of Planned Change* (New York: Harcourt, Brace & Co., 1958).

11. Warren G. Bennis, Kenneth Benne, and Robert Chin, *The Planning of Change* (New York: Holt, Rinehart & Winston, 1962).

12. Hubert S. Coffey and William P. Golden, Jr., "Psychology of Change Within an Institution," in *In-Service Education of Teachers, Supervisors, and Administrators, Fifty-sixth Yearbook of the National Society for the Study of Education,* Part I (Chicago: University of Chicago Press, 1957).

13. Eli Ginzberg and Ewing W. Reilly, *Effecting Change in Large Organizations* (New York: Columbia University Press, 1957).

of change is an important prerequisite to administrative success in secondary education.

It should be noted at the outset that group resistance to change is not always deleterious. Although resistance is often viewed as commitment to the status quo, it sometimes has the positive effect of assuring continuity and stability in the secondary school. But if group resistance keeps an institution from adapting its behavior to meet changing circumstances, it may seriously affect organizational effectiveness—if it does not, in fact, adversely affect possibilities for organizational survival. Thus the reasons behind continued resistance to change become matters of concern to secondary school administrators.

Resistance may be caused by anxiety generated by lack of information concerning the effects of proposed changes upon organizational members. Consultations and factual announcements can do much to relieve anxiety and to quell harmful rumors. Revolutionary proposals for change which indicate to personnel that extensive retraining or study may be necessary for adequate job performance are likely to meet active resistance. Thus, change is likely to be more successful if it is gradual and continuous rather than revolutionary. Often, major resistance to organizational change may be traced to the operation of a strong informal organization which is seeking to control organizational decisions through the enforcement of standards counter to those of the formal organization. Excessive resistance from such a source may indicate serious imbalance between organizational expectations and personnel needs.

Research on group behavior indicates that the organizational group may be viewed from an administrative viewpoint as a *medium* of change, as a *target* of change, and as an *agent* of change.[14] All three approaches are effective for introducing change in secondary school organizations. The strategy for administrative intervention, however, differs in each case.

In viewing the group as a *medium* of change, the administrator recognizes that groups exert strong influence upon their members. Attempts to restructure behavior in new directions may be either accepted or rejected by informal pressures operating within different groups. The essential problem becomes one of intervention—of finding ways to place the individuals to be changed into group situations where sustained con-

14. Dorwin Cartwright, "Achieving Change in People: Some Applications of Group Dynamics Theory," *Human Relations,* Vol. IV, No. 1, 1951, p. 387.

tact with agents of change is possible. In secondary schools this is often possible through committee work, departmental activities, study councils, and the like. Important to the success of this avenue to change is the development of strong "we"-feelings during the group experience, the minimization of psychological distance among group members, and the creation of opportunities for observation, discussion, and internalization of new attitudinal, behavioral, and value patterns. Research indicates that change is likely to be accelerated if the group experience results in increased need satisfaction, prestige, or heightened awareness of the significance of group goals.

In working with groups viewed as the *targets* of change, the administrator uses a somewhat different intervention process. Here, stress is placed upon building and opening channels of communication, upon creating shared perceptions, and upon creating desires for change within the group itself. Ordinarily, this is a difficult task, especially if hostility or lack of trust has stifled group communication and interaction. Chin has noted some of the problems that secondary school administrators may encounter:

A system in equilibrium reacts to outside impingements by (1) resisting the influence of the disturbance, refusing to acknowledge its existence, or by building a protective wall against the intrusion, and by other defensive maneuvers. Example: A small group refuses to talk about a troublesome problem of unequal power distribution raised by a member. (2) By resisting the disturbance through bringing into operation the homeostatic forces that restore or recreate a balance. The small group talks about the troublesome problem of a member and convinces him that it is not "really" a problem. (3) By accommodating the disturbances through achieving a new equilibrium. Talking about the problem may result in a shift in power relationships among members of the group.[15]

Important tasks for the secondary school administrator in working with groups as targets of change are (*a*) getting the group to face and verbalize the underlying problems, even though hostility arises during the process; (*b*) creating shared perceptions of the need for change; (*c*) formulating plans *with* the group for desirable change; and (*d*) making clear the consequences of planned changes.

The use of groups as *agents* of change is commonly practiced in most institutions. An example of a group acting as an agent of change would

15. Robert Chin, "The Utility of System Models and Developmental Models for Practitioners," in Bennis, Benne, and Chin, *op. cit.,* pp. 205-206.

be a committee of secondary school faculty members chosen to study a new organizational pattern, such as team teaching, and charged with the responsibility of making definite recommendations to the faculty and administration. Participants in action research projects undertaken in many school systems perform much the same function. A university survey group that makes recommendations for change in a school is another example. In each instance, the goal is to initiate change. But the apparent pressure for change is shifted from the administrator in the situation to (*a*) a faculty group, or (*b*) an expert outside agency.

2. *In working toward permanent change, the expectations of formal leaders must be both supportive and widely known.* Expectations for change on the part of institutional leaders should seldom, if ever, be greater than the capabilities for achievement of organizational members. Thus, mature judgment is an essential ingredient in the planning and initiation of change. At the same time it should be remembered that the expectations of formal leaders are more powerful movers for change than are individual needs—although both are important. Thus, in the secondary school it is essential that (*a*) staff members *know* the change expectations of key administrators, and (*b*) formal leaders express strong support for desired changes. Without such formal support, movement toward change may be abortive. Organizational members may perceive that the movement is unimportant to, or not desired by, institutional leaders.

3. *Change is costly in terms of time, risk, and demands upon leadership.* Before embarking upon any extensive program of change it is well to consider whether the cost of change will result in sufficient reward to make it desirable. In economic terms, profit equals reward minus cost.

Change requires time—a commodity of considerable value in organizations. It requires time for planning, initiation, communication, implementation, coordination, monitoring and control, and evaluation.

Change involves risk. It creates anxiety and unrest, both of which may be detrimental to organizational effectiveness. Prior to the initiation of change, careful consideration should be directed to this question: Is the change involved worth the possible disturbance in terms of staff morale and satisfaction?

Change poses heavy demands upon leadership. Disagreeable and difficult actions are sometimes necessary during the change process, and the administrator must initiate those actions. Again, it is necessary to give thoughtful consideration to several questions: Is the change worthwhile in terms of the expenditure of psychic energy in the organization? Will the change produce sufficient reward to warrant the disagreeable and difficult actions? Will future efforts toward cooperation be handicapped by the possible unpleasantness and bad feeling generated by the change?

4. *The prestige of organizational effectiveness resulting from change may accrue to all members of the institution.* The promise that change will enhance future status, prestige, security, or power provides powerful motivation for acceptance of change in organizations. Change that increases organizational effectiveness or that provides new visibility and status for the institution may serve to enhance the prestige of all organizational members. This phenomenon has been repeatedly demonstrated in schools that have pioneered in the development of innovations such as team teaching, merit rating, use of technological media in instruction, and a host of others. The fame of schools and school systems that pioneered such innovations as the Winnetka Plan, the platoon system, the Dalton Plan, departmentalization, and the unit method of instruction is legendary.

The administrator should note, however, that successful innovations may become so institutionalized that they become difficult to change when their purpose has been served. Especially is this so when staff members perceive change as a way of divesting personnel—or the system—of valued symbols of prestige, status, or power.

5. *Communication is the major vehicle for promoting change.* Communication is central not only in developing readiness for change but also in implementing and controlling change. Communication is the central process in developing and increasing the common core of values which guide the institution's operations. When formal leaders and staff members are able to perceive and share each other's goals, aspirations, and motivations, their differing orientations and perspectives may stimulate rather than hinder change.

6. *Although change may be engineered through force, lasting change is built upon a foundation of consent.* There should be no doubt in anyone's mind concerning the ability of formal leaders to institute change by force if necessary. Administrators in secondary schools have extensive control of many values important to staff personnel since formal controls over reward, prestige, promotion, and ratings of effectiveness

are lodged with formal leaders. It is generally recognized, however, that change engineered through force must be maintained by force. Thus, change brought about by such means provides an extremely unsatisfactory foundation for organizational effectiveness and efficiency. Change through manifest power chokes communication, inhibits interaction, and introduces studied formality into organizational relationships. In the secondary school setting, consent is a primary requisite to lasting change.

7. *Change requires the acquisition of new skills.* The formulation and acceptance of new goals or new methods of operation usually demand new skills or require the adoption of different behavioral and attitudinal patterns. If change is to be realized and if it is to last, opportunities must be made available for the acquisition and practice of new competences and behaviors. Secondary school administrators can facilitate these ends through (*a*) clarification of the meaning of new goals in terms of the operations required to achieve them, (*b*) providing necessary cues to guide desired behavior, (*c*) rewarding correct responses, (*d*) making available the organizational resources necessary to realizing new levels of proficiency in skill and behavior, and (*e*) relocating work loads to provide time for the practice and perfection of new skills and behaviors.

8. *Effective measuring and feedback devices are essential in the change process.* Change, as a developmental process, requires both evaluation and feedback. Progress made toward new goals should be measured and communicated. Evaluation procedures that are carefully structured and effectively implemented will (*a*) indicate where weaknesses exist, (*b*) suggest areas where corrective action is necessary, (*c*) reveal whether the structured goals are attainable or whether they require revision, and (*d*) provide personnel with guides for assessing the effectiveness of their own performance.

COORDINATING EFFORT

The structuring of effective secondary schools requires more than either the intelligent planning of change or the constant motivation of personnel toward task accomplishment. An additional requirement is coordinated effort. Organizational work-flow patterns must be in phase so that the activities of personnel neither hinder nor nullify the forward movement of organizational effort. Coordination requires not only planned encouragement of some individual and group effort and inhibition of others, but also regulation of organizational communication and resource distribution in terms of timing, direction, and intensity.[16]

Dahl and Lindblom have noted that two models underlie most theories concerning the manner in which coordination is effected in organizations.[17] One of these is the reciprocating model in which work flow and activity are guided and governed by intraorganizational cues and signals. No one person controls or governs others; each individual responds to organizational needs in terms of his perception of the actions of others. The second is the leadership model in which all organizational work flow and activity patterns are guided by stimuli emanating from a central source. In this second model, coordination is effected through the planned actions of both formal leaders and leadership groups. Kaufman has noted certain limitations and strengths of the two models:

> ... channels of distribution often break down when regulated exclusively by reciprocal methods. Information is not always distributed, communications are often incomplete and ambiguous and contradictory. The timing of flows permits the accumulation of excess materials in some places, shortages of the same materials in others. Things and messages go to the wrong people, generate the wrong actions. People undo each other's work, impede each other. The basic processes are all jeopardized.
>
> A leader, or a leadership group, devoting time specifically to the detection of such situations and to the issuance of messages that inhibit some actions, encourage others, slow some down, speed up others, change the directions and intensities of flow, open new channels, and so on, can often end blockages, prevent jams, and thus facilitate the vigorous performance of the basic processes ...[18]

The goal of the secondary school administrator in establishing effective coordination procedures is not, however, to seek replacement of the reciprocating model by the leadership model. His goal is to seek an appropriate "mix" of these two methods of operation. Neither model is sufficient in itself to ensure effective coordination. Both tend to operate within the structure of organization, and both may be used to advantage by the alert administrator. Above all, the secondary school administrator

16. Herbert Kaufman, "Why Organizations Behave as They Do: An Outline of a Theory," in *Administrative Theory* (Austin, Tex.: University of Texas, 1961), p. 46.

17. R. A. Dahl and C. E. Lindblom, *Politics, Economics, and Welfare* (New York: Harper & Row, 1953), pp. 357 ff.

18. Kaufman, *op. cit.*, pp. 58-59.

should be aware that the primary aim of leadership is not the development of monolithic organizations. Leadership is most appropriately used when it is directed toward the development of individual and cooperative patterns of action which facilitate the accomplishment of organizational goals.

REFERENCES

Campbell, Roald F., and Lipham, James M. (eds.), *Administrative Theory as a Guide to Action* (Chicago: Midwest Administration Center, University of Chicago, 1960).

Culbertson, Jack A., and Hencley, Stephen P. (eds.), *Educational Research: New Perspectives* (Danville, Ill.: The Interstate Printers and Publishers, 1963).

Cyert, Richard M., and March, James G., *A Behavioral Theory of the Firm* (Englewood Cliffs, N.J.: Prentice-Hall, 1963).

Griffiths, Daniel, *et al.*, *Organizing Schools for Effective Education* (Danville, Ill.: The Interstate Printers and Publishers, 1962).

Guba, Egon, and Bidwell, Charles E., *Administrative Relationships* (Chicago: Midwest Administration Center, University of Chicago, 1957).

Lucio, William H., and McNeil, John D., *Supervision* (New York: McGraw-Hill Book Co., 1962).

March, James G., and Simon, Herbert, *Organizations* (New York: John Wiley & Sons, 1958).

Marx, F. M. (ed.), *Elements of Public Administration* (Englewood Cliffs, N.J.: Prentice-Hall, 1959).

Miles, Matthew B. (ed.), *Innovation in Education* (New York: Bureau of Publications, Teachers College, Columbia University, 1964).

Presthus, Robert V., *The Organizational Society: An Analysis and a Theory* (New York: Alfred A. Knopf, 1962).

Simon, Herbert A., *Administrative Behavior* (New York: The Macmillan Co., 1959).

Part IV
Operations and
Management

Chapter 13
School Office Functions

T HE entire day-by-day operation of the school centers upon the functions performed in and about the school office. This rather unfortunate term denotes location rather than activity, but it is through the records, procedures, and services that surround the operation of the school office that "school keeps." The office serves as a clearing house, communication center, source of information, and as a coordinating agency, among other important things. The makeup of the office—its staff, records, facilities, and the way it functions—determines to a large extent the effectiveness of the principal and the total staff.

Size of school, resources of the school district and attitudes of the principal have important bearing upon the manner in which school office functions are organized and performed. In some schools, all records, management procedures, even supplies for teachers, are handled through one office; in other schools, functions are delineated and decentralized. Large suburban high schools, for example, provide a main office, business office, guidance office, records and data-processing room, activities office, health office, attendance office, and various departmental offices —sometimes employing a staff of thirty-five to forty clerks and secretaries. Some junior high schools known to the authors have no secretarial help, and some operate with volunteer, student, or perhaps part-time secretarial help. These illustrations indicate the wide variation in practice and reveal as well the variation in type of service available to staff, students, and public.

An understanding of the total management function depends both upon the extent to which each major management task is identified and upon the principal's point of view concerning his responsibility for each task. As the authors attempted to reveal with the model presented in Chapter 1, management functions are designed to maintain the school in its daily operation. If the factors influencing management tasks did not change, little administration at the management level would be needed. Clear-cut routines and well-established procedures should permit the school to operate, insofar as its management is concerned, with only occasional monitoring and supervision by the principal.

In any case, whether change is desirable or not, secondary school programs are not static. Furthermore, teachers do not perform at near-perfect levels; adequate resources are rarely available; numbers of pupils do not remain constant, nor do the kinds of problems they bring into the school. All these factors require administrative attention at the management level. This is not to imply that the principal must spend a large percentage of his time in the management of purely internal operations of the school. It does mean that he must understand school management and be able to analyze management problems, plan procedures, design and use records, and employ the management function as a tool of administration.

MANAGEMENT AND OPERATIONS: AN OVERVIEW

The myriad details of organizing, operating, recording, and reporting that are required in modern junior and senior high schools seem overwhelming when viewed *in toto*. They are indicated by the list given in Figure 13-1, which includes major management functions and types of records and accounts. Although extensive, the list is not exhaustive. Schools operating adult education programs, summer schools, and similar programs will, of course, require additional functions, records, and specific tasks.

In Figure 13-1, student personnel, staff personnel, curriculum, activities, and business represent the broad categories of regular school operation; organizing school and maintaining organizational effectiveness are categories of special concern to management. Each is fundamental to proper administrative direction, control, and stewardship. Together, they tend to give a picture of the total management needs of the modern secondary school. At the same time, they provide a necessary basis for adequate study, planning, development, and evaluation of the school's program.

A useful means of conceptualizing the management process is to analyze it as four distinct parts. These are: functions, tasks, procedures, and records. Functions, illustrated in Figure 13-1, represent major areas of administrative concern in managing schools. Organizing the school— the first function given in Figure 13-1—is clearly an administrative responsibility. It is the category under which a particular collection of specific tasks can be classified. When one administrator tells another that he has spent two weeks organizing the opening of school, the second administrator understands the kinds of activities in which the first has been engaged. The same response would be expected if any of the other functions were indicated by our hypothetical principal. Functions, when referring to school management, represent categories of administrative tasks. Functions are divided into specific tasks; thus, when tasks that make up a particular function are properly completed, that function is said to be fulfilled. Administrative planning entails, as one step, the logical breakdown of a particular function into its component tasks. Making up the master schedule, for example, is one of the necessary tasks of organizing the school. At the other end of the administrative process, assessment reverses the planning procedure. Here, tasks are examined—both in terms of their nature and the manner of their completion—to determine why a particular result occurred. If the opening of school was unsatisfactory in certain respects, some tasks necessary to a successful school opening were omitted or certain tasks were not accomplished properly.

Procedures are the prescriptions by which tasks are to be accomplished. A particular task may need to be specified according to the steps to be taken, the order and timing of accomplishing them, and the assignment of responsibility to particular positions in the organization. This is usually the case when tasks are complex, requiring coordination with other tasks or involving work by several individuals. The task of developing the master schedule may again be used to illustrate this point. First, course offerings, record of the rooms to be assigned particular teachers and classes, and teacher course assignments are necessary materials. The schedule may then be constructed in a particular way—it must include class section, period, teacher's name, and room number for each subject offered by the school. Usually, courses which are offered in only one period must be placed in the schedule first, in such a way that conflicts are avoided; next, double-period classes must be entered, and so on. Other tasks, such as registering students or preparing report

Figure 13-1. Summary of Management Areas and Records

Major Management Function	Breakdown of Function	Types of Records and Accounts
Organizing school	Class scheduling	Room usage record Teacher assignment record Course offerings Student course selections Master schedule Student daily program
	Work schedules and files	School master schedule School calendar with school events Activity calendar Card file of personal information for each student File of students' daily programs Bell schedules Student and faculty procedures handbooks
Student personnel	Information service (records room)	Academic records Activity records Test profiles Record of educational plans Health examinations and histories Attendance records Anecdotal reports Confidential records Summaries of counselor interviews Discipline records
	Attendance	Daily record Record by accounting periods and annual reports
	Reports to parents	Cardex of each student's study program or punched-card system Report cards (by reporting periods) Behavioral report, failure notices, or other intermediate reports Record of parent conferences
	Discipline	Simple record with reports to teachers, counselors, and parent Reports of formal investigations
Staff personnel		Professional growth record Personal and professional data Confidential reports and communications Salary record Teaching certificate, health record, chest X-ray certificate, other required information Reports of conferences with principal and supervisory staff

Major Management Function	Breakdown of Function	Types of Records and Accounts
Curriculum		Record of course offerings with detailed review, course offering description, prerequisites, etc. Curriculum guides, courses of study, resource units Record of prepared materials List of approved texts and required supplies List of special fees for course work Records and reports of studies, curriculum recommendations, etc.
Activities		Activity calendar—including outside groups Assignment of sponsors Code of regulations and procedures Budget, accounting records, purchase orders, report of audit, inventories Information on individual organizations: purposes, activities, dues, sponsors, officers, membership rosters, ceremonies
Business		Budget, accounting records, purchase orders File of state-aid claims and reimbursement reports Payroll data—including substitute and nonacademic personnel Inventories of supplies and equipment Records of auxiliary services Central treasury account (activities) Building maintenance records
Maintenance of organizational effectiveness		Bulletins and announcements Safety and emergency procedures: fire, storm, national defense, accident, and internal emergency Substitute teacher list State reports and records: average daily attendance, nonresident students, enrollments in reimbursed programs (driver training, special education, vocational education, etc.) Accreditation reports and records Bell schedules and special programming of classes Records and reports for district office

cards, require a particular sequence and routing of work flows as a specified procedure. All procedures are designed from the point of view of what is needed at the completion of the task; working backward, steps, timing, and other considerations can be easily determined.

Records are the means of maintaining the data necessary to perform tasks; they are the product of procedures. Records are the means for capturing information needed at a later time. Record keeping itself is always composed of three steps: noting, sorting or collating, and reporting. First the data must be noted, as when a teacher registers a grade or a student writes down his home address, birth date, and last school attended on the school's information card. Second, the data are sorted into an order on a form which anticipates future use, as when teachers' grade cards are sorted into decks by homeroom and then into packets by student name preparatory to making out report cards, or when the student information card is filed in alphabetical order preparatory to making a roster of the school or assignment of students to counselors. Third, data are reported in a form from which decisions can be made or action taken, as when attendance lists are prepared, a roster of each class is made up for teacher use, or a schedule of classes is made in order to assign students.

RECORD KEEPING AND SCHOOL MANAGEMENT

The planning of a record system, design of record forms, and procedures for data collection are important to efficient school management. Unless careful planning is done, considerable duplication of records and record keeping takes place. In some schools, identical records are kept by the school's main office, departmental offices, guidance office, and the homeroom—each laboriously collecting and recording information in its own way. A well-planned system would provide the information needed more efficiently with greater security of basic records and at greatly reduced cost. Some larger secondary schools are designing office space with this in mind by setting up a central records room with its own staff of clerks to serve the needs of the entire school.

Record keeping is an administrative problem primarily because of the varied needs for records; the growing magnitude of records required; the attitudes that records are symptoms of red tape and bureaucratic organization; and the belief—even among administrators—that clerical staff is a wasteful educational expenditure. The point concerning varied needs for records is worth noting because it is a central consideration in planning. Some records are needed because of the requirements of outside agencies, as, for example, accrediting agencies and state departments. Other records are required by the district office; often the forms are standardized for use throughout the district, for example, the budget, report card, and cumulative record. Sound management and effective internal operation of the school place further demands upon a record system. Finally, records also are kept as a service to parents, community agencies, and, in some cases, particular groups. Frequently, the needs of one office do not coincide with those of another. In Illinois, for example, the Office of the Superintendent of Public Instruction requires that each school report pupil attendance by thirty-day periods, beginning with the first day of school. This arrangement does not conform to any standard practice in the schools, where attendance is kept by calendar months for reports to parents, cumulative records, and the like. Further, the same state regulation requires that a student attending school for any five hours on a given day is to be counted as present for that day, and attendance for less than five hours is to be counted as a full day's absence. This necessitates duplications of records and separate sets of attendance procedures throughout the state.

Without an assessment of record-keeping needs, administrators frequently permit the preparation of forms and records for each function, or even each task, independent of that for any other; permit the development of duplicate sets of records, as noted above; allow the collection of information which is never used; and maintain the use of old forms and procedures after major changes in tasks have outdated the type and order of the information collected. A useful method of records assessment is through periodic examination of the kinds of information collected, the records kept by each office, and the forms used. The information thus obtained is then checked against the requirements for such records.

DATA-PROCESSING SYSTEMS

Data-processing systems have come into wide use in secondary schools as a means of attaining a flexible, centralized record-keeping system. Where large amounts of data must be processed—as in scheduling, reports to parents, attendance records, inventories of supplies or books, rosters, and lists—a punch-card or tape system is of proven merit. The advantages of these systems are flexibility of storage and easy access to basic information. Machine systems provide tremendous speed, accuracy, and uniformity of records and reports. The basic record-keeping processes—recording, sorting, and reporting—can all be accomplished by proven machine methods at reasonable cost.

Figure 13-2 presents a complete plan of a student personnel record system. The plan is a flowchart of data-processing steps for the preparation of the master schedule; assignment of students; preparation of class lists, rosters, failure and honors reports, and report cards; posting to a permanent academic record and a cumulative record; and handling of attendance accounting as well as other routine tasks. In addition, the flexibility of the punch-card system permits the retrieval of data for numerous other purposes, including studies of retention, distribution of age groups or sexes by subjects, and marking patterns. Not shown in the chart are the steps involved in the use of standard test scores and marks in ability grouping, the preparation of test profiles, or the recording and reporting of special programs, as, for example, programs in education for the handicapped, remedial reading, and driver education. All of these tasks can be accomplished within the design of the system shown and can be used in either junior or senior high schools.

Computers can also perform the same tasks as the basic accounting machines that use punch cards. With either punch cards, tape, or direct keyboard entry to a computer, the only limits to any of the record-keeping and reporting operations now in use in schools is the design of the program that directs the operation of the computer. In a scheduling problem worked out by one of the authors, a 1540-pupil junior high school was scheduled: multiple copies of each student's daily program were printed; the master schedule was printed—showing course, period, room, teacher, and number of students assigned to each; an alphabetical list was made of students whose subject choices could not be accommodated; and class cards were punched for each class. All this work was completed in fifteen minutes with only twenty-six unscheduled student programs. With this speed, accuracy, and flexibility, schools would not need to be rigid in providing programs of study—they could even re-schedule the entire school each week or each day.

THE PRINCIPAL AND OFFICE ADMINISTRATION

The school office is widely regarded today as a functional unit of any school. Its development has been severely retarded, however, by narrow conceptions of the management needs of schools and of the role of the

Figure 13-2. Secondary School Student Personnel
Record System Designed for Data Processing

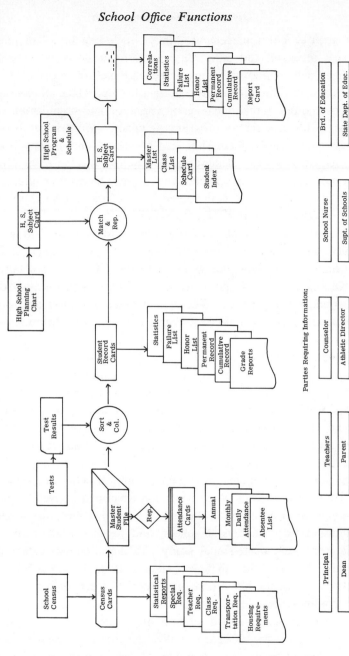

principal in school management. Many—including board of education members, teachers, and even some administrators—view expenditures for office facilities and personnel as educational "overhead." Studies of school organization still largely ignore the importance of management functions and fail to relate management practices to organizational effectiveness. Growth of school programs requiring special supervision, procedures, and records; increasing size of school enrollments and staff; added requirements for accounting and reports; and the recognition that sound planning and development require controlled procedures and improved records have all contributed to a changed conception of the school office and the role of administration.

The functional view of administration presented in Chapter 4, the organization of the secondary school presented in Chapter 7, and the list of management functions given in Figure 13-1 of this chapter indicate the extent to which the operation of the secondary school depends upon sound office practices. The school office is clearly an instrument for organizational communication and coordination. Although control and accountability have been the primary purposes of management provisions, these purposes are rapidly becoming secondary. As the leadership dimension of administration becomes dominant, the management aspects are being altered to support the primary role. Knowledgeable principals are reshaping office practices away from emphasis on regulation and control to those which conserve professional staff time, serve and support the work of the staff, and provide means for studying and improving instruction.

The role of the principal in organizing and directing the school office is crucial to the kind of office operation described above. In too many cases, principals do not plan the use of their own time for supervision; consultation with students, teachers, and parents; leadership in committee work; and professional study and development. When they do not plan, they find that these activities tend to be superseded by the detailed work of the office and that much of their time is taken up by office routines and clerical tasks.

In studies of school board regulations, district directives, and surveys of the principal's work, there is indication that an excessive amount of the principal's time is spent upon clerical tasks and the direction of office routines. Because regulations charge the principal with the responsibility for conducting fire drills or for reporting suspensions of students, this does not mean that these chores must be done by the principal personally. Often principals handle detailed record keeping and reporting because they do not take the time initially to design procedures and train office personnel to handle them. In the main, any regularly recurring activity that does not involve sensitive decision or judgment can be reduced to routine.

The role of the principal in the administration of the school office, in addition to his own preferences, is conditioned by such factors as instructions of the central office, school board regulations, office facilities and clerical staff available, and traditions and practices of the local school system. In most cases, considerable latitude is left to the principal to organize and operate the school office. Both his own staff and those to whom he is responsible expect him to understand the management functions, to be able to specify them in terms of specific tasks, and to design the procedures and records necessary to carry them out in a satisfactory manner. This observation seems to be violated primarily in school systems where the superintendent and his staff exercise rigorous direction over the internal operations of each school and in schools where grossly inadequate facilities and clerical personnel are provided.

Out of the considerations presented thus far, certain principles can be enumerated to guide the administrator in a consideration of his role in school management:

1. Understand the extent to which administrative action, reports, and records are required.
   a. Enumerate and assess requirements made by constituted authority, by request of community agencies, and by the needs of the school.
   b. Develop a list, calendar, or some other organized record of these needs.
2. Understand the major school management functions and the tasks involved in fulfilling them.
3. Develop and periodically evaluate an integrated records system. Avoid duplication and the maintenance of obsolete records wherever possible.
4. Have prepared in writing an outline of procedures necessary to the completion of each major task. Assign responsibility for each phase of each task, including the record keeping and reporting attendant to it.
5. Understand procedures, and check on their usefulness. Gain the skills to design procedures, and take the initiative to make changes which appear necessary.
6. Provide opportunities for the staff—both clerical and professional—to discuss functions, tasks, procedures, and records.

7. Gain experience with records and procedures, but avoid becoming engrossed with detailed clerical tasks.
8. Seek to employ records as a service to the organization rather than primarily as a means of regulating and controlling it or of serving external demands.

These principles seem to the authors to provide an orientation to the administrator who seeks to determine his own point of view in relation to the management function of the secondary school. This is an area of administration that requires thoughtful planning. The administrator who accepts the management conditions of a school as he finds them will soon discover that he has become an administrative head rather than a leader. If he gears management procedures primarily to external requirements, he becomes a bureaucrat. If he becomes enmeshed in detailed record keeping, he becomes a clerk. Not one of these roles is suitable to the professional role of leading educational development; the alternative seems to lie in the direction indicated by the statement of principles above.

TOOLS OF ADMINISTRATION

The administrator requires many tools. Each of the levels of administration—management, institutional leadership, and policy making—noted in the model in Chapter 1, implies processes and procedures that serve as administrative tools. At the management level, the master schedule, school calendar, marking system, budget, and a host of other devices and procedures are administrative tools. How these tools are designed and the ways in which they are used deeply affect the operation of the school and the manner in which it accomplishes its purposes. The administrator who is unaware of or insensitive to the effects of his administrative tools upon the organization may not only be inefficient, he may also be dangerous.

Tools of administration function in two ways: (1) as a means of control, and (2) as a means of analysis and decision. Unfortunately, the management tools of public education have largely been employed as controls. Accreditation reports and state office requirements of various kinds are used to fix minimum requirements. The use of state and federal funds and the accounting devices they entail are to control local school programs for certain purposes. The use of most reports and records within the school itself seems to be for purposes of control. Controls are not to be construed as undesirable. They create structure, provide standards, and—to some extent, at least—ensure that certain functions are performed and that students and public are protected. Still, this is fundamentally a negative feature. Emphasis upon these uses of management tools leaves much to be desired, for it leaves the administrator in a weak position to lead and develop.

While management tools are maintained for control purposes, other emphases are needed—upon the tools at hand, and upon others that might be developed, to analyze and aid in solution of problems already known and to locate important problems that are undetected. The decision-making, problem-solving orientation to educational administration has been stressed throughout this book. If this orientation is to be effective, it must be supported by management tools that emphasize analysis rather than control.

Much of the literature of educational administration reveals the principal as the only person in the school aware of the need to alter purposes and change procedures. This does not conform to the experience of the authors, who see at least three effects of the dominant influence of management as tools of control rather than analysis. First, school administrators become enamored with a few changes, and the satisfaction of attaining initial goals soon freezes into a desire to maintain the status quo. Second, school administrators become so bound up with the intricacies of accounting, data processing, and schedule making that the design and enforcement of these procedural mechanics are mistaken for the administrative process itself. Third, school administrators succumb to the many controls already surrounding them and give up the goals of the school to the major task of meeting requirements. These, the authors suggest, are tendencies that seem to exist in most school administrators —even the most competent. Awareness of them may be sufficient to prevent or minimize their effects. The trappings of administration, including the mechanics of management, are attractive and demanding of the administrator's time and thought. Unless he consciously uses them as tools and maintains his focus upon educational objectives and the processes of educating youth, he cannot function as a leader.

Principals are rarely confronted with the important problems of education or even those of their own organization. Significant problems have to be identified and defined. Creative, positive administration is involved with the identification of problems created by serious attempts to realize objectiyes. Each phase of the entire decision-making process—problem recognition and identification, choice of alternatives, trial of alternatives, feedback, assessment, and action—can be monitored through administrative tools geared to analysis rather than control. Most of the management procedures and records noted in this chapter are amenable to this use.

REFERENCES

Clark, Harold F., *Cost and Quality in Public Education* (Syracuse, N.Y.: Syracuse University Press, 1963).

Holz, Robert E., *School Scheduling Using Computers* (Cambridge: Massachusetts Institute of Technology, 1964).

Kershaw, J. A., and McKean, R. N., *Systems Analysis and Education* (Santa Monica, Calif.: The Rand Corp., 1959).

Knezevich, Stephen J., and Fowlkes, John Guy, *Business Management of Local School Systems* (New York: Harper & Bros., 1960).

National Education Association, *For Better Substitute Teaching,* Research Circular No. 4 (Washington, D.C.: the Association, 1962).

System Development Corporation, "Information-Processing Research," in *Research Directorate Report,* TM 530-004-00 (Santa Monica, Calif.: the Corporation, 1962).

Wengert, E. S., *et al., The Study of Administration* (Eugene, Ore.: School of Business Administration, University of Oregon, 1961).

Yeager, William A., *Administration of the Noninstructional Personnel and Services* (New York: Harper & Bros., 1959).

Chapter 14
Business Management Functions

THE primary focus of the secondary school administrator should, at all times, be upon his central role in maintaining, facilitating, and improving program development, instructional excellence, and educational opportunity. Today, however, the rapid growth of secondary schools is drawing attention to the role of the administrator in managing large numbers of business responsibilities inherent in the operation of the educational enterprise. Where business managers are not provided, principals of large secondary schools are responsible for the efficient handling of many duties of a business nature. Included among these duties are responsibilities related to budget making and financial accounting, managing extracurricular finances, accounting for equipment and supplies, maintaining libraries and free textbook plans, and administering cafeteria and bookstore operations. The need for an administrative officer responsible for business affairs in the secondary school is being recognized in increasing numbers of school districts.

BUDGET MAKING AND FINANCIAL ACCOUNTING

Sound administration of secondary schools requires a carefully planned and ably executed budgetary process. In essence, the budget is a detailed statement of the financial resources necessary to implement desired school programs for the period of one fiscal year. The budget process in the secondary school involves determination of both expenditures and income associated with total school operations.

Expenditures

The determination of educational expenditures involves consideration of each of the following budget categories:

1. *General control.* Included in this category are financial resources allocated to the accomplishment of administrative and managerial tasks. The salaries of administrators, administrative assistants, and the cost of office equipment and supplies are all encompassed under general control.

2. *Instruction.* This budget division includes the cost of teacher salaries and necessary expenditures for textbooks, materials, and equipment required in instruction. Normally, this budget category accounts for 70 to 75 percent of the total budget.

3. *Auxiliary services.* Expenditures related to health and guidance services, the school lunch program, school transportation, and the operation of the school bookstore are encompassed in this category.

4. *Plant maintenance.* The replacement and repair of original equipment, renovation of the school plant, and maintenance and improvement of the school grounds are examples of items in this category.

5. *Operation.* The cost of fuel, utilities, telephone, rentals, and the salaries of custodial personnel are included in this category.

6. *Community services.* This category includes services such as adult education and/or recreation programs offered by the secondary school.

7. *Fixed charges, capital outlay, debt service, and estimation of income.* These important budget categories are significant divisions of the total school district budget. Secondary school administrators, however, have little, if any, responsibility for administering these budget divisions unless their functions include those of district superintendents.

Income

Sources of income are also to be considered during the budget-building process. School district income is usually derived from (1) local taxation; (2) aid from state taxes and from state-administered federal programs; (3) land sales; (4) tuition paid by students living outside district boundaries; and (5) rentals and fees in connection with auditoriums, gymnasiums, laboratories, lockers, books, and so forth. The importance of keeping abreast of new sources of school revenue cannot be overemphasized. Changes in state-support structures, revision of assessment formulas, and participation of the federal government in the support of special areas of education (see Chapter 6) continue to present new opportunities for increasing school income.

Effective business management in secondary schools requires knowledge of the sources of income (local, state, and federal) available to schools and of the methods for using these funds to best advantage. Since proposals for program change or modification inevitably raise questions related to costs, the secondary school administrator needs competence in presenting proposals for expenditure, in translating proposals into monetary terms, and in indicating available sources of income. Competent performance also encompasses efficient administration of internal income funds such as those generated by extracurricular activities.

Involvement in Budget Preparation

The intensity of involvement in budget preparation of secondary school administrators is often a function of school size. The larger the school district, and the greater the number of secondary schools in operation, the greater the likelihood that the principal will carry major responsibilities for budget development. In states such as Illinois, where high schools often function under separate boards of education, the principal may be called upon to assume responsibility for all budgeting and financial operations required of superintendents. Most school situations, however, require the principal's cooperation with the superintendent and other central-office personnel in matters related to budget and finances.

The trend in school districts is toward greater involvement of the secondary school principal in budget development. The limited conception of the principal as custodian of materials and controller of requisitions is rapidly disappearing. Especially is this so in school districts where individual schools are used as basic units in the preparation and operational management of the school budget. In such circumstances, the principal and his staff are centrally involved in all aspects of budget preparation and control that are pertinent to the operation of secondary schools.

Preparing for Effective Involvement

Effective participation in budget development demands both knowledge and planning on the part of secondary school administrators. The focus in budget development should never be oriented merely toward assuring survival levels of operation. Rather, the budget should be seen as one of the major instruments through which the secondary school may achieve its goals in terms of programs and instructional effectiveness. Budget is an expression of policy—it defines commitment to and support of educational objectives in terms of dollars and cents. The formulation of clear educational goals and the structuring of meaningful programs are prerequisites to effective participation in budget development. The budget development process, in essence, involves the translation of activities—including program maintenance, program improvement, administration, instruction, operation, and service—into monetary terms which define commitment to both goal-seeking and organizational maintenance objectives.

Effective participation in school budget making requires not only business acumen but also a clear conception of instructional goals and the educational programs necessary for their achievement. The nature of program goals and factors such as student enrollment become primary considerations in moving from program conceptions to budget considerations. Such factors determine needs in relation to each of the budget categories enumerated earlier.

Thus, effectiveness in budget making requires the development of administrative competence in relation to several dimensions of administrative performance:

1. *Goal development in relation to the objectives and directions of secondary education.* Purpose definition, a central task of all institutional leaders,[1] is a *sine qua non* in effective budget preparation.

2. *Goal translation into viable educational programs.* The conceptualization and formulation of programs aimed at the implementation of institutional goals make up a significant dimension of administrative performance, and generate important implications for budget needs.

3. *Determination of human and material resources necessary to the implementation of desired educational programs.* Included here are clear concepts of needs in relation to (*a*) staff numbers and competences; (*b*) physical plant facilities; (*c*) equipment and supplies; (*d*) auxiliary, operational, and custodial services; and (*e*) administrative services.

4. *Development of accurate budget estimates.* The ability to translate

1. James G. Harlow, "Purpose Defining: The Central Function of the School Administrator," in Jack A. Culbertson and Stephen P. Hencley (eds.), *Preparing Administrators: New Perspectives* (Columbus, Ohio: University Council for Educational Administration, 1962), pp. 61-71.

educational programs into monetary equivalents is important in budget development.

Budget-making activities are neither routine nor mechanical. They involve consideration of basic educational purposes, programs, and goals. Viewed in proper perspective, budget making becomes an important avenue for developing and clarifying concepts of desirable educational ends, and for delineating means for their achievement.

The Budget Process

The relationships outlined in Chapter 4 are appropriate for guiding interaction between the principal and central-office personnel in budget development. The principal must also, however, develop procedures for initiating budget planning and development at the building-unit level. These procedures should include opportunities for broad participation in budget construction for personnel at all levels in the organization.

The budget process at the building-unit level begins with an intensive review of all appropriate budget categories affecting the individual school. Preliminary work necessary is initiated by the principal and carried forward by department heads, library and school store personnel, and personnel in charge of pupil personnel services, cafeteria operations, and extracurricular activities. At this point, judgments are necessary concerning the adequacy or inadequacy of budget allotments in terms of the educational and service programs that must be implemented. Every budget category requires consideration: instruction, control, operations, school and community services, plant maintenance, supplies, equipment, and books.

The principal, or his designate, should plan conferences with every instructional and service department, and with as many individual staff members as possible during the preliminary overview and review of budget categories. Extensive participation in the budget process ensures staff interest in this important activity. Moreover, it serves to further understanding of budget limitations (which staff members sometimes lack) and to make clear to all personnel who will be affected the bases of budget decisions.

Recommendations from individual school departments and service units for budget reappraisal and adjustment should always be made on the basis of careful study and consideration of (1) the educational objectives sought, (2) the necessary resources and services required, and (3) the values expected. Written recommendations for suggested budget changes are ordinarily forwarded to the principal for his joint consideration with the school budget committee. At the same time, supporting documents outlining budget needs and requests—based upon specified goals and program needs—are customarily prepared and submitted by each operating and service unit in the school. Revisions in these requests that are deemed necessary by the principal and budget committee are reviewed with each instructional department and service unit before the total budget is transmitted to the superintendent of schools.

Although the planning of programs, projects, and changes is usually a continuous activity in secondary schools, it should be stressed that a regular time schedule should be established in each school year during which the intensive work of budget preparation can be accomplished. Handicaps, bottlenecks, and emergencies in school operation which are attributable to inadequate budgeting should be identified and recorded during the year by both staff and administration. Such information should be fed into budget deliberations so that significant shortcomings may be corrected.

Prior to adoption of the budget by the board of education, the principal will normally receive a preliminary estimate of the probable maximum appropriation possible from the total district budget for operating his school. At times, the budget appropriation will fail to cover the range of worthy requests generated during the school's budget-building process. To cover this contingency, the principal and his staff should seek to develop a system of priorities for elimination of individual budget items. Staff participation in the development of priority lists of this kind is important in all schools. It is especially important in secondary schools where budget preparation is characterized by extensive staff participation.

Using Cost Analyses

Cost analyses and research on various facets of school expenditures may be used to good advantage in making sound decisions in budget matters. Cost comparisons with similar schools in neighboring districts may also be helpful—so long as these comparisons are not employed solely as means for preserving the status quo. Experience in secondary schools indicates that costs related to instruction generally account for between 70 and 75 percent of the total budget. Typically, other budget categories range between 1 and 10 percent. Extreme deviations from such norms generally indicate (1) the existence of unusual educational conditions, or (2) inappropriate budget allocations which may require attention and correction.

Staff involvement in schoolwide cost studies can provide much of the information required for projecting budget estimates. Data for projecting unit costs should be available in relation to laboratory and shop courses; courses taught by conventional methods and teaching teams; services offered in the areas of health and guidance; costs of maintenance, repairs, renovations, and improvements in school plant and groups; expenditures for equipment, supplies, and textbooks; school library purchases; costs of cafeteria and school store operations; and support required for extracurricular activities. Cost studies should also consider anticipated changes that may result from increased or decreased enrollments, changed teacher-pupil ratios, increased salary scales, and so on. Findings of such studies should be kept current and made available during the budget development process.

Unit-cost studies often serve important ancillary purposes. They reveal areas in which there is overallocation or insufficiency of monetary resources; they identify areas in which concentrated effort is needed to make operations more efficient; and they increase staff understanding of budget decisions and budget limitations.

Since schools are expected to conform to yearly budget allotments, accurate cost analyses in budget building are of paramount importance. Increased budget allotments for individual schools are not normally made unless unusual circumstances arise. Frequent requests for transfers of funds from one account to another often leave the impression of poor planning and inefficient administration.

Financial Accounting

In secondary schools where the administrator has responsibility for overseeing a budget, the development of a suitable accounting system is mandatory. Accounting procedures should never be more complex than necessary, but they should always be complete enough to permit orderly audit procedures. Records that meet audit requirements can be invaluable in developing the cost analyses for budget building.

Standardized procedures for handling requisitions, memorandum accounts for every budget category, and efficient systems for recording receipts, expenditures, and budget allocations are all necessary in a sound accounting system. To ensure that accurate records will be maintained, and to save the possible embarrassment that may result from inadequate control, accounting practices in schools should conform to a number of accepted school business procedures:

1. All moneys received should be traceable through official receipts.
2. All cash receipts should be banked.
3. Individuals responsible for the final safekeeping of school funds should be bonded.
4. All disbursements should be by check—except for small purchases made from petty cash.
5. Official documents (such as requisition forms, memorandum accounts, receipts, canceled checks, and check vouchers) should be on file and accessible for inspection.
6. The records should permit preparations of monthly bank reconciliation statements.
7. Financial statements encompassing all transactions should be prepared monthly and yearly.
8. Copies of yearly audit statements should be placed on file in the school district's central office.

All secondary schools require standardized accounting procedures and regularized channels for processing routine forms. The intensity of demands posed by these concerns varies almost directly with school size, however. The principal in the small high school may find that such matters make relatively minor demands upon his time after channels for handling forms and requisitions have been established. In the large secondary school, on the other hand, the volume of paper work may be formidable and continuous unless arrangements are made to process it during convenient, specified periods.

MEMORANDUM ACCOUNTS. Proper attention to memorandum accounts will ensure the availability of accurate information concerning amounts of money allocated to various budget categories, amounts that have been expended, and remaining balances. Memorandum accounts should be maintained even though the district central office makes periodic statements of budget balances to each school. The memorandum account is a simple form for recording important information about every budget account for which the principal is held responsible. The form makes possible the recording of the amount and date of budget appropriations, the nature and value of goods and materials received and outstanding, and the unused balance in every account.

PERPETUAL INVENTORIES. A growing number of schools have found that both the estimation of yearly requirements of supply items and the elimination of irritating shortages can be handled with ease through the maintenance of perpetual inventories. The perpetual-inventory form facilitates the keeping of cost and performance specifications for every supply item and solves the problem of when orders should be placed. A system of periodic checks of the entries on these forms assists in orderly planning and facilitates yearly budget estimates.

PETTY CASH. Most school districts provide a fund for petty cash to cover the cost of nonrecurring, small purchases that may be necessary in the operation of secondary schools. The principal administers this fund and accounts periodically for expenditures made.

ACCOUNTING FOR SCHOOL ACTIVITY FUNDS

The day has long passed in many secondary schools when it was possible for independent organizations and sponsors to handle their own extracurricular financing and accounting problems. Many large secondary schools have six-figure incomes from ticket sales, dues, and sales of materials. Since schools are the sponsors of such activities, major responsibilities devolve upon secondary school administrators for developing appropriate accounting and control procedures to ensure that these funds are neither misappropriated nor misused.

The importance of formalized control procedures in accounting for school activity funds is receiving increased recognition in many places. In approximately a dozen states, legislation exists to regulate school activity accounting procedures. In approximately an equal number of other states, regulations of the state department of education provide clear guidelines for the sound and efficient handling of these funds. In states where neither of the foregoing regulatory procedures exist, the responsibility for developing local guidelines falls squarely upon the principal. If the board of education has failed to provide operational guidelines, it is crucial that the secondary school administrator institute businesslike accounting procedures in this area. Nothing is so likely to jar public respect for the integrity of school operations as rumor or scandal concerning deficits in school accounts due to mismanagement or misappropriation.

Table 14-1. Minimum Receipt Accounts

---

1. Activity income

    a. Admission
    b. Prorated share of general activity tickets
    c. Dues and fees
    d. Sales
        (1) Books and periodicals
        (2) Confections, goods, and beverages
        (3) Other merchandise
    e. Student rentals from materials
        (1) Rental from books
        (2) Rental from equipment
    f. Advertising
    g. Guarantees
    h. Other activity income

2. Grants from the school district

3. Gifts from other sources

4. Other receipts

SOURCE: Everett V. Samuelson et al. (compilers), Financial
Accounting for School Activities (Washington, D.C.:
U.S. Government Printing Office, 1959), p. 5.

Fortunately, excellent guidelines are available for developing accounting systems for activity funds in secondary schools. A comprehensive publication of the U.S. Office of Education on this subject recommends adoption of a centralized system of accounting, with a central treasurer or the school's business manager in charge of all activity funds.[2] In such a system, a central treasurer is charged with maintaining and overseeing the separate accounts of every school organization and activity.

Accounting Procedures

Samuelson and others have recommended that certain steps be followed in recording receipts, in recording expenditures, and in preparing summary statements for each extraclass account.[3] The forms to be used

2. Everett V. Samuelson *et al.* (compilers), *Financial Accounting for School Activities* (Washington, D.C.: U.S. Government Printing Office, 1959), p. 52.
3. *Ibid.,* p. 59.

with each step are identified in the recommended flowchart of accounting operations shown in Figure 14.1.[4]

RECORDING RECEIPTS. The steps necessary in recording receipts for extraclass activities include (1) issuing official receipts for all money received; (2) depositing money in the bank and completing duplicate deposit slips and an Analysis of Deposit form; (3) recording cash receipts in a Fund Balance Record; (4) entering receipts in the Receipts and Expenditures Register; (5) recording receipts in the Receipts Distribution Ledger; and (6) entering receipts in the Subsidiary Activity Ledger—when such a ledger is used. Minimum receipt accounts, which may be expanded as needs require, are shown in Table 14-1.

RECORDING EXPENDITURES. The steps to be taken in recording expenditures are (1) processing each Activity Purchase Order for payment, (2) making payments by check, (3) entering payments in the Fund Balance Record, (4) entering payments in the Receipts and Expenditures Register, (5) entering payments in the Expenditures Distribution Ledger, and (6) entering payments in the Subsidiary Activity Ledger, if it is used. Minimum expenditure accounts are shown in Table 14-2. These accounts may be expanded as needs arise.

PREPARING SUMMARY STATEMENTS. Summary statements necessary in accounting for each extracurricular activity include (1) a bank reconciliation statement, (2) a monthly financial statement for each fund, (3) a monthly summary statement for all funds, (4) an annual financial statement for each fund, and (5) an annual summary statement for all funds.

THE ACCOUNTING FLOWCHART. The procedure outlined in Figure 14-1 utilizes a cash basis of accounting which encompasses multiple funds in a single-entry system. The procedure is readily adaptable, however, to a double-entry system, to a single-fund system, or to an accrual basis of accounting.

The flowchart indicates the appropriate roles of both the central treasurer and student treasurers in accounting for school activity funds. Although the central treasurer carries the important formal load in the accounting system, valuable learning experiences can be provided for student officers through the keeping of a set of "books" which parallel the record of official receipts and expenditures maintained by the school.

4. *Ibid.,* p. 58.

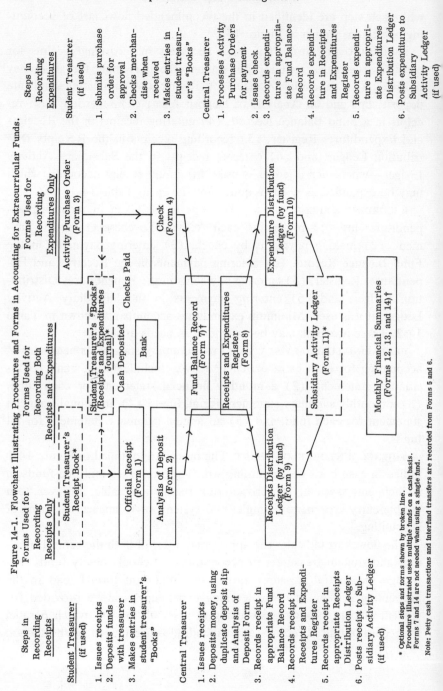

Figure 14-1. Flowchart Illustrating Procedures and Forms in Accounting for Extracurricular Funds.

Table 14-2. Minimum Expenditure Accounts

---

1. Activity expense
   a. Basic operating expenditures
      (1) Personal and contracted services
      (2) Supplies
      (3) Purchases of merchandise
         (a) Books and periodicals
         (b) Confections, foods, and beverages
         (c) Other merchandise
      (4) Other activity expense
         (a) Advertising
         (b) Guarantees
         (c) Travel expense

   b. Supplemental operating expenditures
      (1) Health services
         (a) Personal and contracted services
         (b) Other expense
      (2) Pupil transportation
         (a) Personal and contracted services
         (b) Other expense
      (3) Operation of plant
         (a) Personal and contracted services
         (b) Other expense
      (4) Maintenance of plant
         (a) Personal and contracted services
         (b) Other expense
      (5) Fixed charges
         (a) Employer contributions for retirement
             and social security
         (b) Insurance
         (c) Rental of land and buildings
         (d) Other fixed charges

2. Capital outlay (initial or additional equipment)

SOURCE: Everett V. Samuelson et al. (compilers), <u>Financial
Accounting for School Activities</u> (Washington, D.C.:
U.S. Government Printing Office, 1959), p. 13.

Guidelines to Operation

1. *The principal should assume responsibility for developing policies to guide fund-raising and fund-disbursing activities.* In the last analysis, it is the principal who is held accountable for the manner in which activity funds are raised and expended. It is desirable to establish regula-

tory policies in these areas in cooperation with a school policy committee consisting of both staff members and student representatives. Established policies should be made known throughout the school and should guide decision making among both activity sponsors and student groups.

2. *Control procedures in the school's accounting system should encompass all fund-raising and fund-disbursing transactions associated with extracurricular activities.* Development of accounting procedures similar to those described in this chapter will accomplish this objective. The procedures structured should be inclusive—encompassing every extra-class activity sanctioned by the secondary school. Moreover, the need for an annual audit, especially where large sums of money are involved, cannot be too strongly emphasized.

3. *Transfers of funds from one account to another should be carefully regulated.* Since some school activities are better income producers than others, requests are sometimes made for the transfer of funds to those activities that are operating under financial hardship. Requests of this nature should be handled with discretion. Although educational practice condones fund disbursal on the basis of need, a number of states forbid the spending of activity account moneys for needs not closely related to the activity. All requests for fund transfers should receive the careful consideration of the principal and the school's finance committee. This judgment, after consideration of all related factors, should be final. Legitimate needs that are made apparent by transfer requests should receive further consideration and review when operating budgets are being determined for school organizations engaged in extracurricular activities.

4. *The general school fund should not become the vehicle for providing equipment and purchases which are the responsibility of the board of education.* Although general school funds have, in many places, made possible purchases benefiting the entire school, it is wise to limit acquisitions made through such funds to equipment that cannot normally be secured through district appropriations. Otherwise, undesirable precedents may be established which are difficult to circumvent.

EQUIPMENT AND SUPPLIES

Every secondary school requires a systematic procedure for classifying, requisitioning, handling, storing, and accounting for equipment and supplies. The volume of supplies and equipment used in the conduct of schools is indicated by the many school systems now operating central warehouses in which quantity purchases of supplies and equipment are stored. Deliveries to individual schools are made on the basis of approved requisitioning at various times during the school year. In school districts in which central warehousing is practiced, the need for extensive handling and storing of supplies and equipment at each school building is much decreased.

Where the secondary school does not have the services and the facilities offered by a central warehousing scheme, the problem of administering and storing needed supplies and equipment may be formidable. In such situations it is necessary to provide a room in which purchases may be received, systematically checked for shortages and damage, and recorded on inventory forms. It is also necessary to safeguard the supplies and equipment in the school's possession, to establish routine channels for handling requisitions, to keep strict accounts of all equipment and materials issued, to set standards for quantities of materials to be made available to instructional and service departments, to maintain perpetual inventories of all items, to prevent waste and deterioration of items in storage, and to integrate ordering and accounting procedures into the school's central accounting system.

It is the principal's responsibility to establish simple yet efficient administrative procedures covering all matters related to securing, storing, distributing, and ordering equipment and supplies. He must also keep abreast of new developments in school equipment and in technological media being introduced into secondary education. The principal who keeps up with such developments can make lasting contributions to instructional effectiveness through the excellence of teaching aids available for use in the school.

LIBRARY AND TEXTBOOKS

Library

The library's role as a key link in the teaching-learning process makes it one of the most important parts of the secondary school. A well-planned library provides concentrated learning resources which can efficiently serve the needs of every instructional and service department. Despite its importance, however, the fund for building and improving library facilities and services may be neglected if its cause is not championed by formal leaders. In every secondary school, the strongest advocate of provision of adequate funds for library purchases should be the principal.

General practice in school districts is to structure library funds in terms of a fixed sum of money per pupil per year. Medium-sized schools often strive toward a yearly minimum goal of one dollar per pupil for library improvement. Large secondary schools are often able to maintain excellent library facilities for a lesser amount. Small schools usually seek a fixed sum appropriation for library improvement. Total book and periodical purchases of $300 to $500 per year are not uncommon in small secondary schools.

The development of an adequate and workable library budget should become the concern of the total school. All instructional departments should share in determining library needs and in ensuring judicious allotments of resources to enhance the teaching-learning potential of the total school. The principal's role in coordinating these efforts is important. So, too, is his role in seeing that the library's control and accounting procedures are integrated with the school's central accounting system.

Textbooks

Since neither free textbooks nor rental textbooks are ordinarily accessions of the school library, procedures are required to control and account for such school property. A majority of states presently provide either some or all textbooks to secondary pupils without charge. Where free textbooks are not provided, rental schemes are ordinarily in operation. Regardless of the plan in operation, certain school districts require central storing and annual requisitioning of textbooks. Others prefer to leave reasonable numbers of texts in each school and provide for transfers by requisition when enrollment shifts occur.

Textbook accounting and control procedures in secondary schools ordinarily possess the following characteristics:

1. A central book room is provided for storing unused textbooks and for housing books returned at the end of the year.

2. Textbooks are stamped or labeled to indicate that they are school district property. Each textbook may also be assigned a number.

3. Books are issued by requisition only. All books issued are recorded in appropriate account books.

4. Each teacher maintains a textbook loan record indicating the

names of pupils receiving books, the condition of the books at issue, the state of repair upon return, and the amount of any fines levied.

5. The principal and his assistants have access to perpetual textbook inventories which indicate the need for ordering additional books or replacements.

6. Provisions are made for repairing worn textbooks and for withdrawing damaged books from circulation.

7. Lost and badly misused textbooks are replaced through a system of fines.

CAFETERIA AND BOOKSTORE OPERATIONS

All school enterprises such as the cafeteria and bookstore are operated from service, rather than profit, motives. Economy, standardization, convenience, education, and the promotion of health standards are the real and intangible benefits realized by the school and its pupils through the existence of these facilities. Services of this kind facilitate, but are always ancillary to, the main function of the secondary school: instruction and the improvement of educational opportunity. Despite the need for efficient operation, the secondary school administrator must always guard against the possibility that the management of ancillary school services will place inordinate demands upon his time and energy. Extensive involvement of the administrator in the mechanics of cafeteria and bookstore operations may preclude adequate allocations of his time and energy to educational leadership and instructional improvement activities.

The important responsibilities of the secondary school administrator in managing cafeteria and bookstore operations include:

1. Developing procedures for capitalizing upon advantages accruing from pooled purchases.
2. Developing and managing centralized accounting procedures that encompass all facets of purchasing, sales, inventory, and operation.
3. Developing policies related to the supervision, regulation, and control of all aspects of operation.
4. Developing and maintaining business practices that permit and facilitate orderly audit procedures.

When appropriately handled, a school cafeteria or bookstore can provide avenues for extending the education of selected secondary students through job experiences. Not to be condoned in the secondary school setting, however, are the practices of using students as an inexpensive source of labor or in repetitive, noneducational experiences.

REFERENCES

Burke, Arvid J., *Financing Public Schools in the United States* (New York: Harper & Bros., 1957).

Johns, Roe L., and Morphet, E. L., *Financing the Public Schools* (Englewood Cliffs, N.J.: Prentice-Hall, 1960).

Knezevich, Stephen J., and Fowlkes, John Guy, *Business Management of Local School Systems* (New York: Harper & Bros., 1960).

Linn, Henry H. (ed.), *School Business Administration* (New York: The Ronald Press Co., 1956).

Morrison, H. C., *The Management of School Money* (Chicago: University of Chicago Press, 1932).

Mort, P. R., Reusser, W. C., and Polley, J. S., *Public School Finance* (New York: McGraw-Hill Book Co., 1960).

Ovsiew, Leon, and Castetter, William B., *Budgeting for Better Schools* (Englewood Cliffs, N.J.: Prentice-Hall, 1960).

Samuelson, Everett V., *et al.* (compilers), *Financial Accounting for School Activities* (Washington, D.C.: U.S. Government Printing Office, 1959).

U.S. Office of Education, *School Finance and School Business Administration* (Washington, D.C.: U.S. Government Printing Office, 1958).

Chapter 15
Auxiliary Services
and Custodial Functions

T HE administration of modern secondary schools encompasses responsibility for the maintenance and improvement of both special
services and custodial functions that serve to facilitate the educative
process. Although special services and custodial functions are often taken
for granted and may, in many instances, appear to be peripheral to the
mainstream of teaching-learning activities, they are, nevertheless, indispensable elements in the total configuration of secondary education. The
competent secondary school administrator realizes the direct and indirect benefits accruing to school operation from efficient library, health,
cafeteria, transportation, and custodial services, and strives to obtain
the optimum contribution of each of these areas to total school effectiveness.

In every organization it is necessary to allocate resources not only to
important goal functions but also to functions which—although they
appear to be essentially of a nongoal nature—make significant contributions to effective pursuit of legitimate goals. Thus, although certain special service and custodial functions in secondary schools are characteristically of a nongoal variety, it is important to note and to capitalize
upon the interrelationship between these two kinds of functions in organization. The *enabling* function of nongoal activities is what makes
them worthy of pointed administrative attention. Outstanding school
plant management and operation, for instance—exemplified in high
standards of custodial and maintenance service, in the provision of attractive physical settings for learning activities, and in constant attention
to factors of health, comfort, and safety—provide the climate and en-

vironment which encourage maximum efforts by both faculty and students. Similar benefits accrue from the efficient operation of all other necessary auxiliary school services: library, cafeteria, transportation, and health.

LIBRARY SERVICES

A significant number of smaller secondary schools in this country still offer no more than minimum library services to students. Many have no central library facilities whatsoever. Students in such situations must seek to augment information in basic texts either through the public library or through shared use of limited collections of books and materials housed in individual classrooms. Fortunately, however, secondary schools offering minimum library facilities are decreasing in number; the trend is toward increased service in this area in all schools. Many medium-sized and large high schools provide services of an outstanding nature—services that reflect not only keen appreciation and understanding of the educative process but also commitment to the highest standards of excellence and scholarly effort.

Library Functions

The traditional role of school libraries has centered upon responsibilities associated with the purchase, circulation, repair, and control of books and other educational materials made available to augment, supplement, and enrich the learning opportunities afforded by the educational program of the school. Educational materials other than books which have usually become the custodial responsibility of school libraries have included audiovisual materials, magazines, charts, pamphlets, pictures, and printed materials of other kinds.

The major emphasis and philosophy of operation in school libraries have tended to view the library's holdings as *supplementary* rather than as *primary* learning resources. This traditional view has tended to focus attention upon supplementing the limitations of basic learning situations involving the time-honored ingredients of teacher, learner, and textbook. The use of school library facilities as primary learning resources—in which independent study is the essential ingredient, and in which the mediation of teachers is of a different order from that in conventional classroom situations—is still a distant goal in many secondary schools.

Newer conceptions are tending to view the school library as the most important element in a total learning resources center. Implementation of such concepts involves not only the creation of a single reference and instructional material center for the whole school, but the development of maximum learning capacity through provision of automated instructional devices, listening rooms, viewing rooms, reading rooms, and laboratories in subject areas such as foreign language, English, mathematics, social studies, and science. The library becomes the heart of the learning resources center, with extensive responsibilities for facilitating the use of both primary and supplementary learning resources.

Encouraging Library Use

As the instructional leader in his school, the principal has important responsibilities in developing the instructional and learning potential available in school library facilities. Among his important functions in this area are the following:

1. To act as the consistent advocate of increased financial and attitudinal support in the building of outstanding library facilities.
2. To foster understanding among instructional and library personnel of the library's purposes as a primary as well as a supplementary learning resource.
3. To work toward acceptance of the concept of the library as an important element in a total learning resources center in which many opportunities exist for individual and small-group learning.
4. To encourage optimum use of library resources through free access to its facilities, and to discourage the practice of using the library as a convenient place to assign unscheduled pupils.
5. To facilitate the use of library conference rooms by classroom groups and to encourage the taking of library resources to pupil patrons through use of rolling bookcases and portable bookshelves.
6. To provide necessary resources for establishing and securing storage places, equipment, and facilities and supplies for library administration and book repairs.
7. To coordinate the use of library materials and facilities, learning laboratories, and self-instructional resources to ensure maximum benefit to all instructional departments.

Library Personnel

The need for competent, fully trained library personnel cannot be too strongly stressed if the aims of the secondary school are to encompass optimum service and maximum utilization of library services. School librarians should possess competence in library management and understanding of the total school program. Librarians meeting both qualifications should be afforded the status and pay of regular teachers—with the expectation that their performance will equal the contributions of other faculty members. A degree in library science, appropriate personal qualifications, ability to work well with all age groups, and a good general understanding of secondary education would appear to be minimum qualifications for school library personnel.

The functions of the secondary school administrator in working with library personnel, instructional staff, and the student body to ensure efficient and maximum use of library resources include the following:

1. Coordinating the work of the library personnel and faculty advisory committees in developing policies to cover all aspects of daily operation and library management.

2. Developing procedures for assessing library needs in relation to the instructional aims of various departments of the secondary school.

3. Developing plans and strategies for (*a*) extending and increasing library utilization (including evening, weekend, and summer use), and (*b*) improving library services.

4. Outlining the roles of student volunteers and paid student assistants in library operation.

The school library houses a significant portion of the total educational resources available in the secondary school. Secondary school administrators and library personnel should ensure that the full potential of available library resources is directed toward the sustained improvement of educational opportunities throughout the school.

CAFETERIA SERVICES

School cafeteria services have grown tremendously during the past three decades. Several factors have contributed to the continued growth of these valuable services. First, participation in federal subsidy programs has enabled schools to provide substantial amounts of wholesome food in school lunch programs at minimum cost. Second, the growth of secondary schools and the extension of attendance boundaries have increased the numbers of secondary pupils who willingly patronize school lunch programs. Third, the scheduling practices of many secondary schools have tended to reduce the amount of time available to pupils for traveling between home and school during the lunch period. Finally, the efforts of most secondary schools to provide appealing lunches in surroundings that are clean, comfortable, pleasant, and relaxing have encouraged maximum utilization of this school service.

The minimum goal in school lunch programs is to make available one or more hot dishes which are both tastefully prepared and attractively served. Normally, hot dishes are varied and are augmented with other foods. Milk is always available. Other goals of school lunch programs encompass direct and indirect education through assisting pupils with lunch selections, establishing appropriate behavioral codes for conduct in lunchrooms, fostering health rules and knowledge of adequate dietary requirements, and making pupils aware of desirable social learnings required in a variety of social settings.

Operational Efficiency

The operating efficiency of the cafeteria service is directly related to adequacy of kitchen facilities, arrangement and utility of serving counters, management procedures encompassing cafeteria personnel, appropriateness of service-line procedures, and the physical capacity of the eating area. Close cooperation between the secondary school administrator and the director of cafeteria is necessary if the efficiency of the cafeteria service is to be maintained and improved and if continuous-flow standards in cafeteria operation are to be approximated.

Determination of the number of lunch periods required is one of the first matters to be settled. The seating capacity of the cafeteria and the number of students that can be served per minute are important considerations. Moreover, since each lunch period should be approximately one-half hour long, no more than four lunch periods should be scheduled. Otherwise, some pupils will enter the lunchroom either too early or too late. Where facilities permit, the optimum arrangement is for three lunch periods, each accommodating one-third of the students.

A second factor requiring attention is the control of peak loads during each serving period. Administrative arrangements designed to control peak loads in the cafeteria and to reduce the length of waiting lines usually involve staggering pupil-release times. A continuous-flow plan reduces strain on cafeteria facilities, eliminates student congestion in cafeteria service areas, and facilitates the orderly serving of large numbers of pupils. Efficient scheduling of both the release and return times of classrooms is mandatory. The benefits accruing, however, may be well worth the extra effort involved.

Attempts to increase operational efficiency should direct attention to a number of other related factors. Among the more important of these are the following:

1. Providing sufficient numbers of serving personnel to move six to eight pupils per minute through every point in each service line.
2. Coordinating the serving rate established by service lines with the seating capacity of the eating area.
3. Making sure that kitchen facilities and service equipment will permit fulfillment of established service goals.
4. Directing concerted effort toward reduction of noise and odors.
5. Establishing desired standards of student conduct.
6. Making sure that health standards in relation to food cleanliness, balanced diets, and general sanitation are of a high order and serve as examples from which students may learn and profit.
7. Creating official avenues such as faculty and student committees for channeling suggestions concerning menu improvement, service standards, pupil conduct, and other matters of concern to cafeteria patrons, cafeteria personnel, and administrative officers.

Staffing and Financing

Since school cafeterias are usually managed on a systemwide basis, the secondary school administrator usually does not have direct control over either the selection or the in-service training of cafeteria personnel. Because of the desirability of high standards in cafeteria operation, however, the school administrator should strive to ensure that qualifications and job descriptions for cafeteria personnel are aimed at excellence rather than mediocrity. Personnel in cafeteria work should possess competence in all aspects of food selection, preparation, and service. Moreover, health standards for those who are to prepare food for others should always be maintained at a high level.

In large systems, a systemwide coordinator of cafeterias will have charge of interviewing, hiring, and appointing school cafeteria directors assigned to secondary schools. Once an appointment is made, the relationship between the director and the principal is subject to systemwide policies governing cafeteria operation. Usually, these policies leave some latitude for local option. The principal's responsibility in every instance is to assure that cafeteria procedures not only conform to district policies but meet the operational needs of his educational unit. Often, these objectives can be realized without friction—especially if problems are approached in a cooperative fashion. In situations where cafeteria directors are not directly responsible to principals, the resolution of serious issues can often best be accomplished through appeal to central-office authority.

The financing of school cafeteria operations is a direct responsibility of boards of education. Since service rather than profit is the guiding principle in cafeteria operations, charges to pupils seldom exceed the expense of securing, preparing, and serving food. Salaries of cafeteria assistants are often recovered through food charges; salaries of cafeteria directors, on the other hand, are usually budgeted items. Desirable practice in cafeteria financing takes advantage of federal, state, and local subsidies; seeks service rather than profit as an operating principle; and seeks to serve the needs of those who are unable to take advantage of cafeteria services out of their own financial resources. An important function of the high school principal is to assure that cafeteria service is extended without prejudice to all students under the school's jurisdiction.

TRANSPORTATION SERVICES

The rapid and widespread growth of school transportation is, in many ways, a direct manifestation of concern for equal educational opportunity. It is intimately linked with growth of attendance units, expansion of school program and plant facilities, movements toward school district reorganization, and efforts to broaden the base for educational support. School transportation services have made available outstanding educational opportunities for countless numbers of secondary school pupils.

Since the transportation of secondary school pupils is a matter for systemwide decision, transportation policies have systemwide application. Individual schools rarely determine policies of this kind. The secondary school principal has, however, both a duty and a responsibility for active, professional engagement in policy development concerning pupil transportation. His participation in decision processes becomes highly desirable in view of his interest in protecting the welfare, safety, and health of pupils; developing reasonable regulations covering pupil conduct while en route to and from school; meshing school schedules with transportation schedules; and resolving pupil problems generated by transportation.

Many decisions are necessary concerning the control and regulation of pupil transportation in school districts. The importance of proper regulation of this school service is evidenced in the growing number of state statutes and codes aimed at control and standardization of safety and health procedures and provisions. North Carolina, for example, has seen fit to make pupil transportation a state function. In that state, all aspects of school transportation are subject to state control and regulations. Most other states have developed stringent regulations encompassing school bus operation, inspection, and maintenance. Moreover, the licensing of qualified school bus operators has become a state function.

Determining the form of pupil transportation services is an important decision in areas where provision of facilities is a school district responsibility. Three plans are in common use: (1) the *contract plan* under which school districts contract with individuals or public carriers to provide all equipment, supplies, and drivers needed to transport pupils at agreed prices; (2) the *school-ownership plan* under which the board of education makes all provision necessary for the operation and upkeep of buses and for the hiring and payment of drivers; and (3) the *joint-ownership plan* under which divided responsibilities are structured between carriers and the school district.

In choosing the plan to be adopted, most school districts have given consideration to factors such as the following:

1. The central goals of school transportation encompass both service and pupil safety, health, and welfare.

2. Transportation costs are high regardless of the plan adopted; however, contracted services are guided by profit motives and are subject to taxes from which school district conveyances are exempt.

3. Standards and controls related to bus maintenance, inspection, operation, and routes and to pupil conduct are more amenable to enforcement where there is no division of authority.

Whatever the plan, the secondary school administrator is responsible for ascertaining that transportation practices conform to all state codes and to the regulations adopted by the board of education. Moreover, the principal has responsibility for dealing with deviant pupil conduct occurring on buses. His role encompasses the development of organizational procedures to overcome such problems through cooperative work with bus drivers, student officers, and parents. Other duties related to pupil transportation include (1) informing parents and students of both time schedules and changes in regulations, (2) developing procedures for conducting accident drills, and (3) keeping accurate records on student transportation.

HEALTH SERVICES

Although competent community medical services may one day assume all health responsibilities for secondary schools other than health education, the slow development of general health services has resulted in active school sponsorship of programs in this area. Health inspections, centrally aimed at early discovery of needed medical treatment, dental work, and eye care, are common in secondary schools. Many school systems also provide extensive remedial services—both medical and dental—for pupils requiring them. In many areas the need for health services has generated close working relationships between schools and local and county health authorities and units. It should be noted, however, that in certain rural sections where health services are scarce—and in cities where school systems are financially dependent—organized, systematic school health services may be generally lacking.

The small high school that has developed systematic health services through cooperation with a county health unit is fortunate; many small schools lack services of this kind. Procedures for implementing health services show no consistent pattern in small school systems. Often the service exists outside the secondary school building—at a local medical or health center, at the county health unit, or, in some instances, at the central office serving the district. Where minimal services prevail, the cause is ordinarily attributed to lack of funds for maintaining special services of this nature. Often, however, the cause may be more closely related to lack of appreciation of the importance of health services in situations where many live and work together for extensive periods of time. Since the betterment of health is a goal that is generally accepted in education, it may not be unrealistic for most small secondary schools to seek to establish a school health center—even if its services are limited to those offered by one part-time nurse.

Health Services: An Enabling Function

The amelioration of health defects and the promotion of health standards represent significant enabling functions in the process of education. Good health habits, coupled with physical and mental well-being, are necessary conditions to effective participation in prolonged and arduous tasks associated with acquiring an education. Minimum goals of the school health service should be: (1) to assist in the correction of youth health problems that inhibit the attainment of maximum effectiveness in educative and learning processes, and (2) to guide youth toward understanding and appreciation of the importance of physical and mental health in all aspects of individual, family, and community life.

Whether a secondary school can maintain extensive or minimum health services is dependent upon a number of factors and variables operating in the local situation. Awareness of need for such services is an important variable. Some communities have developed this awareness, have dealt with important underlying issues, and have moved toward resolution of school health problems. Other communities are still progressing through various stages of issue identification and problem resolution. In all school districts, financial and attitudinal support—as reflected in school policies and community sentiment—are important determiners of the scope of school health services that can be offered. Moreover, the willingness of community and county health agencies to provide such services to schools significantly affects the need for developing extensive auxiliary services in school districts. Where cooperation exists, school districts usually elect only to extend the services offered by existing health agencies.

To the secondary school administrator the source of the health service is not so important as its adequacy, availability, and utility in promoting general health standards for youth. Where existing community and county services are available and adequate, there may be less urgency for schools to embark upon extensive auxiliary services in the health field. Where community services are lacking or inadequate, the secondary school administrator should promote awareness and understanding of the need for school health services.

Health Service Activities

Sharp distinctions among health service functions are difficult to maintain, because many of those functions overlap. In general, however, it is possible to categorize health services along four dimensions: custodial, preventative, ameliorative, and educational.

THE CUSTODIAL DIMENSION. Since youth are entrusted to the custody of secondary schools for extended periods, schools possess responsibility for meeting the emergency health problems of pupils in their care.

A minimum responsibility encompasses provision of a suitable place where pupils who are ill may receive care until parents are notified or until medical aid is summoned. Moreover, since accidents of varying severity are likely to occur during school operation, the responsibility for rendering competent first aid is ever present in secondary schools. If a physician or school nurse is not available, someone in the school situation should have the competence necessary to render qualified first-aid treatment.

The custodial dimension of school health services also requires attention to the removal of existing health and accident hazards. Elimination of fire hazards, dangerous heating practices, and accident-producing conditions is necessary through systematic inspection and control procedures.

THE PREVENTATIVE DIMENSION. Periodic examinations of general health, eyesight, hearing, and teeth are important aspects of the preventative dimension of health services. Such examinations reveal the need for medical and dental attention before serious health problems develop. Measures designed to identify and prevent the spread of contagious diseases are also responsibilities of school health services.

THE AMELIORATIVE DIMENSION. Where physicians, dentists, psychologists, or psychiatrists are available in school health programs, significant efforts may be devoted to the correction of both physical and mental health problems. Few school systems, however, are fortunate enough to have the services of enough medical specialists to encompass the full range of corrective services required by secondary school youth. In very large numbers of school systems, ameliorative services are restricted to those that may be offered by a school nurse.

THE EDUCATIONAL DIMENSION. The educational functions of school health services are optimized when close working relationships exist between health services and health education programs. Joint effort among those responsible for *caring for* health and those responsible for *teaching about* health provides an ideal arrangement for pursuing the school's health objectives. The secondary school administrator can contribute significantly to the promotion of such cooperative arrangements.

Health Service Personnel

Indicating the importance of school health services, in part, school districts in this country are the third largest employers of personnel in the mental health field. In the field of counseling alone, the schools in

1961 employed approximately 35,500 individuals. Personnel employed in school health services range from the highly skilled, including psychiatrists and medical doctors, to part-time personnel possessing limited skills such as those required in testing vision.

Lauber has noted that diversity is also apparent among personnel who hold responsibilities for administering and supervising special education activities such as the school health service.[1] Titles of personnel, line and staff responsibilities, and program directions are not always clear in this field. Staub's comments concerning student personnel programs are often equally applicable to school health services:

... Fragments of the student personnel program, in some school districts, are administered by many different people. Counselors, for example, may be responsible to the principal in whose building they work and at the same time be responsible to a Director of Guidance. As a result, guidance personnel often report that they are caught in a web of conflicting role expectations. Teachers of special education classes, their programs usually subsidized, at least in part, by special provisions of a state's foundation program, and holding special certification to perform their tasks, often can live in a world of their own, responsible organizationally to so many that, in fact, they operate responsible only to themselves. The same kinds of illustrations could be given for psychological services, health, attendance, and psychometrics. Personnel who work in these areas often have very little coordination of their efforts. Evaluation frequently is piecemeal, and innovative behavior at times is not tied in with purposeful, directional planning.[2]

For several reasons, the administration of health service personnel presents unique problems to the secondary school administrator. Ideally, such personnel should be responsible to, and should work under the direction of, the school administrator. However, since health service personnel represent highly specialized fields and possess unique professional qualifications, administration and supervision of their functions become a delicate matter. In cases involving professional judgment, the principal is unwise to question medical decisions. Clarification of professional relationships between administrators and school health personnel is still a matter that requires considerable attention.

1. Ellyn G. Lauber, "Special Education Administrative and Supervisory Personnel in Selected States" (Doctoral dissertation, Ohio State University, 1961).

2. W. Frederick Staub, "Common and Specialized Learnings for Student Personnel Administrators," a paper prepared for presentation at the Seventh Career Development Seminar of the University Council for Educational Administration, Michigan State University, November 11-14, 1962.

SCHOOL PLANT MANAGEMENT AND CUSTODIAL SERVICES

Intelligent school plant management, coupled with a systematic program of custodial services, can generate outstanding benefits in secondary school operation. Plant management and custodial services are aimed at the continuous improvement of services, activities, and procedures necessary to keep school plants in peak operating condition.

Five areas of concern are paramount in the work of secondary school administrators in this area:

1. *Enhancing the learning climate.* A clean, comfortable, orderly, and aesthetically pleasing school plant makes an indirect contribution to learning processes. An attractive school environment not only creates an appropriate learning climate but promotes pride and respect for school property and the acquisition of valued qualities of citizenship.

2. *Promoting health and safety.* Custodial responsibilities in secondary schools include the protection of students and staff from conditions that are deleterious to health and safety. Both vigilance and cooperative planning are necessary if safe and healthful conditions are to be maintained.

3. *Maintaining economical operation.* Ensuring the economical operation of the secondary school plant is a responsibility of the principal. Linn [3] has suggested three areas in which attention can eliminate waste and lost time in custodial services: personnel, utilities, and supplies and equipment used in cleaning operations. Since labor generates more than nine-tenths of the costs involved in cleaning school plants, the need for developing efficient and conscientious custodial personnel is obvious.

4. *Protecting the value of property.* At present, more than 1,250,000 classrooms and related facilities are being serviced and maintained by approximately 125,000 custodial personnel.[4] The prevention of depreciation and damage to billions of dollars' worth of school facilities and equipment has become a major goal in school plant management. The protection of school property values encompasses *maintenance* activities, including prompt attention to minor and major repairs; *custodial* activities, which direct attention to cleaning operations; and *prevention*

3. Henry H. Linn, "Economics in School Operation," *The American School and University* (New York: American School Publishing Corp., 1945), pp. 281-289.
4. Samuel Schloss and Carol Jay Hobson, *Fall, 1959, Statistics on Enrollment, Teachers, and School Housing in Full-Time Public Elementary and Secondary Day Schools* (Washington, D.C.: U.S. Government Printing Office, 1959), p. 6.

activities, which protect buildings and grounds from damage, vandalism, and fire hazards.

5. *Promoting an appropriate community image.* The satisfactory impressions created by clean and orderly buildings, well-maintained grounds, and efficient and courteous custodial personnel tend to generate attitudes of support for schools among both citizens and students. It is important to note that direct contact of many community members with schools is often restricted to participation in public functions held in school facilities. Much community goodwill can be prompted through efficient preparation of the school plant for such events. Public gatherings require proper supervision and the helpful assistance of a trained custodial staff. Appropriate attention to lighted entrances, information signs, heating and ventilation, seating, exits, and parking can do much to improve the community's image of school operation.

Working with Custodial Staff

The proper care and management of school facilities require cooperation among all school personnel—administrators, professional staff, students, and building custodians. General responsibility among teachers for facilitating orderly cleaning operations and appropriate student attitudes in relation to school property are often as important to plant maintenance as a well-ordered program of custodial services. Teachers can develop desirable attitudes among pupils by both example and instruction. Appropriate use of wastebaskets, attention to dirt removal from footwear at school entrances, cleanup of clutter created during class activities, avoidance of desk carving and wall marking, and proper storage of books at the end of the day not only promote habits of good citizenship but lessen the load of the custodial staff.

Despite excellent cooperation among custodial personnel, students, and staff members in many schools, there are certain categories of duties which should remain the sole responsibility of the custodial staff. An important function of administrators is to develop proper standards of custodial performance in relation to such duties.

HOUSEKEEPING. A regular schedule is necessary for inspecting the quality of custodial services such as sweeping, damp mopping, dusting, cleaning and polishing, scrubbing, and equipment and supply storage. Inspection should cover classrooms, service areas, corridors, stairs, washrooms, and storage areas. Note should be taken of the cleanliness of blackboards and chalk troughs; the condition of fixtures, towel containers, soap dispensers, washbowls, and toilet bowls; the cleanliness of floors and walls; and the maintenance of school equipment requiring custodial care.

HEALTH AND SAFETY. Adequate school plant care requires attention to a number of factors which may be deleterious to health if overlooked. Health hazards such as inadequate lighting, improper light control, faulty heat regulation, poor sanitation, improper ventilation and air circulation, and unsatisfactory humidification often need attention and correction.

Custodial services must also direct attention to safeguarding occupants and preventing accidents. Finchum has listed the duties of custodial personnel in promoting school safety as follows:

1. Keeping obstructions out of corridors, stairways, and exit lanes.
2. Repairing handrails, stair treads and nosing, playground equipment, and other types of equipment as soon as they are found to be defective.
3. Keeping all doors unlocked and all exit devices operable while the building is in use.
4. Preventing overloading and the consequent possible overfusing of electric circuits.
5. Seeing that fire extinguishers are properly charged and that other fire protective equipment is usable.
6. Observing recognized safety precautions in storing wastepaper, treated mops, and other combustible materials.
7. Inspecting and keeping in working order all automatic safety controls for heating plants.
8. Preventing floor surfaces from becoming slippery, either as the result of cleaning and waxing, or as the result of moisture carried into buildings on shoes.[5]

FIRE PREVENTION. Brainard has estimated that approximately 85 percent of the fires occurring in schools can be traced to faulty maintenance.[6] Thus, custodial personnel have major responsibilities for preventing not only the 30 million dollar annual loss from school fires [7] but also the

5. R. N. Finchum, *Administering the Custodial Program* (Washington, D.C.: U.S. Government Printing Office, 1961), p. 2.
6. Alanson D. Brainard, *Handbook for School Custodians* (Lincoln, Neb.: University of Nebraska Press, 1948), p. 193.
7. Paul William Kearney, "How Fire-Safe Is Your Child's School?" *National Parent-Teacher,* September, 1959, pp. 10-12.

tragic loss of life that sometimes occurs in conflagrations.[8] If systemwide policies in relation to fire-prevention practices are absent, the principal must accept responsibility for seeing that such policies are set out.

The principal must also accept responsibility for structuring a definite plan for evacuation of the building in case of fire. Teachers, students, and custodial personnel should be thoroughly familiar with the plan and have ample opportunities to implement it through a systematic series of announced and unannounced fire drills held at different times during the school day. Teachers, custodians, and student committees should be assigned definite responsibilities designed to cope with all contingencies that are likely to occur during fire emergencies. Alternate evacuation routes should be planned for every area of the building, including the auditorium, library, and cafeteria. Moreover, procedures designed to ensure that no person is left in any part of the building are mandatory.

REPLACEMENTS AND REPAIRS. Although larger school districts ordinarily employ maintenance crews to handle most major replacements and repairs on a systemwide basis, minor maintenance and repairs are often handled by the school's custodial staff. Among the regular duties of many custodians are tasks such as the following: minor repair of furniture, fixtures, and equipment; sealing and varnishing wood floors; replacement of window glass, fuses, light bulbs, and switches; attention to the condition of chalk boards; and repair of grounds equipment.

OTHER DUTIES. Most custodians take responsibility for controlling insect pests and rodents such as cockroaches, ants, termites, silverfish, mice, and rats which not only present health hazards but cause property damage. Moreover, mechanical duties associated with boilers, stokers, motors, fans, gauges, compressors, and the like are usually handled by the custodial staff. In addition, custodial personnel usually care for school grounds, assist with building supervision, and do minimum record keeping and accounting in relation to the total custodial task.

COOPERATIVE PLANNING. The principal works with both staff members and custodians in determining custodial, maintenance, and repair needs in the school. Check lists of required duties should be available to all, and inspections should be conducted on a systematic basis. Revisions in the amount and scope of custodial services required may need to be made from time to time. Involvement of both staff members and

8. National Fire Protection Association, *The Chicago School Fire* (Boston: the Association, 1959), p. 3.

custodians in assessments and studies of custodial needs is desirable practice in secondary schools.

Plant Utilization and Building Traffic

Since secondary school buildings are utilized both during and after school hours by students and community groups and agencies, policies regulating such use are usually necessary. Efficient utilization of building space and effective control of building traffic are important aspects of school plant management.

BUILDING USE DURING SCHOOL HOURS. Most principals find that space requirements in secondary school buildings present allocation problems at one time or another. Frequently it appears that the building is over-crowded in certain areas and underutilized in others. When such conditions prevail, a study of building utilization is indicated. At times, rather startling facts are revealed concerning the amount of unused space available in various parts of the building. Moreover, study of the number of pupil stations available and the time period each is in use provides important clues for both scheduling and over-all school planning. The improvement of school building utilization may call for rescheduling, for increasing numbers of pupil stations in certain school areas, for keeping class sizes at acceptable standards, and for making more pupil stations available through augmented numbers of class periods.

Building use requires effective control of student traffic. Although a military, Spartan atmosphere is unnecessary in secondary schools, studies of traffic flow and the use of hall supervisors and student proctors are helpful in reducing congestion and undisciplined student conduct. The development of poise and self-control among members of the student body and the reduction of unnecessary noise and boisterousness are important considerations in building traffic control.

Traffic regulation is necessary outside the building as well as in. Thus, attention must be directed to the control of bicycles, motorcycles, and automobiles used by the student body in and around the school grounds. Regulations should cover student use of cars as conveyances to school, parking, and the use of cars and other conveyances during lunch periods and when school is in session.

BUILDING USE AFTER SCHOOL HOURS. Intensive utilization of secondary school buildings after school hours is regular practice in many school districts. The concept of the school as a community center is especially evident in areas where school building sites are planned in cooperation with community recreation and park agencies. In such areas, extensive educational and recreational facilities are often available for the combined benefit of both the young and adult members of the community. Employment of teachers and recreation directors in evening and summer jobs is common practice and serves to extend educational and recreational opportunities to a wide spectrum of community members.

Extensive utilization of school buildings for worthwhile purposes serves not only to relieve housing difficulties experienced by many laudable civic and community agencies, but also to generate support for schools among community members. Generally, community use of school facilities is encouraged so long as (1) the activity is worthy and does not conflict with school purposes, (2) school property is respected and carefully used, and (3) the volume of student extracurricular activities leaves room for such use. In most school systems, outside organizations using school buildings must agree to abide by systemwide regulations covering building use.

REFERENCES

Aldrich, Ella V., *Using Books and Libraries* (Englewood Cliffs, N.J.: Prentice-Hall, 3rd ed., 1951).

American Association of School Administrators, *Health in Our Schools, Twentieth Yearbook* (Washington, D.C.: the Association, 1942).

Baker, Joseph J., and Peters, J. S., *School Maintenance and Operation* (Danville, Illinois: Interstate Printers and Publishers, 1963).

Ellsworth, Ralph E., and Wagener, Hobart D., *The School Library: Facilities for Independent Study in the Secondary School* (New York: Educational Facilities Laboratories, 1963).

Fargo, L. F., *The Library in the School* (Chicago: American Library Association, 4th ed., 1947).

Fernalled, Otto K., "How Many Custodians Do You Need?" *School Management,* October, 1958, pp. 62-68.

Finchum, R. N., *Organizing the Maintenance Program* (Washington, D.C.: U.S. Government Printing Office, 1960).

———, *Administering the Custodial Program* (Washington, D.C.: U.S. Government Printing Office, 1961).

Trump, Lloyd J., and Baynham, Dorsey, *Guide to Better Schools* (Chicago: Rand McNally & Co., 1961).

Viles, N. E., *The Custodian at Work* (Lincoln, Neb.: The University Publishing Company, 1941).

Yeager, William A., *Administration of the Noninstructional Personnel and Services* (New York: Harper & Bros., 1959).

Part V
The Administrator
and His
Profession

Chapter 16
Professional
Mission

THREE key words—competence, knowledge, and commitment—
capture the essence and emphasis of the secondary school administrator's professional mission. Leadership and management in the development and maintenance of effective secondary schools demand broad
administrative competence and extensive knowledge and understanding
of the purposes, processes, and technologies underlying education at
the secondary school level. They also require sustained commitment.
Significant dimensions in the pursuit of administrative excellence in
secondary education thus include continuous scholarly effort, awareness
of worthy educational purposes, sensitivity to important professional
movements, alertness to performance and knowledge inadequacies, and
commitment to continuous professional improvement.

The growth of professionalism in all areas of educational administration has shown unusual acceleration during the past fifteen years. Numerous influences have been responsible for this increased momentum.
These include movements to provide a rigorous knowledge base in
administrative preparation; to incorporate relevant knowledge from the
social sciences and humanities into administrative training programs; to
define preparation requirements for various levels of administrative performance; to generate viable concepts and theory to guide research and
action; to augment the flow of superior candidates into preparation programs; to create and test new instructional methodologies and materials;
to define functions and roles of various administrative positions; to
organize and extend existing knowledge about educational purposes,
processes, and technologies; to provide reality-oriented learnings through

field experiences; and to extend significant in-service training opportunities. Outstanding contributions to these movements have been made by individual universities, by the cooperative efforts of member institutions of the University Council for Educational Administration (UCEA), by the National Conference of Professors of Educational Administration (NCPEA), by the stimulus of the Cooperative Program in Educational Administration (CPEA), and by national professional bodies such as the American Association of School Administrators (AASA), the Committee for the Advancement of School Administration (CASA), the National Association of Secondary-School Principals (NASSP), the Department of Elementary School Principals (DESP), and the Association for Supervision and Curriculum Development (ASCD).

Professionalization of educational administration is also evidenced in other movements. The National Council for the Accreditation of Teacher Education is proceeding with the task of accrediting institutions of higher learning that presently prepare school administrators, supervisors, and teachers. The AASA is now requiring two years of graduate study as prerequisite to membership in the organization. Other professional organizations of administrators and supervisors are considering similar requirements for membership. Two years of graduate study are required by law for new appointees to the superintendency in Pennsylvania. The State Board of Education in California has adopted seven years of undergraduate and graduate study as a requirement for individuals who are aspiring to the superintendency. The push toward professionalization in many states is characterized by increasing consideration of longer and more intensive programs of preparation for school administrators. Awareness of and sensitivity to major movements aimed at the development of increasingly vital concepts of school administration are essential to practicing administrators at the secondary school level.

COMPETENCE IN SECONDARY SCHOOL ADMINISTRATION

Contemporary thinking in relation to competences required in secondary school administration is achieving a solid synthesis of past emphases in this important field of study. Even more important, it is directing attention to facets of the administrator's role which, until recently, were largely ignored. For many years, principal emphases in the study and teaching of school administration centered upon the technical-managerial tasks of administrators, upon administrative organization and structure, upon significant administrative processes, upon human relations skills, and upon administration as a social process. In many ways, these were important movements to school administrators whose concerns encompassed the development of increased professional competence.

Beginning around 1950, certain newer emphases began to permeate the field of school administration. Further studies of leadership and human relations, for example, provided new understandings of both organizational effectiveness and efficiency. Psychological and sociological emphases generated new insights concerning social systems phenomena, role relationships, authority, conflict, and behavior in organizations. Studies in public administration and political science made available useful concepts about decision making in both administrative and broad community contexts. Social science models and theories provided alternative "cognitive maps" for dimensionalizing reality and for ordering complex social phenomena occurring in administration. The importance of social science concepts in the milieu of administration was stressed by various writers in statements such as the following:

... concepts drawn from the basic disciplines and humanities ... provide an important eye-opening function for administrators, sensitizing them not only to value patterns but to the factors that motivate human belief and action. The fact that the disciplines and humanities use different spectacles for dimensionalizing the world of actuality creates a resource of tremendous potential for administrators. The theoretical models of a single discipline may be inadequate for understanding and dealing with complex phenomena occurring in the administrator's social system, for such phenomena are rarely unidimensional. An interdisciplinary or multidimensional view appears to hold much more promise for dealing with problems of organized complexity. Different disciplines provide alternative avenues for conceptualizing the world of actuality: each discipline provides a different focus for dimensionalizing reality.[1]

Most recently, however, major attention has been devoted to concerns of a different nature. Open questioning of the viewpoint that the educational leader should be merely "the executor of accepted policies and

1. Stephen P. Hencley, "The School Superintendent and His Role: A Conflict Typology," *Educational Research Bulletin,* Vol. XL, No. 3, March 1961, p. 67. Also, see the discussion of ways of inducing "cognitive reorganization" in W. W. Charters, Jr., "Anthropology and the Study of Administration: Response," in Lawrence W. Downey and Frederick Enns (eds.), *The Social Sciences and Educational Administration* (Edmonton, Alberta, Canada: Division of Educational Administration, University of Alberta, 1963), pp. 85-94.

the patient and deliberate reader of the public will . . ." [2] has led to new appraisals of the administrator's responsibility for the analysis of social change in the educational setting and for active participation in structuring and shaping the purposes and directions of education. Stress has been placed upon the need for educational leaders to become (1) finely attuned to the interrelationship between education and the broader culture, (2) perceptive concerning the role of education in the total ethos of the society, (3) increasingly sensitive to the educational implications of broad social movements, (4) competent in the generation of educational purposes, and (5) concerned with active participation in policy determination and legitimation processes. Basic to this view are theses such as the one advanced by Harlow—that "the United States can no longer afford the simple group addition of assertions such as 'I feel that . . . ,' and 'I believe that . . .' and 'I am convinced that . . .' as a way to define purpose in so significant a group of institutions as its schools." [3] Rather than seeing the administrator as a "patient and deliberate reader of the public will," this view sees the administrator as one who possesses a firm grasp of the history of human purposes; as one who has mastered the intellectual processes necessary to generate goals; as one who seeks active involvement in educational policy making; and as one who is within, rather than outside, the mainstream of societal forces that initiate and guide social reform.

The emergence of this school of thought has added a significant new dimension to the competence pattern envisioned for secondary school administrators. Skill in the conceptualization and development of educational purposes, goals, and policies has become fully as important as high-level competence in the technical and process dimensions of administration. The emerging professional mission of secondary school administrators has become challenging and extremely demanding.

2. John Walton, "New Concepts in Educational Administration," *Proceedings of the Canadian Education Association Short Course* (Banff, Alberta, Canada: the Association 1962).

3. James G. Harlow, "Purpose Defining: The Central Function of the School Administrator," in Jack A. Culbertson and Stephen P. Hencley (eds.), *Preparing Administrators: New Perspectives* (Columbus, Ohio: University Council for Educational Administration, 1962), pp. 70-71.

Purpose Competences

The report of the UCEA Committee on Guides for Improving Preparatory Programs has indicated the significant characteristics of future school administrators as follows:

... the administrator of the future can best be defined as a perceptive generalist. Such a person will have a background of liberal education. While he will need to possess a high degree of intelligence, infinite analysis and pedantic tendencies, which typically prevent or interfere with decisiveness, will not characterize his mind; *rather, he will be intelligent and decisive, penetrating, yet flexible, a sophisticated analyst and a vigorous actor.* . . . He will likely have specialized in a subject matter field as a teacher; however, his capacity to learn new fields of application quickly and to depart from the narrow confines of specialization will lead him to an interest in more general values and relationships.[4]

The development of competence in structuring educational purposes is a major dimension of the total professional mission of the secondary school administrator. Effective administrative performance in this vital area demands abilities that are difficult to acquire in the absence of both sustained professional commitment and continuous study and self-improvement. Among the salient competences underlying effective performance in this area are the following:

1. *Ability to relate educational policy to broad social movements.* The administrator who excels in competences related to purpose definition shows an affinity for "comprehending and making decisions about problems which are characterized by complexity and by tangled relationships."[5] He is concerned with broad social values and possesses a deep appreciation of the role of the school in the social order. He accepts responsibility for analyzing complex educational problems and is able to encompass the social, psychological, economic, and political factors underlying educational choice making. Moreover, he is aware of perva-

4. University Council for Educational Administration, "Improving Preparatory Programs for Educational Administrators in the United States: Some Action Guides," committee report (Columbus, Ohio: the Council, mimeographed, undated). Members responsible for the report were Roald Campbell, Jack Culbertson, Stephen Hencley, Daniel Griffiths, Van Miller, Henry Otto, Truman Pierce, and John Ramseyer. For a cogent discussion of the administrator as a perceptive generalist, see Jack A. Culbertson, "New Perspectives: Implications for Program Change," in Culbertson and Hencley (eds.), *op. cit.,* pp. 151-173.
5. University Council for Educational Administration, *op. cit.,* p. 12.

sive forces affecting the educational enterprise and is adept in analyzing the educational implications of widespread social change. The professional mission of administrators in secondary schools requires attention to the continuous development of these competences. As leaders in important operating units, and as advisors in the superintendent's cabinet, their competence in purpose-definition activities can significantly affect the quality of educational policy making and operation in local school districts.

2. *Ability to formulate ways in which education, as an instrument of society, can implement the purposes of the broader culture.* The professional mission of the secondary school administrator encompasses serious study of cultural change and mandates his active participation in spelling out ways in which education can implement societal purposes.[6]

The rapid advance of knowledge, science, automation, and technology, for example, poses educational implications of the first magnitude for curriculum development, for vocational education, for the reeducation of the technologically unemployed, for general adult education, and for possibilities of implementing systems approaches to education. The need for sound leadership in appraising educational directions is becoming increasingly evident. Educational leaders in the days ahead will need to accept increasing responsibility for promoting constructive solutions to major societal problems through education.

3. *Ability to provide professional leadership in the resolution of significant value dilemmas.* The past decade has witnessed an increasingly broadened interest in education from all levels of society; much of this interest has been generated by conflicting values concerning vital educational issues. Value-laden issues associated with integration, educational excellence, equal educational opportunity, local versus federal control, and adequate financial support have continued to characterize social controversies centering around the educational enterprise.

Providing leadership in the resolution of incompatible educational expectations and community value dilemmas is a high-priority challenge in the professional mission of the secondary school administrator. Effective performance in this area demands development of a defensible, total concept of secondary education that is based upon legitimate purposes, that is aware of the unique role of educational institutions in

6. See Stephen P. Hencley, "Forces Shaping the New Perspectives," in Culbertson and Hencley (eds.), *op. cit.*, pp. 1-8.

relation to other social institutions, and that directs attention to both social and individual purposes. Moreover, effective performance requires competence not only in mediating incompatible proposals concerning secondary school purposes, but in formulating sound educational policies in a matrix of social and ideological conflict.

Process Competences

The professional mission of the secondary school administrator encompasses continuous self-improvement along two major process dimensions. One dimension relates to the improvement of the process of secondary education itself. The other dimension encompasses improvement in administrative processes that are essential to effective performance.

THE PROCESS OF SECONDARY EDUCATION. The process of secondary education is, in reality, a disciplined approach to learning. It is the particular nature of the process of education which makes the secondary school unique among other social institutions. Secondary education encompasses all modes of inquiry which distinguish the important basic disciplines and incorporates these into central teaching-learning processes and activities. The primary objective at this level is not the development of extreme specialization in the mode of inquiry of any single discipline. Rather, the aim is to develop appreciation for, and competence in, several modes of inquiry which have served as basic vehicles in man's search for understanding and knowledge.

Approximation of the true mission of secondary education requires deep insight into significant institutional purposes, into the enabling nature of basic teaching-learning processes, and into the fundamental processes of human learning, human growth, and human development. Secondary school administrators require clear concepts of the significant purposes and processes underlying the total educative task. Only in this way can the process of secondary education become a functioning reality.

ADMINISTRATIVE PROCESSES. As indicated in Chapter 4, sophistication in the use of fundamental processes—decision making, communicating, coordinating, organizing, directing change, appraising, and maintaining morale—is essential (1) in formulating and achieving institutional purposes, (2) in developing operational policies, (3) in unifying and formalizing work-flow patterns, and (4) in maintaining the organizational-environmental exchange system. Sections of preceding chapters have directed attention to the use of these processes in both intraorganizational and extraorganizational settings.

The study entitled Determination of Criteria of Success (DCS) dealing with the administrative behavior of 232 elementary school principals in a simulated elementary school has given some indication of the importance of sophistication in the use of administrative processes. The set of primary factors developed in this study is heavily process-oriented and appears to represent a partial taxonomy of administrative performance:

Factor A′	Exchanging information
Factor B′	Discussing with others before acting
Factor C′	Complying with suggestions made by others
Factor D′	Analyzing the situation
Factor E′	Maintaining organizational relationships
Factor F′	Organizing work
Factor G′	Responding to outsiders
Factor H′	Directing the work of others [7]

Thus, primary goals in the mission of the secondary school principal encompass increased sophistication in the use of all administrative processes, improved competence in human relations skills, and augmented understanding of (1) the operation of role systems, norm systems, and interaction systems in organizations; and (2) the impact of intraorganizational and extraorganizational authority and power systems which affect organizational performance and achievement.

Technical-Managerial Competences

The improvement of technical-managerial competences requires that attention be directed to three important facets of administrative performance. The first involves broad understanding of the total secondary school operation in relation to all technical demands posed. Among these are technical functions related to instruction and curriculum development, pupil personnel, staff personnel, finance and business management, school plant and auxiliary services, and community relations. Mastery of the technical operations in each of these areas is essential in secondary school administration.

7. John K. Hemphill, Daniel E. Griffiths, and Norman Frederiksen, *Administrative Performance and Personality* (New York: Teachers College, Bureau of Publications, Columbia University, 1960), p. 362.

The second facet of technical competence is centered in the area of organizational management. This area encompasses determination of organizational functions necessary for effective accomplishment of legitimized goals and purposes, allocation of functions to positions, development of procedures for allocating authority and responsibility, and structuring of organizational relationships that facilitate decision making and result in integrated organizational work-flow patterns.

The third area encompasses broad understanding of various educational and organizational technologies such as ETV, learning machines, the business and educational uses of computers, team teaching, large-group instruction, instructional "streams," and building designs that promote instructional effectiveness.

It is clear that many technical-managerial competences are more closely associated with organizational *maintenance* than with organizational *leadership*. Nevertheless, activities directed toward organizational maintenance form a significant dimension of administrative performance. Competence and effectiveness in these activities are essential in secondary school administration; continuous improvement of administrative performance in technical-managerial functions is an important facet of the administrator's professional mission.

KNOWLEDGE IN SECONDARY SCHOOL ADMINISTRATION

The avenues to knowledge in secondary school administration are numerous and include preservice preparation, workshops, conferences, in-service activities, formal courses at colleges and universities, work in professional associations, and independent self-study. Each of these avenues offers opportunities for acquiring the knowledge that undergirds competence in the purpose, process, and technical-managerial aspects of administrative performance.

Concepts, models, and knowledge existing in philosophy, the arts, the humanities, and the social sciences have increasingly been found useful in developing administrative competence. Such thinking is becoming increasingly evident in course offerings in many institutions, in staffing arrangements which include interdisciplinary instructional teams, and in joint appointments to social science and education departments.

Although relevant knowledge from these fields can be of substantial importance in developing administrative competence, it is well to be aware of three potential problems associated with interdisciplinary approaches.[8] First, every attempt should be made to avoid superficiality and narrowness in the use of social science content in both self-study and in preparation programs. Second, practicing administrators should avoid the danger of "trained incapacitation." It is necessary both to *know* and to *do* in administration. Thus, social science knowledge should be viewed not as an end but as a guide to action. Finally, although social science knowledge provides important clues to "what is" and to "what might work," it rarely provides or proposes guidelines for "what ought to be." Value decisions are still necessary in administration. Despite these limitations, however, the authors offer the viewpoint that relevant knowledge and concepts gleaned from interdisciplinary content can be of importance in improving purpose, process, and technical competences in school administration.

Knowledge Relevant to Purpose Definition

The social order served by today's secondary school is characterized by interdependence and complexity. The rate of societal change resulting from pervasive national and international influences is exponential in character and is affecting every stratum of society. If today's administrative leaders are to be more than managers of technical operations, they will need to direct attention toward increasing their capacity to engage in purposeful activities that serve to guide and direct accelerated cultural and social transformations. Effective performance in this area requires knowledge—described by Albright as "a network of concepts in terms of which the most pertinent policies can be shaped and the most responsible decisions made." [9] The three kinds of concepts recommended by Albright include:

1. Images formed by generalizations, drawn from the particulars, on what the major problems are and the underlying reasons for these problems. Concepts of this kind provide a fundamental basis for making decisions and inducing behavior that deals with the "real" issues and problems rather than with the symptoms. . . .

2. Ideas on what can be done in situations about the major problems. These ideas, or concepts, obviously relate to assessments of the tolerances for different ways of change in the administrator's community and school system. . . .

8. Luvern L. Cunningham, Lawrence W. Downey, and Keith Goldhammer, "The Social Sciences and the Preparation of School Administrators," in Downey and Enns (eds.), *op. cit.,* pp. 97-109.

9. A. D. Albright *et al., School Administration and the Human Sciences* (Lexington, Ky.: University of Kentucky, 1961), pp. 115-116.

3. Ideas about what should be. Any able administrator has concepts of what characterizes a good society. He knows that personal and organizational purposes gain their deepest meanings from the relationship of these purposes to social goals.[10]

Thus, one of the principal problems confronting the secondary school administrator in fulfilling his assisting role [11] in policy determination and legitimation involves the question of how available knowledge, theory, and research may best be mobilized in developing effective performance. The areas of knowledge that may be most relevant to development of competence in purpose setting and policy making are enumerated below.

CONCEPTS FROM PHILOSOPHY AND THE HUMANITIES. Competence in purpose setting and policy making requires a firmly anchored value system—a value system that has evolved through substantial thought and study in relation to the "good" life and the "good" society, and which has systematically related such considerations to questions of educational purpose. Philosophy and the humanities have, for centuries, been the storehouses of the major mode of civilized thought in relation to questions of values. Concepts from these fields appear essential in dimensionalizing and resolving value-laden issues associated with questions of excellence in education, equal educational opportunity, the focuses of educational curricula, and the allocation of available resources to educational functions.

CONCEPTS FROM POLITICAL SCIENCE. The importance of political sophistication in school administration is evident from Agger's observations that the past twenty-five years have resulted in major changes in the operation of community political systems:

1. Increasing transformations of formerly political decision making into administrative decision making.
2. Increasing acquisition by public administrators of political leadership roles and more political influence vis-à-vis legislators and private citizen participants in both political and administrative decision making.
3. The conversion of hitherto relatively "private" political decision making by relatively consensual political leaderships into openly conflictful public issues with more competitive leadership situations.[12]

10. *Ibid.,* p. 116.
11. See Chapter 4.
12. Robert E. Agger, "Political Science and the Study of Administration," in Downey and Enns (eds.), *op. cit.,* p. 57. See also Stephen Bailey *et al., Schoolmen and Politics* (Syracuse, N.Y.: Syracuse University Press, 1962).

For effective participation in purpose definition, the administrator of the future will require not only knowledge of the political processes, operations, and structures through which social decision making proceeds,[13] but acquaintance with political science concepts concerning the milieu in which educational institutions function. Certainly the administrator will need to understand the operation of community power structures and the manner in which decision making and issue resolution proceed in community settings. Moreover, he will require understanding of the interrelationships of political institutions at the local, state, and federal levels and ways in which these are mobilized in public decision making.[14] Finally, he will need to encompass significant variables affecting levels of support for public education. Numerous issues are relevant in this area, including increased competition for the tax dollar resulting from expanding civic and governmental functions at all levels, questions related to separation of church and state, and conflicts related to respective roles of local, state, and federal governments in financing education.

CONCEPTS FROM SOCIOLOGY. The importance of understanding the functioning and structure of social systems—as well as the impact of such systems upon community behavior—points up the need for sociological concepts in school administration. The concerns of sociology as a field of study encompass numerous areas—many of which are essentially related to purpose definition in education. Sociologists have conducted significant studies in relation to bureaucracies, the family, ethnic groups, religion, health, welfare, industry, education, political behavior, race relations, occupations, science and specialization, social stratification, population, patterns of leisure and recreation, mass communication, and many other areas. Merton has identified more than thirty specialized fields in sociology in which major problems of interest to the educational administrator are receiving study and consideration.[15]

CONCEPTS FROM ECONOMICS. Economics has for many years provided concepts that have been utilized in educational finance and business management. Newer trends in economics as a field of study are providing

13. See Bert E. Swanson (ed.), *Current Trends in Comparative Community Studies* (Kansas City, Mo.: Community Studies, Inc., 1962).

14. See Robert S. Cahill and Stephen P. Hencley (eds.), *The Politics of Education in the Local Community* (Danville, Ill.: The Interstate Printers and Publishers, 1964).

15. R. K. Merton *et al., Sociology Today* (New York: Basic Books, 1959). See also Orville G. Brim, Jr., *Sociology and the Field of Education* (New York: Russell Sage Foundation, 1958).

powerful concepts related to the task of purpose definition in education. Among the economists' contributions which are essentially relevant in this area are those assessing (1) the economic contributions of education,[16] (2) economic changes and their effects on tax systems,[17] (3) resource allocations at various governmental levels, and (4) the societal impacts of automation, technology, and cybernation.[18]

Knowledge Relevant to Administrative Processes

Studies which illuminate basic processes common to bureaucracies and organizations—decision making, communication, control, change, and morale building—have been conducted in many contexts by researchers from various social science disciplines. Knowledge of the results of these studies is important in building competence in the use of administrative processes in both intraorganizational and extraorganizational settings in school administration.

In considering administrative processes, Culbertson has noted that the administrator should direct attention to both scientific content and value content:

... there is always an important value element which the administrator cannot ignore in the processes of communication, decision making, coping with change, and building morale. Not only must he understand "the world" as it *actually is,* but he must also be concerned about what it *should be.* Even though the social sciences may provide him enough knowledge in some situations to control consequences, he must still decide whether or not he should control the consequences.[19]

Psychology and social psychology, for example, have developed scientific methods for determining the way in which groups come to decisions. Knowledge of the work in these fields is valuable in understanding *what is,* but may be of less value for questions of *what ought to be.* Whether the administrator should exercise power, for instance, in guiding a group

16. Theodore W. Schultz, "Investment in Man: An Economist's View," *Social Service Review,* Vol. 33, No. 115, June, 1959.

17. James Tobin, "Growth Through Taxation," *New Republic,* Vol. 143, No. 15, July 25, 1960.

18. See, for example, George Stigler, *The Demand and Supply of Scientific Personnel,* National Bureau of Economic Research (Princeton, N.J.: Princeton University Press, 1957).

19. Jack A. Culbertson, "Common and Specialized Content in the Preparation of Administrators," a paper prepared for presentation at the Seventh Career Development Seminar of the University Council for Educational Administration, Michigan State University, November 11-14, 1962.

to the "right" decision is a question which is more philosophical than psychological in character. And yet, to the administrator, who must function in the world of action, both *is* and *ought* questions are of the utmost importance.

To build knowledge and competence in the *ought* of administrative processes requires acquaintance with the humanities, philosophy, and literature. Concepts relevant to *what is* may be more appropriately gleaned from the fields of sociology, political science, psychology, and social psychology.

The cumulative impact of study in relation to the *is* aspect of the communication process, for example, is illustrated in the communications framework depicted in Figure 16-1. The framework, which was developed by the UCEA Task Force on Communications, dimensionalizes the major concepts and variables which administrators in public schools should understand and encompass in developing communication effectiveness. Important questions related to the *ought* of the communication process (such as those concerned with concealing information, "slanting" information, omitting information, and communicating false information) are not encompassed in such frameworks. On questions of value, social science knowledge is essentially neutral.

Knowledge Related to Technical Areas

Secondary school administration, while recognizing the major importance of knowledge about purpose definition and administrative processes, recognizes as of equal importance knowledge about the technical means for achieving legitimized purposes. In relation to technical-managerial functions, the authors give strong support to the concept of organization which views the operating line as the primary locus of responsibility in relation to the teaching-learning process. This concept highlights the operating line extending from the superintendent through the principal to the classroom teacher, and sees the principal's primary functions in the technical areas as maintaining, facilitating, and improving educational opportunity. Thus, although effective functioning in secondary school administration requires knowledge concerning finance and management, staff personnel, community relations, physical facilities, and organization, the secondary school principal's position is made unique by his specialized functions in instructional leadership, in developing student potential, and in program development.

Many areas of knowledge are relevant to competence building in technical areas. Psychology has much to offer in relation to learning theory, instructional methodology, and pupil guidance. Sociology and political science provide concepts useful in viewing community decision processes and in building community relations programs. Economics offers avenues for developing business management and school finance competences. Social psychology provides valuable insights into staff personnel administration. Educational philosophy supplies required value orientations for program development. Each discipline provides concepts for improving the general competence of administrators in the technical task areas.

Principals are closest to the over-all improvements and supervision of teaching-learning opportunities in building units. Their competence should encompass marshaling and bringing to bear total organizational resources for carrying out the development, maintenance, and enhancement of teaching-learning opportunities. Such competence forms an important part of the secondary school principal's professional mission.

Knowledge in the technical areas of secondary school administration would be incomplete, however, without extensive understanding of the rapidly changing concepts and technologies characterizing the process of secondary education. Many innovations that are influencing this level of education were discussed in Chapters 3 and 11.

COMMITMENT IN SECONDARY SCHOOL ADMINISTRATION

The scope of knowledge and competence projected for secondary school administrators in the previous pages clearly exceeds both present practice and the general aspiration levels of many practitioners. The recommendations posed, however, are neither unrealistic nor unattainable. Nevertheless, it is abundantly clear that high standards of administrative performance are unlikely to become a reality in the absence of long-term commitment, unselfish dedication, and a desire to improve professional competence.

The 1960 AASA Yearbook has listed six criteria which distinguish professions among other vocations, noting that a profession:

a. Differs from other occupations by having a unique body of knowledge that is known and practiced by its members.

Figure 16-1. A COMMUNICATIONS FRAMEWORK

Communication Processes Found in Schools, School Districts, and Communities

I. Two-Way Oral
- A. Two-person
  1. Superior (e.g., principal with superintendent)
  2. Subordinate (e.g., supt. with teacher)
  3. Professional peer (ass't supt. with ass't supt.)
  4. Community leader (supt. with bank president)
  5. Community follower (teacher-parent conference)
- B. Small-group
  1. Professional (principal with teacher's group)
  2. Lay (supt. with citizen's committee)
  3. Lay-professional (supt. with lay-professional salary committee)
- C. Combination of A & B

II. One-Way Oral
- A. Face-to-face audience
  1. Professional (principal to teachers)
  2. Lay (supt. to Lion's Club)
  3. Lay-professional (ass't supt. to PTA)
- B. Unseen audience
  1. Professional
  2. Lay
  3. Lay-professional

III. Written
- A. To an individual
  1. Superior
  2. Subordinate
  3. Professional peer
  4. Community leader
  5. Community follower
- B. To a single public or group
  1. Professional (elementary teachers)
  2. Lay (taxpayers assoc.)
  3. Lay-professional (PTA)
- C. To multiple publics
  1. Professional (high school and elementary teachers)
  2. Lay (newspapermen, YWCA, civic groups)
  3. Lay-professional teachers, pupils, NAM)

Concepts to Describe and Explain Communication Processes

1. Communicator
- 1. Position
  - (1) Teacher
  - (2) Principal
  - (3) Superintendent
  - (4) Leader in non school organization
  - (5) Pupil
  - (6) Noncertificated
  - (7) Other
- 2. Purpose
  - (1) To inform
  - (2) To change attitudes

2. Channel
- 1. Direction
  - (1) Upward
  - (2) Downward
  - (3) Horizontal
  - (4) Outward
- 2. Location
  - (1) Internal
  - (2) External
  - (3) Controlled situation
- 3. Type
  - (1) Formal
  - (2) Informal

3. Medium
- 1. Audio
  - (1) Speech (radio)
  - (2) Panel (radio)
  - (3) Discussion (radio)
  - (4) Telephone
  - (5) Intercom
  - (6) Recordings
- 2. Visual
  - (1) Letter
  - (2) Memo
  - (3) Newsletter

4. Message
- 1. Content
  - (1) Facts
  - (2) Values
  - (3) Rumors
  - (4) Ideas
  - (5) Attitudes
  - (6) Opinions
  - (7) Innuendo
- 2. Form
  - (1) Beginning
  - (2) Ending
  - (3) Paragraphs
  - (4) Sentences
  - (5) General organization

5. Communicatee
- 1. Personal Factors
  - a. Motivation in relationship to:
    - (1) Social goals
    - (2) Economic goals
    - (3) Political goals
    - (4) Religious goals
    - (5) Aesthetic goals
    - (6) Theoretical goals
    - (7) Professional goals

6. Effects
- 1. Message Interpretation
  - a. Accurate interpretation of:
    - (1) Facts
    - (2) Values
    - (3) Rumors
    - (4) Ideas
    - (5) Attitudes
    - (6) Opinions
    - (7) Innuendo
  - b. Distorted interpretation of:
    - (1) Facts
    - (2) Values
    - (3) Rumors

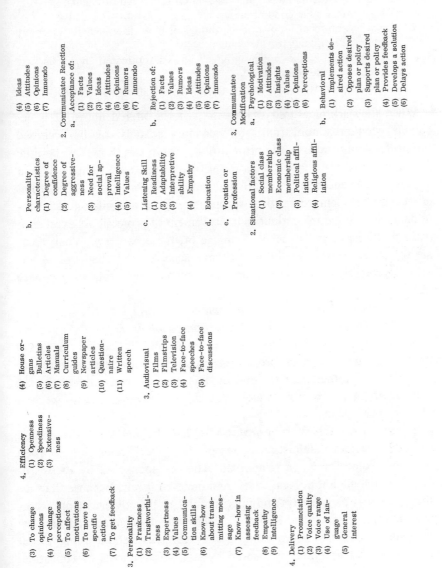

(3) To change opinions
(4) To change perceptions
(5) To affect motivations
(6) To move to specific action
(7) To get feedback

3. Personality
   (1) Frankness
   (2) Trustworthiness
   (3) Expertness
   (4) Values
   (5) Communication skills
   (6) Know-how about transmitting message
   (7) Know-how in assessing feedback
   (8) Empathy
   (9) Intelligence

4. Delivery
   (1) Pronunciation
   (2) Voice quality
   (3) Voice range
   (4) Use of language
   (5) General interest

4. Efficiency
   (1) Openness
   (2) Speediness
   (3) Extensiveness

(4) House organs
(5) Bulletins
(6) Articles
(7) Manuals
(8) Curriculum guides
(9) Newspaper articles
(10) Questionnaire
(11) Written speech

3. Audiovisual
   (1) Films
   (2) Filmstrips
   (3) Television
   (4) Face-to-face speeches
   (5) Face-to-face discussions

b. Personality characteristics
   (1) Degree of confidence
   (2) Degree of aggressiveness
   (3) Need for social approval
   (4) Intelligence
   (5) Values

c. Listening Skill
   (1) Readiness
   (2) Adaptability
   (3) Interpretive ability
   (4) Empathy

d. Education

e. Vocation or Profession

2. Situational factors
   (1) Social class membership
   (2) Economic class membership
   (3) Political affiliation
   (4) Religious affiliation

(4) Ideas
(5) Attitudes
(6) Opinions
(7) Innuendo

2. Communicatee Reaction
   a. Acceptance of:
      (1) Facts
      (2) Values
      (3) Ideas
      (4) Attitudes
      (5) Opinions
      (6) Rumors
      (7) Innuendo
   b. Rejection of:
      (1) Facts
      (2) Values
      (3) Rumors
      (4) Ideas
      (5) Attitudes
      (6) Opinions
      (7) Innuendo

3. Communicatee Modification
   a. Psychological
      (1) Motivation
      (2) Attitudes
      (3) Insights
      (4) Values
      (5) Opinions
      (6) Perceptions
   b. Behavioral
      (1) Implements desired action
      (2) Opposes desired plan or policy
      (3) Supports desired plan or policy
      (4) Provides feedback
      (5) Develops a solution
      (6) Delays action

b. Is characterized by a strong, voluntary association of its members, active in the regulation of professional entrance requirements.

c. Has an enforceable code of ethics.

d. Has a literature of its own, even though it may draw heavily on many academic disciplines for the content.

e. Is ordinarily "in the public service" and is motivated by ideals that transcend purely selfish aims.

f. Is not only professional, but is also perceived by the public as such.[20]

When they are measured against the criteria offered above, it is debatable whether administrators of secondary schools can be accorded full professional status at the present time. There can, however, be little doubt that important movements toward such status are under way and are growing in momentum. More and more avenues to professional improvement are being opened to secondary school administrators; practitioners committed to continuous improvement of professional excellence continue to seek, and to take advantage of, these avenues. What, then, are the characteristics of those who have accepted the challenge of improved professional knowledge and competence? The following appear salient:

1. *An orientation indicating acceptance of, and beliefs in, continuous improvement as a requisite of professional excellence.* The committed professional recognizes his weaknesses and limitations. He looks upon learning as a lifelong process; regards graduation from a university as a stage in, rather than the end of, this process; and recognizes that keeping abreast of new knowledge and developments is a *sine qua non* of every profession.

2. *Active participation in professional learning activities.* Committed secondary school administrators accept the "doer" role, as contrasted with the "joiner" role, in relation to activities sponsored by their professional association at local, state, and national levels. Because they see these activities as gateways and opportunities to the advancement of professional competence and knowledge, they attend regional and national meetings; participate in workshops, study councils, school improvement programs, and programs sponsored by state departments of education; participate in workshops at the school district level and in in-service activities sponsored by universities; and exhibit a continued concern for

20. American Association of School Administrators, *Professional Administrators for America's Schools, Thirty-eighth Yearbook* (Washington, D.C.: the Association, 1960), p. 257.

the advancement of the profession and its membership in every way possible. Committed professionals welcome opportunities to deliberate with colleagues, prepare addresses for professional meetings, participate in serious discussions of professional concerns, and become involved in all forms of productive intellectual pursuit.

3. *A carefully planned program of independent study.* The mastery of the unique body of knowledge required for competence in secondary school administration requires attention not only to the fulfillment of requirements for advanced degree programs but also to programs of continuous self-study in service. A regular reading program encompassing the literature and research of education and related academic disciplines is indispensable for all secondary school administrators seeking professional excellence.

4. *Dedication to development of a well-rounded concept of the principalship.* Professional commitment to secondary school administration involves improvement on a broad front. Narrow specialization must necessarily give way to improved competence in all the dimensions of administrative performance: policy, process, and technical.

That professional status has not always been accorded to secondary school administrators just because they happen to hold such positions is understandable. The body of secondary school administrators includes some who are inadequately prepared and unsuited for administration, and some others who are using the principalship as a steppingstone to other employment. As a consequence, professional recognition is usually afforded on an individual basis. Status is granted to administrators in relation to their preparation, their dedication to administrative excellence, and their consistency in following the ethical standards of their profession. Status does not accrue merely because of membership in the administrative group.

REFERENCES

Albright, A. D., *et al., School Administration and the Human Sciences* (Lexington, Ky.: University of Kentucky, 1961).

American Association of School Administrators, *Professional Administrators for America's Schools, Thirty-eighth Yearbook* (Washington, D.C.: the Association, 1960).

Cahill, Robert S., and Hencley, Stephen P. (eds.), *The Politics of Education in the Local Community* (Danville, Ill.: The Interstate Printers and Publishers, 1964).

Culbertson, Jack A., and Hencley, Stephen P. (eds.), *Preparing Administrators: New Perspectives* (Columbus, Ohio: University Council for Educational Administration, 1962).

Department of Elementary School Principals, National Education Association, *Better Principals for Our Schools* (Washington, D.C.: the Association, 1961).

Downey, Lawrence W., and Enns, Frederick (eds.), *The Social Sciences and Educational Administration* (Edmonton, Alberta, Canada: Division of Educational Administration, University of Alberta, 1963).

Griffiths, Daniel E. (ed.), *Behavioral Science and Educational Administration*. Sixty-third Yearbook, Part II, National Society for the Study of Education (Chicago: University of Chicago Press, 1964).

Hemphill, John K., Griffiths, Daniel E., and Frederiksen, Norman, *Administrative Performance and Personality* (New York: Teachers College, Bureau of Publications, Columbia University, 1960).

Kimbrough, Ralph B., *Political Power and Educational Decision-making* (Chicago: Rand McNally and Co., 1964).

McIntyre, Kenneth E., *Recruiting and Selecting Leaders for Education* (Austin, Tex.: University of Texas, 1956).

Swanson, Bert E. (ed.), *Current Trends in Comparative Community Studies* (Kansas City, Mo.: Community Studies, 1962).

University Council for Educational Administration, "Improving Preparatory Programs for Educational Administrators in the United States: Some Action Guides," committee report (Columbus, Ohio: the Council, mimeographed, undated).

Chapter 17
Challenges
and Opportunities

IMPORTANT challenges facing administrators of secondary schools have been delineated in several of the preceding chapters. The discussion which follows treats, first, the challenges in four major areas: educational purposing, improving teaching-learning opportunities, building institutional relationships, and improving the profession. It concludes with a brief section on career opportunities in secondary school administration.

EDUCATIONAL PURPOSING

Although past pronouncements of various commissions, committees, and national leaders have indicated wide agreement on certain educational aims and goals, it appears clear that educational purposing will continue to be a major challenge confronting school administrators in coming years. The reason for this expectation is well illustrated in the Report of the President's Commission on National Goals:

... All our institutions—political, social, and economic—must further enhance the dignity of the citizen, promote the maximum development of his capabilities, stimulate their responsible exercise, and widen the range of effectiveness of opportunity for individual choice. ... The development of the individual and the nation demand that education at every level and in every discipline be strengthened and its effectiveness enhanced. New teaching techniques must continue to be developed. The increasing population and the growing complexity of the world add urgency. ... [1]

1. President's Commission on National Goals, *Goals for Americans* (Englewood Cliffs, N.J.: Prentice-Hall, 1960).

Statements such as the above are valuable since they reiterate basic goals and values of our culture. Their usefulness is limited, however, because of their broad generality, together with their lack of operational definitions. If the value premises of such pronouncements are to be implemented in school districts, policies must still be formulated, and educational programs must still be structured. Moreover, statements of this kind do not indicate the difficulties that may be encountered in moving from broad objectives to operational specifics, but ways of meeting such difficulties must still be found.

Many disparities exist between the *sacred* values of our culture (as reflected in statements such as the foregoing) and the *secular* values that sometimes guide community action.[2] Although most school administrators are sensitive to the public "mind" and possess some working knowledge of the aspirations of various publics in relation to the schools, they have at times been forcibly reminded that public decision making in relation to educational issues does not always proceed in conformity with the sacred values of our culture. The gulf separating the sacred values from the secular values that frequently guide community decision making has been strikingly illustrated in relation to issues such as integration, the provision of equal educational opportunities, and the availability of adequate financial support for education.

The complexity of the problems surrounding educational policy making and program building can be illustrated in other ways. Educators are agreed, for example, that school programs should encompass desirable values, skills, and concepts. But achieving operational agreements concerning such matters is difficult. The following questions give some indication of the kinds of difficulties that are likely to be encountered:

1. In a pluralistic culture, what values should the public schools espouse? How should these values be identified and made operational?

2. In a society undergoing vast transformations due to automation, technology, and cybernation, what skills should school programs seek to develop?

3. In a world that is witnessing a knowledge explosion, what concepts are necessary to ensure the effective functioning of future citizens?

4. In a society where change has become a cliché, what is the ap-

2. See, for example, Jacob W. Getzels, "Changing Values Challenge the Schools," *School Review*, Vol. LXV, No. 1, March 1957, pp. 92-102.

propriate "mix" of social, intellectual, and attitudinal preparation which will enable learners to meet present and future challenges?

Problems and questions such as those above will continue to pose major challenges in the realm of educational purposing. Meeting such challenges will require insight into the role of education in the total society; sensitivity to the implications of cultural transformations; competence in generating cogent educational purposes; concern for active participation in policy-determination processes; and motivation to engage in difficult tasks aimed at forging societal and professional agreements concerning the directions of education in the public schools.

Improving Teaching-Learning Opportunities

Significant strides are presently being made in the development of new instructional systems, in perfecting technological aids in education, in revamping entire curricula, in developing new patterns of organization, and in evaluating and revising total educational programs. Each of these movements presents challenges. Keeping abreast of new developments is a challenge in itself. But the increasing opportunities available for improving the entire educational enterprise are of even greater consequence.

Five teaching-learning challenges presently face secondary school administrators:

1. *Refinement and revision of strategies of inquiry in secondary education.* The proliferation of new knowledge in all fields has served to emphasize the futility of overdependence on so-called "factual" knowledge as the sole foundation for secondary school programs.

New emphases in program construction have recognized that many "facts" are obsolete almost as soon as they are learned. There is a definite movement toward the structuring of new modes of inquiry which utilize concepts rather than facts as the building blocks in school programs. Instructional system prototypes have begun the dual task of reordering knowledge and of creating new knowledge structures for instructional purposes.

The restructuring of knowledge for instructional purposes is still in its infancy. Continuing progress in this area will create unique challenges for secondary school administrators. The conceptualization and implementation of newer, more viable programs will not be achieved without considerable administrative effort. Changing fixed attitudes in relation to cherished, traditional subject matter will be a task of growing importance in the years ahead.

2. *Mastery of new technologies having relevance to teaching-learning tasks.* Testing potential contributions of new technologies to learning processes is a second challenge. The following are among the important new developments that require assessment in learning situations:

a. *Television*—airborne, closed-circuit, broadcast, video tape, low-power translators.
b. *Learning laboratories*—language laboratories, mobile laboratories, computer-based instructional systems.
c. *Autoinstructional devices*—programmed and scrambled books, reading pacers, viewing and listening devices, learning machines.
d. *Additional techniques*—multiple projection systems, 8 mm sound films, telephone recorders, teletest systems, thermoplastic recordings.

The complexity of technological developments which have relevance to learning processes has been illustrated by Stolurow in relation to teaching machines and systems approaches to instruction.[3] Ten critical requirements have been posited for teaching by machine:

1. Display (presentation)	6. Collator-recorder
2. Response	7. Selector
3. Pacing	8. Library or storage
4. Comparator	9. Programming
5. Knowledge of results or feedback	10. Computer [4]

The interrelationships among these requirements, as seen by Stolurow, are shown in Figure 17-1. Computer-based systems (such as the CLASS facility described in Chapter 3) are in a stage of rapid development and may be available for school use in the near future.

The revolution in instruction that will be ushered in by widespread use of systems approaches to learning will present major challenges to administrators of secondary schools. Testing of electronic devices in the instructional process, continuous assessment of the instructional results of system programs, redeployment and regrouping of both teachers and

3. Lawrence M. Stolurow, *Teaching by Machine* (Washington, D.C.: U.S. Government Printing Office, 1961).
4. *Ibid.,* p. 6.

Figure 17-1. Adaptive Teaching Machine System

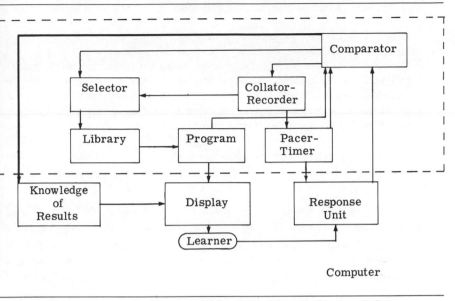

SOURCE: Lawrence M. Stolurow, <u>Teaching by Machine</u> (Washington, D.C.:
U.S. Government Printing Office, 1961).

students, maintenance of flexibility in programming and scheduling to
fit new instructional patterns, use of self-directed pupil learning in various learning laboratories—these are but a few of the major challenges
to be met.

3. *Development of sharpened insight into factors that have a bearing
upon program development and effectiveness.* Program building at the
secondary school level requires broad understanding of significant variables affecting human behavior and learning. Attention must be directed
not only to problems and circumstances to be faced by students following
graduation, but to such important considerations as the needs, interests,
and developmental levels of pupils; the unique contributions of various
program elements to the development of needed knowledge, skills, attitudes, and values; the formulation of clear educational objectives to
guide teaching-learning activities; and the evaluation of goal attainment.

The development of understanding and competence in relation to each
of the above factors is a formidable task in secondary school administration. Of the factors mentioned, probably none are more critical than
those relating to (*a*) clearly defined objectives, and (*b*) means for as-

sessing goal achievement. Flanagan has noted the critical interrelationship between these two factors as follows:

Unless the status and progress of a student can be evaluated in terms of each specific educational objective, it is extremely difficult to plan a program or determine its effectiveness. Only when instruments which provide meaningful measures of educational objectives are available can an effective instructional program which produces significant student progress be distinguished from a program which represents no improvement but merely innovation and change from former programs.[5]

Clear goal definition and the development of reliable means to assess goal attainment continue to be significant frontiers in secondary school administration.

4. *Provision of leadership in optimizing the development of both staff and student personnel.* A major task in the improvement of teaching-learning opportunities centers around the development of professional personnel in the utilization of available resources in educational improvement. The need for dynamic leadership in this process is paramount. New developments affecting the process of secondary education require the acquisition of new skills, attitudes, and perspectives on the part of professionals in the schools. The role of tomorrow's teacher will encompass competence in the management of new learning situations and a greatly expanded number of learning resources and processes. The secondary school administrator as an instructional leader must provide opportunities for staff members to acquire and practice the full range of competences required.

5. *Maintenance of a climate that is supportive of research endeavors.* Clark has observed that the educational enterprise has frequently undervalued the importance of research in improving teaching-learning performance:

Research seems unable to find an appropriate place in the field of education. Practitioners have not used research as a basis for their operations. The paths to school improvement have been directed toward the provision of more of what already exists—more classrooms, more books, more audio-visual aids, more teachers, more buses—and the improvement of practice on the basis of what is already known. Research has had no dynamic role to

5. John C. Flanagan, "Implications of Research for American Secondary Education," in Stanley Elam (ed.), *New Dimensions for Educational Progress* (Bloomington, Ind.: Phi Delta Kappa, 1962), p. 69.

play and, as a consequence, has lacked the resources needed to play a dynamic role.[6]

Maintaining a climate that encourages both the doing and the using of research in secondary schools is important to the development of educational excellence. There are many areas in which educational knowledge can be substantially improved through sustained research effort. Six important areas identified by Clark include: (1) the characteristics of the learner; (2) the teaching-learning process and learning theory; (3) the education of special groups of learners; (4) the social, historical, and philosophical foundations of education; (5) the personnel, organization, facilities, and finance of education; and (6) the substance of the curriculum.[7]

BUILDING INSTITUTIONAL RELATIONSHIPS

The maintenance and improvement of institutional relations at local, regional, and state levels constitute a challenge to every member of the administrative performance system. The secondary school principal, as a member of this system, shares certain responsibilities in this area with other administrators; other responsibilities are unique to his position. Generally speaking, the principal has responsibility for maintaining and improving relations with schools in the local system, with the board of education, with colleges and universities, with regional associations, and with state departments of education.

Relations with Local Schools

The establishment and improvement of institutional relations among schools in the local school district pose a number of important tasks and challenges to secondary school administrators. They demand continuous cooperation among all school units in building a defensible system of education within a common framework of school policies. They require continued attention to articulation so that students may progress from lower to higher schools with little difficulty and with few major problems. They necessitate the building of programs of study which reflect a common philosophy of education and a shared understanding

6. David L. Clark, "Educational Research: A National Perspective," in Jack A. Culbertson and Stephen P. Hencley (eds.), *Educational Research: New Perspectives* (Danville, Ill.: The Interstate Printers and Publishers, 1963), p. 8.
7. *Ibid.*, p. 15.

of teaching-learning purposes and processes at different educational levels. Above all, they demand cooperative effort among teachers, principals, central-office personnel, and the superintendent in solving common school problems, in shaping general and operational policies, and in improving education practices and opportunities at all school levels.

Board of Education Relations

Although few secondary school principals meet regularly with boards of education, they have opportunities, nonetheless, both for influencing and for improving relations with this body. Principals often meet with board of education members to explain school programs, to outline certain educational needs, and to present special problems. Opportunities of this kind are usually made available by the superintendent, who normally is anxious to open communication channels between individual school units and board of education members. Many principals also serve as members of the superintendent's cabinet and have extended opportunities for shaping positive educational policies for recommendation to the board of education.

Still other opportunities for building good relations are afforded through visits of board members to individual schools. During such visits the principal faces the challenge of ensuring that board members receive a clear and accurate picture of the school's programs, educational facilities, problems, and aspirations. Objective and accurate reporting during these occasions not only improves relations and increases mutual trust, but also ensures that board members will leave the school with the kind of information necessary for adequate policy making.

Relations with Colleges and Universities

Great increases in the numbers of college-bound youth, growing competition among high schools for meeting entrance requirements to better colleges and universities, nationwide influences such as the National Merit Scholarship Program, and increased community pressures for outstanding college preparatory programs have all combined to create unique challenges for secondary school principals. Building, maintaining, and improving relations with colleges and universities have already become urgent in many school districts. Moreover, the steadily growing demand for use of the limited facilities in institutions of higher learning will tend to intensify existing problems during the next decade.

Secondary school principals have traditionally sought to build bridges into institutions of higher learning through cultivation of relations with college faculties and admissions officers, through improvement of performance standards on College Board Examinations and National Merit Scholarship tests, and even through the assistance and intervention of influential people having ties with colleges and universities. Few delusions exist concerning the equality of existing relationships between high schools and institutions of higher learning. Colleges and universities will more than ever be able to maintain independence in, and control of, selection procedures in future years.

Improving the competence of high school graduates who will seek entrance to institutions of higher learning is one of the best ways to meet this challenge. Continuous attention should be directed to:

1. Improving programs of preparation to enable students seeking college entrance to attain high levels of scholarly competence.
2. Providing continuous counseling about career choices and about requirements for various fields of study.
3. Assisting students with choices of colleges and universities best suited to their abilities and career interests.
4. Providing institutions of higher learning with accurate estimates and descriptions of the potential of students seeking college entrance.

It should be noted that a number of states have provided statutes which require colleges to accept high school graduates for advanced study. Even in these states, however, the great numbers of students seeking admission have resulted in selective admissions and an accelerated attrition rate during the freshman and sophomore years. Despite the ever mounting barriers to entrance into certain institutions, it should be stressed that almost all high school graduates seeking college preparation will be able to find a college to which they will be admitted for study. Thus, the secondary school administrator's responsibility encompasses building institutional relationships with a wide range of colleges and universities. Only in this way can he best serve the interests of all students.

Relations with Regional Associations

Six regional associations covering the entire nation are now operating as media through which high schools and institutions of higher learning can direct attention to common educational problems. The regional associations presently in operation include: the Northwestern Association of Secondary and Higher Schools, the North Central Association, the New England Association, the Middle States Association, the Western Association of Colleges and Secondary Schools, and the Southern Association.

Four primary purposes have guided the operation of the six regional associations:

1. The development of educational standards and the accreditation of schools.
2. The control of undesirable practices in athletics and other areas.
3. The development of evaluative criteria by which each school may judge its own performance and capabilities.
4. The provision of professional leadership in the improvement of educational practices.

Where state departments of education do not possess legal authority to accredit high schools and colleges, the associations have served the useful purpose of developing and maintaining acceptable educational standards. School officials, however, have sometimes questioned the wisdom of permitting the regional association to wield both legislative and judicial powers in relation to standards and accreditation.

The challenges facing secondary school administrators in working with regional associations are fourfold:

1. To ensure that schools meet at least minimum educational criteria set by regional associations.
2. To seek to develop maximum educational capabilities which surpass minimum accreditation criteria in all aspects of school operation.
3. To bring unprofessional and/or undesirable educational practices to the attention of regional associations.
4. To assist in the professional task of improving standards and accreditation practices in high schools and colleges.

Regional associations control educational standards over wide geographical areas; therefore, broad opportunities exist for maximizing professional educational development through membership and active participation in the work of such bodies.

Relations with State Departments of Education

The increased stress placed upon leadership functions by many state departments is providing varied opportunities and challenges for administrators in local districts. Major projects in educational improvement and development sponsored by these agencies of government are opening the way to increased cooperative action between state officials and local school administrators. Such joint action appears to be an important new frontier in educational improvement.

Close cooperation between state departments of education and school districts will result in varied tasks and challenges for secondary school administrators. New opportunities will be available for:

1. Participation in "pilot" work to test innovation and change in secondary school programs, methods, and practices.
2. Participation in large-scale developmental and research efforts.
3. Participation in decision making about new projects to be undertaken, and in planning the organization and implementation of such projects.

Since state appropriations for public education presently approximate eight billion dollars, the resources for effecting improvement through cooperative effort are not lacking. A major challenge will continue, however, in the development of appropriate cooperative frameworks between state and local levels for wise use of these resources.

IMPROVING THE PROFESSION

Building the profession of educational administration is an arduous task requiring careful planning and thought, together with dedicated service on many levels. Although the improvement of professional status in educational administration presents many significant challenges, the following four appear to be critical.

More Exact Definition of the Values, Skills, and Knowledges Required by Professional Practitioners

Such definitions are basic to the development of appropriate certification codes. Since certification governs entry into the profession, the definition of the values, skills, and knowledges required by practitioners is a matter of vital concern to school administrators. Present certification patterns in the fifty states show little uniformity; [8] there is lack of consensus on both the knowledge and length of training required for suc-

8. Earl W. Armstrong and T. M. Stinnett, *A Manual on Certification Requirement for School Personnel in the United States* (Washington, D.C.: National Education Association, 1959).

cessful practice in school administration. The job of building such consensus is essential to any group seeking professional status.

A publication of the Department of Elementary School Principals has indicated some of the steps that lie ahead in improving certification standards for school administrators. The steps recommended by DESP appear equally applicable to secondary school administrators:

1. State organizations of . . . school principals should seek the cooperation of other professional organizations in the state, of the state department of education, and of staff members of institutions which prepare administrative personnel, in working for the improvement of state certification requirements for principals and other education personnel. The problem should be faced as a problem of the education profession, not as a problem of any one group alone. One reason the certification picture is not better than it is, is the fact that the profession has for too long a time spoken with many different tongues.

2. Strong efforts should be devoted to the development of reciprocity between and among states which develop similar certification codes. Principals' groups at the state and national level should seek the cooperation of other professional groups in this respect.

3. Responsibility for the certification of principals, as in teacher certification, should be primarily a function of the preparing institutions. The states should assume the role of approving institutional preparation programs. Certification would follow when a student completed the program.

4. . . . teaching should be a requirement of all certification codes, preferably specifying a minimum of two years.

5. Completion of a master's degree program in administration should be the minimum requirement for the initial or "provisional" or "temporary" state certificate for the . . . school principalship. Completion of a two-year graduate program in administration should be required for the "permanent" or "standard" certificate.

6. "Permanent" or "standard" certification should require renewal at stated intervals, renewals to be based on evidence of continued study and efforts to "keep up" with significant changes in education.[9]

Development of Strong State Associations and a Powerful National Organization

Although most states have some form of association for secondary school administrators, typically these associations have been hampered by sporadic operation, lack of funds, lack of support, and lack of full-

9. Department of Elementary School Principals, National Education Association, *Better Principals for Our Schools* (Washington, D.C.: the Association, 1961), pp. 41-42.

time officers who could devote time and energy to professional development. Action-planning and decision-making meetings are infrequently held, and major progress on professional matters is still the exception rather than the rule. The building of strong state associations which could work in cooperative fashion with the state departments of education and with other associations of school administrators is a prerequisite to professional advancement.

Strong support of the National Association of Secondary-School Principals in its work on the national level is also indicated. Secondary school administrators acting through NASSP possess unique opportunities for joining forces with other national associations (see Chapter 16) to advance the cause of professionalism in educational administration.

Development of a Code of Ethics to Guide Professional Behavior

The development of an appropriate code of ethics is a necessary prerequisite to the attainment of professional status. The code adopted by the Executive Committee of the AASA in November, 1962, is a model worth considering by secondary school administrators. The principal policies of the AASA code are as follows:

1. The professional school administrator constantly upholds the honor and dignity of his profession in all his actions and relations with pupils, colleagues, school board members, and the public.
2. The professional school administrator obeys local, state, and national laws; holds himself to high ethical and moral standards, and gives loyalty to his country and to the cause of democracy and liberty.
3. The professional school administrator accepts the responsibility throughout his career to master and to contribute to the growing body of specialized knowledge, concepts, and skills which characterize school administration as a profession.
4. The professional school administrator strives to provide the finest possible educational experiences and opportunities to all persons in the district.
5. The professional school administrator applying for a position or entering into contractual agreements seeks to preserve and enhance the prestige and status of his profession.
6. The professional school administrator carries out in good faith all policies duly adopted by the local board and the regulations of state authorities and renders professional service to the best of his ability.
7. The professional school administrator honors the public trust of his position above any economic or social rewards.

8. The professional school administrator does not permit considerations of private gain or personal economic interest to affect the discharge of his professional responsibilities.[10]

Development of Expanded·Opportunities for In-Service Growth

The report of the AASA Commission on In-Service Education for School Administration has indicated that although a great number of in-service training programs for administrators are in operation, relatively small numbers of school systems are being reached by worthwhile programs.[11] Expanding opportunities for school administrators to gain the knowledge and competence necessary in meeting challenges are necessary.

At the present time, four major avenues to in-service growth are available to secondary school administrators. Each avenue offers opportunities for administrators motivated toward increasing their professional competence:

1. Workshops, meetings, and conferences sponsored by institutions of higher learning, professional associations, state agencies, and local school districts.
2. Consultant services offered by colleges and universities, state departments of education, and private consultant firms.
3. Credit courses offered by universities and colleges.
4. Self-study of the growing body of professional literature in both administration and secondary school education.

The school administrator who takes his profession seriously will take full advantage of the opportunities offered by each of these avenues.

CAREER OPPORTUNITIES IN SECONDARY SCHOOL ADMINISTRATION

It has been estimated that there will be 35,000 secondary schools by 1970. The total number of administrative personnel required to man these schools will be more than double this figure, and many new administrative positions will be available to qualified personnel. Culbertson has estimated that the total demand for newly prepared secondary school

10. American Association of School Administrators, *Policies to Govern the Ethical Professional Behavior for School Administrators* (Washington, D.C.: the Association, undated).

11. American Association of School Administrators, *In-Service Education for School Administration* (Washington, D.C.: the Association, 1963), p. 105.

principals alone will be in the neighborhood of 12,000 in the period 1963-1970.[12] Table 17-1 indicates that approximately 60 percent of the total demand will be generated by newly created positions. The remainder will be associated with the need to replace personnel presently in service.

Table 17-1. Estimated Demands for Newly Prepared Principals for Secondary Schools, 1963-1970

Year	Newly-created Positions	Replacements	Total
1963-1964	1,678	1,089	2,767
1965-1966	1,824	1,158	2,982
1967-1968	1,936	1,232	3,168
1969-1970	2,018	1,310	3,328
Total	7,456	4,789	12,245

SOURCE: Jack A. Culbertson, "How Much Money Is Needed, and Where Will It Come from for Financing Quality University Programs in School Administration?" a paper delivered at the American Association of School Administrators Convention, Atlantic City, New Jersey, February 19, 1962.

The estimated demand shown in Table 17-1 does not encompass positions such as assistant principal, dean, and department head. Thus the total demand for administrative personnel in secondary schools in the period 1963-1970 will offer wide opportunities for those preparing for service at this level.

Salaries

As indicated by Figure 17-2, there is a great range in the median salaries paid to principals in secondary schools. The median salary of the principal in a metropolitan area is about three times that of the principal of a small high school: salaries of principals tend to increase in relation to the size of communities.

Although beginning salaries are often modest for secondary school administrators, the data presented in Table 17-2 indicate that maximum scheduled salaries in many districts make the principalship relatively

12. Jack A. Culbertson, "How Much Money Is Needed, and Where Will It Come from for Financing Quality University Programs in School Administration?" a paper delivered at the American Association of School Administrators Convention, Atlantic City, N.J., February 19, 1962.

Figure 17-2. Median Annual Salaries of Principals, Urban Schools and
Small High Schools, 1960-1961

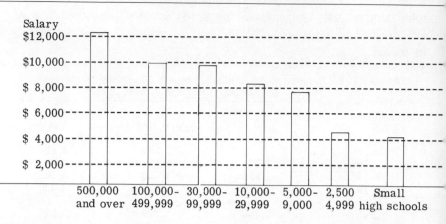

SOURCE: NEA Research Bulletin, Vol. 41, No. 1, February, 1963, p. 18.

desirable as a career position. Moreover, since nearly half of the super-intendents presently in service were high school principals at one time, the possibility for promotion to positions with higher salary levels is often present in secondary school administration.[13]

Opportunities for Expanded Responsibilities

The 1960 AASA *Yearbook* has indicated that varied opportunities exist for the advancement of secondary school administrators who aspire toward expanded responsibilities. Of the superintendents surveyed by AASA, 83 percent had been building principals at one time. Nearly 50 percent had been secondary school administrators. The *Yearbook* has also noted that the common career route in smaller communities is teacher—principal—superintendent. In cities of over 100,000, the pattern most frequently reported is teacher—principal—central-office administrator—superintendent.[14]

For those secondary school administrators who (1) are willing to seek the necessary training; (2) are serious students of both education and administration; (3) seek constantly improved standards of perform-

13. American Association of School Administrators, *Professional Administrators for America's Schools, Thirty-eighth Yearbook* (Washington, D.C.: the Association, 1960), pp. 36-41.
14. *Ibid.,* p. 40.

Table 17-2. Average Maximum Scheduled Salaries for Administrators, 1962-1963, for Highest Preparation Recognized

	School Systems with Enrollments of			
Position	25,000 or More	12,000-24,999	6,000-11,999	Selected Suburban Systems
Supervising Principals				
Elementary	$10,597	$10,103	$10,351	$12,812
Junior high	11,297	10,902	11,289	13,504
Senior high	12,064	11,785	11,851	14,718
Assistant Principals				
Elementary	9,882	9,235	9,666	11,283
Junior high	10,186	9,881	10,708	11,608
Senior high	10,298	10,234	10,991	12,533
Other Building Positions				
Counselor	9,094	9,170	9,356	10,850
Head of department	9,327	9,228	9,121	10,780
Central-office Personnel				
Supervisor	11,040	9,776	9,314	11,518
Coordinator	11,781	10,283	10,300	12,302
Director	13,043	11,848	11,848	13,828
Asst. superintendent	15,990	14,179	13,865	16,274
Superintendent	22,018	17,655	16,534	19,530

SOURCE: NEA Research Bulletin, Vol. 41, No. 1, February, 1963, p. 10.

ance in their present positions; and (4) possess insight into the realities of school administration in our time, opportunities for advancement to positions of expanded responsibility are ordinarily available.

As the authors have indicated throughout this volume, the principalship as it exists today is a worthy and challenging career. Optimum performance in this position demands vision, broad competence, extensive knowledge, and deep commitment to important educational goals. The secondary school principalship has become one of the significant career positions in American education.

REFERENCES

American Association of School Administrators, *Professional Administrators for America's Schools, Thirty-eighth Yearbook* (Washington, D.C: the Association, 1960).

————, *In-Service Education for School Administration, Forty-first Yearbook* (Washington, D.C.: the Association, 1963).

————, *Policies to Govern the Ethical Professional Behavior of School Administrators* (Washington, D.C.: the Association, undated).

Culbertson, Jack A., and Hencley, Stephen P. (eds.), *Preparing Administrators: New Perspectives* (Columbus, Ohio: University Council for Educational Administration, 1962).

Department of Elementary School Principals, National Education Association, *Better Principals for Our Schools* (Washington, D.C.: the Association, 1961).

Foster, Charles R. "Current Challenges to Educational Leadership," *Phi Delta Kappan,* Vol. 43, No. 106, December, 1961.

Index